THE FUNDAMENTALS OF THE TRUTH

Walk in His Truth Because He Is the God of Our Salvation

GOD IS SPIRIT, AND THOSE WORSHIPING HIM MUST WORSHIP IN SPIRIT AND TRUTH.—JOHN 4:24

Updated and Expanded

R. A. TORREY & EDWARD D. ANDREWS

EDITED BY JOAN PHILLIPS

THE FUNDAMENTALS OF THE TRUTH

Walk in His Truth Because He Is the God of Our salvation

R. A. Torrey & Edward D. Andrews

Edited by Joan Phillips

Updated and Expanded

Christian Publishing House
Cambridge, Ohio

Copyright © 2016 Christian Publishing House

All rights reserved. Except for brief quotations in articles, other publications, book reviews, and blogs, no part of this book may be reproduced in any manner without prior written permission from the publishers. For information, write, support@christianpublishers.org

Unless otherwise stated, Scripture quotations are from *The Holy Bible, Updated American Standard Version (UASV)*®, Copyright © 2016 by Christian Publishing House, Professional Conservative Christian Publishing of the Good News.

THE FUNDAMENTALS OF THE TRUTH: Cause Me to Walk in Your Truth Because You Are the God of My salvation [Updated and Expanded]

ISBN-10: 1-945757-15-9

ISBN-13: 978-1-945757-15-0

CHRISTIAN PUBLISHING HOUSE

Christian Classics

Table of Contents

PREFACE 1
CHAPTER I The History of Higher Criticism 2
   Canon Dyson Hague 2
CHAPTER II The Mosaic Authorship of the Pentateuch 20
   George Frederick Wright 20
CHAPTER III Fallacies of the Higher Criticism 27
   Franklin Johnson 27
CHAPTER IV The Bible and Modern Criticism 39
   Bettex Translation David Heagle 39
CHAPTER V Holy Scripture and Modern Negations 49
   James Orr 49
CHAPTER VI Christ and Criticism 56
   Robert Anderson 56
CHAPTER VII Old Testament Criticism and New Testament Christianity 65
   W. H. Griffith Thomas 65
CHAPTER VIII The Tabernacle in The Wilderness: 78
Did It Exist? 78
   David Heagle, Translator Bremen Lectures 78
CHAPTER IX The Internal Evidence of the Fourth Gospel Canon 102
   G. Osborne Troop 102
CHAPTER X The Testimony of Christ to the Old Testament 107
   William Caven 107
CHAPTER XI The Early Narrative of Genesis 123
   James Orr 123
CHAPTER XII One Isaiah 130
   George L. Robinson 130
CHAPTER XIII The Book of Daniel 141
   Joseph D. Wilson 141
CHAPTER XIV Inspiration – Or to What Extent Is The Bible Inspired of God?
.... 149
   R. A. Torrey 149

CHAPTER XV Three Peculiarities of the Pentateuch that Are Incompatible with the Graf-Wellhausen Theories of Its Composition 160
    Andrew Craig Robinson 160

CHAPTER XVI The Testimony of the Monuments to the Truth of the Scriptures..163
    George Frederick Wright 163

CHAPTER XVII My Personal Experience with Higher Criticism 175
    J. J. Reeve..175

CHAPTER XVIII Bible Difficulties Explained 186
    Edward D. Andrews 186

CHAPTER XIX The Documentary Hypothesis 209
    Edward D. Andrews 209

CHAPTER XX The Authorship and Unity of Isaiah 249
    Edward D. Andrews 249

CHAPTER XXI Daniel Misjudged 261
    Edward D. Andrews 261

Other Books By Christian Publishing House Classics 278
    Exapanded and Updated 278

PREFACE

In 1909 God moved two Christian laymen to set aside a large sum of money for issuing twelve volumes that would set forth the fundamentals of the Christian faith, which were to be sent free to ministers of the gospel, missionaries, Sunday School superintendents, and others engaged in aggressive Christian work throughout the English-speaking world. A committee of men who were known to be sound in the faith was chosen to have the oversight of the publication of these volumes. Dr. A. C. Dixon was the first executive secretary of the Committee, and upon his departure for England, Dr. Louis Meyer was appointed to take his place. Upon the death of Dr. Meyer, the work of the executive secretary devolved upon me.

We were able to bring out these twelve volumes according to the original plan. Some of the volumes were sent to 300,000 ministers, missionaries, and other workers in different parts of the world. On the completion of the twelve volumes, as originally planned, the work was continued through The King's Business, published at 536 South Hope St., Los Angeles, California. Although a larger number of volumes were issued than there were names on our mailing list, the stock became exhausted, and appeals for them continued.

As the fund was no longer available for this purpose, the Bible Institute of Los Angeles, to whom the plates were turned over when the Committee closed its work, has decided to bring out the various articles that appeared in The Fundamentals in four volumes at the least expensive price possible. All the articles that appeared in The Fundamentals, with the exception of a few that did not seem to be in exact keeping with the original purpose of The Fundamentals, will be published in this series.

R. A. TORREY

CHAPTER I The History of Higher Criticism

Canon Dyson Hague

What is the meaning of the higher criticism? Why is it called higher? Higher than what?

At the outset, it must be explained that the word "higher" is an academic term, used in this connection in a purely special or technical sense. It is not used as the common definition of "higher," nor is it meant to convey the idea of superiority. It is simply used to contrast the phrase, "lower criticism."

One of the most important branches of theology is called the Science of Biblical Criticism, which has for its object the study of the history, contents, origins, and purposes of the various books of the Bible. In the early stages of the science, Biblical criticism was devoted to two branches: the lower and the higher. The lower criticism was employed to designate the study of the text of the Scripture, including the investigation of the manuscripts and the different readings in various versions to be sure we have the original words as they were written by the divinely inspired writers. (See *Briggs, Hex.*, page 1.) The term generally used today is "textual criticism."

Higher criticism, on the contrary, was employed to designate the study of the historic origins, dates, and authorship of the various books of the Bible as well as the study of the technical language of modern theology known as "Introduction." A valuable branch of Biblical science, higher criticism is essential in the interpretation of the Word of God. By its researches, the Scriptures are illuminated.

The term "higher criticism" means nothing more than the study of the literary structure of the Bible, specifically the Old Testament. Now this in itself is most laudable. It is indispensable. It is the work every minister or Sunday school teacher does when he takes up his Peloubet's Notes[1] to find out all he can with regard to the portion of the Bible he is studying.

Why Is Higher Criticism Identified with Unbelief?

How is it, then, that higher criticism has become identified in the popular mind with attacks upon the Bible and the supernatural character of the Holy Scriptures?

No study requires more devotion or faith in the supernatural as the pursuit of the higher criticism, which demands at once the ability of the scholar and the simplicity of the believing child of God. For without faith, no one can explain the Holy Scriptures; and without scholarship no one can investigate historic origins.

There is a higher criticism that is reverent in tone and scholarly in work. Ernst Wilhelm Hengstenberg, the Lutheran theologian from Germany, and John Horne Tooke, the English clergyman, may be taken as examples. Perhaps the greatest work in English on higher criticism is Horne's *Introduction to the Critical Study and Knowledge of the Holy*

---

[1] A strategic curriculum created by Francis Nathan Peloubet (1830–March 27, 1920) to train and equip ministers and Bible teachers

Scripture, a massive work that is invaluable in its vast reach of information for the study of the Holy Scriptures.

Horne's *Introduction* is too large a work, too cumbersome for use in this contemporary age. It is the work of a Christian believer; constructive, not destructive; fortifying faith in the Bible, not rationalistic. But the work of the higher critic has not always been pursued in a reverent spirit nor in the spirit of scientific and Christian scholarship.

Subjective Conclusions

The critics who were the leaders, the men who have given name and force to the whole movement, have been men who have based their theories largely upon their own subjective conclusions of the author's style and supposed literary qualifications. Generally, the greater the writer the more versatile his power of expression; and the Bible isn't to be studied as a mere classic by human scholarship without any regard to the Spirit. The Bible, as has been said, has no revelation to make to unbiblical minds. Just because a man is a philological expert does not mean he is able to understand the integrity or credibility of a passage of Scripture without the infilling of the Holy Spirit.

The qualification for the perception of biblical truth is neither philosophic nor philological knowledge but spiritual insight. The primary qualification of the musician is that he be musical; of the artist, that he have the spirit of art. So the merely technical, mechanical, and scientific mind is disqualified for the recognition of the spiritual and infinite. A thoughtful man must honestly admit that the Bible is to be treated as unique in literature, and, therefore, ordinary rules of critical interpretation are inadequate without the direction of the Holy Spirit.

Anti-Supernaturalists

The dominant men of the movement were men with a strong bias against the supernatural. Some of the men who have been most distinguished as the leaders of the higher critical movement in Germany and Holland have been men who have no faith in the God of the Bible, and no faith in either the necessity or the possibility of a personal supernatural revelation. The men who have been the voices of the movement, of whom the great majority, less widely known and less influential, have been mere echoes.

The men who manufactured the articles the others distributed have been notoriously opposed to the miraculous.

We must not be misunderstood. We distinctly repudiate the idea that all the higher critics were or are anti-supernaturalists. Not so. The British-American School embraces within its ranks many earnest believers. What we do say, as we will presently show, is that the dominant minds which have led and swayed the movement, who made the theories that the others circulated, did not believe in miracles.

Therefore, the higher critical movement has not followed its true and original purposes in investigating the Bible for the purposes of confirming faith, or of helping believers to understand the beauties and appreciate the its origin. It has become identified with a system of criticism that is based on hypotheses and suppositions, apparently not to confirm the authenticity and credibility of the Scriptures but to discredit them.

The Origin of the Movement

Who, then, were the men whose views have molded the views of the leading teachers and writers of the higher critical school of today?

It is not easy to say who is the first so-called higher critic or when the movement began, but it is not a contemporary undertaking. Broadly speaking, it has passed through three stages:

1. The French-Dutch
2. The German
3. The British-American

In its origin, the higher critical ideology was Franco-Dutch; speculative if not skeptical. The views now accepted as axiomatic by the Continental and British-American schools of Higher Criticism seem to have been first hinted at by Carlstadt in 1521 in his work on the Canon of Scripture, as well as by Andreas Masius, a Belgian scholar who published a commentary on Joshua in 1574; and a Roman Catholic priest, Peyrere or Pererius, in his *Systematic Theology*, 1660. (LIV. Cap. i.)

Arguably, it has been said to have originated with Spinoza, the rationalist Dutch philosopher. In his *Tractatus Theologico-Politicus* (Cap. vii-viii, 1670), Spinoza came out boldly and impugned the traditional date and Mosaic authorship of the Pentateuch, or the first five books of the Bible, and ascribed the origin of the Pentateuch to Ezra or to some other late compiler.

Spinoza was really the fountain-head of the movement, and his line was taken in England by the British philosopher Hobbes. He went deeper than Spinoza as an outspoken antagonist of the necessity and possibility of a personal revelation. Also, he denied the Mosaic authorship of the Pentateuch.

A few years later, a French priest, Richard Simon of Dieppe, pointed out the supposed varieties of style as indications of various authors in his *Historical Criticism of the Old Testament*, "an epoch-making work."

In 1685, another Dutchman, Clericus (or Le Clerk), advocated still more radical views, suggesting an Exilian and priestly authorship for the Pentateuch and that the New Testament's first five books were composed by the priest sent from Babylon in about 678, B. C., (2 Kings, 17) and also a kind of later editor or redactor theory. Clericus is said to have been the first critic who set forth the theory that Christ and his Apostles did not come into the world to teach the Jews criticism and that it is only to be expected that their language would be in accordance with the views of the day.

In 1753, a Frenchman named Astruc, a medical man and reputedly a free-thinker of wasteful life, advocated for the first time the Jehovistic and Elohistic divisive hypothesis and opened a new era. (Briggs' *Higher Criticism of the Pentateuch*, p. 46.) Astruc said that the use of the two names, Jehovah and Elohim, showed the book was composed of different documents. (The idea of the Holy Ghost employing two words, or one here and another there, or both together as He wills, never seems to enter the thought of the higher critical.) His work was called "*Conjectures Regarding the Original Memoirs in the Book of Genesis*" and was published in Brussels.

Astrue may be called the father of the documentary theories. He asserted there are traces of no less than ten or twelve different memoirs in the Book of Genesis. He denied its Divine authority and considered the book to be disfigured by useless repetitions, disorder, and contradiction. (Hirschfelder, p. 66.) For fifty years Astruc's theory was unnoticed. The rationalism of German input was as yet undeveloped, so that the body was not yet prepared to receive the germ, or the soil the weed.

The German Critics

The next stage was largely German. Johann Gottfried Eichhorn is the greatest name in this period, the eminent professor at Gottingen, who published his work on the Old Testament introduction in 1780. He put into different shape the documentary hypothesis of the Frenchman and did his work so ably that his views were generally adopted by the most distinguished scholars.

Eichhorn's formative influence has been incalculably great. Few scholars refused to do honor to the new sun; it is through him that the name "higher criticism" has become identified with the movement. He was followed by Johann Severin Vater and later by A. T. Hartmann, with their fragment theory that practically undermined the Mosaic authorship, made the Pentateuch a heap of fragments carelessly joined by one editor, and paved the way for the most radical of all divisive hypotheses.

In 1806, Wilhelm Martin Leberecht De Wette, Professor of Philosophy and Theology at Heidelberg, published a work that ran through six editions in four decades. His contribution to the introduction of the Old Testament instilled the same general principles as Eichhorn and, in the supplemental hypotheses, assumed that Deuteronomy was composed in the age of Josiah (2 Kings 22:8).

Not long after, Vatke and Leopold George (both Hegelians) unreservedly declared the post-Mosaic and post-prophetic origin of the first four books of the Bible. Then came Friedrich Bleek, who advocated the idea of the Grundschift or original document and the redactor theory. Next was Ewald, the father of the Crystallization theory; and then Hupfield (1853), who held that the original document was an independent compilation; and Graf, who wrote a book on the historical books of the Old Testament in 1866 and advocated the theory that the Jehovistic and Elohistic documents were written hundreds of years after Moses' time. Graf was a pupil of Reuss, the redactor of the Ezra hypothesis of Spinoza.

Then came a most influential writer, Professor Kuenen of Leyden in Holland, whose work on the Hexateuch, the first six books of the Bible, was edited by Colenso in 1865, and his *"Religion of Israel and Prophecy in Israel,"* published in England in 1874–1877. Kuenen was one of the most advanced exponents of the rationalistic school. Last, but not least, of the continental higher critics is Julius Wellhausen, a theological professor in Germany, who published in 1878 the first volume of his history of Israel and won by his scholarship the attention if not the allegiance of a number of leading theologians. (See *Higher Criticism of the Pentateuch*, Green, p. 59–88.)

It will be observed that nearly all these authors were Germans, and most of them were professors of philosophy or theology.

The British-American Critics

The third stage of the movement is the British-American. The best known names are those of Dr. Samuel Davidson, whose "*Introduction to the Old Testament*," published in 1862, was largely based on the fallacies of the German rationalists. The supplementary hypothesis passed over into England through him and with strange incongruity, he borrowed frequently from Baur. Dr. Robertson Smith, the Scotchman, recast the German theories in an English form in his works on the Pentateuch, *The Prophets of Israel*, and the *Old Testament in the Jewish Church*, first published in 1881, and followed the German school, according to Briggs, with great boldness and thoroughness. A man of deep piety and high spirituality, Smith combined with a sincere regard for the Word of God a critical radicalism that was strangely inconsistent, as did also his namesake, George Adam Smith, the most influential of the present-day leaders and a man of great insight and scriptural acumen, who, in his works on Isaiah and the twelve prophets, adopted some of the most radical and least demonstrable of the German theories. He took his later work, "*Modern Criticism and the Teaching of the Old Testament*," still farther in the rationalistic direction.

Another well-known higher critic is Dr. S. R. Driver, the Regius professor of Hebrew at Oxford, who, in his "*Introduction to the Literature of the Old Testament*" published ten years later and his work on the Book of Genesis, has elaborated with remarkable skill and great detail of analysis the theories and views of the continental school. Driver's work is able, but it lacks originality and English independence. The hand is the hand of Driver, but the voice is the voice of Kuenen or Wellhausen.

The third well-known name is that of Dr. C. A. Briggs, professor of Biblical Theology in the Union Theological Seminary of New York. An equally earnest advocate of the German theories, Briggs published in 1883 his "*Biblical Study*"; in 1886, his "*Messianic Prophecy*," and a little later his "*Higher Criticism of the Hexateuch*." Briggs studied the Pentateuch, as he confesses, under the guidance chiefly of Ewald. (*Hexateuch*, page 63.)

Of course, this list is a very partial one, but it gives most of the names that have become famous in connection with the movement, and the reader who desires more will find a complete summary of the literature of the higher criticism in Professor Bissell's work on the Pentateuch (Scribner's, 1892). Briggs, in his "*Higher Criticism of the Hexateuch*" (Scribner's, 1897), gives an historical summary also.

Now, we must investigate another question—the religious views of the men most influential in this movement. In making the statement that we are about to make, we desire to deprecate entirely the idea of there being anything uncharitable, unfair, or unkind, in stating what is simply a matter of fact.

The Views of the Continental Critics

Regarding the views of the continental critics, three things can be confidently asserted of nearly all, if not all, of the real leaders. First, they were men who denied the validity of miracle and the validity of any miraculous narrative. What Christians consider to be miraculous they considered legendary or mythical; "legendary exaggeration of events that are entirely explicable from natural causes."

Second, these men denied the reality of prophecy and the validity of any prophetical statement. What Christians have been accustomed to consider prophetical, they called dexterous conjectures, coincidences, fiction, or imposture.

Finally, they denied the reality of revelation, in the sense in which it has ever been held by the universal Christian Church. They were avowed unbelievers of the supernatural. Their theories were devised on pure grounds of human reasoning. Their hypotheses were constructed on the assumption of the falsity of Scripture. As to the inspiration of the Bible, as to the Holy Scriptures from Genesis to Revelation being the Word of God, they had no such belief.

We may take them one by one. Spinoza repudiated absolutely a supernatural revelation, and he was one of their greatest. Eichhorn discarded the miraculous and considered that the so-called supernatural element was an Asian exaggeration; and Eichhorn has been called the father of higher criticism, and was the first man to use the term. De Wette's views as to inspiration were entirely infidel. Vatke and Leopold George were Hegelian rationalists, and regarded the first four books of the Old Testament as entirely mythical.

Kuenen, says Professor Sanday, wrote in the interests of an almost avowed Naturalism. That is, he was a free-thinker, an agnostic; a man who did not believe in the Revelation of the one true and living God. (*Brampton Lectures*, 1493, page 117.) He wrote from an avowedly naturalistic standpoint, says Driver (page 205).

According to Wellhausen the religion of Israel was a naturalistic evolution from heathendom, an emanation from an imperfectly monotheistic kind of semi-pagan idolatry. It was simply a human religion.

The Leaders Were Rationalists

In one word, the formative forces of the higher critical movement were rationalistic forces, and the men who were its chief authors and expositors, who "on account of purely philological criticism have acquired an appalling authority," were men who had discarded belief in God and Jesus Christ Whom He had sent. The Bible, in their view, was a mere human product. It was a stage in the literary evolution of a religious people. If it was not the result of a fortuitous concourse of Asian myths and legendary accretions, and its Yahweh, the excogitation of a Sinaitic clan, it certainly was not given by the inspiration of God and is not the Word of the living God.

"Holy men of God spoke as they were moved by the Holy Ghost," said Peter. "The prophets," said Kuenens, "were not moved to speak by God. Their utterances were all their own." (Sanday, page 117.)

These then were their views and these were the views that have so dominated modern Christianity and permeated modern ministerial thought in the two great languages of the modern world. We cannot say that they were men whose rationalism was the result of their conclusions in the study of the Bible. Nor can we say their conclusions with regard to the Bible were wholly the result of their rationalism. But we can say, on the one hand, that inasmuch as they refused to recognize the Bible as a direct revelation from God, they were free to form hypotheses *ad libitum*.

As they denied the supernatural, the animus that animated them in the construction of the hypotheses was the desire to construct a theory that would explain away the supernatural. Unbelief was the antecedent, not the consequent, of their criticism—a statement of fact which modern authorities most freely admit.

The School of Compromise

When we come to the English-writing higher critics, we approach a much more difficult subject. The British-American higher critics represent a school of compromise. On the one hand, they practically accept the premises of the continental school with regard to the antiquity, authorship, authenticity, and origins of the Old Testament books. On the other hand, they refuse to go with the German rationalists in altogether denying their inspiration, yet still they claim to accept the Scriptures as containing a revelation from God. But do they not hold their own peculiar views with regard to the origin, date, and literary structure of the Bible without endangering either their own faith or the faith of Christians in general?

This is the very heart of the question. In order that the reader may see the seriousness of the adoption of the critics' conclusions, a brief resume will be given.

The Point in a Nutshell

According to the faith of the universal church, the Pentateuch is one consistent, coherent, authentic, and genuine composition inspired by God. According to the testimony of the Jews, the statements of the books, the reiterated corroborations of the rest of the Old Testament, and the explicit statement of the Lord Jesus (Luke 24:44, John 5:46–47), the Pentateuch was written by Moses (with the exception, of course, of Deuteronomy 34, possibly written by Joshua or probably by Ezra) at a period of about fourteen centuries before the advent of Christ and 800 years or so before Jeremiah.

Moreover, this portion of the Bible is foundational to the whole revelation of God, not because it is merely the literature of an ancient nation, but because it is the introductory section of the Word of God. It bears His authority and is given by inspiration of the Holy Spirit through His servant Moses. That is the faith of the Church.

The Critics' Theory

According to the higher critics:

1. The Pentateuch consists of four completely diverse documents that were the primary sources of what they call the Hexateuch: (a) The Yahwist or Jahwist, (b) the Elohist, (c) the Deuteronomist, and (d) the Priestly Code, the Grundschift, the work of the first Elohist (Sayce *Hist. Heb.*, 103), now generally known as J.E.D.P. for convenience.

2. These different works were composed at various periods of time, not in the fifteenth century, B. C., but in the ninth, seventh, sixth and fifth centuries; J and E being referred approximately to about 800 to 700 B.C.; D to about 650 to 625 B.C., and P to about 525 to 425 B.C. According to the Graf theory, accepted by Kuenen, the Elohist documents were post-exilian, that is, they were written

only five centuries or so before Christ. Genesis and Exodus as well as the Priestly Code, that is, Leviticus and part of Exodus and Numbers were also post-exilic.

3. Moreover, these different works represent different traditions of the national life of the Hebrews and are at variance in most important particulars.

Furthermore, the conjecture is that these four suppositive documents were not compiled and written by Moses but were probably constructed somewhat after this fashion: For some reason, at some time, and in some way, someone, no one knows who, or why, or when, or where, wrote J. Then someone else wrote another document, which is now called E, again with no knowledge of its origin.

Later, the critics only know who, or why, or when, or where, an anonymous personage, whom we may call Redactor I, took in hand the reconstruction of these documents, introduced new material, harmonized the real and apparent discrepancies, and divided the inconsistent accounts of one event into two separate transactions.

Then some time after this, perhaps one hundred years or more, once again without knowledge of the details, D was written. And after a while another anonymous author, whom we will call Redactor II, took this in hand, compared it with J and E, revised the document with considerable freedom and introduced new material.

And still, someone else, probably between 525 and 425 B.C., wrote P; and then another anonymous Hebrew, whom we may call Redactor III, undertook to incorporate this with the triplicated composite, with what they call redactional additions and insertions. (Green, p. 88, cf. Sayce, *Early History of the Hebrews*, p. 100–105.)

It may be well to state at this point that this is not an exaggerated statement of the higher critical position. On the contrary, we have given here what has been described as a position "established by proofs, valid and cumulative" and "representing the most sober scholarship." The more advanced continental higher critics, Green says, distinguish the writers of the primary sources according to the supposed elements as J1 and J2, E1 and E2, P1, P2 and P3, and D1 and D2, nine different originals in all by the different redactors who completed the Hexateuch by combining P with J, E, and D. (*H. C. of the Pentateuch*, p. 88.)

A Discredited Pentateuch

These four documents are alleged to be internally inconsistent and undoubtedly incomplete. How far they are incomplete was not agreed upon. How much is missing and when, where, how and by whom it was removed; whether it was some thief who stole, or copyist who tampered, or editor who falsified, they do not declare.

In this redactory process, no limit apparently is assigned by the critic to the work of the redactors. It is declared that they inserted misleading statements with the purpose of reconciling incompatible traditions; that they amalgamated what should have been distinguished, and split apart that which should have united.

In one word, it is an axiomatic principle of the divisive hypothesizers that the redactors "have not only misapprehended, but misrepresented the originals" (Green, p. 170). They were animated by "egotistical motives." They confused varying accounts and erroneously ascribed them to different occasions. They not only gave false and colored impressions but also destroyed valuable elements of the suppositive documents and tampered with the dismantled remnant.

Worst of all, the higher critics are unanimous in the conclusion that these documents contain three species of material:

1. The probably true

2. The certainly doubtful

3. The positively spurious

"The narratives of the Pentateuch are usually trustworthy, though partly mythical and legendary. The miracles recorded were the exaggerations of a later age." (Davidson, *Introduction*, p. 131.) In his *"Modern Criticism and the Preaching of the Old Testament,"* George Adam Smith says that the framework of the first eleven chapters of Genesis is woven from the raw material of myth and legend. He denies their historical character and says that he can find no proof in archaeology for the personal existence of characters of the Patriarchs themselves. Later on, however, in a fit of apologetic repentance, he makes the condescending admission that it is extremely probable that the stories of the patriarchs have at the heart of them historical elements. (Smith, p. 90–106.)

Such is the view of the Pentateuch that is accepted as conclusive by "the sober scholarship" of a number of the leading theological writers and professors of the day. It is to this the higher criticism reduces what the Lord Jesus called the writings of Moses.

A Discredited Old Testament

As to the rest of the Old Testament, it may be said that the critics have dealt with it with an equally confusing hand. The time-honored traditions of the Catholic Church and its thesis of inspiration, genuineness, and authenticity have been derided. As to the Psalms, the harp that was once believed to be the harp of David was not handled by the sweet Psalmist of Israel but generally by some anonymous post-exilist; and Psalms that are ascribed to David by the omniscient Lord Himself are daringly attributed to some anonymous Maccabean. Ecclesiastes, written, nobody knows when, where, and by whom, possesses just a possible grade of inspiration, though one of the critics "of cautious and well-balanced judgment" denies that it contains any at all. "Of course," says another, "it is not really the work of Solomon." (Driver, p. 470.)

The Song of Songs is an idyl of human love and nothing more. There is no inspiration in it; it contributes nothing to the sum of revelation. (Sanday, p. 211.) Esther, too, adds nothing to the sum of revelation and is not historical (p. 213). Isaiah was, of course, written by a number of authors. The first part, chapters 1 to 40, by Isaiah; the second by a Deutero-Isaiah and a number of anonymous authors. As to Daniel, it was a purely pseudonymous work, written probably in the second century B.C.

With regard to the New Testament, the critics have confined themselves mainly to the Old Testament, but if Professor Sanday, who passes as a most conservative and moderate representative of the critical school, can be taken as a sample, the historical books are "yet in the first instance strictly histories put together by ordinary historical methods, or, in so far as the methods on which they are composed, are not ordinary, due rather to the peculiar circumstances of the case, and not to influences, which need be specially described as supernatural" (page 399).

The Second Epistle of Peter is pseudonymous, its name counterfeit, and, therefore, a forgery, just as large parts of Isaiah, Zachariah and Jonah, and Proverbs were supposititious and quasi-fraudulent documents. This is a straightforward statement of the position taken by what is called the moderate school of Higher Criticism. It is their own admitted position, according to their own writings.

The difficulty, therefore, that presents itself to the average man of today is this: How can these critics still claim to believe in the Bible as the Christian Church has ever believed it?

A Discredited Bible

There can be no doubt that Christ and His Apostles accepted the whole of the Old Testament as inspired in every portion of every part. From the first chapter of Genesis to the last chapter of Malachi, all was implicitly believed to be the inspired Word of God Himself, And ever since their day, the view of the universal Christian Church has been that the Bible is the Word of God; as the twentieth article of the Anglican Church terms it, it is God's Word written.

The Bible is inspired—God-breathed. "All that is written is God-inspired." The Bible does not merely *contain* the Word of God; it *is* the Word of God. It contains a revelation. "All is not revealed, but all is inspired." This is the conservative and, up to the present day, the almost universal view of the question. There are many theories of inspiration. But whatever view or theory of inspiration men may hold—plenary, verbal, dynamical, mechanical, superintendent, or governmental—they refer either to the inspiration of the men who wrote or to the inspiration of what is written. They imply throughout the work of God the Holy Ghos, and are bound up with the concomitant ideas of authority, veracity, reliability, and truth divine. (The two strongest works on the subject from this standpoint are by Gaussen and Lee. Gaussen on the *Theopneustia* is published in an American edition by Hitchcock & Walden, Cincinnati; and Lee on the *Inspiration of Holy Scripture* is published by Rivingtons. Bishop Wordsworth, on the "Inspiration of the Bible," also is scholarly and strong. Rivingtons, 1875.)

According to the critics, the Bible can no longer be viewed in this light. It is not the Word in the old sense of that term, not the Word of God in that all of it is given by the inspiration of God. It simply *contains* the Word of God. In many of its parts it is just as uncertain as any other human book. It is not even reliable history. Its records of what it does narrate as ordinary history are full of falsifications and blunders. The origin of Deuteronomy, e.g., was "a consciously refined falsification." (See Möller, page 207.)

The Real Difficulty

However, do they still claim to believe that the Bible is inspired? Yes—in a measure. As Dr. Driver says in his preface, "Criticism in the hands of Christian scholars does not banish or destroy the inspiration of the Old Testament; it pre-supposes it." Criticism in the hands of Christian scholars is safe, but the preponderating scholarship in Old Testament criticism has admittedly *not* been in the hands of men who could be described as Christian scholars. It has been in the hands of men who disavow belief in God and Jesus Christ Whom He sent. Criticism in the hands of Horne and Hengstenberg does not banish or destroy the inspiration of the Old Testament. But, in the hands of Spinoza, Graf, Wellhausen, and Kuenen, inspiration is neither pre-supposed nor possible.

Dr. Briggs and Dr. Smith may avow earnestly belief in the Divine character of the Bible, and Dr. Driver may assert that critical conclusions do not touch either the authority or the inspiration of the Scriptures of the Old Testament, but from first to last, they treat God's Word with an indifference almost equal to that of the German critics, handling the Old Testament as if it were ordinary literature. And in all their theories they seem like plastic wax in the hands of the rationalistic molders. However, they still claim to believe in Biblical inspiration.

A Revolutionary Theory

Their theory of inspiration must then be different from that held by the average Christian. In the Bampton Lectures for 1903, Professor Sanday of Oxford, as the exponent of the later and more conservative school of higher criticism, came out with a theory that he termed the inductive theory. It is not easy to describe what is fully meant by this, but it appears to mean the presence of what is called "a divine element" in certain parts of the Bible. Sanday does not cohesively explain what he means, using vague language whenever he speaks of it.. "It is present in different books and parts of books in different degrees. In some the Divine element is at the maximum; in others at the minimum," he says, sounding unsure.

Sanday is sure there is not a divine element in Esther, Ecclesiastes, or Daniel. If it is in the historical books, it is there as conveying a religious lesson rather than as a guarantee of historic veracity; rather as interpreting than as narrating. At the same time, if the histories as far as textual construction was concerned were "natural processes carried out naturally," it is difficult to see where the divine or supernatural element comes in. It is an inspiration that seems to have been devised as a hypothesis of compromise. In fact, it is tenuous, equivocal, and indeterminate, the amount of which is as indefinite as its quality. (Sanday, p. 100–398; cf. Driver, Preface, ix.)

But its most serious feature is this: It is a theory of inspiration that completely overturns the traditional ideas of the Bible and its unquestioned standard of authority and truth. For whatever this so-called divine element is, it appears to be quite consistent with defective argument, incorrect interpretation, if not what the average man would call forgery or falsification.

It is, in fact, revolutionary. To accept it, the Christian will have to completely readjust his ideas of honor and honesty, of falsehood and misrepresentation. Men used to think that forgery was a crime and falsification a sin. Pusey, in his great work on Daniel, said that "to write a book under the name of another and to give it out to be his is in any case a forgery, dishonest in itself, and destructive of all trustworthiness." (Pusey, *Lectures on Daniel*, page 1.) But according to the Higher Critical position, all sorts of pseudonymous material, and not a little of it believed to be true by the Lord Jesus Christ Himself, is to be found in the Bible, and no antecedent objection ought to be taken to it.

Men used to think that inaccuracy would affect reliability and that proven inconsistencies would imperil credibility. But now it appears that there may not only be mistakes and errors on the part of copyists, but forgeries, intentional omissions, and misinterpretations on the part of authors. Yet, marvelous to say, faith is not to be destroyed, but to be placed on a firmer foundation. (Sanday, p. 122.) They have, according to Briggs, enthroned the Bible in a higher position than ever before. (Briggs, "*The Bible, Church and Reason,*" p. 149.)

Sanday admits that there is an element in the Pentateuch derived from Moses himself. An element! But he adds, "However much we may believe that there is a genuine Mosaic foundation in the Pentateuch, it is difficult to lay the finger upon it and to say with confidence, here Moses himself is speaking. The strictly Mosaic element in the Pentateuch must be indeterminate. We ought not, perhaps, to use them (the visions of Ex. 3 and 33) without reserve for Moses himself.f" (p. 172–174–176) The ordinary Christian, however, will say: Surely, if we deny the Mosaic authorship and the unity of the Pentateuch, we must undermine its credibility. The Pentateuch claims to be Mosaic. It was the universal tradition of the Jews. It is expressly stated in nearly all the subsequent books of the Old Testament. The Lord Jesus said so most explicitly. (John 5:46–47.)

If not Moses, Who?

For this thought must surely follow to the thoughtful man: If Moses did not write the Books of Moses, who did?

If there were three, four, six, or nine authorized original writers, why not fourteen, or sixteen, or nineteen? And then another and more serious thought must follow that: Who were these original writers, and who originated them? If there were manifest evidences of alterations, manipulations, inconsistencies, and omissions by an indeterminate number of unknown and unknowable and undateable redactors, then the question arises, who were these redactors, and how far had they authority to redact, and who gave them this authority? If the redactor was the writer, was he an inspired writer, and if he was inspired, what was the degree of his inspiration; was it partial, plenary, inductive or indeterminate?

This is a question of questions: What is the guarantee of the inspiration of the redactor, and who is its guarantor? Moses, Samuel, and Daniel we know, but who are the anonymous and pseudonymous? The Pentateuch, with Mosaic authorship, as Scripturally, divinely accredited, is upheld by Catholic tradition and scholarship, and appeals to reason. But a mutilated scrap-book of anonymous compilations, with its pre- and post-exilic redactors and redactions, is confusion at its worst.

At least, that is the way it appears to the average Christian, who may not be an expert in philosophy or theology, but his common sense must surely be allowed its rights. And that is the way it appears, too, to such an illustrious scholar and critic as Dr. Emil Reich. (Contemporary Review, April, 1905, p. 515.)

It is not possible then to accept the Kuenen-Wellhausen theory of the structure of the Old Testament and the Sanday-Driver theory of its lack of inspiration without undermining faith in the Bible as the Word of God. For the Bible is either the God's written Word, or it is not. The children of Israel were the children of the only Living and True God, or they were not. If their Jehovah was a mere tribal deity, and their religion a human evolution; if their sacred literature was natural with mythical and pseudonymous admixtures; then the Bible is dethroned as the exclusive, authoritative, Divinely inspired Word of God. It simply ranks as one of the sacred books of the ancients with similar claims of inspiration and revelation. Its inspiration is an indeterminate quantity, and any man has a right to subject it to the judgment of his own critical insight and to receive just as much of it as inspired as he or some other person believes to be inspired. When the contents have passed through the sieve of his judgment, it is simply the ancient literature of a religious people containing somewhere the Word of God; "a revelation of no one knows what, made no one knows how, and lying no one knows where, except that it is to be somewhere between Genesis and Revelation, but probably to the exclusion of both." (Pusey, Daniel, xxviii.)

No Final Authority

Another serious consequence of the higher critical movement is that it threatens the Christian system of doctrine and the entire fabric of systematic theology. Up to the present time, text from any part of the Bible was accepted as a proof-text for the establishment of any truth of Christian teaching, and a statement from the Bible was considered an end of controversy. The doctrinal systems of the Anglican, Presbyterian, Methodist, and other Churches are all based upon the view that the Bible contains the truth, the whole truth, and nothing but the truth. (See 39 *Articles Church of England*, vi, ix, xx, etc.) They accept as an axiom that the Old and New Testaments, in part and as a whole, have been given and sealed by God the Father, God the Son, and God the Holy Ghost.

All the doctrines of the Church of Christ, from the greatest to the least, are based on this. All the proofs of the doctrines are based also on this. No text was questioned; no book was doubted; all Scripture was received by the great builders of our theological systems with that unassailable belief in the inspiration of its texts, which was the position of Christ and His apostles. But now the higher critics think they have changed all that. They claim that the science of criticism has dispossessed the science of systematic theology.

Canon Henson tells us that the day has gone by for proof-texts and harmonies. It is not enough now for a theologian to turn to a book in the Bible and bring out a text in order to establish a doctrine. It might be in a book or in a portion of the Book that the German critics have proved to be a forgery or an anachronism, such as Deuteronomy, Jonah, or Daniel, which caseit would be out of the question to accept it. The Christian system, therefore, will have to be readjusted if not revolutionized; every text and chapter and book will have to be inspected and analyzed in the light of its date, origin, circumstances, authorship, and so on. Only after it has passed the examining board of the modern Franco-Dutch-German criticism will it be allowed to stand as a proof-text for the establishment of any Christian doctrine. But the most serious consequence of this theory of the structure and inspiration of the Old Testament is that it overturns the juridic authority of our Lord Jesus Christ.

What of Christ's Authority?

The attitude of Christ to the Old Testament Scriptures must determine ours. He is God. He is the Truth. His is the final voice. He is the Supreme Judge. There is no appeal from that court. Christ Jesus the Lord believed and affirmed the historic veracity of the whole of the Old Testament writings implicitly (Luke 24:44). And the Canon, or collection of Books of the Old Testament, was precisely the same in Christ's time as it is today. And further, Christ Jesus our Lord believed and emphatically affirmed the Mosaic authority of the Pentateuch (Matt. 5:17–18; Mark 12:26–36; Luke 16:31; John 5:46–47).

That is true, the critics say, but neither Christ nor His Apostles were critical scholars. Perhaps not in the twentieth century sense of the term. But, as a German scholar said, if they were not critical scholars, they were scholars of truth who did not come into the world to fortify popular errors by their authority. But then they say, Christ's knowledge as man was limited. He grew in knowledge (Luke 2:52). Surely that implies His ignorance. And if His ignorance, why not His ignorance with regard to the science of historical criticism? (Gore, *Lux Mundi*, page 360; Briggs, *H. C. of Hexateuch*, p. 28.) Or even if He did know more than His age, He probably spoke as He did in accommodation with the ideas of His contemporaries! (Briggs, p. 29.)

In fact, what they mean is that Jesus did know perfectly well that Moses did not write the Pentateuch but taught and allowed His disciples to believe that Moses did simply because He did not want to upset their simple faith in the whole of the Old Testament as the actual and authoritative and Divinely revealed Word of God. (Driver, p. 12.) Or Jesus imagined, like any other Jew of His day, that Moses wrote the books that bear his name, and believed, with the childlike Jewish belief of His day, the literal inspiration, Divine authority and historic veracity of the Old Testament and yet was completely mistaken, ignorant of the simplest facts, and wholly in error. In other words, He could not tell a forgery from an original or a pious fiction from a genuine document.

This, then, is their position: Christ knew the views He taught were false, and yet taught them as truth, or Christ didn't know they were false and believed them to be true when they were not true. In either case, the Blessed One is dethroned as True God and True Man. If He did not know the books to be inauthentic; if He accepted legendary tales as trustworthy facts, then He was not and is not omniscient. He was not only intellectually fallible, He was morally fallible, for He was not true enough "to miss the ring of truth" in Deuteronomy and Daniel.

And further, if Jesus did know the books lacked authenticity, if He did know the stories of the Fall, Lot and Abraham, Jonah and Daniel to be allegorical and imaginary, if not unverifiable and mythical, then He was neither trustworthy nor good. "If it were not so, I would have told you." Those who love and trust Him believe that if these stories were not true, He would have told us so. It is a matter that concerned His honor as a Teacher as well as His knowledge as our God. As Canon Liddon has conclusively pointed out, if our Lord was unreliable in these historic and documentary matters of inferior value, how can He be followed as the teacher of doctrinal truth and the revealer of God? (John 3:12.) (Liddon, *Divinity of Our Lord*, p. 475–480.)

After the Kenosis

These critics say that part of the humiliation of Christ was His being touched with the infirmities of our human ignorance and fallibilities. They dwell upon the so-called doctrine of the *Kenosis*, or the emptying of one's own will, as explaining satisfactorily His limitations. But Christ affirmed after His glorious resurrection that "all things must be fulfilled which were written in the law of Moses, and in the prophets, and in the Psalms concerning Me" (Luke 24:44). This was not a statement made during the time of the *Kenosis*, when Christ was a mere boy, or a youth, or a mere Jew after the flesh (1 Cor. 13:11). It is the statement of Him who has been declared the Son of God with power. It is the Voice that is final and overwhelming. The limitations of the *Kenosis* are all abandoned now, and yet the Risen Lord not only does not give a shadow of a hint that any statement in the Old Testament is inaccurate, not only solemnly declared that those books which we receive as the product of Moses were indeed the books of Moses but also authorized with His Divine "license" to publish as authentic the whole of the Old Testament Scriptures from beginning to end.

However, two or three questions may be raised, as they will have to be faced by every student of present day concerns. The first is this: Is not refusal of the higher critical conclusions mere opposition to light and progress and the position of ignorant alarmists and obscurantists?

Not Obscurantists

It is necessary to be perfectly clear on this point and to remove all misunderstanding. The desire to receive all the light that the most fearless search for truth by the highest scholarship can yield is the desire of every true believer in the Bible. No really healthy Christian mind can advocate obscurantism—the practice of deliberately preventing the facts or full details of something from becoming known.

The obscurant who opposes the investigation of scholarship, and would throttle the investigators, has not the spirit of Christ. In heart and attitude he is a Mediævalist. To use Bushnell's famous apologue, he would try to stop the dawning of the day by wringing the neck of the crowing cock. No one wants to put the Bible in a glass case. But it is the duty of every Christian who belongs to the noble army of truth-lovers to test all things and to hold fast that which is good. He also has rights even though he is, technically speaking, unlearned, and to accept any view that contradicts his spiritual judgment simply because it is that of a so-called scholar, is to abdicate his franchise as a Christian and his birthright as a man. (See that excellent little work by Professor Kennedy, "Old Testament Criticism and the Rights of the Unlearned," F. H. Revell.) And in his right of private judgment he is aware that while the privilege of investigation is conceded to all, the conclusions of an avowedly prejudiced scholarship must be subjected to a peculiarly searching analysis.

The most ordinary Bible reader is learned enough to know that the investigation of the Book that claims to be supernatural by those who are avowed enemies of all that is supernatural, and the study of subjects that can be understood only by men of humble and contrite hearts must certainly be received with caution. (See Parker's striking work, "*None Like It*," F. H. Revell, and his last address.)

The Scholarship Argument

The second question is also serious: Are we not bound to receive these views when they are advanced, not by rationalists but by Christians, and not by ordinary Christians but by men of superior and unchallengeable scholarship?

There is a widespread idea among younger men that the so-called higher critics must be followed because their scholarship settles the questions. This is a great mistake; no expert scholarship can settle questions that require a humble heart, a believing mind, and a reverent spirit as well as a knowledge of Hebrew and philology. No scholarship can be relied upon as expert that is manifestly characterized by a biased judgment, a curious lack of knowledge of human nature, and a still more curious deference to the views of men with a prejudice against the supernatural.

No one can read such a suggestive and inspiring writer as George Adam Smith without a feeling of sorrow that he has allowed this bias of mind to lead him into such an assumption of infallibility in many of his positions and statements. It is the same with Driver. With an air of command, he introduces assertions and propositions that would require exponential documentation to substantiate.

On page after page, his "must be," and "could not possibly be," and "could certainly not," extort from the average reader the natural exclamation: "But why?" "Why not?" "Wherefore?" "On what grounds?" "For what reason?" "Where are the proofs?" But of proofs or reason there is not a trace. The reader must be content with the writer's assertions, reminiscent of the "we may well suppose," and "perhaps" the Darwinian offers as the sole proof of the origination of a different species in his random supposition! ("*Modern Ideas of Evolution*," Dawson, p. 53–55.)

A Great Mistake

There is a widespread idea also among younger students that because Graf, Wellhausen, Driver, and Cheyne are experts in Hebrew that their deductions as experts in language must be received. This, too, is a mistake. There is no such difference in the Hebrew of the so-called original sources of the Hexateuch as some suppose. The argument from language, says Professor Bissell ("*Introduction to Genesis in Colors*," p. vii), requires extreme care for obvious reasons; there is no visible line among the supposed sources. The vast difference between the English of Tennyson and Shakespeare, and Chaucer and Sir John de Mandeville is obvious. But no scholar in the world ever has or ever will be able to tell the dates of each and every book in the Bible by the style of the Hebrew. (See Sayce, "*Early History of the Hebrews*," p. 109.)

The unchanging East knows nothing of the swift lingual variations of the West. Pusey, with his masterly scholarship, has shown how even the Book of Daniel, from the standpoint of philology, cannot possibly be a product of the time of the Maccabees. ("*On Daniel*," p. 23–59.) The late Professor of Hebrew in the University of Toronto, Professor Hirschfelder, in his scholarly work on Genesis, says: "We would search in vain for any peculiarity either in the language or the sense that would indicate a two-fold authorship." As far as the language of the original goes, "the most fastidious critic could not possibly detect the slightest peculiarity that would indicate it to be derived from two sources" (p. 72). Dr. Emil Reich also, in his "*Bankruptcy of the Higher Criticism*," in the Contemporary Review, April, 1905, says the same thing.

Not All on One Side

A third objection remains, a most serious one. It is that all the scholarship is on one side. The old-fashioned, conservative views are no longer maintained by men with pretension to scholarship. The only people who oppose the higher critical views are the ignorant, the prejudiced, and the illiterate. (Briggs, "*Bible, Church and Reason*," p. 240–247.)

This, too, is a matter that needs some clarity. In the first place, it is not fair to assert that the upholders of what are called the old-fashioned or traditional views of the Bible are opposed to the pursuit of scientific Biblical investigation. It is equally unfair to imagine that their opposition to the views of the Continental school is based upon ignorance and prejudice.

What the Conservative school oppose is not Biblical criticism, but Biblical criticism by rationalists. They do not oppose the conclusions of Wellhausen and Kuenen because they are experts and scholars; they oppose them because the Biblical criticism of rationalists and unbelievers can be neither expert nor scientific. A criticism that is characterized by the most arbitrary conclusions from the most spurious assumptions has no right to the word scientific. And further. Their adhesion to the traditional views is not only conscientious but intelligent. They believe that the old-fashioned views are as scholarly as they are Scriptural. It is the fashion in some quarters to cite the imposing list of scholars on the side of the German school and to sneeringly assert that there is not a scholar to stand up for the old views of the Bible.

This is not the case. Hengstenberg of Basle and Berlin was as profound a scholar as Eichhorn, Vater, or De Wette; and Keil, Kurtz, Zahn, and Rupprecht were competent to compete with Reuss and Kuenen. Wilhelm Möller, who confesses that he was once "immovably convinced of the irrefutable correctness of the Graf-Wellhausen hypothesis," has revised his former radical conclusions on the ground of reason and deeper research as a higher critic. Professor Winckler, who has of late overturned the assured and settled results of the higher critics from the foundations, is, according to Orr, the leading German scholar of the East and a man of enormous learning.

Sayce, the professor of Assyriology at Oxford, has a right to rank as an expert and scholar with Cheyne, the Oriel professor of Scripture Interpretation. Margoliouth, the Laudian professor of Arabic at Oxford, as far as learning is concerned, is in the same rank with Driver, the Regius professor of Hebrew, and the conclusion of this great scholar with regard to one of the widely boasted theories of the radical school, is almost amusing in its terseness.

"Is there then nothing in the splitting theories," he says in summarizing a long line of defense of the unity of the book of Isaiah; "is there then nothing in the splitting theories? To my mind, *nothing at all!*" ("*Lines of Defense*," p. 136.)

Green and Bissell are as able scholars, if not more, than Robertson Smith and Professor Briggs, and both of these men, as a result of the widest and deepest research, have come to the conclusion that the theories of the German higher critics are unscientific, unhistorical, and unscholarly. The last words of Professor Green in his excellent work on the "*Higher Criticism of the Pentateuch*" are most suggestive. "Would it not be wiser for them to revise their own ill-judged alliance with the enemies of evangelical truth and inquire whether Christ's view of the Old Testament may not, after all, be the true view?"

Yes! After all, that is the great and final question. We trust we are not ignorant. We feel sure we are not malignant. We desire to treat no man unfairl, or set down anything at all in malice.

However, we desire to stand with Christ and His Church. If we have any prejudice, we would rather be prejudiced against rationalism. If we have any bias, it must be against a teaching which unsteadies heart and unsettles faith. Even at the expense of being thought behind the times, we prefer to stand with our Lord and Savior Jesus Christ in receiving the Scriptures as the Word of God, without objection and without a doubt.

A little learning, and a little listening to rationalistic theorizers and sympathizers may incline us to uncertainty. But deeper study and deeper research will incline us, as it inclined Hengstenberg and Möller, to the profoundest conviction of the authority and authenticity of the Holy Scriptures and to cry, "Your word is pure; therefore, Your servant loves it."

CHAPTER II The Mosaic Authorship of the Pentateuch

George Frederick Wright

During the last quarter of a century an influential school of critics has deluged the world with articles and volumes attempting to prove that the Pentateuch did not originate during the time of Moses and that most of the laws attributed to him did not come into existence until several centuries after his death, and many of them not till the time of Ezekiel. By these critics, the patriarchs are relegated to the realm of myth or dim legend and the history of the Pentateuch generally is discredited.

In answering these destructive contentions and defending the history which they discredit we can do no better than to give a brief summary of the arguments of Mr. Harold M. Wiener, a young orthodox Jew, who is both a well-established barrister in London, and a scholar of the widest attainments. What he has written on the subject during the last ten years would fill thousands of pages; while our condensation must be limited to less than twenty. In approaching the subject it comes in place to consider:

I. The Burden of Proof

The Mosaic authorship of the Pentateuch has until recent times been accepted without question by both Jews and Christians. Such acceptance, coming down to us in unbroken line from the earliest times of which we have any information, gives it the support of what is called general consent, which, while perhaps not absolutely conclusive, compels those who would discredit it to produce incontrovertible opposing evidence. But the evidence that the critics produce is wholly circumstantial, consisting of inferences derived from a literary analysis of the documents and from the application of a discredited evolutionary theory concerning the development of human institutions.

II. Failure of the Argument from Literary Analysis

Evidence of Textual Criticism

It is an instructive commentary upon the scholarly pretensions of this whole school of critics that, without adequate examination of the facts, they have based their analysis of the Pentateuch upon the text that is found in our ordinary Hebrew Bibles. While the students of the New Testament have expended an immense amount of effort in the comparison of manuscripts, and versions, as well as quotations to determine the original text, these Old Testament critics have done scarcely anything in that direction. This is certainly a most unscholarly proceeding, yet it is admitted to be the fact by a higher critic of no less eminence than Principal J. Skinner of Cambridge, England, who has been compelled to write: "I do not happen to know of any work that deals exhaustively with the subject, the determination of the original Hebrew texts from the critical standpoints."

Now the fact is that while the current Hebrew text, known as the Massoretic, was not established until about the seventh century A. D., we have abundant material with which to compare it and carry us back to nearer the time of the original composition of the books. First, the Greek translation known as the Septuagint was made from Hebrew manuscripts two or three centuries before the Christian era. It is from this version that most of the quotations in the New Testament are made. Of the 350 quotations from the Old Testament in the New, 300, while differing more or less from the Massoretic text, do not differ materially from the Septuagint.

Second, the Samaritans broke away early from the Jews and began the transmission of a Hebrew text of the Pentateuch on an independent line which has continued down to the present day. Next, three other Greek versions were made long before the establishment of the Massoretic text. The most important of these was one by Aquila, who was so methodical that he transliterated the word "Jehovah" in the old Hebrew characters instead of translating it by the Greek word "Lord," as was done in the Septuagint.

Next, early Syriac material often provides much information concerning the original Hebrew text. Additionally, the translation into Latin, known as the *Vulgate*, preceded the Massoretic text by some centuries` and was made by Jerome, who was noted as a Hebrew scholar. But Augustine thought it sacrilegious not to be content with the Septuagint.

All this material furnishes ample ground for correcting in minor particulars the current Hebrew text; and this can be done on well-established scientific principles which largely eliminate conjectural modifications. This argument has been elaborated by a number of scholars, notably by Dahse, one of the most brilliant of Germany's younger scholars. At the time of this publications, no German critic has yet produced an answer to it. In England and America, Dr. Redpath and Mr. Wiener have driven home the argument. (See Wiener's "*Essays in Pentateuchal Criticism*", and "*Origin of the Pentateuch*.")

On bringing the light of this evidence to bear upon the subject, some remarkable results are brought out; the most important relate to the very foundation upon which the theories concerning the fragmentary character of the Pentateuch are based. The most prominent clue to the documentary division is derived from the supposed use by different writers of the two words, "Jehovah" and "Elohim," to designate the deity. Jehovah was translated in the Septuagint by a word meaning "Lord," which appears in our authorized version in capitalized form, "LORD." The revisers of 1880, however, have transliterated the word, so that "Jehovah" usually appears in the revision wherever "LORD" appeared in the authorized version. Elohim is everywhere translated by the general word for deity, "God."

Now the original critical division into documents was made on the supposition that several hundred years later than Moses, there arose two schools of writers: one, in Judah, used the word "Jehovah" when they spoke of the deity, and the other, in the Northern Kingdom, "Elohim." And so the critics came to designate one set of passages as belonging to the "J" document and the other to the "E" document. They supposed the passages had been cut up and pieced together by a later editor to make the existing continuous narrative. But when one of these words is found in passages where it is thought the other word should have been used, it is supposed wholly on theoretical grounds that a mistake had been made by the editor, or the "redactor," and so with no further ceremony, the objection is arbitrarily removed without consulting the direct textual evidence.

However, upon comparing the early texts, versions, and quotations, it appears that the words, "Jehovah" and "Elohim" were so nearly synonymous that there was originally little uniformity in their use. Jehovah is the Jewish *name* of the deity, and Elohim the *title*. The use of the words is precisely like that of the English in referring to their king or the Americans to their president. In ordinary usage, "George V", "the king," and "King George" are synonymous in their meaning. Similarly "Taft," "the president," and "President Taft" are used by Americans during his term of office to indicate an identical concept. So it was with the Hebrews. "Jehovah" was the name, "Elohim" the title, and "Jehovah Elohim"—LORD God—signified nothing more.

Consulting the evidence, it appears that while in Genesis and the first three chapters of Exodus (where this clue was supposed to be most decisive) Jehovah occurs in the Hebrew text 148 times; in 118 of these places, other texts have either Elohim or Jehovah Elohim. In the same section, while Elohim alone occurs 179 times in the Hebrew, one or the other designation takes its place in 49 of the passages. In the second and third chapters of Genesis where the Hebrew text has Jehovah Elohim (LORD God) 23 times, there is only one passage in which all the texts are unanimous on this point.

These facts, which are now amply verified, utterly destroy the value of the clue which the higher critics have all along conspicuously put forward to justify their division of the Pentateuch into conflicting "E" and "J" documents, and this the critics themselves are now compelled to admit. The only answer they are able to give is, in Dr. Skinner's words, that the analysis is correct even if the clue that led to it was false, adding "even if it were proved to be so altogether fallacious, it would not be the first time that a wrong clue has led to true results."

On further examination, in the light of present knowledge (as Wiener and Dahse abundantly show), legitimate criticism removes a large number of the alleged difficulties that are put forward by higher critics and renders of no value many of the supposed clues to the various documents. We have space to notice only one or two of these:

In the Massoretic text of Exodus 18:6 we read that Jethro says to Moses, "I thy father-in-law Jethro am come," while in the seventh verse it is said that Moses goes out to meet his father-in-law and that they exchange greetings and then come into the tent. But how could Jethro speak to Moses before they had had a meeting? The critics say that this confusion arises from the bungling patchwork of an editor who put two discordant accounts together without attempting to cover up the discrepancy. But scientific textual criticism completely removes the difficulty. The Septuagint, the old Syriac version, and a copy of the Samaritan Pentateuch, instead of "I thy father-in-law Jethro am come", read, "And one said unto Moses, *behold* thy father-in-law Jethro" comes. Here the corruption of a single letter in the Hebrew gives us "behold" in place of "I". When this is observed the objection disappears entirely.

Again in Genesis 39:20–22, Joseph is said to have been put into the prison "where the king's prisoners were bound . . . And the *keeper of the prison*" promoted him. But in chapter 40:2–4, 7, it is said that he was "in ward of the house of the *captain of the guard*

. . . and the captain of the guard" promoted Joseph. But this discrepancy disappears as soon as an effort is made to determine the original text. In Hebrew, "keeper of the prison" and "captain of the guard" both begin with the same word, and in the passages where the "captain of the guard" causes trouble by its appearance, the Septuagint either omitted the phrase or read "keeper of the prison," in one case being supported also by the *Vulgate*.

In many other instances also, attention to the original text removes the difficulties that have been manufactured from apparent discrepancies in the narrative.

Delusions of Literary Analysis

But even on the assumption of the practical inerrancy of the Massoretic text, the arguments against the Mosaic authorship of the Pentateuch drawn from the literary analysis are seen to be the result of misdirected scholarship and are incorrect. The long lists of words cited as characteristic of the writers to whom the various parts of the Pentateuch are assigned are thought to be motivated by the different objects targeted in the portions from which the lists are made.

However, it is necessary to add that besides the "E" and "J" documents, the critics suppose that Deuteronomy, which they designate "D", is an independent literary production written in the time of Josiah. Furthermore, the critics pretend to have discovered by their analysis of another document, which they call the Priestly Code and designate as "P". This provides the groundwork of most of the narrative and comprises the entire ceremonial portion of the law.

This document, which, according to these critics did not come into existence till the time of Ezekiel, largely consists of special instructions to priests, telling them how they were to perform the sacrifices and public ceremonials and how they were to determine the character of contagious diseases and unsanitary conditions.

Such instructions are necessarily made up largely of technical language, such as is found in the libraries of lawyers and physicians, and it is easy enough to select from such literature a long list of words that are not found in contemporary literature. Furthermore, an exhaustive examination (made by Chancellor Lias) of the entire list of words found in this "P" document attributed to the time of Ezekiel shows absolutely no indication of their belonging to an age later than that of Moses.

The absurdity of the claims of the higher critics to having established the existence of different documents in the Pentateuch by a literary analysis has been shown by a variety of examples. The late Professor C. M. Mead, the most influential of the American revisers of the translation of the Old Testament, in order to exhibit the fallacy of their procedure, took the Book of Romans and arbitrarily divided it into three parts, according as the words "Christ Jesus," "Jesus," or "God" were used; and then by analysis showed that the lists of peculiar words characteristic of these three passages were even more remarkable than those drawn up by the destructive critics of the Pentateuch from the three leading fragments into which they had divided it.

The argument from literary analysis after the methods of these critics would prove the composite character of the Epistle to the Romans as fully as that of the critics would prove the composite character of the Pentateuch. A distinguished scholar, Dr. Hayman, formerly headmaster of Rugby, by a similar analysis demonstrated the composite character of Robert Burns' little poem addressed to a mouse, half of which is in the purest English and the other half in the broadest Scotch dialect. By the same process it would be easy to prove three Macaulays and three Miltons by selecting lists of words from the documents prepared by them, when holding high political offices and from their various prose and poetical writings.

III. Misunderstanding Legal Forms and the Sacrificial System

Another source of fallacious reasoning into which these critics have fallen arises from a misunderstanding of the sacrificial system of the Mosaic law. The critics assert that there was no central sanctuary in Palestine until several centuries after its occupation under Joshua, and that at a later period all sacrifices by the people were forbidden except at the central place when offered by the priests, unless it was where there had been a special appearance by God. But these statements indicate an entire misunderstanding or misrepresentation of the facts. In what the critics reckon as the oldest documents ("J" and "E"), the people were required three times a year to present themselves with sacrifices and offerings "*at the house of the Lord*" (Exodus 34:26; 23:19).

Before the building of the temple this "house of the Lord was at Shiloh" (Joshua 18:1; Judges 18:31; 1 Samuel 2:24). The truth is that the critics upon this point make a most humiliating mistake in repeatedly substituting "sanctuaries" for "altars," assuming that since there was a plurality of altars in the time of the Judges, there was therefore a plurality of sanctuaries. They have completely misunderstood the permission given in Exodus 20:24: "An altar of earth thou shalt make unto Me and shalt sacrifice thereon thy burnt offerings, and thy peace offerings, thy sheep, and thine oxen . . . where I record My name I will come unto thee and I will bless thee. And if thou make Me an altar of stone, thou shalt not build it of hewn stones."

In reading this passage we are likely to be misled by the erroneous translation. Where the revisers read in "every place" and the authorized version in "all places" the correct translation is "in all the place" or "in the whole place." The word is in the singular number and has a definite article before it. The whole place referred to is Palestine, the Holy Land, where sacrifices such as the patriarchs had offered were always permitted to laymen, provided they made use only of an altar of earth or unhewn stones, which was kept free from the adornments and accessories characteristic of heathen altars.

These lay sacrifices were recognized in Deuteronomy as well as in Exodus. (Deuteronomy 16:21.) But altars of earth or unhewn stone, often used randomly and having no connection with a temple of any sort, are not houses of God and will not become such on being called sanctuaries by critics several thousand years after they have fallen out of use.

In accordance with this command and permission, the Jews have always limited their sacrifices to the land of Palestine. When exiled to foreign lands, the Jews, to this day, have ceased to offer sacrifices. It is true that an experiment was made of setting up a sacrificial system in Egypt for a time by a certain portion of the exiles, but this was soon abandoned. Ultimately a synagogue system was established and worship outside of Palestine was limited to prayer and the reading of Scriptures.

But besides the lay sacrifices, which were continued from the patriarchal times and guarded against perversion, there were two other classes of offerings established by statute; namely, those individual offerings that were brought to the "house of God" at the central place of worship and offered with priestly assistance and the national offerings described in Numbers 28 that were brought on behalf of the whole people and not of an individual.

A failure to distinguish clearly between these three classes of sacrifices has led the critics into endless confusion, and error has arisen from their inability to understand legal terms and principles. The Pentateuch is not mere literature but contains a legal code. It is a product of statesmanship consisting of three distinct elements, which have always been recognized by lawgivers: the civil, the moral, and the ceremonial, or what Wiener calls the "jural laws," the "moral code," and "procedure."

The jural laws are those infractions that can be brought before a court, such as "Thou shalt not remove thy neighbor's landmark." But "Thou shalt love thy neighbor as thyself" can be enforced only by public sentiment and Divine sanctions. The Book of Deuteronomy is largely occupied with the presentation of exhortations and motives, aiming to secure obedience to a higher moral code, and is largely followed by the prophets of the Old Dispensation and the preachers of the present day. The moral law supplements the civil law. The ceremonial law consists of directions to the priests for performing the various technical duties and were of as little interest to the mass of people as are the legal and medical books of the present time.

All these strata of the law were naturally and necessarily in existence at the same time. In putting them successively, with the ceremonial law last, the critics have made an egregious and misleading blunder.

IV. The Positive Evidence

Before proceeding to give in conclusion a brief summary of the circumstantial evidence supporting the ordinary belief in the Mosaic authorship of the Pentateuch, it is important to define the term. By it we do not mean that Moses wrote *all* the Pentateuch with his own hand or that there were *no* editorial additions made after his death. Moses was the author of the *Pentateuchal Code*, as Napoleon was of the code which goes under his name.

Apparently the Book of Genesis is largely made up from existing documents, of which the history of the expedition of Amraphel in chapter 14 is a noted specimen; while the account of Moses' death, and a few other passages are evidently later editorial additions. But these are not enough to affect the general proposition. The Mosaic authorship of the Pentateuch is supported by the following, among other weighty considerations:

1. The Mosaic era was a literary epoch in the world's history when such codes were common. It would have been strange if such a leader had not produced a code of laws. The Tel-el-Amarna tablets and the Code of Hammurabi testify to the literary habits of the time.

2. The Pentateuch so perfectly reflects the conditions in Egypt at the period assigned to it that it is difficult to believe that it was a literary product of a later age.

3. Its representation of life in the wilderness is so perfect and so many of its laws are adapted only to that life that it is incredible that literary men a thousand years later should have imagined it.

4. The laws themselves bear indubitable marks of adaptation to the stage of national development to which they are ascribed. It was the study of Maine's works on ancient law that set Mr. Wiener out upon his re-investigation of the subject.

5. The little use that is made of the sanctions of a future life is, as Bishop Warburton ably argued, evidence of an early date and of a peculiar Divine effort to guard the Israelites against the contamination of Egyptian ideas upon the subject.

6. The omission of the hen from the lists of clean and unclean birds is incredible if these lists were made late in the nation's history after that domestic fowl had been introduced from India.

7. As Rev. A. C. Robinson showed in Volume VII of this series, it is incredible that there should have been no intimation in the Pentateuch of the existence of Jerusalem, or of the use of music in the liturgy, nor any use of the phrase, "Lord of Hosts," unless the compilation had been completed before the time of David.

8. The subordination of the miraculous elements in the Pentateuch to the critical junctures in the nation's development is such as could be obtained only in genuine history.

9. The whole representation conforms to the true law of historical development. Nations do not rise by virtue of inherent resident forces but through the struggles of great leaders enlightened directly from on high or by contact with others who have already been enlightened.

The defender of the Mosaic authorship of the Pentateuch has no occasion to flinch in presence of the critics who deny that authorship and discredit its history. He may boldly challenge their scholarship, deny their conclusions, resent their arrogance, and hold on to his confidence in the well authenticated historical evidence, which sufficed for those who first accepted it. Those who now at second hand are popularizing in periodicals, Sunday school lessons, and volumes of greater or less pretentions, the errors of these critics must answer to their consciences as best they can, but they should be made to feel that they assume a heavy responsibility in putting themselves forward as leaders of the blind when they themselves are not able to see.

CHAPTER III Fallacies of the Higher Criticism

Franklin Johnson

The errors of the higher criticism of which I write pertain to its very substance. Those of a secondary character the limits of my space forbid me to consider. My discussion might be greatly expanded by additional masses of illustrative material, and hence I close it with a list of books that I recommend to those who desire to pursue the subject further.

Definition of "Higher Criticism"

As an introduction to the fundamental fallacies of the higher criticism, I will state what the higher criticism is and what the higher critics tell us they have achieved. The name "higher criticism" was coined by Eichhorn, who lived from 1752 to 1827. Zenos,[2] after careful consideration, adopts the definition of the name given by its author: "The discovery and verification of the facts regarding the origin, form, and value of literary productions upon the basis of their internal characters."

The higher critics are not blind to some other sources of argument. They refer to history, where they can gain any polemic advantage by doing so. The background of the entire picture they bring is the assumption that the theory of evolution is true; but their chief appeal is to the supposed evidence of the documents themselves.

Other names for the movement have been sought. It has been called the "historic view," on the assumption that it represents the real history of the Hebrew people, as it must have unfolded itself by the orderly processes of human evolution. But, as the higher critics contradict the testimony of all the Hebrew historic documents, their theory might better be called the "unhistoric view." The higher criticism has sometimes been called the "documentary hypothesis." But as all schools of criticism and all doctrines of inspiration are equally hospitable to the supposition that the biblical writers may have consulted documents, and may have quoted them, the higher criticism has no special right to this title. We must fall back, therefore, upon the name "higher criticism" as the very best at our disposal and upon the definition of it as chiefly an inspection of literary productions in order to ascertain their dates, their authors, and their value, as they themselves interpreted in the light of the hypothesis of evolution, may yield the evidence.

"Assured Results" of Higher Criticism

What do the higher critics profess to have found out by this method of study? The "assured results" on which they congratulate themselves are stated variously. In this country and England they commonly assume a form less radical than that given them in Germany, though sufficiently startling and destructive to arouse vigorous protest and a vigorous demand for the evidences, which, as we shall see, have not been produced and cannot be produced. The less startling form of the "assured results" announced in England and America may be owing to the brighter light of Christianity in these countries. Yet it

---

[2] *"The Elements of the Higher Criticism."*

should be noticed that there are higher critics who go beyond the principal German representatives of the school in their zeal for the dethronement of the Old Testament and the New, in so far as these holy books are presented to the world as a special revelation from heaven as the very Word of God.

The following statement from Zenos may serve to introduce us to the more moderate form of the "assured results" reached by the higher critics. It is concerning the analysis of the Pentateuch, or rather of the Hexateuch, the Book of Joshua being included in the survey.

> The Hexateuch is a composite work whose origin and history may be traced in four distinct stages: (1) A writer designated as J. Jahvist, or Jehovist, or Judean prophetic historian, composed a history of the people of Israel about 800 B. C. (2) A writer designated as E. Elohist, or Ephraemite prophetic historian, wrote a similar work fifty years later, or about 750 B. C. These two were used separately for a time but were fused together into JE by a redactor [an editor] at the end of the seventh century. (3) A writer of different character wrote a book constituting the main portion of our present Deuteronomy, during the reign of Josiah or a short time before 621 B. C. This writer is designated as D. To his work were added an introduction and appendix, and with with these appendages, it was united with JE by a second redactor, constituting JED. (4) Simultaneously with Ezekiel, the ritual law began to be reduced to writing, first appearing in three parallel forms. These were codified by Ezra slightly before 444 B. C. Between that date and 280 B. C., it was joined with JED by a final redactor. Thus no less than nine or ten men were engaged in the production of the Hexateuch in its present form, and each one can be distinguished from the rest by his vocabulary and style and his religious point of view.

Such is the analysis of the Pentateuch, as usually stated in the United States. But in Germany and Holland, its chief representatives carry the division of labor much further. Wellhausen distributes the total task among twenty-two writers and Kuenen among eighteen. Many others resolve each individual writer into a school of writers, multiplying the numbers enormously. There is no agreement among the higher critics concerning this analysis; therefore, the cautious learner may well wait for those who represent the theory to tell what they desire to learned.

While some of the "assured results" of higher critics are in doubt, certain things are matters of general agreement, such as Moses wrote little or nothing, if he ever existed. A large part of the Hexateuch consists of unhistorical legends. We may grant that Abraham, Isaac, Jacob, Ishmael and Esau existed, or we may deny this. In either case, what is recorded of them is chiefly myth. These denials of the truth of the written records follow as matters of course from the late dating of the books, and the assumption that the writers could set down only the national tradition. They may have worked in part as collectors of written stories to be found here and there. But, if so, these written stories were not ancient, and they were diluted by stories transmitted orally. These fragments, whether written or oral, must have followed the general law of national traditions, and have presented a mixture of legendary chaff, with a grain of historic truth to be sifted out.

> The Psalms are so full of references to the Hexateuch that they must have been written after it, hence after the captivity, perhaps beginning about 400 B. C. David may possibly have written one or two of them, but probably he wrote none, and the strong

conviction of the Hebrew people that he was their greatest hymn-writer was a total mistake.

These revolutionary processes are carried into the New Testament, which also is found to be largely untrustworthy as history, as doctrine, and as ethics. It may be a good book, with expression to high ideals that influence the spiritual life, but it can have no divine authority. The Christian reader should consider carefully this invasion of the New Testament by the higher criticism. So long as the movement was confined to the Old Testament, many good men looked on with indifference, not reflecting that the Bible, though containing many parts by many writers and trecording a progressive revelation, is, after all, one book.

The limits of the Old Testament have long since been overpassed by the higher critics, and it is demanded of us that we abandon the immemorial teaching of the Church concerning the entire volume. The picture of Christ portrayed in the New Testament is in many respects mistaken. The doctrines of primitive Christianity were well enough for the time but have no value for us today. Its moral precepts are fallible, and we should accept them or reject them freely, in accordance with the greater light of the twentieth century. Even Christ could err concerning ethical questions, and neither His commandments nor His example need constrain us.

The foregoing may serve as a brief introductory sketch of the higher criticism and as a basis of the discussion of its fallacies, now immediately to follow.

First Fallacy: The Analysis of the Pentateuch

The first fallacy is higher criticism's analysis of the Pentateuch. First, we cannot fail to observe that these various documents and their authors and editors are only imagined. As Green has said, "There is no evidence of the existence of these documents and redactors and no pretense of any, apart from the critical tests that determined the analysis. All tradition and historical testimony as to the origin of the Pentateuch are against them. The burden of proof is wholly upon the critics. And this proof should be clear and convincing in proportion to the gravity and the revolutionary character of the consequences that is proposed."

Moreover, we know what can be done, or rather what cannot be done, in the analysis of composite literary productions. Some of the plays of Shakespeare are called his "mixed plays," because it is known that he collaborated with another author in their production. The very keenest critics have sought to separate his part in these plays from the rest, but they confess that the result is uncertainty and dissatisfaction. Coleridge professed to distinguish the passages contributed by Shakespeare by a process of feeling, but Macaulay pronounced this claim to be nonsense, and the entire effort, whether made by the analysis of phraseology and style or by esthetic perceptions, is an admitted failure in spite of the fact that the style of Shakespeare is one of the most peculiar and inimitable.

The Anglican Prayer Book is another composite production which the higher critics have often been invited to analyze and distribute to its various sources. Some of the authors of these sources lived centuries apart. They are now well known from the studies of historians. But the Prayer Book itself does not reveal one of them, though its various vocabularies and styles have been carefully interrogated. Now if the analysis of the Pentateuch can lead to such certainties, why should not the analysis of Shakespeare and the Prayer Book do as much? How can men accomplish in a foreign language what they cannot accomplish in their own? How can they accomplish in a dead language what they cannot accomplish in a living language? How can they distinguish ten or eighteen or twenty-two collaborators in a small literary production, when they cannot distinguish two? These questions have been asked many times, but the higher critics have given no answer whatever, preferring the safety of a learned silence; "The oracles are dumb."

Much has been made of differences of vocabulary in the Pentateuch, and elaborate lists of words have been assigned to each of the supposed authors. However, these distinctions fade away when subjected to careful scrutiny, and Driver admits that "the phraseological criteria are slight." Orr, who quotes this testimony, adds, "They are slight, in fact, to a degree of tenuity that often makes the recital of them appear like trifling."

Second Fallacy: The Theory of Evolution Applied to Literature and Religion

A second fundamental fallacy of the higher criticism is its dependence on the theory of evolution as the explanation of the history of literature and of religion. The progress of the higher criticism towards its present state has been rapid and assured since Vatke discovered in the Hegelian philosophy of evolution a means of biblical criticism. The Spencerian philosophy of evolution, aided and reinforced by Darwinism, has added greatly to the confidence of the higher critics. As Vatke, one of the earlier members of the school, made the hypothesis of evolution the guiding presupposition of his critical work, so today does Professor Jordan, the very latest representative of the higher criticism. "The nineteenth century," he declares, "has applied to the history of the documents of the Hebrew people its own magic word, evolution. The thought represented by that popular word has been found to have a real meaning in our investigations regarding the religious life and the theological beliefs of Israel."

Thus, were there no hypothesis of evolution, there would be no higher criticism. The "assured results" of the higher criticism have been gained, after all, not by an inductive study of the biblical books to ascertain if they present a great variety of styles, vocabularies, and religious points of view. They have been attained by assuming that the hypothesis of evolution is true and that the religion of Israel must have unfolded itself by a process of natural evolution. They have been attained by an interested cross-examination of the biblical books to constrain them to admit the hypothesis of evolution. The imagination has played a large part in the process, and the so-called evidences upon which the "assured results" rest are largely imaginary.

However, the hypothesis of evolution, when applied to the history of literature, is a fallacy, leaving us utterly unable to account for Homer, or Dante, or Shakespeare, the greatest poets of the world, yet all of them writing in the dawn of the great literatures of the world. It is a fallacy when applied to the history of religion, leaving us unable to account for Abraham, Moses, and Christ, requiring us to deny that they could have been such men as the Bible declares them to have been. The hypothesis is a fallacy when applied to the history of the human race in general.

Our race has made progress under the influence of supernatural revelation, but progress under the influence of supernatural revelation is one thing and evolution is another. Buckle[3] undertook to account for history by an application of the hypothesis of evolution to its problems; but no historian today believes that he succeeded in his effort, and his work is universally regarded as a brilliant curiosity.

The types of evolution advocated by different higher critics are widely different from one another, varying from the pure naturalism of Wellhausen to the recognition of some feeble rays of supernatural revelation; but the hypothesis of evolution in any form, when applied to human history, blinds its and renders us incapable of beholding the glory of God in its more signal manifestations.

Third Fallacy: The Bible a Natural Book

A third fallacy of the higher critics is the doctrine concerning the Scriptures they teach. If a consistent hypothesis of evolution is made the basis of our religious thinking, the Bible will be regarded as only a product of human nature working in the field of religious literature—merely a natural book. If there are higher critics who recoil from this application of the hypothesis of evolution and who seek to modify it by recognizing some special evidences of the divine in the Bible, the inspiration of which they speak rises but little higher than the providential guidance of the writers.

The Church doctrine of the full inspiration of the Bible is almost never held by the higher critics of any class, even of the more believing. Here and there we may discover one who tries to save some fragments of the Church doctrine, but they are few and far between; and the salvage to which they cling is so small and poor that it is scarcely worthwhile. Throughout their ranks, the storm of opposition to the supernatural in all its forms is so fierce as to leave little place for the faith of the Church that the Bible is the very Word of God to man.

However, the fallacy of this denial is evident to every believer who reads the Bible with an open mind. He knows by an immediate consciousness that it is the product of the Holy Spirit. As the sheep know the voice of the shepherd, so the mature Christian knows that the Bible speaks with a divine voice. On this ground, every Christian can test the value of the higher criticism for himself. The Bible manifests itself to the spiritual perception of the Christian as in the fullest sense both human and divine. This is true of the Old Testament as well as the New.

Fourth Fallacy: The Miracles Denied

Yet another fallacy of the higher critics is found in their teachings concerning the biblical miracles. If the hypothesis of evolution is applied to the Scriptures consistently, it will lead us to deny all the miracles recorded. But if applied timidly and waveringly, as it is by some of the English and American higher critics, it will lead us to deny a large part of the miracles and to inject as much of the natural as possible into the rest. We shall strain out as much of the gnat of the supernatural as we can and swallow as much of the camel

---

[3] *"History of Civilization in England."*

of evolution as we can. We shall probably reject all the miracles of the Old Testament, explaining some of them as popular legends and others as coincidences.

In the New Testament we shall pick and choose, and no two of us will agree concerning those to be rejected and those to be accepted. If the higher criticism shall be adopted as the doctrine of the Church, believers will be left in a distressing state of doubt and uncertainty concerning the narratives of the four Gospels and unbelievers will scoff and mock. A theory that leads to such wanderings of thought regarding the supernatural in the Scriptures must be fallacious. God is not a God of confusion.

Among the higher critics who accept some of the miracles there is a notable desire to discredit the virgin birth of our Lord. Their treatment of this event presents a good example of the reasoning they would use to abolish many of the other miracles. One feature of their argument may suffice as an exhibition of all. It is the search for parallels in the pagan mythologies. There are many instances in pagan stories of the birth of men from human mothers and divine fathers that the higher critics could reference to create the impression that the account of the birth of Christ was influenced by these fables to emulate them, thus securing for Him the honor of a celestial paternity. It turns out, however, that these pagan fables do not in any case present to us a virgin mother; the child is always the product of commerce with a god who assumes a human form for the purpose.

The despair of the higher critics in this hunt for events of the same kind is well illustrated by Cheyne, who cites the record of the Babylonian king Sargon, about 3,800 B.C. This monarch represents himself as having "been born of a poor mother in secret and as not knowing his father." There have been many millions of such instances, but we do not think of the mothers as virgins. Nor does the Babylonian story affirm that the mother of Sargon was a virgin or that his father was a god. It is plain that Sargon did not intend to claim a supernatural origin, for, after saying that he "did not know his father," he adds that "the brother of his father lived in the mountains."

It was a case like multitudes of others in which children, early orphaned, have not known their fathers but have known the relations of their fathers. This statement of Sargon is quoted from a translation of it made by Cheyne in the "*Encyclopedia Biblica.*" He continues, "There is reason to suspect that something similar was originally said by the Israelites of Moses." To substantiate this he adds, "See Encyclopedia Biblica, 'Moses,' section 3 with note 4." On turning to this reference, the reader finds that the article was written by Cheyne himself and that it contains no evidence whatever.

Fifth Fallacy: The Testimony of Arachaeology Denied

The limitation of the field of research as far as possible to the biblical books as literary productions has rendered many of the higher critics reluctant to admit the new light derived from archaeology. This is granted by Cheyne. "I have no wish to deny that the so-called 'higher critics' in the past were as a rule suspicious of Assyriology as a young and self-assertive science and that many of those who now recognize its contributions to knowledge are somewhat too mechanical in the use of it and too skeptical as to the influence of Babylonian culture in relatively early times in Syria, Palestine, and even Arabia." This grudging recognition of the testimony of archaeology may be observed in several details.

It was said that the Hexateuch must have been formed chiefly by the gathering up of oral traditions, because it is not to be supposed that the early Hebrews possessed the art of writing and recordkeeping. But the entire progress of archaeological study refutes this. In particular, the discovery of the Tel el-Amarna tablets has shown that writing in cuneiform characters and in the Assyrio-Babylonian language was common to the entire biblical world long before the exodus. The discovery was made by Egyptian peasants in 1887. There are more than three hundred tablets, which came from various lands, including Babylonia and Palestine.

Other finds have added their testimony to the fact that writing and the preservation of records were the peculiar passions of the ancient civilized world. Under the constraint of the overwhelming evidences, Professor Jordan writes, "The question as to the age of writing never played a great part in the discussion." He falls back on the supposition that the nomadic life of the early Hebrews would prevent them from acquiring the art of writing. He treats us to such reasoning as the following: "If the fact that writing is very old is such a powerful argument when taken alone, it might enable you to prove that Alfred the Great wrote Shakespeare's plays."

It was easy to treat Abraham as a mythical figure when the early records of Babylonia were but little known. The entire coloring of those chapters of Genesis, which refer to Mesopotamia, could be regarded as the product of the imagination. This is no longer the case. Thus Clay,[4] writing of Genesis 14, says: "The theory of the late origin of all the Hebrew Scriptures prompted the critics to declare this narrative to be a pure invention of a later Hebrew writer. The patriarchs were relegated to the region of myth and legend. Abraham was made a fictitious father of the Hebrews. Even the political situation was declared to be inconsistent with fact. Weighing carefully the position taken by the critics in the light of what has been revealed through the decipherment of the cuneiform inscriptions, we find that the very foundations upon which their theories rest, with reference to the points that could be tested, totally disappear.

The truth is that wherever any light has been thrown upon the subject through excavations, their hypotheses have invariably been found wanting." However, the higher critics are still reluctant to admit this new light. Thus, Kent says, "The primary value of these stories is didactic and religious, rather than historical."

The books of Joshua and Judges have been regarded by the higher critics as unhistorical on the ground that their portraiture of the political, religious, and social condition of Palestine in the thirteenth century B. C. is incredible.

This cannot be said any longer, for the recent excavations in Palestine have shown us a land exactly like that of these books. The portraiture is so precise and is drawn out in so many distinct features, that it cannot be the product of oral tradition floating down through a thousand years. In what details the accuracy of the biblical picture of early Palestine is exhibited may be seen perhaps best in the excavations by Macalister[5] at Gezer. Here again, there are absolutely no discrepancies between the Land and the Book, for the Land lifts up a thousand voices to testify that the Book is history and not legend.

---

[4] *"Light on the Old Testament from Babel."* 1907. Clay is Assistant Professor and Assistant Curator of the Babylonian Section, Department of Archaeology, in the University of Pennsylvania.

[5] *"Bible Side-Lights from the Mound of Gezer."*

It was held by the higher critics that the legislation which we call Mosaic could not have been produced by Moses, since his age was too early for such codes. This reasoning was completely neutralized by the discovery of the code of Hammurabi, the Amraphel[6] of Genesis 14. This code is very different from that of Moses; it is more systematic, and it is at least seven hundred years earlier than the Mosaic legislation.

In short, from the origin of the higher criticism till this present time, the discoveries in the field of archaeology have given it a succession of serious blows. The higher critics were shocked when the passion of the ancient world for writing and the preservation of documents was discovered. They were shocked when primitive Babylonia appeared as the land of Abraham. They were shocked when early Palestine appeared as the land of Joshua and the Judges. They were shocked when Amraphel came back from the grave as a real historical character, bearing his code of laws. They were shocked when the stele of the Pharaoh of the exodus was read, and it was proved that he knew a people called Israel, that they had no settled residence, that they were "without grain" for food, and that in these particulars they were quite as they are represented by the Scriptures to have been when they had fled from Egypt into the wilderness.[7]

The embarrassment created by these discoveries is manifest in many of the writings of the higher critics, in which, however, they still cling heroically to their analysis and their late dating of the Pentateuch and their confidence in the hypothesis of evolution as the key of all history.

Sixth Fallacy: The Psalms Written After the Exile

The Psalms are usually dated by the higher critics after the exile. The great majority of the higher critics are agreed and tell us that these varied, magnificent lyrics of religious experience all come to us from a period later than 450 B. C. A few of the critics admit an earlier origin, but they do this begrudgingly and against the general consensus of opinion among their fellows. In the Bible, a large number of the Psalms are ascribed to David, and these, with a few insignificant and doubtful exceptions, are denied to him and brought down, like the rest, to the age of the second temple. This leads to the following observations:

1. Who wrote the Psalms? Here, the higher critics have no answer. Of the period from 400 to 175 B. C., we are in almost total lack of knowledge. Josephus knows almost nothing about it, nor has any other writer told us more. Yet, according to the theory, it was precisely in these centuries of silence—when the Jews had no great writers—that they produced this magnificent outburst of sacred song.

---

[6] On this matter see any dictionary of the Bible, art. "*Amraphel.*"

[7] The higher critics usually slur over this remarkable inscription, and give us neither an accurate translation nor a natural interpretation of it. I have, therefore, special pleasure in quoting the following from Driver, "Authority and Archaeology," page 61: "Whereas the other places named in the inscription all have the determinative for 'country,' Ysiraal has the determinative for 'men': it follows that the reference is not to the land of Israel, but to Israel as a tribe or people, whether migratory, or on the march." Thus this distinguished higher critic sanctions the view of the record which I have adopted He represents Maspero and Naville as doing the same.

2. This is the more remarkable when we consider the well-known men to whom the theory denies the authorship of any of the Psalms. The list includes such names as Moses, David, Samuel, Nathan, Solomon, Isaiah, Jeremiah, and more. We are asked to believe that these men composed no Psalms and that the entire collection was contributed by men so obscure that they have left no single name by which we can identify them with their work.

3. This will appear still more extraordinary if we consider the times in which, it is said, no Psalms were produced, and contrast them with the times in which all of them were produced. The times in which none were produced were the great times, times of growth, mental unrest, of conquest, imperial expansion, disaster, and recovery. The times in which none were produced were the times of the splendid temple of Solomon. The times in which none were produced were the heroic times of Elijah and Elisha, when the people of Jehovah struggled for their existence against the abominations of the pagan gods. On the other hand, the times that actually did produce them were the times of growing legalism, obscurity, and of inferior abilities. All this is incredible. We could believe it only if we first came to believe that the Psalms are works of slight literary and religious value. This is actually done by Wellhausen, who says, "They certainly are to the smallest extent original, and are for the most part imitations that illustrate the saying about much writing."

The Psalms are not all of an equally high degree of excellence, and there are a few of them which might give some faint color of justice to this depreciation of the entire collection. But as a whole they are exactly the reverse of this picture. Furthermore, they contain absolutely no legalism, but are as free from it as are the Sermon on the Mount and the Pauline epistles. Yet further, the writers stand out as personalities that must have left a deep impression upon their contemporaries. Finally, they were full of the fire of genius kindled by the Holy Spirit. It is impossible for us to attribute the Psalms to the unknown mediocrities of the period that followed the restoration.

4. Many of the Psalms plainly appear to be ancient. They sing of early events and have no trace of allusion to the age that is said to have produced them.

5. The large number of Psalms attributed to David have attracted the special attention of the higher critics. They are denied to David on various grounds: He was a wicked man, hence incapable of writing these praises to the God of righteousness. He was an iron warrior and statesman, so not gifted with the emotions found in these productions. He was so busy with the cares of conquest and administration that he had no leisure for literary work. Finally, his conception of God was utterly different from that which moved the psalmists.

The larger part of this catalogue of inabilities is manifestly erroneous. David, with some glaring faults and a single enormous crime, for which he was profoundly penitent, was one of the noblest of men. He was indeed an iron warrior and statesman, but he also was one of the most emotional of all great historic characters. He was busy, but busy men not seldom find relief in literary occupations, such as George Washington, who poured forth a continual tide of letters during the Revolutionary War, and as Cæsar, Marcus Aurelius, and Gladstone, while burdened with the cares of empire, composed immortal books.

When he began his career, David's concept of God was indeed narrow (1 Samuel 26:19). But did he learn nothing in all his later experiences, and his associations with holy priests and prophets? He was certainly teachable: did God fail to make use of him in further revealing Himself to His people? To deny these Psalms to David on the grounds of his limited views of God in his early life denies God's revelations to David wherever He found suitable channels?

Further, if we consider the unquestioned skill of David in the music of his nation and his age (1 Samuel 16:14–23), this will constitute a presupposition in favor of his interest in sacred song. If, finally, we consider his personal career of danger and deliverance, this will appear as the natural means of awakening in him the spirit of varied religious poetry. His times were much like the Elizabethan period, which ministered unexampled stimulus to the English mind.

From all this we may turn to the singular verdict of Professor Jordan: "If a man says he cannot see why David could not have written Psalms 51 and 139, you are compelled to reply as politely as possible that if he did write them, then any man can write anything." So also we may say that if Shakespeare, with his small Latin and less Greek, did write his incomparable dramas, that if Dickens, with his mere elementary education, did write his great novels, or if Lincoln, who had no early schooling, did write his Gettysburg address, "then any man can write anything."

Seventh Fallacy: Deuteronomy Not Written by Moses

One of the fixed points of the higher criticism is its theory of the origin of Deuteronomy. In 1 Kings 22 we have the history of the finding of the book of the law in the temple, which was being repaired. Now the higher critics present this finding not as the discovery of an ancient document but as the finding of an entirely new document, which had been concealed in the temple in order that it might be found, accepted as the production of Moses to produce an effect by its assumed authorship. It is not supposed for a moment that the writer innocently chose the fictitious dress of Mosaic authorship for merely literary purposes. On the contrary, it is steadfastly maintained that he *intended* to deceive, and that others were with him in the plot to deceive. This statement of the case leads me to the following reflections:

1. According to the theory, this was an instance of pious fraud that was prepared deliberately. The manuscript must have been soiled and frayed by special care, for it was at once admitted to be ancient. This supposition of deceit must always repel the Christian believer.

2. Our Lord draws from the Book of Deuteronomy all the three texts with which He foils the tempter, Matthew 4:1–11, Luke 4:1–14. It should shock the devout student to hear that his Saviour would select His weapons from an armory founded on deceit.

3. This may be called an appeal to ignorant piety rather than to scholarly criticism, but surely the moral argument should have some weight in scholarly criticism. In the sphere of religion, moral impossibilities are as insuperable as physical and mental.

4. If we turn to consideration of a literary kind, it is to be observed that the higher criticism runs counter here to the statement of the book itself that Moses was its author.

5. It runs counter to the narrative of the finding of the book and turns the finding of an ancient book into the forgery of a new book.

6. It runs counter to the judgment of all the intelligent men of the time who learned of the discovery. They judged the book to have come down from the Mosaic age and to be from the pen of Moses. We hear of no dissent whatever.

7. It seeks support in a variety of reasons, such as style, historical discrepancies, and legal contradictions, all of which prove of little substance when examined fairly.

Eighth Fallacy: Priestly Legislation Not Enacted until the Exile

Another case of forgery is found in the origin of the priestly legislation, if we are to believe the higher critics. This legislation is contained in a large number of passages scattered through Exodus, Leviticus, and Numbers. It has to do chiefly with the tabernacle and its worship, with the duties of the priests and Levites, and with the relations of the people to the institutions of religion. It is attributed to Moses in scores of places. It has a strong coloring of the Mosaic age and of the wilderness life. It affirms the existence of the tabernacle, with an orderly administration of the ritual services. But this is all imagined, for the legislation is a late production.

Before the exile there were temple services and a priesthood, with certain regulations concerning them, either oral or written. Use was made of this tradition; but as a whole the legislation was enacted by such men as Ezekiel and Ezra during and immediately after the exile, or about 444 B. C.

The name of Moses, the fiction of a tabernacle, and the general coloring of the Mosaic age were given it in order to render it authoritative and to secure the ready obedience of the nation. But now:

1. The moral objection here is overwhelming. The supposition of forgery so cunning, so elaborate, and so minute, is abhorrent. If the forgery had been invented and executed by wicked men to promote some scheme of selfishness, it would have been less odious. But when it is presented as the expedient of holy men for the advancement of the religion of the God of righteousness, which afterwards blossomed out into Christianity, we must revolt.

2. The theory gives us a portraiture of such men as Ezekiel and Ezra which is utterly alien from all that we know of them. The expedient might be worthy of the prophets of Baal or of Chemosh; it was certainly not worthy of the prophets of Jehovah, and we dishonor them when we attribute it to them and place them upon a low plane of craft and cunning of which the records concerning them are utterly ignorant.

3. The people who returned from the exile were among the most intelligent and enterprising of the nation, or they would not have returned; they would not have been deceived by the sudden appearance of Mosaic laws forged for the occasion and never before heard of.

4. Many of the regulations of this legislation are drastic. It subjected the priests and Levites to a rule that must have been extremely exasperating, and it would not have been lightly accepted. We may be certain that if it had been a new thing fraudulently ascribed

to Moses, these men would have detected the deceit and would have refused to be bound by it. But we do not hear of any revolt or even criticism.

Such are some of the fundamental fallacies of the higher criticism. They constitute an array of impossibilities. I have stated them in their more moderate forms that they may be seen and weighed without the remarkable extravagances that some of their advocates indulge. In the very mildest interpretation given them, they are repugnant to the Christian faith.

No Middle Ground

But might we not accept a part of this system of thought without going to any hurtful extreme? Many today are seeking to do this. They present to us two diverse results.

1. Some who stand at the beginning of the tide find themselves in a position of doubt. If they are laymen, they know not what to believe. If they are ministers, they know not what to believe or to teach. In either case, they have no firm footing, and no Gospel, except a few platitudes, which do little harm and little good.

2. The majority of those who struggle to stand here find it impossible to do so and give themselves up to the current. There is intellectual consistency in the lofty Church doctrine of inspiration. There may be intellectual consistency that all things have had a natural origin and history under the general providence of God, as distinguished from His supernatural revelation of Himself through holy men and especially through His co-equal Son, so that the Bible is as little supernatural as the "Imitation of Christ" or the "Pilgrim's Progress." But there is no position of intellectual consistency between these two, and the great mass of those who try to pause at various points along the descent are swept down with the current. The natural view of the Scriptures is a sea that has been rising higher for three-quarters of a century. Many Christians bid it welcome to pour lightly over the walls that the faith of the Church has always set up against it in the expectation that it will prove a healthful and helpful stream. It is already a cataract, uprooting, destroying, and slaying.

CHAPTER IV The Bible and Modern Criticism

Bettex Translation David Heagle

It is undeniable that the universe, including ourselves, exists. Whence comes it all? For any clear-thinking mind there are only three possibilities. Either the universe has existed always, it produced itself, or it was created by a Divine, a Supreme Being.

The Universe Not Eternal

The eternity of the universe is most clearly disproved by its evolution. From a scientific point of view, that hypothesis is now discredited and virtually abandoned. Astronomers, physicists, biologists, philosophers, are beginning to recognize more and more, and men like Secchi, Dubois-Reymond, Lord Kelvin, Dr. Klein and others, unanimously affirm that creation has had a beginning. It always tends toward an entropy, that is, toward a perfect equilibrium of its forces, a complete standstill. The fact that it has not yet reached such a condition is proof that it has not always existed. However, should creation ever come to a standstill, it could never again put itself in motion. It has had a beginning, and it will have an end.

That is demonstrated most clearly by its still unfinished evolution. Should anyone say to us of a growing tree or of a young child that either of these forms of life has existed forever, we would at once reply, "Why has it not then long ago grown up so as to reach the heaven of heavens? In like manner, reasons that great astronomer William Herschel with regard to the Milky-Way, that just as its breaking up into different parts shows that it cannot always endure, so we have in this same fact proof that it has not eternally existed.

God, the Author of all Things

There remains, therefore, only this alternative: either the world produced itself, or it was created. That all things came into existence spontaneously, without any cause, and without the use of means became a something is the most unreasonable assumption that could possibly be attributed to a human being. How could anything act before it existed or a thing not yet created produce something? There is nothing more unreasonable than the creed of the unbeliever, notwithstanding all his prating about the excellence of reason.

But if this world did not produce itself, then it must have been created by some Higher Power, some Cause of all causes, such as was that First Principle upon which the dying Cicero called. Or, to use the words of Dr. Klein, that originating cause must have been a "Supreme Intelligence that has at its command unlimited creative power" (*Kosmologische Briefe*, p. 27). Hence what that Intelligence does is both unlimited and unfathomable and can at any time either change this world or make a new one. It is therefore *prima facie* silly for us, with our prodigiously narrow experience, to set any kind of bounds to the Supreme Being. A god who works no miracles and is the slave of his own laws implanted in nature, such a god as the New Theology preaches, is as much lacking in being a true divinity as is the unconscious but all-wise "cosmic ether" of Spiller, or the "eternal stuff" of other materialists.

We conclude, then, that the universe was created—that God is the author of all things.

Revelation in Nature

But now the question arises whether God, who is both the Creator of all things and the Father of spirits, has revealed Himself to his creatures or to His own children, the work of His hands. Such a question might surely provoke one's laughter. For what is the entire universe, this created nature of which we form a part? What is air, water, and fire? What are all organized beings, bodies with many parts put together in such a highly artistic and inscrutable fashion. What about the soul with its infinite capabilities but so little understood?

What are all these matters but a progressive revelation of God, given to us, as it were, in a series of concentric circles rising one above another toward their Source? For this purpose God created the visible so that through it we might perceive the invisible, and for this purpose, the whole creation was made so that through it the invisible things of God, even his eternal power and godhead might be manifested. (Romans 1:20). Creation is only the language of "the Word that was in the beginning, and was with God, and was God, and by Whom all things were made" (John 1:1–3). What does this Word declare? What else but the great infinite name of God the Father, the primal source of all things, the name that must be hallowed? There was a time, however, even before the world was, when there existed nothing but God and His name. All the different works of creation are only letters in this great name.

Revelation in the Bible

There is another revelation that God has given of Himself to men—a more definite and personal one. He declared Himself to Adam and through Enoch and Noah before the Flood and again after the Flood to other generations through Noah and his sons. But because at the building of the tower of Babel, men turned stubbornly away from God. So He gave them up to the thoughts of their own heart and selected one man, Abraham, to go out from his friends and kindred, so that in his seed all the nations of the world might be blessed. Out of Abraham came the people of Israel, to whom were committed the oracles of God; and from this period began the history of the written Word. Moses narrates the beginning of things, also records the law, and holy men of God speak and write as they are moved by the Holy Spirit. That is inspiration—a divine *in-breathing*.

But here a distinction must be made. The Bible reports matters of history, and in doing so includes many genealogies which were composed, first of all, not for us, but for those most immediately concerned and for the angels (1 Corinthians 4:9). Also it reports many sins and shameful deeds. The Bible undertakes to represent not only God but also man just as he is. Moreover, in giving these narratives, it may be said that God, who numbers the very hairs of our head, exercised a providential control so that what was reported by His chosen men should be the real facts and nothing else. To what extent He inspired those men with the very words used by them, it is not for us to know but probably more fully than we suspect.

But after having communicated the law to Moses on Mount Sinai and in the Tabernacle, God communes with him as a friend, and Moses writes "all the words of this law in a book" (Deuteronomy. 28:58; 31:24); then Moses really becomes the pen of God. When God speaks to the prophets, "Behold, I put my words in your mouth," and "all the words that you hear you shall say to this people," then these prophets become the very mouth of God. When Christ appears to John on Patmos, and says, "To the angel of the church write these things," this is an instance of verbal dictation.

But just here we are amused at those weak-minded critics who, with their overused phrases, talk so glibly about "mechanical instruments" and "mere verbal dictation." Does then a self-revelation of the Almighty and a making known of His counsels, a gracious act which exalts the human agent to be a coworker with Jehovah, annihilate personal freedom? Or does it not rather enlarge that freedom and lift it up to a higher and more joyous activity? Am I then a "mechanical instrument" when with deep devotion and enthusiasm I repeat after Christ, word for word, the prayer which He taught his disciples? The Bible is, consequently, a book which originated according to the will and with the cooperation of God. As such, it is our guide to eternity, conducting humankind with absolute certainty from the first creation to the New Jerusalem (*Comp.* Genesis 2:8–10 with Revelation 21:1, 2).

Proof of the Bible's Inspiration

How does the Bible prove itself to be a divinely inspired, heaven-given book, a communication from a Father to His children, and thus a revelation? First, as does no other sacred book in the world does, it condemns man and all his works apart from God. It does not praise either man's wisdom, his reason, his art, or any progress that he has made but represents him as being a sinner in the sight of God, incapable of doing anything good and deserving only death and endless perdition. Truly, such a book that causes millions of men, troubled in conscience, to prostrate themselves in the dust, crying, "God be merciful to me a sinner," must contain more than mere ordinary truth.

Second, the Bible exalts itself far above all mere human books by its announcement of the great incomprehensible mystery that, "God so loved the world that He gave His only begotten Son; that whosover believeth in Him should not perish, but have everlasting life" (John 3:16). Where is there a god among all the heathen nations, be he Osiris, Brahma, Baal, Jupiter, or Odin, that would have promised those people that by taking upon himself the sin of the world and suffering its punishment, he would thus become a savior and redeemer to them?

Third, the Bible sets the seal of its divine origin upon itself by means of the prophecies. Appropriately God inquires through the prophet Isaiah, "Who, is like Me? Let him proclaim it. Let him declare and lay out before me what has happened sincie I established my ancient people, and what is yet to come—yes, let them foretell what will come" (Ch. 44:7). Or, addressing Pharaoh, "Where are your wise men? Let them tell you what the Lord of Hosts hath purposed upon Egypt" (Ch. 19:12).

Again we say, where is there a god, or gods, a founder of religion, such as Confucius, Buddha, or Mohammed, who could, with such certainty, have predicted the future of even his own people? Or where is there a statesman who in these times can foretell what will be the condition of things in Europe ten years from now? Nevertheless the prophecies of Moses and his threatened judgments upon the Israelites have been literally fulfilled. Literally also have been fulfilled the prophecies respecting the destruction of those great ancient cities, Babylon, Nineveh, and Memphis. Who in these times would believe a like prophecy respecting London, Paris, or New York? Moreover, in a literal way has been fulfilled what the prophets David and Isaiah foresaw concerning the last sufferings of Christ—His death on the cross, His drinking of vinegar, and the casting of lots for His garments. And there are other prophecies that will fulfilled, such as the promises made to Israel, the final judgment, and the end of the world. "For," as Habakkuk says, "the vision is yet for an appointed time, and will not lie. Though it tarry, wait for it; it will surely come" (Ch. 2:3).

Furthermore, the Bible has demonstrated its peculiar power by its influence with the martyrs. Think of the hundreds of thousands who, at different times and among different peoples, have sacrificed their all, their wives, their children, all their possessions, and finally life itself on account of this book. Think of how they have, on the rack and at the stake, confessed the truth of the Bible and borne testimony to its power. However, you critics and despisers of God's Word, if you will only write such a book and then die for it, we will believe you.

Last, the Bible shows itself every day to be a divinely given book by its benevolent influence among all kinds of people. It converts to a better life the ignorant and the learned, the beggar on the street and the king upon his throne, the poor, the greatest poet and the profoundest thinker, civilized people and uncultured savages. Despite all the scoffing and derision of its enemies, it has been translated into hundreds of languages and has been preached by thousands of missionaries to millions of people. It makes the proud humble and the dissolute virtuous; it consoles the unfortunate and teaches man how to live patiently and die triumphantly. No other book or collection of books accomplishes for man the exceeding great benefits accomplished by this book of truth.

Modern Criticism and its Rationalistic Method

In these times there has appeared a criticism that constantly grows bolder in its attacks upon this sacred book and now decrees, with all self-assurance and confidence, that the Bible is simply a human production. It is declared to be full of errors, many of its books to be fraudulent, written by unknown men at later dates than those assigned. But we ask, upon what fundamental principle, what axiom, is this verdict of the critics based? It is upon the idea that, as Renan expressed it, reason is capable of judging all things but is itself judged by nothing. That is surely a proud dictum but an empty one if its character is really noticed. To be sure, God has given reason to man, so that, in his customary way of planting and building, buying and selling, he may make practical use of created nature that surrounds him.

But is reason, even as respects matters of this life, in accord with itself? By no means. For if that were so, where does all the strife and contention in all walks of life come from? Does it not all proceed from the conflicts of reason? The entire history of our race is the history of millions of men gifted with reason who have been in perpetual conflict one with another. Is it with such reason, then, that such a sentence is to be pronounced upon a divinely given book? A purely rational revelation would certainly be a contradiction of terms; besides, it would be wholly superfluous. But when reason undertakes to speak of things entirely supernatural, invisible and eternal, it talks as a blind man does about colors, speaking of matters of which it knows nothing. It has not ascended up to heaven, neither has it descended into the deep; and therefore a purely rational religion is no religion at all.

Incompetency of Reason for Spiritual Truth

Reason alone has never inspired men with great sublime conceptions of spiritual truth, whether in discovery or invention; but usually it has at first rejected and ridiculed such matters. And just so it is with these rationalistic critics, they have no appreciation or understanding of the majesty in God's Word. They understand neither the excellence of Isaiah, the pathos of David's repentance, the audacity of Moses' prayers, the philosophic depth of Ecclesiastes, nor the wisdom of Solomon that "raises her voice in the streets." (Proverbs 1:20)

According to higher critics, ambitious priests at a later date than is commonly assigned compiled all those books to which we have alluded. Also, they wrote the Sinaitic law and invented the whole story of Moses' life. ("A magnificent fiction"—so one of the critics calls that story.) But if all this is so, then we must believe that cunning falsifiers, who were devout men, genuine products of their day; that is to say, we must believe not only that shallow-minded men have uncovered for us eternal truths and the most distant future but also that gross liars have declared to us the inexorable righteousness of a holy God! Of course, all that is nonsense; no one can believe it.

But if these critics speak with great self-assurance upon topics such as the history of Israel, the peculiar work of the prophets, revelation, inspiration, the essence of Christianity, the difference between the teachings of Christ and those of Paul, anyone who intelligently reads what they say is impressed with the idea that they do not really understand the matters concerning which they speak.

In like manner, they speak with the appearance of intimate knowledge about men with whom they have only a far-off acquaintance; and they discuss events in the realm of the Spirit where they have had no personal experience. Thus they both illustrate and prove the truth of the Scripture teaching that "the natural man does not the things of the Spirit of God."

These critics say that God, not being a man, cannot speak; consequently there is no word of God! Also, God cannot manifest Himself in visible form; therefore all the accounts of such epiphanies are mythical tales! Inspiration, they tell us, is unthinkable; so all representations of such acts are diseased imagination! Of prophecy, there is none; what purports to be such was written after the events! Miracles are impossible; therefore, all the reports of them, as given in the Bible, are mere fiction. Thus it is explained that men always seek their own advantage and personal glory, and so it was with those "prophets of Israel."

Such is what they call "impartial science," "unprejudiced research," "objective demonstration."

Nothing New under the "New Views"

Moreover, these critics claim for their peculiar views that they are the "new theology," and the "latest investigation." But that also is untrue. Even in the times of Christ, the famous rabbi Hillel and his disciple Gamaliel substituted for the Mosaic law all manner of "traditions" (Matthew 15:2–9; 23:16–22). Since then, other learned rabbis, such as Ben Akiba, Maimonides and others, have engaged in Bible criticism, not only casting doubts upon the genuineness of various books of the Old Testament but also denying the miracles and talking learnedly about "myths." Even eighteen hundred years ago, Celsus brought forward the same objections as those now raised by modern criticism; and in his weak and bungling production, the "*Life of Jesus*," David Strauss has in part repeated them. Also there have been other noted heretics, such as Arius (317 A. D.), who denied the divinity of Christ, and Pelagius in the fifth century, who rejected the doctrine of original sin.

Indeed this exceedingly new theology adopts even the unbelief of those old Sadducees who said "there is no resurrection, neither angel nor spirit" (Acts 23:8), and whom Christ reproved with the words, "Ye do err, not knowing the Scriptures nor the power of God" (Matthew 22:29). It certainly does not argue for the spiritual progress of our race that such a threadbare and outworn unbelieving kind of science should again, in these days, deceive and even fool thousands of people.

No Agreement among the Critics

Do these critics then agree with one another? Far from it. To be sure, they unanimously deny the inspiration of the Bible, the divinity of Christ and of the Holy Spirit, the fall of man and the forgiveness of sins through Christ; also prophecy and miracles, the resurrection of the dead, the final judgment, heaven and hell. But when it comes to their supposed sure results, not any two of them affirm the same things; and their numerous publications create a flood of disputable, self-contradictory, and mutually destructive hypotheses.

For example, the Jehovah of the Old Testament is made to be some heathen god, either a nomadic god, the weather-god Jahu, or the god of West-Semitism. It was David who first introduced this divinity; and according to some authors the peculiar worship of this god was, with its human sacrifices, only a continuation of the Baal-Moloch worship! It is sometimes reported that Abraham never existed, but at other times that he was a Canaanite chief, dwelling at Hebron. Or he is the myth of the Aurora; and Sarah, or Scharratu, is the wife of the moon-god Sin, and so on. The twelve sons of Jacob are very probably the twelve months of the year. As to Moses, some teach there never was such a man, also that the ten commandments were composed in the time of Manasseh.

The more moderate writers say that Moses is a historical character. It was in Midian that he learned about Jah, the tribal god of the Kenites; and he determined with this divinity to liberate his people. Elijah is simply a myth, or he was some unfortunate prophet who had perhaps been struck by lightning. And so, too, this modern criticism knows for sure that it was not Solomon but an unknown king, living after the time of Ezra, who wrote Ecclesiastes; also there never was a Daniel but, again, some unknown author wrote the book bearing that name. Moreover, Kautsch tells us that this book first made its appearance in January, 164 B. C., while other critics are positive that it was in 165. One must wonder why that unknown author could not have been named Daniel?

Wellhausen also knows of twenty-two different authors—all of them, to be sure, unknown—for the books of Moses, while Kuenen is satisfied with sixteen. The noted English critic, Canon Cheyne, is said to have taken great pains to tear the book of Isaiah's prophecies into one hundred sixty pieces, all by unknown writers; which pieces were scattered through ten different epochs including four and a half centuries ("*Modern Puritan*," 1907, p. 400).

Likewise this critic knows that the first chapter of 1 Samuel originated with an unknown writer living some five hundred years after the time of that prophet; also that Hannah's glory-song, as found in 2 Kings, was written by some other "unknown." That Eli ruled over Israel for forty years is, "in all likelihood," the unauthentic statement of a later day (Hastings' Bible Dictionary). The book of Deuteronomy was written, we are told, in 561 B. C., and Ecclesiastes in 264 B. C.; and a German critic, Budde, is certain that the book of Job has somehow lost its last chapter, and that fifty-nine verses of this book should be wholly expunged.

Such are a few illustrations of the way in which Holy Scripture is treated by the criticism we are considering.

Criticism Applied to the New Testament

Of course, this modern criticism does not stop short of the New Testament. This part of the Bible, Harnack says, narrates for us incredible stories respecting the birth and childhood of Christ. "Nevermore," he goes on to assert, "shall we believe that he walked upon the sea and commanded the storm." It stands to reason that He did not rise from the dead. The Fourth Gospel is phony and so also is the Epistle to the Romans. The Book of Revelation is only the occasion for derisive laughter on the part of these skeptical critics; and because it is so, the curse mentioned in its last chapter is made applicable to them (vs. 18, 19).

Nevertheless, these men sin most seriously against Christ. In their view the Son of God, the Word that was in the beginning with God, and that was God, and without Whom nothing exists, is only a fanatical young rabbi; entangled in the peculiar views and superstitions of his people. He died upon the cross only because he misconceived of the character of his own mission and the nature of his times. Jesus "is not indispensable to the Gospel," writes Harnack.

Now all this is what is denominated Biblical criticism. It is a jumble of mere hypotheses, imaginings and assertions, brought forward often without even the shadow of proof, and with no real certainty. Still, in these times it represents itself to thousands of nominal Christians and to hundreds of miserably deceived theological students who are to become preachers of God's word, as being the "assured results of the latest scientific research."

What Are the Fruits of this New Criticism?

Now, if these people were of the truth and believed Him who says, "I am the Way, the Truth and the Life," they would not be under the necessity of tediously working through numerous publications (statistics show that there appear in Europe and America annually some eight hundred of these works); but they would find in His teaching a simple and sure means for testing the character of these critical doctrines.

"Ye shall know them by their fruits," is what Christ says of the false teachers who came in His name. "Do men gather grapes of thorns, or figs of thistles?" (Matthew 7:16). Are the fruits of modern criticism good? Has not this criticism already robbed, perhaps forever, thousands of people of their first love, their undoubting faith, and their joyous hope? Has it not sown dissension, fostered pride and self-conceit, and injured before all the world the authority of both the Church and its ministers? Has it not offended Christ's "little ones?" (Matthew 18:6, 7). And does it not furnish the enemies of God with opportunities for deriding and scorning the truth? Where are the souls that it has led to God—comforting, strengthening, purifying and sanctifying them? Where are the individuals who even in the hour of death have continued to rejoice in the benefits of this criticism?

In the study room it ensnares and lecture halls it makes great pretenses, it is still serviceable. But when the thunders of God's power break in upon the soul, when despair at the loss of all one has loved takes possession of the mind, when remembrance of a miserable lost life or of past misdeeds is felt and realized, when one is on a sick-bed and death approaches, and the soul, appreciating that it is now on the brink of eternity, calls for a Savior—just at this time when its help is most needed, this modern religion utterly fails.

In 1864, in Geneva, one of those modern theologians was summoned to prepare for execution a young man who had committed murder and robbery. But he candidly exclaimed, "Call someone else, I have nothing to say to him." This incompetent criticism did not know of any consolation for the sin-burdened soul; therefore an orthodox clergyman was obtained, and the wretched man, murderer though he was, died reconciled to God through the blood of Christ.

But suppose that all the teachings of this criticism were true; what would it avail us? It would put us in a sad condition indeed. For then, sitting beside ruined temples and broken down altars, with no joy as respects the hereafter, no hope of everlasting life, no God to help us, no forgiveness of sins, we should be utterly unable either to know or believe anything more. Can such a view of the world, such a religion, be true? No! If this modern criticism is true, then away with all so-called Christianity, which only deceives us with idle tales! Away with a religion which has nothing to offer us but the commonplace teachings of morality! Away with faith! Away with hope! Let us eat and drink, for tomorrow we die!

These Teachings in the Light of Scripture

This is what God's Word has to say on the subject:

2 Peter 1:21: [21] "or no prophecy was ever produced by the will of man, but men carried along by the Holy Spirit spoke from God."

2 Timothy 3:16–17: [16] All Scripture is inspired by God and profitable for teaching, for reproof, for correction, for training in righteousness; [17] so that the man of God may be fully competent, equipped for every good work.

Galatians 1:11-12: " For I would have you know, brothers, that the gospel that was preached by me is not according to man. For I neither received it from man, nor was I taught it, but I received it through a revelation of Jesus Christ."[8]

---

[8] I.e. *human origin*, Lit *uncovering; disclosure;* Gr *apokalypseos*

Romans 1:16: "For I am not ashamed of the gospel, for it is the power of God for salvation to everyone who believes, to the Jew first and also to the Greek."

Acts 20:30: and from among your own selves men will arise, speaking twisted things, to draw away the disciples after them.

2 Peter 2:1: "But false prophets also arose among the people, just as there will also be false teachers among you, who will secretly introduce destructive heresies, even denying the Master who bought them, bringing swift destruction upon themselves. "

1 Corinthians 1:20–21: [20] Where is the wise man? Where is the scribe? Where is the debater of this age? Has not God made foolish the wisdom of the world? [21] For since, in the wisdom of God, the world through its wisdom did not know God, God was pleased through the foolishness of preaching to save those who believe.

Colossians 2:4: [4] This I am saying so that no one may delude you with persuasive arguments.

1 Corinthians 3:19: [19] For the wisdom of this world is foolishness before God. For it is written, "He is the one who catches the wise in their craftiness;"[9]

1 Corinthians 2:4-5: [4] and my message and my preaching were not in persuasive words of wisdom, but in demonstration of the Spirit and of power, [5] so that your faith would not rest on the wisdom of men, but on the power of God.

1 Corinthians 2:12-13: [12] Now we have received, not the spirit of the world, but the Spirit who is from God, so that we may know the things freely given to us by God, [13] which things we also speak, not in words taught by human wisdom, but in those taught by the Spirit, combining spiritual thoughts with spiritual words.

Colossians 1:21: [21] And you, who once were alienated and enemies in your minds, doing evil works,

2 Corinthians 10:5: [5] We are destroying speculations and every lofty thing raised up against the knowledge of God, and we are taking every thought captive to the obedience of Christ,

Galatians 1:9: [9] As we said before, and now I say again, if anyone is proclaiming a gospel to you contrary to[10] what you have received, let him be accursed![11]

1 Corinthians 15:17: [17] and if Christ has not been raised, your faith is futile; you are still in your sins.

2 John 1:7–11: [7] For many deceivers have gone out into the world, even those who do not confess the coming of Jesus Christ in the flesh. This is the deceiver and the antichrist. [8] Watch yourselves, that you do not lose what we have worked for, but that you may receive a full reward. [9] Everyone who goes on ahead and does not remain in the teaching of Christ, does not have God; the one who remains in the teaching, he has both the Father and the Son. [10] If anyone comes to you and does not bring this teaching, do not

---

[9] Quotation from Job 5:13

[10] Or *other than*

[11] Gr *anathema*

receive him into your house or give him any greeting; ¹¹ for the one who gives him a greeting shares in his evil deeds.

Luke 11:52: ⁵² Woe to you lawyers! For you have taken away the key of knowledge; you yourselves did not enter, and you hindered those who were entering."

Conclusion

Let us then, by repudiating this modern criticism, show our condemnation of it. What does it offer us? Nothing. What does it take away? Everything. Do we have any use for it? No! It neither helps us in life nor comforts us in death; it will not judge us in the world to come. For our biblical faith we do not need either the glowing praise of men nor the approval of a few poor sinners. We will not attempt to improve the Scriptures and adapt them to our liking, but we will believe them. We will not criticize them, but we will be directed by them. We will not exercise authority over them, but we will obey them. We will trust Him who is the Way, the Truth, and the Life. His Word shall make us free.

Respice finem, "consider the end"—that is what even the old Romans said. True rationalism adjudges all things from the standpoint of eternity; and it asks of every religion, "What can you do for me with regard to the great beyond?" What does this Biblical criticism offer us here? Only fog and mist or, at best, an endless state of indecision; something impersonal and inactive, just like its god, whose very nature is inconceivable. "Eternal life," writes one of these modernists, "is only the infinitely weak vestige of the present life." Here also the maxim proves itself true, "By their fruits ye shall know them."

Just as for our present life this criticism offers us no consolation, no forgiveness of sins, no deliverance from "the fear of death, through which we are all our lifetime subject to bondage," so also it knows nothing respecting the great beyond—nothing with regard to that new heaven and new earth wherein righteousness shall dwell; nothing with regard to that golden city that shines with eternal light; nothing with regard to a God who wipes away all tears from our eyes. It is utterly ignorant of the glory of God, and on that account it stands condemned.

John 6:68-69: ⁶⁸ Simon Peter answered him, "Lord, to whom shall we go? You have the words of eternal life, ⁶⁹ and we have believed, and have come to know, that you are the Holy One of God."

Revelation 3:11: ¹¹ I am coming quickly; hold fast what you have, so that no one will take your crown.

CHAPTER V Holy Scripture and Modern Negations

James Orr

Today, is there a tenable doctrine of Holy Scripture for the Christian Church and for the world? If there is, what is that doctrine? That is the pressing question for the present time. Is there a book can be regarded as the repository of a true revelation of God and an infallible guide in the way of life, and as to our duties to God and man? This is a question of immense importance to everyone. Fifty years ago, perhaps less than that, the question hardly needed to be asked among Christian people. It was universally conceded that there is such a book, the book that we call the Bible. Here, it was believed, is an inspired record of the whole will of God for man's salvation. Accepted as true and inspired, one cannot stumble, cannot err in attaining the supreme end of existence, in finding salvation, in grasping the prize of a glorious immortality.

Now, a change has come. There is no disguising the fact that we live in an age when, even within the Church, there is much uneasy and distrustful feeling about the Holy Scriptures—a hesitancy to lean upon them as an authority and to use them as the weapons of precision they once were. Additionally, there is a corresponding anxiety to find corroboration from external Church authority, or with others, in Christ Himself, or in a "Christian consciousness"—a surer basis for Christian belief and life. Today, There is often heard reference in Protestantism to the substitution of an "infallible Bible for an infallible Church." The implication is that the one idea is just as baseless as the other.

It has been suggested that the thought of an external authority must be wholly given up; that only that can be accepted which carries its authority within itself by the appeal it makes to reason or to our spiritual being. Therein lies the judge for us of what is true and what is false.

That proposition has an element of truth in it; it may be true or may be false according as we interpret it. However, as it is frequently interpreted, it leaves the Scriptures—but more than that, it leaves Jesus Christ Himself—without any authority for us except with what our own minds see fit to clothe Him.

But in regard to the infallible Bible and the infallible Church, it is proper to point out that there is a considerable difference between these two things—between the idea of an authoritative Scripture and the idea of an infallible Church or an infallible Pope, in the Roman sense of that word. It may be a clever antithesis to say that Protestantism substituted the idea of an infallible Book for the older Romish dogma of an infallible Church; but the antithesis, the contrast, unfortunately has one fatal inaccuracy about it. The idea of the authority of Scripture is not younger, but older than Romanism. It is not a late invention of Protestantism. It is not something that Protestants invented and substituted for the Roman conception of the infallible Church; but *it is the original conception that lies in the Scriptures themselves.*

There is a great difference there. It is a belief in the Holy Scripture that was accepted and acted upon by Christ's Church from the first. The Bible itself claims to be an authoritative Book and an infallible guide to the true knowledge of God and of the way of salvation. This view is implied in every reference made to it, so far as it then existed by Christ and His Apostles. That the New Testament does not stand on a lower level of inspiration and authority than the Old Testament. And in that sense, as a body of writings of Divine authority, the books of the Old and New Testament were accepted by the Apostles and by the Church of the post-apostolic age.

Take the writings of any of the early Church fathers, Tertullian, or Origen, or others, and you will find their words saturated with references to Scripture. You will find the Scriptures treated in precisely the same way as they are used in contemporary Biblical literature, namely, as the ultimate authority on the matters of which they speak. I really do the fathers an injustice in this comparison, for I find things said and written about the Holy Scriptures by teachers of the Church today that those early fathers would never have permitted themselves to utter. It has now become fashionable among a class of religious teachers to speak disparagingly of or belittle the Holy Scriptures as an authoritative rule of faith for the Church. The leading cause of this has undoubtedly been the trend that the criticism of the Holy Scriptures has assumed during the last half century or more.

By all means, let criticism have its rights. Let purely literary questions about the Bible receive full and fair discussion. Let the structure of books be impartially examined. If a reverent science has light to throw on the composition or authority or age of these books, let its voice be heard. If this thing is of God, we cannot overthrow it. No fright, therefore, need be taken at the mere word, "Criticism."

On the other hand, we are not bound to accept every wild critical theory that any critic may choose to put forward and assert as the final word on this matter. We are entitled—we are bound—to look at the presuppositions on which each criticism proceeds, and to ask, "How far is the criticism controlled by those presuppositions?" We are bound to look at the evidence by which the theory is supported and to ask, "Is it really borne out by that evidence?" And when theories are put forward with every confidence as fixed results, and we find them as we observe them still in constant process of evolution and change, becoming more complicated, more extreme, more fanciful, we are entitled to inquire, "Is this the certainty that it was alleged to be?"

Now that is my complaint against much of the current criticism of the Bible—not that it is criticism but that it starts from the wrong basis, that it proceeds by arbitrary methods, and that it arrives at demonstrably false results. That is a great deal to say, no doubt, but perhaps I shall have some justification to offer for it before I am done.

I am not going to enter into any general tirade against criticism, but it is useless to deny that a great deal of what is called criticism is responsible for the uncertainty and unsettlement of feeling existing at the present time about the Holy Scriptures. I do not speak especially of those whose philosophical standpoint compels them to take up an attitude of negation to supernatural revelation or to books which profess to convey such a revelation. Criticism of this kind, criticism that starts from the basis of the denial of the supernatural, must be reckoned with. In its hands, everything is engineered from that basis.

There is the denial to begin with that God ever has entered into human history in word or deed or any supernatural way. The necessary result is that whatever in the Bible affirms or flows from such interposition of God is expounded or explained away. The Scriptures on this showing, instead of being the living oracles of God, become simply the fragmentary remains of an ancient Hebrew literature, the chief value of which would seem to be the employment it affords to the critic to dissect it into its various parts, to overthrow the tradition of the past in regard to it and to frame new theories of the origin of the books and the so-called legends they contain. Leaving, however, such futile, rationalistic criticism out of account, there is certainly an immense change of attitude on the part of many who still sincerely hold faith in the supernatural revelation of God.

I find it difficult to describe this tendency, for I am desirous not to describe it in any way that would do injustice to any Christian thinker, and it is attended by so many signs of an ambiguous character. Jesus is recognized by the majority of those who represent it as "the Incarnate Son of God," though with shadings off into more or less indefinite assertions even on that fundamental article, which makes it sometimes doubtful where the writers exactly stand.

The process of thought in regard to Scripture is easily traced. First, there is an ostentatious disposal of what is called the verbal inspiration of Scripture—a very much abused term. Jesus is still spoken of as the highest revealer, and it is allowed that His words furnish the highest rule of guidance for time and for eternity. But even criticism, we are told, must have its rights. In the New Testament the Gospels go into the crucible, and in the name of synoptical criticism, historical criticism, they are subject to wonderful processes, in the course of which much of the history gets meted out or is peeled off as Christian characteristics. Jesus, we are reminded, was still a man of His generation, liable to error in His human knowledge, and allowance must be made for the limitations in His conceptions and judgments. Paul is alleged to be still largely dominated by his inheritance of Rabbinical and Pharisaic ideas. He had been brought up a Pharisee, brought up with the rabbis, and when he became a Christian, he carried a great deal of that into his Christian thought, so we must discard that thought when studying Paul's Epistles. Therefore, he is a teacher not to be followed further than our own judgment of Christian truth, ridding us of a great deal that is inconvenient about Paul's teaching.

The Old Testament and the Critics

If these things are done in the "freshness" of the New Testament, it is easy to see what will be done in the Old. The conclusions of the more advanced school of critics are generally accepted as once for all settled, with the result that the Old Testament is immeasurably lowered from the place it once held in reverence. Its earlier history, down to about the age of the kings, is largely resolved into myths and legends and fictions. It is ruled out of the category of history proper.

We are told that the legends are just as good as the history, and perhaps a little better, and that the ideas they convey sufficient, as if they came in the form of fact. But legends lack Divine authority. They are the products of human minds at various ages. Their prophecies are the utterances of men who possessed indeed the Spirit of God, which is only in fuller degree what other good men and religious teachers have possessed. In this confusion of theories—you will find them in magazines, encyclopedias, and many books that appear to annihilate the conservative believers—is it any wonder that many should be disquieted and unsettled? The question comes back with fresh urgency: What is to be said of the place and value of Holy Scripture?

Is there a Tenable Doctrine for Today's Christian Church?

A prime need of the Church must be a replacement of Holy Scripture. But then, is such a position tenable? In the fierce light of criticism that beats upon the documents and upon the revelation of God's grace they profess to contain, can this position be maintained? Indeed, I am very sure that we can have a tenable doctrine of Holy Scripture.

For a satisfactory doctrine of Holy Scripture, three things are indispensably necessary. First, a more positive view of the structure of the Bible than at present. Second is the acknowledgment of a true supernatural revelation of God in the history and religion of the Bible. Third must be the recognition of a true supernatural inspiration in the record of that revelation. Can we affirm these three things? Will they bear the test? I think they will.

The Structure of the Bible

For the structure of the Bible, there a more positive idea of that structure is needed. The current criticism disintegrates the Bible in many ways. For example, it is said that the books are made up of many documents written later than and by various authors other than what was originally scribed. Therefore the Bible cannot claim accurate historical value. They were merely the invention of priests and scribes in the post-exilian period that were brought before the Jews upon their return from Babylon, and accepted as the law of life. Thus, you have the history of the Bible turned pretty much upside down, and things take on a new aspect altogether.

Must we then, in deference to criticism, accept these theories, and give up the structure which the Bible presents? Taking the Bible as it stands, I find what seems to be evidence of a definite internal structure, each part leading to the next, making up a unity of the whole in that Bible. The Bible is distinguished from all other sacred books in the world, from Koran, Buddhist, and Indian scriptures to every other kind of religious book. It is distinguished by the fact that the Bible is the embodiment of a great plan or purpose of Divine grace, extending from the beginning of time through successive ages and dispensations down to its culmination in Jesus Christ and the Pentecostal outpourings of the Spirit.

The *history* of the Bible is the history of that development of God's redemptive purpose. Its *promises* mark the stages of its progress and its hope. The Bible's *covenants* stand before us in the order of its unfolding. Genesis lays the foundation and leads up to the Book of Exodus, which with its introduction of the law-giving, leads up to what follows. Deuteronomy looks back upon the history of the rebellions and the laws given to the people, and leads up to the conquest. Later developments through the monarchy and prophecies and the rest, are mostly fulfilled in the New Testament. The Bible closes with the Gospels, Epistles, and the Apocalypse of Revelation fulfilling all the ideas of the Old Testament. There the circle completes itself with the new heaven and the new earth.

Herein lies structure that creates unity of purpose extending through this Book and binding all its parts together. Is that structure an illusion? Do our eyes deceive us when we think we see it? Or has somebody of a later date invented it? I would like to find the mind capable of inventing it and working it into a history once they got the idea itself. But if not invented, it belongs to the reality and the substance of the history; it belongs to the facts; and therefore to the Book that records the facts.

Some have said, "Now, that is all very well but there are facts on the other side; there are those manifold proofs which our critical friends adduce that the Bible is really a collection of fragments and documents of much later date, and that the history is really quite a different thing from what the Bible represents it to be." Do we accept their dictum on that subject without evidence? When I turn to the evidence, I do not find them to have that convincing power that our critical friends assign to them.

I am not rejecting this kind of critical theory because it goes against my prejudices or traditions; I reject it simply because it seems to me the evidence does not sustain it, and that the stronger evidence is against it. Case in point: this post-exilian origin of the Levitical law is the theory that is stated repeatedly. That would mean that the exiles had returned from Babylon, organized into a new community, and rebuilt their temple. Then many years later, those two great men, Ezra and Nehemiah, publicly proclaimed this law of God by the hand of Moses, which he had brought from Babylon.

A full description of what happened is given in the eighth chapter of the Book of Nehemiah. Ezra reads the law from his pulpit of wood day after day to the people, and the interpreter gives the sense. Remember, most of the things in this law, in this book that he is reading to the people, had never been heard of before—never had existed; priests and Levites such as are there described had never existed. The law itself was long and complicated and burdensome, but the marvelous thing is that the people meekly accept it all as true—as law—and submit to it, and take upon themselves its burdens without a murmur of dissent.

That is a very remarkable thing to start with. But further, it was not a community with oneness of mind but keenly divided. There were strong opposing factions in that community, with parties strongly opposed to Ezra and Nehemiah and their reforms. Many, were religiously faithless in that community. Amazingly, all accept this new, burdensome, and unheard of law as the law of Moses. There were priests and Levites in that community who knew something about their own origin; they had genealogies and knew of their past.

According to the new theory, these Levites were quite a new order; they had never existed at all before the time of the exile,\ and had come into existence through the sentence of degradation that the prophet Ezekiel had passed upon them in the forty-fourth chapter of his book. History is quite silent about this degradation. There is no specific explanation about its origin.

The priests and Levites stand and listen without astonishment as they learn from Ezra how the Levites had been set apart long centuries before in the wilderness by the hand of God, with an ample tithe provision set apart for them to live in. People know a little about their past. These cities never had existed except on paper, but they accept the heavy tithe burdens without argument and make a covenant with God pledging themselves to faithful obedience to all those commands. The tithe laws had no actual relation to their situation at all; the priests were only to get the tithe of a tenth, but in this restored community there were a great many priests and few Levites. The tithe laws did not apply at all, but they accepted these as laws of Moses, according to the critics.

Thus, the tabernacle, priests, rituals, sacrifices, and Day of Atonement in their post-exilian form had never existed; they were spun out of the inventive brains of scribes. Yet the people accepted them all? Was ever such a thing heard of before? Try in any city to get the people to take upon themselves a series of heavy burdens of taxation or tithes on the ground that it had been handed down from the middle ages to the present time. Try to get them to believe and obey it, and you will find the difficulty. I am convinced that the structure of the Bible vindicates itself, and these counter theories by higher critics break down.

A Supernatural Revelation

I think it is essential, in fact the core of the matter, in a tenable doctrine of Scripture that it contains a record of true supernatural revelation. That is what the Bible claims to be—not a development of man's thoughts about God or what the authors of the books of the thought about God but a supernatural revelation of t God revealing Himself in word and deed to men in history. And if that claim to a supernatural revelation from God falls, the Bible falls, because it is bound up with it from beginning to end.

It is here that a great deal of modern thought parts company with the Bible. Many who accept these newer critical theories claim to be just as firm believers in Divine revelation and in Jesus Christ and all that concerns Him. I rejoice in the fact and I believe that they are warranted in saying you cannot expunge or explain on any other hypothesis but Divine revelation.

But what I maintain is that this theory of the religion of the Bible that has evolved into the "critical view" originated from men who did not believe in the supernatural revelation of God in the Bible. This school as a whole holds the fundamental position—the position known as the "modern mind"—that miracles did not happen because they are impossible; therefore its followers have to rule everything called a supernatural miracle out of the Bible record.

I have never been able to see how that position is plausible to those who believe in a living, personal God who loves and desires to bless them. If there is a dogmatism in the world, it is that of the man who claims to limit the Author of the universe by this finite bound. We are told sometimes that it is a far higher thing to see God in the natural than to see Him in something that transcends the natural; a far higher thing to see God in the orderly regular working of nature than to suppose that there has ever been anything transcending that ordinary natural working. I hope all try to see God there, but doesn't the natural have its limits? And do we bind God that He cannot enter into communion with man in a supernatural economy of grace, revelation, and salvation? Are we to deny that He has done so?

That is really the dividing line both in Old and New Testament between the different theories—*revelation!* I believe that it is an essential part of the answer, the true doctrine of Scripture, to say, "Yes, God has so revealed Himself; the Bible is the record of that revelation, and that revelation shines in its light from the beginning to the end of it." Unless there is a wholehearted acceptance of the fact that God has entered, in word and deed, into human history for man's salvation, for man's renovation, for the deliverance of this world—a revelation culminating in the great Revealer Himself—unless we accept that, we do not get the foundation for the true doctrine of Holy Scripture.

The Inspired Book

In conclusion, I do not think that anyone will weigh the evidence of the Bible without saying that it claims to be an *inspired book*. There is hardly anyone who will doubt that Jesus Christ treats the Old Testament as an imperfect stage of revelation. Christ, as the Son of Man, takes up a lordly, discretionary attitude towards that revelation, and He supersedes what is in it by something higher. But He recognizes that there was true Divine revelation there and that He was the goal of it all; He came to fulfill the law and the prophets. The Scriptures are the last word with Him—"Haven't you read?" and "You are in error because you do not know the Scriptures or the power of God."

It is just as certain that the Apostles treated the Old Testament the same way and that they claimed the Spirit of God was in them, and in their word was laid "the foundation on which the Church was built"—Jesus Christ, Himself, as the substance of their testimony, being the chief cornerstone "built upon the foundation of the Apostles and Prophets."

The Bible's Own Test of Inspiration

What does the Bible itself give us as the test of its inspiration? What does the Bible itself name as the qualities that inspiration imparts to it? Paul speaks in Timothy of the Sacred Writings that were able to make wise unto salvation through faith which is in Christ Jesus. He goes on to tell us that all Scripture is given by inspiration of God and is profitable for doctrine, for reproof, for correction, for instruction in righteousness, in order that the man of God may be perfect, furnished unto all good works.

When you go back to the Old Testament and its praise of the Word of God. you will find the qualities of inspiration are just the same. "The law of the Lord is perfect." Those are the qualities that the inspired Book is alleged to sustain—qualities that only a true inspiration of God's Spirit could give—qualities beyond which we surely do not need anything more.

Does anyone doubt that the Bible possesses these qualities? Look at its structure; look at its completeness; look at it in the clearness, fullness, and holiness of its teachings; look at it in its sufficiency to guide every soul that truly seeks light unto the saving knowledge of God. Take the Book as a whole, in its whole purpose, its whole spirit, its whole aim and tendency, and the whole setting of it, and ask, "Isn't it evident that God's Holy Spirit truly was in the men who wrote the Bible?"

CHAPTER VI Christ and Criticism

Robert Anderson

In his Founders of Old Testament Criticism, Professor Cheyne of Oxford gives the foremost place to Eichhorn, hailing him as *the* founder of the cult. According to this same authority, what led Eichhorn to enter on his task was "his hope to contribute to the winning back of the educated classes to religion."

The rationalism of Germany at the close of the eighteenth century would accept the Bible only on the terms of bringing it down to the level of a human book, and the problem that had to be solved was to eliminate the element of miracle, which pervades it. Working on the labors of his predecessors, Eichhorn achieved this to his own satisfaction by appealing to the Eastern habit of thought, which seizes upon ultimate causes and ignores intermediate processes. This commended itself on two grounds: It had an undoubted element of truth, and it was consistent with reverence for Holy Scripture. For of the founder of the "higher criticism," it was said what cannot be said of any of his successors—that "faith in that which is holy, even in the miracles of the Bible, was never shattered by Eichhorn in any youthful mind."

In the view of his successors, however, Eichhorn's hypothesis was open to the fatal objection that it was altogether inadequate. So the next generation of critics adopted the more drastic theory that the Mosaic books were "Mosaic" in the sense that they were literary forgeries of a late date, composed of materials supplied by ancient documents, myths, and legends of the Hebrew race.

Though this theory has been modified from time to time during the last century, it remains substantially the "critical" view of the Pentateuch. But it is open to two main objections, either of which would be fatal—it is inconsistent with the evidence, and it directly challenges the authority of the Lord Jesus Christ as a teacher, for one of the few undisputed facts in this controversy is that our Lord accredited the books of Moses as having divine authority.

The True and the Counterfeit

We must distinguish between the true higher criticism and its counterfeit. The rationalistic higher criticism, when putting the Pentateuch on trial, enters upon its inquiries with an open mind and pursues them without prejudice. "The proper function of the higher criticism is to determine the origin, date, and literary structure of an ancient writing."

This is Professor Driver's description of *true* criticism. But the aim of the counterfeit is to disprove the genuineness of the ancient writings. The justice of this statement is established by the fact that Hebraists and theologians of the highest eminence, whose investigation of the Pentateuch problem has convinced them of the genuineness of the books, are not recognized at all.

In Britain, at least, no theologian of the first rank has adopted their "assured results." But the judgment of such men as Pusey, Lightfoot, and Salmon is contemptuously ignored;

the rationalistic higher critic is not one who investigates the evidence but one who accepts the verdict.

The Philological Inquiry

If, as its proponents sometimes urge, the higher criticism is a purely philological inquiry, two obvious conclusions follow. The first is that its verdict must be in favor of the Mosaic books, for each of the books contains distinctive words suited to the time and circumstances of which it is traditionally assigned. This is admitted, and the critics attribute the presence of such words to the Jesuitical skill of the priestly forgers. But this only lends weight to the further conclusion that higher criticism is wholly incompetent to deal with the main issue it claims to resolve.

The genuineness of the Pentateuch must be decided on the same principles that the genuineness of ancient documents is dealt with in our courts of justice. The language of the documents is only one part of the needed evidence and not the most important part. Dealing with evidence depends upon qualities to which Hebraists, as such, have no special claim. Indeed, their writings afford signal proofs of their unfitness for inquiries that they insist on regarding as their special preserve.

Take, for example, Professor Driver's grave assertion that the presence of two Greek words in Daniel (they are the names of musical instruments) *demand* a date for the book subsequent to the Greek conquest. It has been established by Professor Sayce and others that the intercourse between Babylon and Greece i, and before the days of Nebuchadnezzar would amply account for the presence in the Chaldean capital of musical instruments with Greek names. And the respected authority of Colonel Conder considers the words to be Akkadian, not Greek at all! Apart from all this, we can imagine the reception that would be given to such a statement by any competent tribunal.

The story bears repeating—it is a record of facts—that at a church bazaar in Lincoln years ago, the alarm was raised that pickpockets were at work, and two ladies had lost their purses. The empty purses were afterwards found in the pocket of the Bishop of the Diocese! On the evidence of the two purses, the Bishop should be convicted as a thief, and on the evidence of the two words, the book of Daniel should be convicted as a forgery!

Historical Blunder

Here is another typical item in the critics' indictment of Daniel. The book opens by recording Nebuchadnezzar's siege of Jerusalem in the third year of Jehoiakim, confirmed by history, sacred and secular. Berosus, the Chaldean historian, tells us that during this expedition, Nebuchadnezzar received news of his father's death, and that, committing to others the care of his army and of his Jewish prisoners, "he himself hastened home across the desert."

But the German skeptics, having decided that Daniel was a forgery, had to find evidence to support their verdict. And so they made the brilliant discovery that Berosus was here referring to the expedition of the following year, when Nebuchadnezzar won the battle of Carchemish against the army of the king of Egypt and had not time invaded Judea at that time.

But Carchemish is on the Euphrates, and the idea of "hastening home" from there to Babylon across the desert is worthy of a schoolboy's essay! That he crossed the desert is proof that he set out from Judea; and his Jewish captives were, of course, Daniel and his companion princes. The invasion of Judea took place before Nebuchadnezzr's accession in Jehoiakam's *third* year, whereas the battle of Carchemish was fought after his accession, in the king of Judah's *fourth* year, as the biblical books record. However, this grotesque blunder of Bertholdt's "*Book of Daniel*" in the beginning of the nineteenth century is gravely reproduced in Professor Driver's "*Book of Daniel*" at the beginning of the twentieth century.

Critical Profanity

As for Moses, according to "the critical hypothesis," the books of the Pentateuch are literary forgeries of the Exilic Era, the work of the Jerusalem priests of those evil days. From the Book of Jeremiah, we know that those men were profane apostates; and if "the critical hypothesis" be true, they were infinitely worse than even the prophet's inspired denunciations of them indicate. For no eighteenth century atheist ever sank to a lower depth of profanity than is displayed by their use of the Sacred Name.

In the preface to his "*Darkness and Dawn*," Dean Farrar claims that he "never touches the early preachers of Christianity with the finger of fiction." When his story makes Apostles speak, he has "confined their words to the words of a revelation." The authors of the Pentateuch "touched with the finger of fiction" not only the holy men of the ancient days, but their Jehovah God. "Jehovah spoke to Moses, saying" or similar phrases are repeated numerous times in the Mosaic books. To call it fiction is inconceivable, unless it be that of the man who fails to be shocked and revolted by it.

However, facts prove that this judgment is unjust. For men of unfeigned piety and deep reverence for divine things can be so blinded by the superstitions of "religion" that the *endorsement* of the Church enables them to regard these discredited books as Holy Scripture. As critics they brand the Pentateuch as a tissue of myth, legend, and fraud, but as religionists they assure us that this "implies no denial of its inspiration or disparagement of its contents."[12]

Errors Refuted by Facts

In controversy, it is of the greatest importance to hear opposing statements, thus Professor Driver's statement of the case against the Books of Moses:

> We can only argue on grounds of probability derived from our view of the progress of the art of writing, of literary composition, or of the rise and growth of the prophetic tone and feeling in ancient Israel. Also to be considered is the period at which the traditions are recorded, the probability that they would have been written down before the impetus, and similar consideration of plausible arguments may be advanced, a standard on which we can confidently rely scarcely admits of being fixed. ("*Introduction*," 6th ed., p. 123.)

---

[12] "*The Higher Criticism: Three Papers*," by Professors Driver and Kirkpatrick.

This modest reference to "literary composition" and "the art of writing" is characteristic and intended to gloss over the abandonment of one of the chief points in the original attack. Had *"Driver's Introduction"* appeared twenty years earlier, the assumption that such a literature as the Pentateuch could belong to the age of Moses would doubtless have been branded as a credible account of what was recorded by its true author, Moses.

For one of the main grounds on which the books were assigned to the latter days of the monarchy was that the Hebrews of six centuries earlier were an illiterate people. And after that error had been refuted by archaeological discoveries, it was still maintained that a code of laws so advanced and elaborate as that of Moses could not have originated in such an age. This figment, however, was in its turn exploded, when the spade of the explorer brought to light the now famous Code of Khammurabi, the Amraphel of Genesis, who was king of Babylon in the time of Abraham.

However, instead of donning the white sheet when confronted by this new witness, the critics, with great effrontery, pointed to the newly found Code as the original of the Sinai laws. Such a conclusion is natural on the part of men who treat the Pentateuch as merely human. But the critics cannot have it both ways. The Moses who copied Khammurabi must have been the real Moses of the Exodus, not the mythical Moses of the Exile, who wrote long centuries after Khammurabi had been forgotten!

An Incredible Theory

The evidence of the Khammurabi Code refutes an important count in the critics' indictment of the Pentateuch; but we can call another witness whose testimony demolishes their whole case. The Pentateuch alone constitutes the Bible of the Samaritans. Who, then, were the Samaritans? And how and when did they obtain the Pentateuch? Here again the critics shall speak for themselves.

Among the distinguished men who have championed their crusade in Britain, there has been none more esteemed, none more scholarly, than the late Professor Robertson Smith; and here is an extract from his "Samaritans" article in the *"Encyclopedia Britannica"*:

> They (the Samaritans) regard themselves as Israelites, descendants of the twelve tribes, and claim to possess the orthodox religion of Moses. The priestly law, which is based on the practice of the priests in Jerusalem before the Captivity, was reduced to form after the Exile and was published by Ezra as the law of the rebuilt temple of Zion. The Samaritans must, therefore, have derived their Pentateuch from the Jews after Ezra's reforms.

In the same paragraph he says that, according to the contention of the Samaritans, "not only the temple of Zion but also the earlier temple of Shiloh and the priesthood of Eli were schismatical." And yet, as he goes on to say, "The Samaritan religion was built on the Pentateuch alone."

Now mark what this implies. We know something of racial bitterness and of the fierce bitterness of religious strife; both these elements combined to alienate the Samaritans from the Jews. More than this, in the post-exilic period, distrust and dislike were turned to intense hatred. Smith uses the term "abhorrence" by the sternness and contempt with which the Jews spurned their proffered help in the work of reconstruction at Jerusalem and refused to acknowledge them in any way. Yet we are asked to believe that, at this very time and in these very circumstances, the Samaritans, while denouncing the whole Jewish cult as schismatical, not only accepted these Jewish books relating to that cult as the "service books" of their own ritual but also adopted them as their "Bible" to the exclusion even of the writings of their own Israelite prophets and the sacred books that record the history of their kings—an incredibly preposterous theory!

Another Unreasonable Position

No less unreasonable are the grounds on which this conclusion is delivered, stated in the standard textbook of the cult, Hasting's *Bible Dictionary*:

> There is at least one valid ground for the conclusion that the Pentateuch was first accepted by the Samaritans after the Exile. Why was their request to be allowed to take part in the building of the second temple refused by the heads of the Jerusalem community? Very probably because the Jews were aware that the Samaritans did not as yet possess the Law Book. It is hard to suppose that otherwise they would have met with this refusal. Further, anyone who, like the present writer, regards the modern criticism of the Pentateuch as essentially correct, has a second decisive reason for adopting the above view. (Professor König's article, "*Samaritan Pentateuch*," page 68.)

Here are two "decisive reasons" for holding that "the Pentateuch was first accepted by the Samaritans after the Exile." First, because "very probably" it was because they didn't have those forged books that the Jews spurned their help; and so they went home and adopted the forged books as their Bible! Second, because "higher criticism" has proven that the books were not in existence till then. To characterize the writings of these scholars as they deserve is not a grateful task, but the time has come to expose anything that would have us tear from our Bible the Holy Scriptures on which our Divine Lord based His claims to Messiahship.

The Idea of Sacrifice a Revelation

The refutation of the higher criticism does not prove that the Pentateuch is inspired of God; neither does it decide questions that lie within the legitimate province of the true higher criticism; for example, the authorship of Genesis. It is incredible that for the thousands of years that elapsed before the days of Moses, God left His people on earth without a revelation. It is plain, moreover, that many of the ordinances divinely entrusted to Moses were but a renewal of an earlier revelation. The religion of Babylon is clear evidence of such a primeval revelation. How else can the universality of sacrifice be accounted for? Could such a practice have originated with humanity?

If someone conceived the idea that killing a beast before his enemy's door would propitiate him, his neighbors would no doubt have suppressed him. The fact that sacrifice prevailed among all races can be explained only by a primeval revelation. And the Bible student will recognize that God thus sought to impress on men that death was the penalty of sin, and to lead them to look forward to a great blood shedding that would bring life and blessing to mankind.

But Babylon was to the ancient world what Rome has been to Christendom. It corrupted every divine ordinance and truth and perpetuated them as thus corrupted. And in the Pentateuch, we have the divine re-issue of the true cult. The figment that the debased and corrupt version was the original may satisfy some professors of Hebrew, but no one who has any practical knowledge of human nature would entertain it.

Insufficient Evidence

At this stage, what concerns us is not the divine authority of the Books but the human error and folly of the critical attack upon them. The only historical basis of that attack is the fact that in the revival under Josiah, "the book of the law" was found in the temple by Hilkiah, the high priest, to whom the young king entrusted the duty of cleansing and renovating the long neglected shrine. A most natural discovery it was, seeing that Moses expressly commanded that it should be kept there (2 Kings 22:8; Deuteronomy 31:26). But according to the critics, the whole business was a detestable trick of the priests, who forged the books and invented the command, and then hid the product of their infamous work where they knew it would be found.

Apart from this, the only foundation for "the assured results of modern criticism," as they themselves acknowledge, consists of "grounds of probability" and "plausible arguments." A habitual criminal would not be convicted of petty larceny on such evidence as this, and yet it is on these grounds that we are called upon to give up the sacred books that our Divine Lord accredited as "the Word of God" and made the basis of His doctrinal teaching.

Christ or Criticism?

This brings us to the second and incomparably the graver objection to "the assured results of modern criticism." That the Lord Jesus Christ identified Himself with the Hebrew Scriptures, and in a very special way with the Book of Moses, no one disputes. This being so, we must make choice between Christ and "criticism." For if "the critical hypothesis" of the Pentateuch is correct, the conclusion is seemingly inevitable: either He was not divine, or the records of His teaching are untrustworthy.

Which alternative shall we adopt? If the second, then every claim to inspiration must be abandoned, and agnosticism must supplant faith in the case of every fearless thinker. Inspiration is far too great a question for incidental treatment here; but two remarks with respect to it may not be inopportune. Behind the frauds of Spiritualism there lies the fact, attested by men of high character, including scientists and scholars, that definite communications are received in precise words from the world of spirits.[13] This being so, to deny that the Spirit of God could thus communicate truth to men, or, in other words, to reject verbal inspiration theory, betrays the ignorance of systematized unbelief. It is amazing that anyone who regards the coming of Christ as God's supreme revelation of Himself can imagine that the Divine Spirit would fail to ensure a trustworthy and true record of His mission and His teaching.

---

[13] The fact that, as the Christian believes, these spirits are demons who personate the dead, does not affect the argument.

A More Hopeless Dilemma

But if the Gospel narrative be authentic, we are driven back upon the alternative that He of whom they speak could not be divine. "Not so," the critics protest, "for did He not Himself confess His ignorance? And is not this explained by the Apostle's statement that in His humiliation He emptied Himself of His Deity?" The inference drawn from this (to quote the standard text-book of the cult) is that the Lord of Glory "held the current Jewish notions respecting the divine authority and revelation of the Old Testament."

But even if this conclusion—as portentous as it is profane—could be established, instead of affording an escape from the dilemma in which the higher criticism involves its devoted followers, it would only serve to make that dilemma more hopeless and terrible. For what concerns us is not that the Lord's doctrinal teaching was false but that in unequivocal terms, and with extreme solemnity, He declared again and again that His teaching was not His own but His Father's, and the very words in which He conveyed it were God-given.

A few years ago, the devout were distressed by the proceedings of a certain Chicago "prophet," who claimed divine authority for his meditations. The man was regarded as a profane fool. Shall the higher critics betray us into forming a similarly indulgence?

Will it be believed that the only scriptural basis offered us for this astounding position is a verse in one of the Gospels and a word in one of the Epistles! Indeed, it is strange that men who handle Holy Scripture with such freedom when it conflicts with their "assured results" should attach such importance to an isolated verse or a single word, when it can be misused to support them. The verse is Mark 13:32, where the Lord says, with reference to His coining again: "But concerning that day or the hour no one knows, neither the angels in heaven nor the Son, but only the Father." But this follows immediately upon the words: "Heaven and earth shall pass away, but My words shall not pass away."

The Words of God

The Lord's words were not "inspired." They were the words of God in a higher sense. "The people were astonished at His teaching," we are told, "for He taught them as one having *exousia*." Exousia, Greek for authority, occurs again in Acts 1:7, where He says that times and seasons "the Father hath put in His own *exousia*." And this is explained by Philippians 2:6, 7: "He counted it not a prize (or a thing to be grasped) to be on an equality with God, but *emptied* Himself"—the word on which the *kenosis* theory of the critics depends. He not only stripped Himself of His glory as God; He gave up His liberty as a man. For He never spoke His own words, but only the words which the Father gave Him to speak. And this was the limitation of His "authority"; so that, beyond what the Father gave Him to speak, He knew nothing and was silent.

However, when He spoke, "He taught them as one who had authority, and not as the scribes." From their scribes they received definite teaching, but it was teaching based on "the law and the prophets." However, here was One who stood apart and taught them from a different plane. "For," He declared, "I did not speak of my own initiative, but the Father himself who sent me has given me a commandment as to what to say and what to speak. **50** I know that his commandment is eternal life; therefore the things I speak, I speak just as the Father has told me." (John 12:49–50).

It was not merely the substance of His teaching that was divine but the very language in which it was conveyed; so that in His prayer on the night of the betrayal He could say, "For I gave them the words you gave me and they accepted them."[14]

Therefore, His words about Moses and the Hebrew Scriptures were not with such daring and seeming profanity of a superstitious and ignorant Jew; they were the words of God and conveyed truth that was divine and eternal.

When in the dark days of the Exile, God needed a prophet who would speak only as He gave him words, He struck Ezekiel dumb. Two judgments already rested on that people—the seventy years' servitude to Babylon and the Captivity—and they were warned that continued impenitence would bring on them the still more terrible judgment of the seventy years' desolations. And till that last judgment fell, Ezekiel remained dumb (Ezekiel 3:26; 24:27; 33:22). However, the Lord Jesus Christ needed no such discipline. He came to do the Father's will, and no words ever passed His lips save the words given Him to speak.

In this connection, moreover, two facts, which are strangely, overlooked claim prominent notice. The first is in Mark 13: the antithesis is not at all between man and God but between the Son of God and the Father. The second is that He had been reinvested with all that, according to Philippians 2; He laid aside in coming into the world. "All things have been delivered unto Me of My Father," He declared. And this was at a time when the proofs that "He was despised and rejected of men" were pressing on Him. His reassuming the glory awaited His return to heaven, but here on earth the all things were already His. (Matt. 11:27)

After the Kenosis

The foregoing is surely an adequate reply to the *kenosis* figment of the critics; but if any should still doubt, there is another answer that is complete and crushing. Whatever may have been the limitations under which He rested during His ministry on earth, He was released from them when He rose from the dead. It was in His post-resurrection teaching that He gave the fullest and clearest testimony to the Hebrew Scriptures.

It was while talking to the two men on the road to Emmaus after His resurrection that, "beginning from Moses and all the Prophets, he interpreted to them in all the Scriptures the things concerning himself." (Luke 24:27) And again, confirming all His previous teaching about those Scriptures, "he said to them, 'These are my words that I spoke to you while I was still with you, that all things which are written about me in the law of Moses and the Prophets and the Psalms must be fulfilled.'" (Luke 24:44). The record adds, "Then he opened their minds to understand the Scriptures." (Luke 24:45) The rest of the New Testament is the fruit of that ministry, enlarged and unfolded by the Holy Spirit, given to lead them into all truth. In every part of the New Testament, the Divine authority of the Hebrew Scriptures, especially of the Books of Moses, is either taught or assumed.

---

[14] Both the λόγος and the ῥὴματα John 17:8, 14; as again in Ch. 14:10; 24.

The Vital Issue

It is certain that the vital issue in this controversy is not the value of the Pentateuch but the deity of Christ, yet the present article does not pretend to deal with the truth of the deity. Its humble aim is not even to establish the authority of the Scriptures but merely to discredit the critical attack upon them by exposing its real character and its utter feebleness. The writer's method, therefore, has been mainly destructive criticism. Thus, the critics' favorite weapon is turned against them.

A Demand for Correct Statement

It is distressfu to think that certain distinguished men whose reverence for divine things is beyond reproach are subjected to such criticism, perhaps similar to what is felt by those who have experience in negotiating issues of sedition or rioting. But when men who are entitled to consideration and respect thrust themselves into "the line of fire," they must be prepared for the effects and will not fail to receive the full regard to which they are entitled, if they will dissociate themselves from the dishonesty of this crusade and acknowledge that their "assured results" are mere hypotheses, repudiated by Hebraists and theologians as competent and eminent as themselves.

Things to Fear

The effects of this "higher criticism" are extremely grave, for it has dethroned the Bible in the home, and the practice of family worship is rapidly dying out. National interests are involved as well; the prosperity and power of the Protestant nations of the world are due to the influence of the Bible upon character and conduct. Races of men who for generations have been taught to think for themselves in matters of the highest moment will naturally excel in every sphere of effort or of enterprise.

More than this, no one who is trained in the fear of God will fail in his duty to his neighbor but will prove himself a good citizen. But the dethronement of the Bible leads practically to the dethronement of God; in Germany and America, and now in England, the effects of this are declaring themselves in ways, and to an extent, well fitted to cause anxiety for the future.

Christ Supreme

If a personal word may be pardoned in conclusion, the writer would appeal to every book he has written in proof that he is no champion of a rigid, traditional "orthodoxy." With a single limitation, he would advocate full and free criticism of Holy Scripture. And that one limitation is that the words of the Lord Jesus Christ shall be deemed a bar to criticism and "an end of controversy" on every subject expressly dealt with in His teaching. "The Son of God is come," and by Him came both grace and TRUTH. From His hand we have received the Scriptures of the Old Testament.

CHAPTER VII Old Testament Criticism and New Testament Christianity

W. H. Griffith Thomas

A large number of Christians feel compelled to doubt the present attitude of many scholars to the Scriptures of the Old Testament. It is being taught that the patriarchs of Jewish history are not historic persons; that the records connected with Moses and the giving of the law on Sinai are unhistorical; that the story of the tabernacle in the wilderness is a fabricated history of the time of the Exile; that the prophets cannot be relied on in their references to the ancient history of their own people or in their predictions of the future. Furthermore, it is asserted that the writers of the New Testament, who assuredly believed in the records of the Old Testament, were mistaken in the historical value they assigned to those records; that our Lord Himself in His repeated references to the Scriptures of His own nation, in His assumption of the Divine authority of those Scriptures, and in the reality of the great names they record, was only thinking and speaking as an ordinary Jew of His day and was as liable to err in matters of history and of criticism as any of them were.

The present paper is intended to give expression to some of the questions that have arisen in the course of personal study in connection with collegiate work and also during several years of ordinary pastoral ministry. It is often urged that problems of Old Testament criticism are for experts alone and can only be decided by them. We venture to question the correctness of this view, especially when it is remembered that to many people "experts" means experts in Hebrew philology only. By all means, let us have all possible expert knowledge; but, as Biblical questions are complex and involve several considerations, we need expert knowledge in archaeology, history, theology, and even spiritual experience, as well as in philology. Every available factor must be taken into account, and the object of the present paper is to emphasize certain elements, which appear liable to be overlooked, or at least insufficiently considered.

We do not question for an instant the right of Biblical criticism considered in itself. On the contrary, it is a necessity for all who use the Bible to be "critics" in the sense of constantly using their "judgment" on what is before them. What is called "higher" criticism is not only a legitimate but also a necessary method for all Christians, for by its use we are able to discover the facts and the form of the Old Testament Scriptures. Our hesitation, consequently, is not intended to apply to the method, but to what is believed to be an illegitimate, unscientific, and unhistorical use of it. In fact, we base our objections to much of the modern criticism of the Old Testament on what we regard as a proper use of a true higher criticism.

1. Is the testimony of nineteen centuries of Christian history and experience of no account in this question?

For nearly eighteen centuries these modern views of the Old Testament were not heard of. Yet this is not to be accounted for by the absence of intellectual power and scholarship in the Church. Men like Origen, Jerome, Augustine, Thomas Aquinas, Erasmus, Calvin, Luther, Melancthon, to say nothing of the English Puritans and other divines of the seventeenth century, were not intellectually weak or inert, nor were they wholly void of critical acumen with reference to Holy Scripture. Yet they, and the whole Church with them, never hesitated to accept the view of the Old Testament, which had come down to them, not only as a heritage from Judaism but also as endorsed by the apostles.

Omitting all reference to our Lord, it is not open to question that the views of St. Paul, St. Peter, and St. John about the Old Testament were the views of the whole Christian Church until the end of the eighteenth century. And, making every possible allowance for the lack of historical spirit and of modern critical methods, are we to suppose that the whole Church for centuries never exercised its mind on such subjects as the contents, history, and authority of the Old Testament?

Besides, this is a matter that cannot be decided by intellectual criticism alone. Scripture appeals to conscience, heart, and will, as well as to mind. The Christian consciousness, the accumulated spiritual experience of the body of Christ, is not to be lightly regarded, much less set aside, unless it is proved to be unwarranted by fact. While we do not say that "what is new is not true," the novelty of these modern critical views should give us pause before we virtually set aside the spiritual instinct of centuries of Christian experience.

2. Does the new criticism readily agree with the historical position of the Jewish nation?

The Jewish nation is a fact in history, and its record is given to us in the Old Testament. There is no contemporary literature to check the account given, and archaeology affords us assistance on points of detail only, not for any long or continuous period. This record of Jewish history can be proven to have remained the same for many centuries. Yet much of modern criticism is compelled to reconstruct the history of the Jews on several important points. It involves, for instance, a very different idea of the character of the earliest form of Jewish religion from that seen in the Old Testament as it now stands; its views of the patriarchs are largely different from the conceptions found on the face of the Old Testament narrative; its views of Moses and David are essentially altered from what we have before us in the Old Testament.

Now what is there in Jewish history to support all this reconstruction? Absolutely nothing. We see through the centuries the outstanding objective fact of the Jewish nation, and the Old Testament is at once the means and the record of their national life. It rose with them, grew with them, and it is to the Jews alone we can look for the earliest testimony to the Old Testament canon.

In face of these facts, it is bare truth to say that the fundamental positions of modern Old Testament criticism are utterly incompatible with the historic growth and position of the Jewish people. Are we not right to pause before we accept this subjective reconstruction of history? Let anyone read Wellhausen's article on "Israel" in the *Encyclopaedia Britannica* and then ask himself whether he recognizes at all therein the story as given in the Old Testament.

3. Are the results of the modern view of the Old Testament really established?

It is sometimes said that modern criticism is no longer a matter of hypothesis; it has entered the domain of facts. Principal George Adam Smith has gone so far as to say that "modern criticism has won its war against the traditional theories. It only remains to fix the amount of the indemnity." But is this really so? Can we assert that the results of modern criticism are established facts? Dr. Smith has himself admitted, since writing the above words, that there are questions still open which were supposed to be settled and closed twenty years ago.

First, is the excessive literary analysis of the Pentateuch at all probable or even thinkable on literary grounds? Let anyone work through a section of Genesis as given by Dr. Driver in his "Introduction," and see whether such a complex combination of authors is at all likely or, if likely, the various authors can now be distinguished? Is not the whole method far too purely subjective to be probable and reliable?

Further, the critics are not agreed as to the number of documents or to the portions to be assigned to each author. A simple instance of this may be given. It is not so many years ago when criticism was content to say that Isaiah 40–66, though not by Isaiah, was the work of one author, an unknown prophet of the Exile. But the most recent writers like Duhm, Macfadyen, and Wade consider these chapters to be the work of two writers and the whole Book of Isaiah (from three authors) did not receive its present form until long after the return from the Exile.

Then, these differences in literary analysis involve different interpretations and differences of date, character, and meaning of particular parts of the Old Testament. To prove this, we bring attention to the following excerpts from a review of a work on Genesis by Professor Gunkel of Berlin. The review is by Professor Andrew Harper of Melbourne and appeared in the "Critical Review" in January 1902. Professor Harper's own position would, we imagine, be rightly characterized as generally favorable to the moderate position of the critical movement. His comments on Gunkel's book are, therefore, all the more noteworthy and significant.

> It will change the whole direction of the conflict as to the early books of the Pentateuch and lead it into more fruitful directions, for it has raised the fundamental question whether the narratives in Genesis are not far older than the authors of the documents marked J. E. P. and whether they are not faithful witnesses to the religion of Israel before prophetic times. His conclusion will, in many respects, be welcome to those who have felt how incredible some of the assumptions of the Kuenen-Wellhausen school of critics are.
>
> It will be obvious at a glance what an upsetting of current conceptions in regard to the history of religion must follow if it be accepted. They are sufficient, if made good, to upset the whole of the current reconstructions of the religion of Israel. To most readers it will be seen that he has in large part made them good."
>
> There can be no doubt that his book most skillfully begins a healthy and much-needed reaction. It should, therefore, be read and welcomed by all students of the Old Testament whose minds are open.

In view of Gunkel's position thus endorsed by Professor Harper, is it fair to claim victory for the modern critical theories of the Old Testament? When an able scholar like Professor Harper can speak of a new work as "sufficient to upset the whole of the current reconstructions of the religion of Israel," it is surely premature to speak even in a moment of rhetorical enthusiasm, as Dr. George Adam Smith does, of "victory" and "indemnity."

Dr. Smith himself now admits that Gunkel has overturned the Wellhausen theory of the patriarchal narratives. And the same scholar has told us that distinction in the use of the name for God is "too precarious" as the basis of arguments for distinctions of sources.

For ourselves, we heartily endorse the words of an American scholar when he says:

> We are certain that there will be no final settlement of Biblical questions on the basis of the higher criticism that is now commonly called by that name. Many specific teachings of the system will doubtless abide. But so far forth as it goes upon the assumption that statements of fact in the Scriptures are pretty generally false, so far forth it is incapable of establishing genuinely permanent results.[15]

Sir W. Robertson Nicoll, editor of the *British Weekly*, remarked quite recently that the "assured results" seem to be vanishing, that no one really knows what they are.

4. is the position of modern criticism really compatible with a belief in the old testament as a divine revelation?

The problem before us is not merely literary, nor only historical; it is essentially religious, and the whole matter resolves itself into one question: Is the Old Testament the record of a Divine revelation? This is the ultimate problem. It is admitted by both sides to be almost impossible to minimize the differences between the traditional and the modern views of the Old Testament. As a reviewer of Dr. George Adam Smith's book *Modern Criticism and the Preaching of the Old Testament* rightly says:

> The difference is immense; they involve different conceptions of the relation of God to the world; different views as to the course of Israel's history, the process of revelation, and the nature of inspiration. We cannot be lifted from the old to the new position by the influence of a charming literary style, or by the force of the most enthusiastic eloquence.[16]

In view of this fundamental difference, the question of the trustworthiness of the Old Testament becomes acute and pressing. In order to test this fairly and thoroughly, let us examine some of the statements made on behalf of the modern view.

We may consider first the rise and progress of religion in Israel. Dr. G. A. Smith says, "It is plain, then, that to whatever heights the religion of Israel afterwards rose, it remained before the age of the great prophets not only similar to but also in all respects above-mentioned identical with the general Semitic religion, which was not a monotheism but a polytheism with an opportunity for monotheism at the heart of it, each tribe being attached to one god, as to their particular Lord and Father."[17]

Consider what is meant by the phrase, "in all respects above-mentioned identical with the general Semitic religion," as applied to the religion of Israel previous to the eighth century B. C. Can this view be fairly deduced from the Old Testament as we now have it?

---

[15] Dr. G. A. Smith, "Modern Criticism and the Preaching of the Old Testament", p. 35. Dr. Willis J. Beecher, in "The Bible Student and Teacher," January, 1904.

[16] "American Journal of Theology", Vol. VI., p. 114.

[17] "Mordern Criticism", p. 130.

Still more, is such a view conceivable in the light of the several preceding centuries of God's special dealings with Israel? Wherein, on this assumption, consisted the uniqueness of Israel from the time of Abraham to the eighth century B. C.?

We may next take the character of the narratives of Genesis. The real question at issue is the historical character. Modern criticism regards the account in Genesis as largely mythical and legendary. Yet it is certain that the Jews of the later centuries accepted these patriarchs as veritable personages and the incidents associated with them as genuine history. Apostle Paul and the other New Testament writers assuredly held the same view. If, then, they are not historical, surely the truths emphasized by prophets and apostles from the patriarchal stories are so far weakened in their supports?

Again, take the legislation, which in the Pentateuch is associated with Moses and almost invariably introduced by the phrase, "The Lord spoke unto Moses." Modern criticism regards this legislation as unknown until the Exile—a thousand years after the time of Moses. Is it really possible to accept this as satisfactory? Are we to suppose that "The Lord spoke to Moses" is only a well-known literary device intended to invest the utterance with greater importance and more solemn sanction? This position, together with the generally accepted view of modern criticism about the invention of Deuteronomy in the days of Josiah, cannot be regarded as in accordance with historical fact or ethical principle.

Canon Driver and Dr. G. A. Smith strongly assert the compatibility of the new views with a belief in the Divine authority of the Old Testament, and so far as they themselves are concerned, we of course accept their statements *ex animo*. But we wish they would give us more clearly and definitely the grounds on which this compatibility may be said to rest.

To deny historicity, to correct dates by hundreds of years, to reverse judgments on which a nation has rested for centuries, to traverse views that have been the spiritual sustenance of millions, and then to say that all this is consistent with the Old Testament being regarded as a Divine revelation is at least puzzling and does not afford mental or moral satisfaction to many who do not dream of questioning the *bona fides* of scholars who hold the views now criticized. The extremes to which Dr. Cheyne has gone seem to many the logical outcome of the principles with which modern criticism, even of a moderate type, starts.

Facilis descensus Averno, and we should like to be shown the solid and logical halting place where those who refuse to go with Cheyne think that they and we can stand. Sir W. Robertson Nicoll, commenting March 12, 1903, on a speech delivered by the then Prime Minister of Great Britain (Mr. Balfour) in connection with the Bible Society's Centenary, made the following significant remarks:

> The immediate results of criticism are in a high degree disturbing. So far they have scarcely been understood by the average Christian. But the plain man who has received everything in the Bible as a veritable Word of God cannot fail to be perplexed, and deeply perplexed, when he is told that much of the Old Testament and the New is unhistorical and when he is asked to accept the statement that God reveals Himself by myth and legend as well as by the truth of fact.

Mr. Balfour must surely know that many of the higher critics have ceased to be believers. More than twenty years ago while walking with Julius Wellhausen in the quaint streets of Greifswald, I asked him whether, if his views were accepted, the Bible could retain its place in the estimation of the common people. "I cannot see how that is possible," was his sad reply."

It is no mere question of how we may use the Old Testament for preaching or how much is left for use after the critical views are accepted. But even our preaching will lack a great deal of the note of certitude. If we are to regard certain biographies as unhistorical, it will not be easy to draw lessons for conduct, and if the history is largely legendary, our deductions about God's government and providence must be essentially weakened.

But the one point to be faced is the historic credibility of those parts of the Old Testament questioned by modern criticism and the historical and religious value of the documents of the Pentateuch. Meanwhile, we ask to have clear proof of the compatibility of the modern views with the acceptance of the Old Testament as the record of a Divine revelation.

5. Is modern criticism based on a sound philosophy that Christians can accept?

At the foundation of much modern thought is the philosophy known as Idealism, which, as often interpreted, involves a theory of the universe that finds no room for supernatural interpositions of any kind. The great law of the universe, including the physical, mental, and moral realms, is said to be evolution, and though this doubtless presupposes an original Creator, it does not, on the theory now before us, permit of any subsequent direct intervention of God during the process of development. This general philosophical principle applied to history has assuredly influenced, if it has not almost molded, a great deal of modern criticism of the Old Testament. It is not urged that all who accept even the position of a moderate criticism go the full length of the extreme evolutionary theory; but there can be no reasonable doubt that most of the criticism of the Old Testament is materially affected by an evolutionary theory of all history, which tends to minimize Divine intervention in the affairs of the people of Israel. It is certainly correct to say that the presupposition of much present-day critical reasoning is a denial of the supernatural, and especially of the predictive element in prophecy.

As to the theory of evolution regarded as a process of uninterrupted differentiation of existences, under purely natural laws and without any Divine intervention, it will suffice to say that it is "not proven" in the sphere of natural science, while in the realms of history and literature it is palpably false. The records of history and literature reveal from time to time the great fact and factor of personality, the reality of personal power, and this determinative element has a peculiar way of setting at naught all idealistic theories of a purely natural and uniform progress in history and letters.

The literature of today is not necessarily higher than that produced in the past; the history of the last century is not in every way and always superior to that of its predecessors. Even a "naturalistic" writer like Professor Percy Gardner testifies to the fact and force of personality in the following remarkable terms:

> There is, in fact, a great force in history which is not, so far as we can judge, evolutional, and the law of which is very hard to trace—the force of personality and character.

And quite apart from such instances of personality as have arisen from time to time through the centuries, there is one Personality who has not yet been accounted for by any theory of evolution—the Person of Jesus of Nazareth. There are sufficient data in current Old Testament criticism to warrant the statement that it proceeds from presuppositions concerning the origins of history, religion, and the Bible, which, in their essence, are subversive of belief in a Divine revelation. And such being the case, we naturally look with grave suspicion on results derived from so unsound a philosophical basis.

6. Can purely naturalistic premises be accepted without coming to purely naturalistic conclusions?

Kuenen and Wellhausen are admittedly accepted as masters by our leading Old Testament "higher critics" in England, Scotland, and America, and the results of their literary analysis of the Pentateuch are generally regarded as conclusive by their followers. On the basis of this literary dissection, certain conclusions are formed as to the character and growth of Old Testament religion. As a result, the history of the Jews is reconstructed. The Book of Deuteronomy is said to be mainly, if not entirely, a product of the reign of Josiah; the accounts of the tabernacle and worship are of exilic date; monotheism in Israel was of late date and was the outcome of a growth from polytheism; and the present Book of Genesis reflects the thoughts of the time of its composition or compilation in or near the date of the Exile.

Now it is known that Kuenen and Wellhausen deny the supernatural element in the Old Testament. This is the "presupposition" of their entire position. Will anyone say that it does not materially affect their conclusions? And is there any safe or logical halting-ground for those who accept so many of their premises? The extreme subjectivity of Canon Cheyne ought not to be a surprise to any who accept the main principles of modern higher criticism; it is part of the logical outcome of the general position. We gladly distinguish between the extremists and the other scholars who see no incompatibility between the acceptance of many of the literary and historical principles of Kuenen and Wellhausen and a belief in the Divine source and authority of the Old Testament. But we are bound to add that the unsatisfying element in the writings of moderate men like Canon Driver and Principal George Adam Smith is that, while accepting so much of the "naturalism" of the German school, they do not give us any clear assurance of the strength of the foundation on which they rest and ask us to rest. The tendency of their position is certainly towards a minimizing of the supernatural in the Old Testament.

Take, as one instance, the Messianic element. In spite of the universal belief of Jews and Christians in a personal Messiah, a belief derived in the first place solely from the Old Testament and supported for Christians by the New Testament, modern criticism will not allow much clear and undoubted prediction of Him. Insight into existing conditions is readily granted to the prophets, but they are not allowed to have had much foresight into future conditions connected with the Messiah. Yet Isaiah's glowing words remain, and demand a fair, full exegesis such as they do not get from many modern scholars. Dr. James Wells, of Glasgow, wrote in the *British Weekly* some time ago of the new criticism on this point:

> The fear of prediction in the proper sense of the term is ever before its eyes. It gladly enlarges on fore-shadowings, a moral historical growth which reaches

its culmination in Christ; and anticipations of the Spirit of Christ; but its tendency is always to minimize the prophetic element in the Old Testament.

Another example of the tendency of modern criticism to minimize and explain away the supernatural element may be given from a book entitled, *The Theology and Ethics of the Hebrews*, by Dr. Archibald Duff, professor at Yorkshire College, Bradford. This is his account of Moses at the burning bush:

> He was shepherding his sheep among the red granite mountains . . . The man sat at dawn by the stream, and watched the fiery rocks. Yonder gleamed the level sunlight across the low growth. Each spine glistened against the rising sun. The man was a poet, one fit for inspiration. He felt that the dreams of his soul were the whisperings of his God, the place His sanctuary. He bowed and worshipped (p. 6.).

This, at least, is not the *lat prima facie* impression derived from the account given in Exodus.

One more illustration may be given of modern critical methods of dealing with narratives of the Old Testament that were evidently intended to be regarded as historical. In the *International Critical Commentary* on Numbers, Dr. G. B. Gray, of Mansfield College, Oxford, thus writes on what he terms "the priestly section of the book":

> For the history of the Mosaic age the whole section is valueless. The historical impression given by (P) of the Mosaic age is altogether unhistorical, and much of the detail ... can ... be demonstrated to be entirely unreal, or at least untrue of the age in question. This history is fictitious.

These statements at once set aside the history contained in more than three quarters of the Book of Numbers. Dr. Gray's verdict is by no means reassuring, and he clearly does not possess much confidence in even the small quantity that escapes his condemnation. The brazen serpent is said to be an invention on the part of some "who had come under the higher prophetic teaching" before Hezekiah and is meant "to controvert the popular belief" in the healing power of the serpent by ascribing it to Jehovah. As to the story of Balaam, Dr. Gray wrote:

> It may, indeed, contain other historical features, such as the name of Balak, who may have been an actual king of Moab; but no means at present exist for distinguishing any further between the historical or legendary elements and those which are supplied by the creative faculty and the religious feeling of the writers.

What is any ordinary earnest Christian to make of all these statements? The writer of the Book of Numbers evidently composed what professes to be history, and what he meant to be read as history, and yet according to Dr. Gray all this has no historical foundation. We can only say that the Christian Church will require very much more convincing proofs before they can accept the critical position. It does not facilitate our acceptance of this wholesale process of invention to be told that it is due to "the creative faculty and the religious feeling of the writers."

As to the fact that so many of our British and American higher critics are firm believers in the Divine authority of the Old Testament, and of a Divine revelation embodied in it, we cannot but feel the force of the words of the late Dr. W. H. Green, of Princeton:

> They who have themselves been thoroughly grounded in the Christian faith may, by a happy inconsistency, hold fast their old convictions, while admitting principles, methods, and conclusions that are logically at war with them. But who can be surprised if others shall with stricter logic carry what has been thus commended to them to its legitimate conclusions?

7. Can we overlook the evidence of archaeology?[18]

It is well known that during the last sixty years a vast number of archaeological discoveries have been made in Egypt, Palestine, Babylonia, and Assyria. Many of these have shed remarkable light on the historical features of the Old Testament. A number of persons and periods have been illuminated by these discoveries and are now seen with a clearness never before possible.

Now it is a simple and yet striking fact that not one of these discoveries during the whole of this time has given any support to the distinctive features and principles of the higher critical position. On the other hand, many of them have afforded abundant confirmation of the traditional and conservative view of the Old Testament.

Let us consider a few of these discoveries. Only a little over forty years ago the conservative *Speaker's Commentary* actually had to take into consideration the critical arguments then so prevalent in favor of the late invention of writing, an argument, never heard in critical circles. The change of attack is most striking. While forty or fifty years ago it was argued that Moses could not possibly have had sufficient learning to write the Pentateuch, now, as the result of these modern discoveries, it is argued that he would have been altogether behind his contemporaries if he had not been able to write. Again, the Babylonian story of the flood agrees in long sections with the account in Genesis, and it is known that the Babylonian version was in existence for ages before the dates assigned to the Genesis narrative by the critical school. Professor Sayce rightly calls this a crucial test of the critical position. The historicity of the kings mentioned in Genesis 14 was once seriously questioned by criticism, but this is impossible today, for their historical character has been proved beyond all question.

In particular, it is now known that the Amraphel of that chapter is the Hammurabi of the Monuments and a contemporary with Abraham. The puzzling story of Sarah and Hagar is also now seen to be in exact agreement with Babylonian custom. Then again, the Egypt of Joseph and Moses is true to the smallest details of the life of the Egypt of that day and is altogether different from the very different Egypt of later ages. Sargon, who for centuries was only known from the one reference to him in Isaiah 20:1, is now seen to have been one of the most important kings of Assyria. And the Aramaic language of Daniel and Ezra, which has so often been accused of lateness, is proved to be in exact

---

[18] Remember, archaeology has advanced one hundred years since this book was initially published. Therefore, whatever was said above, emphasize that a thousand fold. – Christian Publishing House.

accord with the Aramaic of that age, as shown by the Papyri discovered at Elephantinè in Egypt.

Now these, and others like them, are tangible proofs that can be verified by ordinary people. Hebrew philology is beyond most of us and is too subjective for any convincing argument to be based upon it, but archaeology offers an objective method of putting historical theories to the test.

Not the least important feature of the archaeological argument is that a number of leading archaeologists who were formerly in hearty agreement with the critical school, have now abandoned this view and oppose it. As Sir William Robertson Nicoll has forcibly said, "The significant fact is that the great firsthand archaeologists, as a rule, do not trust the higher criticism. This means a great deal more than can be put on paper to account for their doubt. It means that they are living in an atmosphere where arguments that flourish outside do not thrive."

Professor Flinders Petrie, the great Egyptologist, reported:

> I have come to the conclusion that there is a far more solid basis than seems to be supposed by many critics . . . I have not the slightest doubt that contemporary documents give a truly solid foundation for the records contained in the Pentateuch . . . The essential point is that some of these critical people support from an *a priori* basis instead of writing upon ascertained facts. We should remember that writing at the time of the Exodus was as familiar as it is now . . . The fact is that it is hopeless for these people by means merely of verbal criticism to succeed in solving all difficulties that arise.

8. Are the views of modern criticism consistent with the witness of our lord to the Old Testament?

The Christian Church approaches the Old Testament mainly and predominantly from the standpoint of the resurrection of Christ. We naturally inquire what our Master thought of the Old Testament, for if it comes to us with His authority and we can discover His view of it, we ought to be satisfied. In the days of our Lord's life on earth, one pressing question was, "What do you think of the Christ?" Another was, "What is written in the Law? How do you read it?" These questions are still being raised in one form or another, and today, as of old, the two great problems—two "stormcenters", as they have well been called—are Christ and the Bible.

The two problems really resolve themselves into one, for Christ and the Bible are inseparable. If we follow Christ, He will teach us of the Bible. If we study our Bible, it will point us to Christ. Each is called the Word of God.

Let us, first of all, be quite clear as to our meaning of our Lord as "the Word of God." The Book of John reads, "In the beginning was the Word." A word is an oral or visible expression of an invisible thought. The thought needs the word for its expression, and the word is intended to represent the thought accurately, if not completely. We cannot in any degree be sure of the thought unless we can be sure of the word. Therefore, our Lord as the Word is the personal and visible expression of the invisible God. (John 14, Hebrews 1:3) We believe that He is an accurate "expression" of God and, as the Word, He reveals God and conveys God's will to us in such a way as to be inerrant and infallible. As the Incarnate Word, He is infallible.

He came, among other things, to bear witness to the truth (John 18:37), and it is a necessary outcome of this purpose that He should bear infallible witness. He came to reveal God and God's will, and this implies and requires special knowledge. It demands that every assertion of His be true. The Divine knowledge did not, because it could not, undergo any change by the Incarnation. He continued to subsist in the form of God even while He existed in the form of man. (Philippians 2:6. See Dr. Gifford's *The Incarnation*.)

In view of this position, we believe that, as Bishop Ellicott (*Christus Comprobator*) says that we have a right to make this appeal to the testimony of Christ to the Old Testament. The place it occupied in His life and ministry is sufficient warrant for referring to His use of it. It is well known that, as far as the Old Testament canon is concerned, our highest authority is that of our Lord Himself. What is true of the Old Testament as a whole is surely true of these parts to which our Lord specifically referred.

Let us be clear, however, as to what we mean in making this appeal. We do not intend to close all possible criticism of the Old Testament. There are numbers of questions quite untouched by anything our Lord said, and there is consequently ample scope for sober, necessary, and valuable criticism. But what we do say is that anything in the Old Testament stated or implied by our Lord as a fact is thereby closed for those who hold Christ to be infallible. Criticism can do anything that is not incompatible with the statements of our Lord, but where Christ has spoken, surely "the matter is closed."

What, then, is our Lord's general view of the Old Testament? There is no doubt that His Old Testament was practically, if not actually, the same as ours, and that He regarded it as of Divine authority—the final court of appeal for all questions connected with it. The way He quotes it shows this. To the Lord Jesus, the Old Testament was authoritative and final because Divine.

No one can go through the Gospels without being impressed with the deep reverence of Jesus for the Old Testament and His constant use of it in all matters of religious thought and life. "Have ye never read," "It is written," and "Ye search the Scriptures" (R. V) are indicative of His view of the Divine authority of the Old Testament as we have it. He sets His seal to its historicity and its revelation of God. He supplements but never supplants it. He amplifies and modifies but never nullifies it. He fulfills but never makes void.

This general view is confirmed by His detailed references to the Old Testament. Consider His testimonies to the persons and to the facts of the old covenant. There is scarcely a historical book, from Genesis to 2 Chronicles, to which our Lord does not refer, while it is perhaps significant that His testimony includes references to every book of the Pentateuch, to Isaiah, to Jonah, to Daniel, and to miracles—the very parts most called in question today.

Above all, it is surely of the deepest moment that at His temptation He should use the Old Testament three times about which there has, perhaps, been most controversy of all. Therefore, we say that everything to which Christ referred or used as fact is thereby sanctioned and sealed by the authority of our Infallible Lord. "*Dominus locutus est; causa finita est.*"

This position cannot be taken that Christ simply adopted the beliefs of His day without necessarily sanctioning them as correct. To the contrary, He went directly against the prevailing opinion of some of the most important issues of His day. His teaching about God, righteousness, the Messiah, tradition, women, divorce, and more, were diametrically opposed to what was promoted at the time and was deliberately grounded on the Old Testament, which our Lord charged religious leaders with misinterpreting.

The one and only question of difference between Him and the Jews as to the Old Testament was that of interpretation. Not a vestige of proof can be cited that He and they differed at all in their general view of its historical character or Divine authority. If the current Jewish views were wrong, would our Lord would have been silent on the matter of a book that He cites or alludes to more than four hundred times, and that He made reference to concerning Himself? If the Jews were wrong, Jesus either knew it or He did not. If He knew it, why did He not correct them as in so many other detailed instances? Nor can this witness to the Old Testament be met by asserting that the limitation of our Lord's earthly life kept Him within current views of the Old Testament which need not have been true views. This statement ignores the essential force of His personal claim to be "the Word."

On more than one occasion our Lord claimed to speak from God and that everything He said had the Divine warrant. Notice carefully what this involves. It is sometimes said that our Lord's knowledge was limited and that He lived here as man, not as God. Suppose we grant this for argument's sake: as man He lived in God and on God, and He claimed that everything He said and did was from God and through God. If, then, the limitations were from God, so *also were the utterances.* And, as God's warrant was claimed for every one of these, they are therefore Divine and infallible. (John 5:19, 5:30; 7:13, 8:26, 12:49, 14:24, 17:8)

Even though we grant to the full a theory that will compel us to accept a temporary disuse or non-use of the functions of deity in the Person of our Lord, yet the words actually uttered as man are claimed to be from God. Therefore, we hold them to be infallible and rest upon Jesus' personal claim to say all and do all by the Father, from the Father, and for the Father.

There is, of course, no question of partial knowledge after the resurrection, when our Lord was free from all limitations of earthly conditions. Yet it was after His resurrection that He set His seal to the Old Testament. (Luke 24:44) We conclude that our Lord's positive statements on the subject of the Old Testament are not to be rejected without charging Him with error. If on these points, on which we can test and verify Him, we find that He is not reliable, what real comfort can we have in accepting His higher teaching, where verification is impossible? We believe we are on absolutely safe ground when we say that what the Old Testament was to our Lord, it must be and shall be to us.

Conclusion

We ask a careful consideration of these eight inquiries. Taken separately, they carry weight. Taken together, they have a cumulative effect and should be seriously pondered by all who are seeking to know the truth on this momentous subject. We may be perfectly sure that no criticism of the Old Testament will ever be accepted by the Christian Church as a whole, because it does not fully satisfy the following conditions:

1. It must admit in all its assumptions and take fully into consideration the supernatural element, which differentiates the Bible from all other books.

2. It must be in keeping with the enlightened spiritual experience of the saints of God in all ages and make an effectual appeal to the piety and spiritual perception of those who know by personal experience the power of the Holy Ghost.

3. It must be historically in line with the general tradition of Jewish history and the unique position of the Hebrew nation through the centuries.

4. It must be in unison with that apostolic conception of the authority and inspiration of the Old Testament that is manifest in the New Testament.

5. Above all, it must be in accordance with the universal belief of the Christian Church in our Lord's infallibility as a Teacher and as "the Word made flesh."

If and when modern higher criticism can satisfy these requirements, it will not merely be accepted but also will command the universal, loyal, and even enthusiastic adhesion of all Christians. Until then, we wait and maintain our position that "the old is better."

CHAPTER VIII The Tabernacle in The Wilderness: Did It Exist?

A Question Involving the Truth or Falsity of the Entire Higher-Critic Theory

David Heagle, Translator Bremen Lectures

Introduction

The question as to whether or not the old Mosaic Tabernacle ever existed is one of far greater consequence than most people imagine, particularly because of the very intimate connection existing between it and the truth or falsity of the higher-critic theory in general. If that theory is all that the critics claim for it, then of course the Tabernacle had no existence; and this is the view held by at least most of the critics. But if, on the other hand, the old Mosaic Tabernacle did really exist, and the story of it as given in the Bible is not, as the critics assert, merely a fiction, then the higher critic scheme cannot be true.

The question, therefore, to be discussed in the following pages is whether or not the Mosaic Tabernacle really existed and would have wide-reaching significance, which will become more apparent as the discussion goes forward. With this brief introduction, we take up the subject that this article was originally prepared as a booklet, in which shape it contained a considerable amount of matter not appearing here.

The Discussion

One peculiarity of the higher criticism is what may be called its unbounded audacity in attacking and attempting to destroy many of the most solidly established facts of the Bible. No matter with what amount of evidence any particular Scripture fact may be capable of demonstration, if it happens to oppose any of the more fundamental notions of the critical hypothesis, it must be dismissed as unworthy of acceptance by so-called "science," or at all events, the entire array of critical doubts and imaginings is brought to bear in order to cast suspicion or get rid of it in some way.

I. The Bible Side of the Question

A striking illustration of such procedure is furnished by the peculiar treatment accorded by the critics to that old religious structure which, being built by Moses near Mt. Sinai, is usually named the Tabernacle or the Tabernacle in the Wilderness. That such a structure not only existed but also was for some five hundred years a very conspicuous object in ancient Israelite history is a fact to which the Bible itself lends no small amount of evidence. For example, there are found in the Book of Exodus alone some thirteen chapters devoted to a minute description of the plan and construction of that building.

Then, as explanatory of the Tabernacle's services, dedication, means of transportation, work of the priests and Levites, and various other matters connected with the structure, the entire Book of Leviticus and ten chapters in Numbers may be cited. Besides, scattered all through both the Old and New Testaments, there are many allusions and notices—some of them merely incidental, but others more historical in nature—all of which go toward establishing the Tabernacle's historicity. And finally—perhaps the most convincing testimony of all—we have in the New Testament the Epistle to the Hebrews, which concerns, especially from a Christian point of view, the typology and religious significance of that old building.

II. The Higher-Critic View

With so much evidence, therefore, to be presented from the Scriptures in support of the Tabernacle's historicity, one would think that it requires at least some literary bravery, not to mention presumptuous audacity, for any individual or class of men to assail with the expectation of overthrowing a fact so solidly established as would seem to be that of the Tabernacle's real existence. Nevertheless, difficult as such task may appear, the critics have not hesitated most vigorously to undertake it. According to their notion, the whole story of the Tabernacle as recorded in the Bible is simply a fiction or, more properly speaking, a literary forgery concocted perhaps by some of those priestly scribes who returned with Ezra from the Babylonian exile. Their special purpose in devising such a story being to help in the introduction of a new temple ritual at Jerusalem, or perhaps it was also to glorify the distant past in the history of the Israelites.[19]

III. The Question Fully Stated

Thus we have presented to us two widely different and opposing views respecting the Tabernacle's existence. One of them, which is the view of at least most higher critics, is that this old structure never existed at all. On the other hand, the orthodox and Biblical conception is that not only in the days of Moses but also long afterward this fabric had a most interesting and important history. Which, then, of these two so widely different doctrines do we accept?

IV: Importance of this Discussion

Whichever one is accepted by us is a matter of no little consequence. Such a discussion is important, first of all, because of the light it will throw upon all of the history of God's first chosen people—the Israelites. It will at least tell us something about the kind of civilization this ancient people must have had. More particularly, it will tell us whether that civilization was, as the higher critics represent, one low down on the scale or whether these Israelites had already made a good degree of progress in all the arts, disciplines, and branches of knowledge that usually belong to a moderately high state of civilization. Surely, then, there is at least some benefit to be derived from the study before us.

But another advantage that will come from this same study is that it will help us to a solution of a somewhat curious yet important, historical problem—whether as a matter of history the Temple preceded the Tabernacle, as the higher critics claim, and, therefore, that the Tabernacle must be regarded as only "a diminutive copy" of the Temple or vice versa, whether, as is taught by the Bible, the Tabernacle went first, and hence the Temple was in its construction patterned after the Tabernacle. To be sure, at first sight this does

---

[19] As explained by Nödelke, another purpose of this forgery was "to give pre-existence to the temple and to the unity of worship." But this is virtually included in the two purposes above named.

not appear to be a very important question, yet when the historical, literary, and other connections involved in it are considered, it does become a question of no little significance.

But the most determinative and therefore the most significant interest we have in a discussion of the question as proposed is the bearing it has upon the truth or falsity of the higher criticism. As is known to persons conversant with that peculiar method of Bible study, one of its main contentions is that the whole Levitical or ceremonial law—that is, the law of worship as recorded especially in Exodus, Leviticus, and Numbers—did not originate, or at all events did not make its appearance, until somewhere near the close of the Babylonian exile or about the time when Ezra first appears in Jewish history.

By thus removing all that part of the Pentateuch down the centuries, from the time of Moses to the time of Ezra, the critics are able not only to deny the Mosaic authorship of this Pentateuchal literature but also to construct a scheme of their own by which all the separate "documents" into which they are accustomed to divide the Pentateuch can be put together in a kind of whole, with each particular document being singled out and designated according to its date, authorship, and other peculiarities, such as the critics suppose belong to it. Moreover, in this way the Pentateuch is all torn to pieces, and instead of its being really a connected, organic whole, such as the orthodox world has always conceived it to be, it is by this peculiar higher-critic method transformed into a mere patchwork, a disjointed affair, having no more Divine authority or inspiration connected with it than any other piece of human literature that has come into being through the law of evolution.

Such, however, is exactly what the critics would make of the Pentateuch, and indeed of much else in the Bible, if they could have their way.

But now suppose that after all the old Mosaic Tabernacle did really exist, what effect would that have upon the success of the critical hypothesis? It would absolutely frustrate all attempts to carry this hypothesis successfully through. Such would necessarily be the result, because, first of all, if that portion of the Pentateuch which contains the ceremonial or Levitical law is transferred down to Ezra's time, the old Tabernacle, for the services of which this law was designed, must necessarily come with it. But then, in the second place, a really existing Tabernacle so far down the centuries, or long after the Temple at Jerusalem had been built and was regarded by the Jews as their great central place of worship, would have been not only an architectural curiosity but also an anachronism such as even the critical imagination could scarcely be accused either of devising or accepting.

Therefore, the only way for the critics, if they are still to hold fast their theory, is for them to do precisely what they have undertaken, namely, to blot out or destroy the Tabernacle as a real existence and then to reconstruct the Bible's account in the form of fiction. This they have really attempted.

However, by doing this, the critics must confess that the foundation upon which they build is very insecure, because it is simply an assumption. If, therefore, in opposition to such assumption, this article shall be able to demonstrate that the old Mosaic Tabernacle actually existed, then the underpinning of the critical hypothesis is at once removed, and the entire edifice with all of its many stories must collapse. And if all this is true, then it is not too much to say, as is affirmed in the sub-title of this article, that the whole truth or falsity of the critical scheme depends upon what may be proven true respecting the Tabernacle's non-existence or existence. Thus, the exceeding importance of the discussion we have undertaken is made evident.

V. Quotations from the Higher Critics

What do the higher critics say with regard to this matter of the Tabernacle's real existence? To quote from only a few of them, Wellhausen, e.g., who is the great leader of the higher-critic doctrine, writes as follows:

> The Temple, which in reality was not built until Solomon's time, is by this document [the so-called Priestly Code] regarded as so indispensable, even for the troubled days of the wilderness before the settlement, that it is made portable, and in the form of a tabernacle set up in the very beginning of things. For the truth is that the Tabernacle is a copy, not the prototype, of the temple at Jerusalem" (*Proleg.*, Eng. trans., p. 37).

So also Graf, who preceded Wellhausen in higher-critic work, affirms that the Tabernacle is only "a diminutive copy of the Temple," and that "all that is said about this structure in the middle books of the Pentateuch is merely post-exilic accretion."

To hear from a more recent authority, Dr. A. R. S. Kennedy, in Hastings' *Dictionary of the Bible*, has these words:

> The attitude of modern Old Testament scholarship to the priestly legislation as now formulated in the Pentateuch, and in particular to those sections of it which deal with the sanctuary and its worship, is opposed to the historicity of P's [that is, the old Mosaic] Tabernacle.

The same or a similar representation is given by Benzinger in the *Encyclopaedia Biblica*, and, in fact, is and must necessarily be the attitude of all consistent higher critics toward the matter under consideration. For it would never do for the adherents of the critic theory to admit that in the Mosaic times the Tabernacle, with all its elaborate ritual and lofty moral and spiritual ideas, could have existed because that would be equivalent to admitting the falsity of their own doctrine. Accordingly, with one voice, the critics stoutly proclaim that no historicity whatever must be allowed to Moses' Tabernacle.

VI. Certain Great Presumptions

To come then to the actual discussion of our subject, it might be said that there are certain great presumptions that lie in the way of our accepting the higher-critic theory as true. One of these presumptions is that this whole critic hypothesis goes on the assumption that what the Bible tells us regarding the real existence of the Tabernacle is not true; in a large part of its teachings, the Bible speaks falsely. Can we believe that? Most assuredly not, so long as we have any real appreciation of the lofty system of moral truth that is taught in this wonderful book that, more than any other ever produced, has taught the entire world common honesty in literary work or other acts. Therefore, regarding this whole matter of the Bible's speaking falsely, *Judaeus Apella credat, non ego*! Let the higher critics believe that if they will, but surely not we!

Robert Burns has a poem, in which he says of lying in general:

> Some books are lies frae end to end,
> And some great lies were never penned;
> E'en ministers, they hae been kenned,
> In holy rapture,
> A rousing whid at times to vend,
> An' nail it wi' Scripture.

Surely, the higher critics would not undertake to reduce our Christian Scriptures to the level of a book that has in it no truth from beginning to end, yet it must be confessed that one serious tendency of their theory is to lessen the general credibility of this sacred volume.

Another presumption lying against the truthfulness of this higher criticism is that it makes all the civilized ages from Ezra down to the present time to be so utterly lacking both in historic knowledge and literary sagacity, that, excepting a few higher critics, no one ever supposed the whole world was being deceived by this untrue story of the Tabernacle's real existence, when, if the facts were told, all these numerous ages have not only been themselves deceived but have been also instrumental in propagating that same old falsehood down the centuries!

Again we say: *Judaeus Apella credat, non ego!* The higher-critic pretensions to having a greater wisdom and knowledge than is possessed by all the rest of the world are very well known, but this illustration of that peculiarity seems to us rather to cap the climax.

Here, if we choose to go farther, it might be shown that, if this peculiar doctrine is true, then the Savior and all of his Apostles were mistaken. For certainly Christ (see Matthew 12:3-4), and perhaps all the Apostles without exception, did believe in the Tabernacle as a real existence. One of the Apostles, or at least an apostolic writer, went so far in the Book of Hebrews as to compose what may be termed an extensive and inspired commentary on that sacred structure—on its apartments, furniture, priesthood, and services, bringing out particularly from a Christian point of view the rich typical significance of all those matters. Now that all these inspired men and the Savior Himself should either have been deceived or should try to deceive others with regard to an important matter of Old Testament history is surely incredible.

VII. External Evidence

Here, however, we desire to introduce some considerations of a different nature. There exists even outside of the Bible a small amount of evidence in support of the Tabernacle's existence, and although we have already alluded to a part of this testimony under the head of favoring presumptions, yet it will bear repetition or rather a fuller consideration. Now, as we conceive of this evidence, it consists of various notices or full descriptions of the Tabernacle as a real existence that are found in very ancient writings. Some of these writings are quite different from our Christian Scriptures. To be sure, a large part of this literature is copied in one way or another from the Bible, and none of it dates anything like so far back in time as do the earlier books of the Old Testament. Yet, as we shall see, some of it is sufficiently enough to give it a kind of confirmatory force in support of what the Bible has to say concerning the matter in hand.

The first testimony, then, of this sort to which we allude, is a full description of the Tabernacle in all its parts, services, priesthood, and history. It is nearly the same as what is given in our modern Bibles, which can be found in the earliest translation ever made of the Old Testament—the Septuagint. This translation appeared some two or three centuries before the time of Christ, and it ought to be pretty good evidence of at least what its contemporaries, or those far-off times, held to be true with regard to the matter under consideration. Then another testimony of like character comes from the Greek Apocrypha to the Old Testament, a work that appeared, or at least most of it, before the time of Christ, where are found various allusions to the real existence of the Tabernacle, e.g., in Judges 9:8; Wisdom of Solomon 9:8; Ecclesiastes. 24:10, 15; and 2 Macabees. 2:5. Moreover, in his *Antiquities*, Josephus, who wrote toward the end of the first century, gives another full description of that old structure in its every part, including also something of its history. (See *Antiquities* III., Chs. six to twelve; Book V, Ch. 1., Sec. 19; Ch. 2., Sec. 9; Ch. 10., Sec. 2; Bookk. VIII., Ch. four., Sec. 1.)

And finally, in that vast collection of ancient Jewish traditions, comments, laws, speculations, etc., that are found under the name of the Talmud, there are not infrequent references made to this same old structure; and one of the treatises (part of the Bereitha)[20] in that collection is devoted exclusively to a consideration of this building.

With so much literature considered direct testimony to the Tabernacle's existence at least when the last part of the Old Testament was written, they must have been acquainted with the best traditions of their day regarding what is taught in that part of our Bible. Therefore, they must have known more about the truth of matters connected with the Tabernacle and its real existence than the mere guesswork speculations of modern higher critics possibly can, or are in a condition to know.[21]

But there is another kind of evidence, of this external nature which is more direct and independent; therefore, it is more significant to the Tabernacle's existence. That evidence is what may be called the archaeology contribution to our argument. Part of it will be given later; but here we will simply call attention to the fact that in Mt. Sinai region there is at least some evidences of the possible presence there, even as is recorded in the Bible of the Israelites at the time when they built the Tabernacle. Moreover, there have recently been made some discoveries in the Holy Land connected with the different places where the Bible locates the Tabernacle during the long period of its history in that country, which, to say the least, are not contradictory but rather confirmatory of Biblical statements.

---

[20] The Bereitha (or Baraitha) is an apocryphal part of the Talmud; but it is very old, and embodies about the same quality of tradition in general as does the compilation made by Jehudah ha-Nasi, which is usually considered the genuine Mishna, or basis of the Talmud.

[21] The value of this evidence is of course only that which belongs to tradition; still it should be remembered that this tradition is a written one, dating away back to near the times of the Old Testament. Moreover, it could be shown that this same kind of written tradition reaches back through the later books of the Old Testament, at least in a negative way, even to the time of Ezra; who surely ought to know whether, as the critics say, the story of the Tabernacle as a fact of history was invented in his own day and generation. But inasmuch as Ezra does not tell us anything about that matter, it stands to reason, that as has since been reported by this long line of tradition, most of it being of a positive nature, no such invention ever took place, but that this story is simply a narrative of actual fact. At all events, as said in the text, it is far more likely that this old and long-continued tradition is correct in what it asserts, than is any of the denials of the higher critics.

One such discovery, as we will call it, is connected with a fuller exploration recently made of that old site where for approximately 365 years, according to Jewish tradition, the old Mosaic Tabernacle stood and where it underwent the most interesting of its experiences in the Holy Land. That site was the little city of Shiloh, located near the main thoroughfare leading up from Bethel to Shechem. In the year 1873 the English Palestine Exploration Fund through some of its agents made a thorough examination of this old site. Among its very interesting ruins was found a place that Colonel Charles Wilson thinks is the *very spot* where the Tabernacle stood. That particular place is at the north of a rather low "tell," or mound where the ruins are located, of which Colonel Wilson's says, "slopes down to a broad shoulder across a sort of local court about 77 feet wide and 412 feet long that has been cut out. The rock is in places scarped to a height of five feet, and along the sides are several excavations and a few small cisterns." This is the locality where, as Colonel Wilson thinks, the Mosaic Tabernacle once really stood, and confirming his conclusion, he further says that this spot is the only one connected with the ruins that is large enough to receive a building of the dimensions of the Tabernacle. Therefore, his judgment is that it is "not improbable" that this place was originally "prepared" as a site for that structure.

Now whether the general judgment of men either at present or in the future will coincide with Colonel Wilson as to the matter in hand we do not know; but we will simply repeat Colonel Wilson's words and say that it is *not improbable* that this site, as indicated, is a real discovery as to the place where the old Tabernacle once stood and is good evidence that this building once existed.

VIII. Positive Biblical Evidence

More conclusive evidence of the Tabernacles existence consists in numerous historical notices scattered throughout the Old Testament that would seem to prove beyond all possibility of doubt that the Old Mosaic Tabernacle really existed.[22] However, the critics claim here that it is only the earlier historical books of the Old Testament that can be legitimately used for proving a matter so far in the past as was this structure.

Testimony of I Kings

Complying then with that requirement, at least in part, we begin our investigation with the Book of I Kings. This is a piece of literature against the antiquity and general credibility of which the critics can raise no valid objection; hence it should be considered credible evidence. Moreover, it might be said of this book, that having probably been constructed out of early court records as they were kept by the different kings of Judah and Israel, at least some of those original documents are records of times of Solomon and David or to the period when, as we shall soon see, the Mosaic Tabernacle was still standing at Gibeon. This was also the general period during which the Tabernacle, having been taken down, was removed from Gibeon and stored away in Solomon's temple at

---

[22] According to Bishop Hervey, in his *Lectures on Chronicles* (p. 171), mention is made of the Tabernacle some eighteen times in the historical books following the Pentateuch—that is, in Joshua, Judges, 1 and 2 Samuel, 1 and 2 Kings, and 1 and 2 Chronicles; and in the Pentateuch itself, which the higher critics have by no means proven to be unhistorical, that structure is mentioned over eighty times.

Jerusalem. It is to this account of transference that our attention is now directed. In 1 Kings 8:4, we read: "And they brought up the ark of Jehovah, the tent of meeting, and all the holy vessels that were in the tent; the priests and the Levites brought them up."

A mere cursory reading of these words gives one the impression that the "tent of meeting," which was brought up from somewhere by the priests and Levites, was the old Mosaic Tabernacle. Where it was brought from we are not told in the Scriptures, but a comparison of texts (see 2 Chronicles 1:3 and 1 Kings 3:1, 4) would seem to indicate that the Tabernacle was first transported from Gibeon to Mt. Zion, where the ark of the covenant was at this time. Afterward it was carried up to Mt. Moriah, along with other sacred articles, where it was stored in the temple.

All this seems to be sufficiently clear; only now the question arises whether this was really the old Mosaic structure or some other tent, as, e.g., the one built by David in Jerusalem, which seems at this time to have been still in existence.[23] Most of the critics, including Wellhausen, are agreed that the words, "tent of meeting" (*ohel moed*), as used in this and various other texts of Scripture, do really signify the old Mosaic structure. One reason for their agreement is that those words form a kind of technical expression by which that old structure was commonly, or at least often, denoted in the Bible.[24] Only one other term is used as frequently as this is to indicate that structure—in Hebrew, *mishkan*, usually translated in English versions as "tabernacle" and means "dwelling-place."

Now if the rendering of those words is correct, we would seem to have already reached the goal of our endeavor; we have actually found the Tabernacle in existence. It existed as an undeniable reality in the times of David and Solomon or at least in those of Solomon, as recorded in 1 Kings 8:4.

But the higher critics, especially Wellhausen, are not so easily to be caught with an admission as to an interpretation of words; even though Wellhausen does concede that the words "tent of meeting" indicate the Tabernacle, he undermines their real force by asserting that in this passage they are an interpolation or that they do not belong to the original Hebrew text. However, neither he nor any other higher critic has ever yet been able to give any textual authority for such an assertion; they only try to argue the matter from internal evidence. But internal evidence alone, and especially such slim evidence of that kind as the critics have been able to adduce in this connection, is insufficient to establish the end desired. Besides, those words, "tent of meeting," are certainly found in our present Hebrew text, as also in the Septuagint version— both of which items being so, it is not likely that Wellhausen's *ipse dixit* will have the effect of changing them.

Such being the case, we may conclude that the structure that was carried by the priests and Levites up to Mt. Moriah and stored away in the temple, was really the old Mosaic Tabernacle.

We quote only one other passage from I Kings 3:4, the account of Solomon going to Gibeon and of his offering sacrifice there: "And the king went to Gibeon to sacrifice there, for that was the great high place; Solomon offered a thousand burnt offerings on that

---

[23] See 2 Sam. 6:17 and 7:2; 1 Chron. 15:1 and 16:1. Cf. 1 Kings 1:29.

[24] The words *ohel moed* seem to have been used first to designate the smaller tent, which Moses used as a place of communion between Jehovah and his people; hence it was called the "tent of meeting." But afterwards, when the regular tabernacle became such a place, the words were applied also to that structure.

altar:" In the second verse of this same chapter, the king's conduct in thus going to Gibeon is further explained by the statement that the people sacrificed in the high places because "there was no house built for the name of Jehovah until those days." The "days" indicated are, as is explained by the preceding verse, those in which "Solomon made an end of building his own house and the house of Jehovah," and the entire passage then would signify that at least one reason why Solomon offered sacrifice in Gibeon was because this was the customary way among the people. They offered sacrifices in the high places before the temple at Jerusalem was built but not ordinarily, or legitimately, afterwards.

Then there is another reason indicated why Solomon went particularly to Gibeon—this was the "*great*" high place." Why it was so called must have been because of some special fact or circumstance connected with it. Among the explanations given, none appear so natural with other teachings of Scripture as the suggestion that this distinction was applied to Gibeon because the old Mosaic Tabernacle with the brazen altar was still there. That would certainly be a sufficient reason for accrediting peculiar eminence to this one of all the many high places that were understood to have existed in the Holy Land. Accordingly, Solomon went over to Gibeon and offered sacrifice there. In the night following this devotional act, the king had a dream in which Jehovah appeared to him and made extraordinary promises. Now this epiphany of Jehovah at Gibeon is really another reason to believe that the Tabernacle was located at this place. For it is not to be supposed that any Jewish author, writing after the temple was built (when this account of Solomon's dream was written), would allow it to be said that the great and idolatry-hating God of the Israelites had made a gracious and extraordinary revelation of himself at any of the Gentile high places in the Holy Land.

If the Tabernacle was located at Gibeon, then all becomes clear, both why Solomon went there to offer sacrifice, why Jehovah revealed himself here, and why this, of all the high places in the Holy Land, was called "great." Moreover, it might be said that we have surely demonstrated the existence of the Tabernacle not only as taught by this passage from First Kings but also by another.

Testimony of Chronicles

In the Books of Chronicles, we find a number of passages that clearly teach the Tabernacle existed at Gibeon not only in the time of Solomon but also before. The two books are a kind of commentary extension of the Books of Samuel and Kings, which is the opinion of many competent scholars. One reason for their conclusion is that the Books of Samuel and Kings were among the principal sources from which the author of Chronicles drew his information, although it must be acknowledged that he used other sources as well. Writing then at a somewhat distant date, say one or two hundred years from the time of the final composition or redaction of Kings and Samuel,[25] and doubtless having at his command a considerable amount of tradition besides his written sources, the

---

[25] It is claimed by the critics that all the historical books of the Old Testament underwent a revision during the exile; and according to the best authorities, Chronicles was composed shortly after the Persian rule, or about 330 B. C. Selecting, then, about the middle of the exilic period (586 to 444 B. C.) as the date for the final revision of Kings and Samuel would make the composition of Chronicles fall near 200 years after that revision. But of course, Samuel and Kings were originally composed, or compiled, at a much earlier date; the former appearing probably about 900 and the latter about 600 B. C.

Chronicler must have been in very good condition to write what may be considered a kind of interpretive commentary upon not only the books of Samuel but also upon the First Book of Kings. If that was so, and the two books of Chronicles are to be understood as giving additional information as to what is found in Kings, then the historical notices in I Kings are illuminated and made stronger and more positive in their nature than when considered alone. For instance, in I Kings we were told that Solomon went to Gibeon and offered sacrifice there, because "that was the great high place." In 1 Chronicles 1:3, it is explained how Gibeon came to be so-called and what Solomon's reason was for going there to offer sacrifice. As taught in Chronicles, it was because *"the tent of meeting of God which Moses the servant of. Jehovah had made in the wilderness"* was at that time in Gibeon. Thus the rather uncertain mention of matters at Gibeon given in I Kings is made clear and positive by what is said in Chronicles. Also, in 1 Chronicles 21:29, which is a part of the account given of David's offering sacrifice on the threshing floor of Ornan, we have stronger language used than is found in Kings, telling us of the existence of the old Mosaic Tabernacle. In explaining David's conduct, the Chronicler says, "For the tabernacle of the Lord, which Moses had made in the wilderness, and the altar of burnt offering were at that time in the high place at Gibeon."

Whatever of uncertainty or lack of positive indication may exist as connected with the passages we have quoted from Kings, there is no such uncertainty in Chronicles. On the contrary, these two books that give plentiful information respecting the Tabernacle are clear. It might be added that the statements made in Chronicles have sometimes been taken as a guide to the study of the Tabernacle history in general.

However, here again the critics are "up in arms" against any use to be made of these two books of Chronicles for determining a matter of ancient history. They say that of all the untrustworthy historical literature to be found in the Old Testament, there is nothing quite so bad as I Chronicles. Wellhausen goes so far as to say that one special purpose served by these two books is that they show how an author may use his original sources with such freedom as to make them say what he pleases according to his own ideas. (See *Proleg.*, Eng. trans., p. 49.) So also Graf, DeWette, and others have energetically attacked the credibility of these two books. But against all that is said by the critics we will put the testimony of one of the higher critics themselves. It is what Dillman, who is acknowledged to be among the very foremost of all the critics, says with regard to Kings and Chronicles, "It is now recognized that the Chronicler has worked according to sources, and there can be no talk with regard to him of fabrications or misrepresentations of the history."

So also Dr. Orr observes that there is no reason for doubting "the perfect good faith" of the author of Chronicles. Professor James Robertson, of Glasgow University, further adds that such matters as the critics have urged against the Chronicler's "misuse" or "invention of sources" are "superficial and unjust." He adds, "There is no reason to doubt the honesty of the author in the use of such materials as he has command of, nor is there any to question the existence of the writings to which he refers."

We take it; therefore, that these two books of Chronicles embody not only the best historical knowledge, but also the best traditions still in existence at their date. That being the case, it is clearly incontrovertible that, as is so unmistakably taught in these books, the old Mosaic Tabernacle must have existed. So long as the critics are unable to impeach the testimony of these books, which would seem to be impossible, that testimony must stand.[26]

Testimony of Samuel

Certainly, the Books of Samuel offer another piece of literature against the general credibility of the higher criticism. These books reveal much respecting the Tabernacle's history. First, they claim the Mosaic Tabernacle was located at Shiloh, in the Ephraimite district. Next, we learn that at least one of the great festivals connected with the Tabernacle services—the "yearly sacrifice"—was still being observed. Also, this is the place where Samuel's parents, Elkanah and Hannah, went up every year to partake in that sacrifice. Moreover, it was in the sanctuary at Shiloh, or in some one of its apartments, that Samuel slept at the time when he had those extraordinary revelations of Jehovah talking with him and where also he came into such intimate and important relations with the aged Eli and his house.

Additionally, one item reported invites special attention. In 1 Samuel 2:22, mention is made of certain "women that did service at the door of the tent meeting." It was with these women that Eli's two sons, Hophni and Phinehas, committed at least a part of their wickedness, for which they were severely condemned and afterward punished by Jehovah. Whatever else this passage may signify, it teaches by its use of the words "tent of meeting" that in the time of Samuel the old Mosaic Tabernacle was in existence at Shiloh. The words "tent of meeting" formed a characteristic expression by which in Old Testament times the Tabernacle was often designated and known. This much even Wellhausen is willing to admit.

However, the critics raise here two objections. One of them is that the sanctuary at Shiloh was not really a tent or tabernacle but rather a solid structure built out of stone, wood, or some other material. The special reason given by the critics for this view is that, in Samuel's account of the structure at Shiloh, there are "posts," "doors," and some other matters usually indicative of a solid structure mentioned. But this difficulty can be easily explained from a statement made in the Jewish Mishna,[27] which is that the lower part of the sanctuary at Shiloh "was of stone," but that above this there was a tent. A more decisive answer to this objection is that in various Scriptures (such as 2 Samuel 7:6; Psalm 78:60; 1 Kings 8:4; Joshua 18:1, and others) the structure under consideration is positively called "a tent" and "a tabernacle."

---

[26] It is claimed by the critics, and especially by Wellhausen, that during the exile the Jewish notions respecting the past of their national and tribal history underwent a radical change, so much so that nearly all the religious features of that history were conceived of as having been very different from what they really were. In other words, the Jewish writers of the exilic period were, so the critics tell us, accustomed to project religious and priestly matters belonging to their history in a much later period back to the earliest times. Consequently the general ideas of the temple and the temple service were projected back to the days of Moses. In this way, it is explained, the notion of a Mosaic Tabernacle with an elaborate ritualistic service came into being. But there is no evidence in the Old Testament writings that the Jews knew anything about such a change taking place. Hence, the critics are decidedly wrong when they represent that the author of Chronicles was only influenced by the spirit of his age when he undertook to misrepresent numerous matters connected with the past history of this people. The truth is that the Chronicler was either a base falsifier or what he tells us in his history must be received as genuine facts.

[27] See Conder's "*Tent Work in Palestine*," Vol. 2, p. 84.

The other objection raised by the critics is that the words "tent of meeting" found in 1 Samuel 2:22 are not authentic. The reason which they give for such an assertion is that this passage is not found in the Septuagint. But in reply to such objection, it may be said, first, that this is not the only passage in the Bible in which mention is made of these women "at the door of the tent of meeting." In Exodus 38:8, as mention was made and as Dr. Orr has observed, it is inconceivable even on the supposition of a post-exilic origin of the last passage. In other words, the genuineness of the text in Exodus argues for the genuineness of the text in Samuel. Besides, as Dr. Orr has again suggested, there may have been some special reason of delicacy or of regard for the good moral reputation of the Israelites, on the account of which the makers of the Septuagint version threw out this item respecting the wickedness of Hophni and Phinehas as connected with these women.

Moreover, as an offset to the Septuagint's authority—which owing to the known faultiness of its present text and its general inexactness as a translation is surely not great—it can be urged that the entire clause containing the words "tent of meeting" is found alike in the old Syriac or Peshito version, in the *Vulgate*, and in the only extant Targum (that of Jonathan Ben Uzziel), all of which very ancient authorities[28] render it as certain that the old original text in 1 Samuel 2:22 was exactly as it is now in our present-day Hebrew Bible.

Finally, it can be affirmed that, for English readers at least, there exists one authority easy to be consulted that would seem to put beyond all reasonable doubt the genuineness of this text. That authority is our Revised English Version of the Scriptures—a literary work that in point of scholarship and general reliability stands perhaps second to none produced in recent years—in which this entire disputed passage is retained, or that the many eminent scholars, both English and American, who studied this translation are agreed that the words, "tent of meeting," or *ohel moed*, as in Hebrew, are genuine and belong to this passage.

Such being the case, the critics' credibility begs to be questioned. Of course, anyone can make what he pleases of any passage of Scripture, provided he only has the privilege of doctoring it sufficiently beforehand. And with regard to this particular passage it may be said that neither Wellhausen nor any other higher critic can do anything to alter it; because so long as those words *ohel moed*, or "tent of meeting," remain in the various textual authorities that have been quoted, it will be impossible to expunge them from our present Hebrew Bible. No matter what authorities the critics may be able to quote as omitting these words, the preponderance of authority will always be in favor of their retention. We claim then a real victory here in being able to substantiate so conclusively the genuineness of this text in Samuel.

But what now is the general result of our examinations with regard to the testimony that Samuel gives us? If our conclusion with regard to the passage just examined is correct, and we are fully persuaded that it is, then we surely have demonstrated in the clearest way that not only in the days of Samuel but also probably long before did the Tabernacle exist and was located at Shiloh.

---

[28] The Targum on Samuel, which is attributed to Jonathan Ben Uzziel, is commonly believed to have been produced some time during the first century; the Peshito version of the Scriptures is thought to have been made somewhat later, probably in the second century; while the Latin *Vulgate*, by Jerome, was completed between the years 390 and 405 A. D.

Testimony of Jeremiah and Psalm 78

If we go further in this investigation, we might find some very interesting testimony to the Tabernacle's historicity in Psalm 78 and in the prophecy of Jeremiah. One of these passages is found in Psalm 78:59–60: "When God heard, he was filled with wrath, and greatly abhorred Israel; So that he abandoned the dwelling place at Shiloh, the tent which he had pitched among men , , ,"

Another passage from Jeremiah 7:12–14 reads: "But go now to my place which was in Shiloh, where I made my name dwell at the first, and see what I did to it because of the wickedness of my people Israel. And now, because you have done all these things," declares the Lord, "and I spoke to you, rising up early and speaking, but you did not hear, and I called you but you did not answer, therefore, I will do to the house which is called by my name, in which you trust, and to the place which I gave you and your fathers, as I did to Shiloh."

Still another passage may be found in Jeremiah 26:6, and reads: "then I will make this house like Shiloh, and this city I will make a curse to all the nations of the earth."[29]

All these passages compare the Temple at Jerusalem with the Tabernacle at Shiloh; and they express the threat, that, unless the Israelites repented, God would destroy the Temple at Jerusalem as he had long before destroyed or removed the Tabernacle at Shiloh.

Testimony of Judges and Joshua

Yet once more, in order to make our story of the Tabernacle complete, it is necessary for us to go back in history, so we quote from the Books of Judges and Joshua. In Joshua 18:1 we read, "Then the whole congregation of the sons of Israel assembled themselves at Shiloh, and set up the tent of meeting there; and the land was subdued before them."

Judges 18:31, we again read about the idolatrous images set up in Dan, that these continued there " . . . all the time that the house of God was at Shiloh."

From these two passages we learn not only how the "house of God" came to be located at Shiloh—because the children of Israel, probably under the leadership of Joshua, set it up there—but also that the two descriptive terms, "tent of meeting" and "house of God," signify the same thing. It is hardly possible that the "tent of meeting" erected at Shiloh in the days of Joshua had been replaced in the time of the Judges by a different structure now called the "house of God."

---

[29] These passages in Jeremiah are important as evidence in favor of the Tabernacle's real existence, since even the higher critics must admit that the chapters containing them were written a considerable time before the exile. Therefore these passages could not, except upon the violent theory of redaction, have been affected by writings appearing either during or after the exile. And as to Psalm 78, which is even more explicit about the structure at Shiloh's being the old Mosaic Tabernacle, it is much easier to say, as the critics do, that this Psalm is post-exilic, than it is to prove such assertion.

Argument from History of the Sacred Ark

Before we give the entire story of the Tabernacle, we notice another argument, which is drawn from the history of the sacred ark. There does not seem to be any notice of the Tabernacle as a structure by itself in the book of Deuteronomy, but in chapter 10, verses 1–5, an account is given of the construction, not of the Tabernacle. What must be considered as its most important piece of furniture is the Ark of the Covenant, as it is usually called (the critics prefer to term it the Ark of Jahweh or Jehovah). Now, although the critics take a very different view regarding the date and authority of Deuteronomy from that which has always been accepted by orthodox scholars, especially upon the ground of the passage referred to, they are willing to admit that at least some kind of a sacred ark was constructed even in the days of Moses. Moreover, if consistent with the facts as recorded in the Bible, the critics cannot deny that this same sacred ark, whatever its form or purpose, was not only carried by the Israelites on all their journeys through the wilderness but also was finally located by them at Shiloh, when, after undergoing various fortunes, it was deposited in the holy of holies of Solomon's Temple. This the critics in general admit, and they are compelled to do so by their own accepted documents of "J," "E," etc.

Now, that being the case, it follows that if the history of the sacred ark can be traced from the days of Solomon's Temple to the days of Moses, somewhat the same thing can be done also with the Tabernacle. For the Tabernacle, as is evident from what the critics call the Priestly Document, was built to house the sacred ark. The same documentary evidence that establishes that fact also confirms further that for a long period such was really the case. That is to say, the sacred ark and the old Mosaic Tabernacle went together, according to Biblical history, down to the times of Shiloh. They were, after some period of separation, even brought together again at the dedicatory services of Solomon's Temple. To be sure, not all of this is admitted by the critics, but they cannot deny that the same ark, which, according to Deuteronomy 10:1–5, was built by Moses and finally deposited in Solomon's Temple.[30] With this much conceded, all the rest that we have claimed must necessarily follow. In other words, the admitted history of the Ark of Jehovah establishes also the historicity of the Mosaic Tabernacle, or at least helps to do so.

Entire Story of the Tabernacle

Now we are prepared to give the entire story of that old structure that was built at Mt. Sinai; only one item still is lacking. This we can learn from 1 Samuel, chapters 21 and 22. For a brief period, the Tabernacle seems to have been located at Nob, some distance south of Shiloh. With this item supplied, our story may go forward, as vouched for by the different historic notices.

Built by the Israelites near Mt. Sinai, the Tabernacle was afterward carried by that people all through the wilderness. Then, having crossed the Jordan with them and being

---

[30] Wellhausen positively states that according to the Law, or the Priestly Document, the Tabernacle is "the inseparable companion of the ark and that "The two things necessarily belong to each other." He also admits, on the grounds of other Biblical evidence, that toward the end of the period of judges there are distinct traces of the ark as existing. Moreover, that this same "ark of Jehovah" was finally deposited in Solomon's Temple. (See *Proleg.*, Eng. Trans., pp. 41, 42.)

set up at Shiloh, it seems for a long time to have remained in that place. Next, for a brief period, it would appear to have been located at Nob, down in the Benjaminite country; and from this point it was carried to Gibeon, where it remained for many years. Finally, it was transferred to Jerusalem upon the erection of the temple. This is the last notice that the Bible gives of it as a matter of history. It had served its purpose, and the time came now for it to be laid aside as a memorial or to give place for another and a more imposing structure.

Intimate Connection of this Story with other Biblical History

Speaking somewhere of the extraordinary influence exerted by Christianity in our world, Renan says that any attempt to separate this religion from the history of humanity would be like "tearing up the tree of civilization by its roots." Very much like that, it seems to us, is the intimacy of relation existing between the history of the Tabernacle and all the rest of the history recorded in the Old Testament. Any attempt to remove the Tabernacle as a matter of fact from Old Testament history, or to turn it into a mere fiction, would necessarily result in failure. It would do so because the effect of it would be really to destroy all the surrounding and connected history given in the Old Testament, which is, of course, impossible. The very extravagance, therefore, of this higher-critic theory, or the vastness of its undertaking, is a sure proof of its inherent falsity.

Dr. Valpy French, considering only the peculiar construction of this Tabernacle story, how wide reaching it is, and how it is made to conform so accurately with many details of archaeology and topography, pronounces it, if viewed as a mere fiction, "a literary impossibility." He suggests that a simpler method to be employed by the critics, in getting rid of this troublesome story, would be for them "to credit the last redactor with the authorship of the whole Old Testament Scriptures." So also Professor Sayce affirms that, regarded as an invention, the Tabernacle story is "too elaborate, too detailed to be conceivable."

Objections of the Higher Critics

To render our discussion complete, it remains for us to notice a few of the many objections that the higher critics have brought forward against the Tabernacle's historicity. These objections, however, are frivolous in character, lacking in support either from fact or reason, and do not really deserve an answer. Nevertheless, to furnish the reader with some notion of their real character, we will give them a cursory examination.

They may all be divided into four classes. The first class embraces all those objections that are based on the idea that the account given in the Bible of the Tabernacle's construction and services is unrealistic or impractical in its nature. A second class proceeds on the notion that the Mosaic Tabernacle is altogether too costly, highly artistic, and cumbersome to have been produced by the Israelites at Mt. Sinai and carried by them through the wilderness.

Another of these classes—really only one objection—represents that in the very oldest sources out of which the Pentateuch was constructed, there is mention made of another tent much smaller than was the Mosaic Tabernacle and different from that structure also in other respects. Therefore, this second tabernacle, as it may be called by the higher critics, being better substantiated by literary documents than is the Mosaic structure, it is not consistent with an acceptance of all the facts in the case to allow that the larger or Mosaic tent really existed.

And finally, there is still a single objection that boldly affirms that in all the earlier historic books of the Old Testament, even from Judges to 2 Kings, there is no sure mention made of the Tabernacle as a real existence.

If we were to try to answer all the objections, it might be said of the last one that it is already answered. We have answered that objection by showing not only that there is mention made in those earlier historic books of the Old Testament of the Tabernacle as a real existence but also that this mention is both sure and abundant. The many historical notices we have examined, all telling about the Tabernacle's construction and history, is positive proof to that effect.

Furthermore, there is mention of another tent different from the Mosaic structure. We have to say with respect to this objection that it is far from being proven that there are in the Pentateuch any such oldest sources as the critics allege. That item is only a part of the still unproven theory of the higher critics in their interpretation of the Old Testament.[31] We might say that it is a difficulty that orthodox scholars have often noticed and have explained in various ways. Perhaps the best explanation is to allow the reality of the difficulty and to attribute it to some obscurity or seeming contradiction existing in the Pentateuchal notices. But whatever the real difficulty may be, it certainly is not insuperable; a good explanation of it is that there were really two tents, but one of them, that is, the smaller tent, was only a kind of provisional structure, perhaps the dwelling place of Moses, which was used also for religious purposes, while the larger or Sinaitic Tabernacle was being prepared.[32] With some allowance for one or two statements made in the Pentateuch that seem not fully to agree with this view, it will answer all the real exigencies of the case. Or, at all events, nearly any explanation that preserves the integrity of the Pentateuchal literature and tries to reconcile its seeming differences of statement, on the ground that this literature deals with facts and is not in large share pure fiction, is vastly preferable to any of the theories the critics have advanced with regard to this matter.

---

[31] The fact of the higher-critic theory being as yet in an unproven state might be urged as one important consideration in favor of the Tabernacle's real existence; and especially could such an argument be legitimately made, inasmuch as the proof of the correctness of that theory does not all come from an assured non-existence of the Mosaic structure. But since an argument of that kind would be, to some extent at least, "reasoning in a circle," we do not make use of it.

[32] Notices of a smaller tent seem to be made in Exodus 33:7–11; Numbers 11:16; 12:4, 5, and Deuteronomy 31:14, 15. From these various passages the critics claim that they can discover at least three points of difference existing between this smaller tent and the larger or Levitical one. These differences are as follows: (1) The smaller tent was always pitched outside the camp; but according to the priestly or Levitical history the larger tent was located within the camp. (2) The smaller tent was only a place of Jehovah's revelation or of his communing with his people; but the larger or priestly structure was a place of most elaborate worship. (3) In the Levitical or larger tent the priests and Levites regularly served, but in the smaller structure it was only Joshua, the "servant" of Moses, who had charge of the building.

All these differences, however, are easily explained by the theory given above of two tents. Besides, it should be observed that after Moses' death no further mention is made in the Scriptures of this smaller structure, which would seem to be a strong proof that the smaller one of the two tents was, primarily at least, a private structure used by Moses.

There remain then only two classes of objections that need to be answered. Although the objections put forward are quite numerous, yet a single illustration of them will show how utterly lacking in substantial reasonableness each of them really are. The illustration of which we will make use is taken from Bishop Colenso's famous attack upon the truthfulness of the Pentateuch and the Book of Joshua. In that attack he puts forward the singular objection that the Tabernacle was, in its dimensions, far too small to accommodate all the vast host of the Israelites standing before its door, as the Scriptures seem to indicate was the case with them on a few occasions.[33] That vast host must have numbered, according to the data given in the Pentateuch, as many at least as some two millions of people. Colenso makes the objection that this great host, standing in ranks of nine, as he suggested, one rank behind another in front of the Tabernacle door would have formed a procession some sixty miles long. which, surely, would have been not only a practical impossibility so far as their gathering at the door of the Tabernacle was concerned but also would have been a complete demonstration of the untruthfulness or unreliability of this Pentateuchal record.

However, there is one thing connected with this record which Bishop Colenso seems not to have understood. It is that when the author of it was speaking of the whole congregation of Israel as standing, or gathered, in front of the Tabernacle door, he was speaking only in general terms. His language then would imply not that every individual belonging to the vast Israelite host stood at the place mentioned, but only that a large and representative multitude of these people was thus gathered. Or the words might signify that even the whole congregation of the Israelites was, on a few occasions, gathered about the Tabernacle, as it had been gathered around Mt. Sinai when the law was given—not all the people near the Tabernacle door but only the leaders, while the great body of the congregation stood behind them or around the structure, like a great sea of human beings stretching away in the distance.

Either of these explanations would meet all the demands of the language used and, as Dr. Orr has remarked, some least particle of common sense must be allowed to the writer of this Pentateuchal record, or, with the "crude absurdities" attributed to him by Bishop Colenso, he could never have written anything in the least degree rational that would bear a moment's reflection even by himself. Besides, as Dr. Orr has noticed, it is only a customary way of speaking to say that a whole town or even a large city was gathered together in mass-convention, when the place of such meeting was perhaps only some large hall or good-sized church. Before attacking so eagerly with his arithmetical calculations the truthfulness of the Biblical account, this higher-critic bishop would have done well to have reflected a little upon the common use of language. That would have saved him from falling into a bigger blunder than he tries to fasten upon the writer of this Pentateuchal record.

Greatest Objection

However, there is still one objection raised by the critics that seems to be more serious, based on what may be called a physical impossibility or the incompetency of the Israelites, while at Mt. Sinai or journeying through the desert to construct or carry with

---

[33] Vid. Leviticus 8:35; Numbers 10:3, and 27:18–22. Also *Comp.* Numbers 16:16–19.

them such a ponderous, highly artistic, and costly a fabric as was the Sinaitic Tabernacle. These people in the desert and at Mt. Sinai, we are told, were the merest wandering Bedouins, having but little civilization and being "poor even to beggary." And of course, such a people possessed neither the means nor the intellectual capability necessary for the construction and transportation of the Tabernacle.

This peculiar objection, however, rests upon at least two mistakes. The first one is that the Israelites at this time were in such extreme poverty. The Bible tells us that when the children of Israel left Egypt they went out "every man armed," and they carried with them all their herds and flocks, leaving "not a hoof behind." Moreover, by means of the many gifts or exactions of "jewels of silver" and "jewels of gold" they received from the Egyptians, they "utterly spoiled" that people. Such is the representation given in the Bible. When these Israelites came to Mt. Sinai, according to the reports of modern travelers and explorers, they could have found various materials necessary for constructing the Tabernacle, such as an abundance of copper existing in mines, various kinds of precious stones, as well as the shittim-wood or acacia tree, which grew well in the region and out of which the boards, pillars, and most of the furniture of the Tabernacle were actually constructed. Therefore, as possessing the means necessary for a construction of the Tabernacle was concerned, these people would seem to have been pretty well supplied.

With regard to the other mistake made by the critics, viz., that these Israelites were intellectually incompetent to build the Tabernacle, this assertion also is not substantiated by facts. It should be remembered that all these Hebrews had from their birth dwelt in Egypt, a country which, of all lands in the world, was at that time the most advanced in all kinds of mechanical, architectural. and industrial art. This was the country where the great pyramids had been produced, and where existed, at that time, at least most of the magnificent temples, tombs, obelisks, statues and palaces, the ruins of which still remain. Accordingly, when the children of Israel came out of Egypt, they must have brought with them a good amount of the architectural and mechanical wisdom peculiar to that country. Moreover, we are taught in the Bible that these people, while in Egypt, dwelt in houses, which they must have built for themselves. Also, as slaves, their lives had been made bitter by "all manner of service in the field," and by "hard service in brick and in mortar," and that they had built "store-cities," such as Pithom and Raamses. Putting, therefore, all these experiences which the Israelites had in Egypt together, it can be easily seen how they could have learned, even from the Egyptians, sufficient wisdom to construct and transport the Tabernacle.

But if we are required yet to name any one particular achievement ever accomplished by these people that was great enough to warrant the belief of their being able to construct and carry with them all through the wilderness the Sinaitic Tabernacle, then we point to that very extraordinary conquest they made of the Holy Land, and also to the almost equally extraordinarily long march made by them through the wilderness. We wish to say that any people who could accomplish two such prodigious deeds as were these could easily have accomplished the so much easier task of building and transporting the old Mosaic "tent of meeting."

Our conclusion, therefore, is that, all teachings of the higher critics to the contrary notwithstanding, those Israelitish people were abundantly competent, both in point of intellectual ability and of material supplies, to accomplish all of the works that are accredited them in the Bible.

Marks of Egypt and the Desert

But this line of argument is one that can be pursued to a much greater extent, and it can be shown that instead of the conditions surrounding the Israelites at Mt. Sinai and while they were in the wilderness being against the truthfulness of the Biblical record appertaining to those matters, such conditions are really in favor of that record's truthfulness, as well as of the Tabernacle's real existence. For illustration, we are told in the Bible that the wood out of which a large part of the Tabernacle was constructed was not taken from the lofty cedars growing in Lebanon nor from the sycamores growing in the Palestinean valley, but they came from the humble acacia or shittim-wood tree, which, as we have already seen, flourishes quite plentifully in the Sinaitic region—all of which particulars accord fully with the topographical facts in the case. So also, if we are to believe in the testimonies of ancient Egyptian monuments and the results of modern Egyptian explorations, there are many resemblances found to exist between matters connected with old Egyptian temples, their structure, furniture, priesthood and services, and other like matters pertaining to the Tabernacle. Indeed, some of these resemblances go so far in their minute details as to an arrangement of buildings according to the points of compass—a peculiarity that was found both in Egypt and in connection with the Tabernacle, including different apartments in the structure, graded according to sanctity; the possession of a sacred ark or chest, peculiarly built and located; strange winged figures, which as existing in the Tabernacle were called "cherubim;" a gradation of the priests; priestly dress and ornaments; the breast-plate and mitre worn by the high-priest; different animals offered in sacrifice; the burning of incense, etc. The impression left upon the mind of a person who knows about these things as existing in ancient Egypt and then reads in the Bible about similar matters connected with the Tabernacle is that whoever wrote this Biblical account must himself have been in Egypt and have seen the old Egyptian worship and temples in order to make his record conform in so many respects to what was found in that country.[34]

So also if we give attention to the peculiar experiences had by the Israelites during their march through the wilderness, we see from what the Bible tells us about their setting up and taking down the Tabernacle; about the wagons furnished for its transportation; about the pillar of cloud going before it or resting upon it, in connection with their long march; the necessity of going outside of the camp in order to perform some of the Tabernacle services. From all these and various other indications given in the Bible, we can surely perceive that the conditions of these people were such as to warrant the belief that they did indeed, as the Bible represents, journey through a wilderness, and that they carried with them their tent of worship.

In his book, entitled "Nature and the Supernatural," Dr. Horace Bushnell tells of an important legal case that once was gained by one of the lawyers noticing, in the web of a sheet of paper that he held, certain "watermarks" that had been made in the paper during the process of its manufacture. These water-marks being indelible, they served as the best kind of proof of certain facts which it was desired to establish. So we would characterize

---

[34] Prof. Sayce undertakes to show that the foreign influences affecting the structure of the Tabernacle and the nature of its services came rather from Babylonia and Assyria than from Egypt. Yet, so far as all the topographical items mentioned above are concerned, they can all be abundantly substantiated by facts from history and archaeology.

all those evidences coming from a correspondence of the Bible account with archaeological facts, which have to do with the Israelites being in Egypt and their journeying through the Sinaitic desert, as so many watermarks left indelibly in the very web of the Biblical record, proving not only the undeniable truthfulness of this record but also the real existence of the Tabernacle.

Summary of the Argument

To sum up the different points we have made in our argument, it will be remembered that, after having outlined our general proposition and the importance of various considerations, we affirmed that there are certain great presumptions that lie in the way of our accepting the higher-critic theory as true. Next, we introduced some archaeological testimony external to the Bible that we found to be helpful in proving the Tabernacle's historicity. Then we established, as a matter beyond all reasonable doubt, the actual historicity of this structure, showing how it was built near Mt. Sinai and then was known to exist continuously for some five hundred years—from the time of Moses until the time of David and Solomon. Finally, to make our argument as complete as possible, we noticed the many objections the higher critics have raised against the Tabernacle's existence, showing that none of these objections are valid, even turning the last one into a positive proof on our side of the question.

Conclusion

Now, if there remains yet anything which needs to be said, it seems to us it is only the assertion that, whether the higher critics will admit it or not, the old Mosaic Tabernacle surely did exist. If there are persons who, in spite of all the numerous important testimonies we have adduced from the Bible and other sources to the Tabernacle's historicity, still persist in denying such evidence and saying that the whole matter was only a priestly fiction, then what the Savior says, with respect perhaps to some of the skeptics living in his day, is quite applicable: "If they believe not Moses and the prophets, neither would they believe though one rose from the dead." Or, to state the case a little differently and somewhat humorously, it might be said that the fact of any person's denying the real existence of the Tabernacle, when so much positive evidence exists in favor of it, reminds one of what Lord Byron says with regard to Bishop Berkeley's philosophical denial of the existence of matter:

> When Bishop Berkeley says it is no matter.
>
> Then 'tis no matter what he says.

However, if the Tabernacle in the wilderness did really exist, then what becomes of the peculiar theory of the higher critics? That necessarily falls to the ground or is proven to be untrue, for, as was shown in the early part of this discussion, the entire critic hypothesis rests upon or has for one of its main pillars the assumed non-existence of the Tabernacle or what amounts to the same thing, the alleged late origin of the Mosaic ritualistic law. Both of these premises being now demonstrated to be unsound, the Tabernacle "which Moses made in the wilderness" will very likely remain where the Bible puts it—among the great undeniable facts of the world's history, and not, as the critics would have it, among fictions or forgeries.

ADDENDA: Various facts respecting places where the Tabernacle was built or located

I. Mount Sinai—its location and present appearance

Dr. J. W. Dawson, in his "Modern Science in Bible Lands," gives the following facts with regard to the location and present appearance of the mountain near which the Tabernacle was built.

"The actual position of Mount Sinai has been a subject of keen controversy, which may be reduced to two questions: Was Mount Sinai in the peninsula of that name or elsewhere? and Which of the mountains of the peninsula was the Mount of the Law? As to the first of these questions, the claims of the peninsula are supported by an overwhelming mass of tradition and of authority, ancient and modern.

"If this question be considered as settled, then it remains to inquire which of the mountain summits of that group of hills in the southern end of the peninsula that seem to be designated in the Bible by the general name of Horeb should be regarded as the veritable 'Mount of the Law?' Five of the mountain summits of this region have laid claim to this distinction, and their relative merits the explorers [those of the English Ordnance Survey] test by seven criteria that must be fulfilled by the actual mountain. These are: (1) A mountain overlooking a plain on which the millions of Israel could be assembled. (2) Space for the people to 'remove and stand afar off' when the voice of the Lord was heard and yet to hear that voice. (3) A defined peak distinctly visible from the plain. (4) A mountain so precipitous that the people might be said to stand under it and to touch its base. (5) A mountain capable of being isolated by boundaries. (6) A mountain with springs and streams of water in its vicinity. (7) Pasturage to maintain the flocks of the people for a year.

"By these criteria the surveyors reject two of the mountains, Jebel el Ejmeh and Jebel Ummalawi, as destitute of sufficient water and pasturage. Jebel Katharina, whose claims arise from a statement of Josephus that Sinai was the highest mountain of the district, which this peak actually is, with the exception of a neighboring summit twenty-five feet higher, they reject because of the fact that it is not visible from any plain suitable for the encampment of the Israelites. Mount Serbal has in modern times had some advocates, but the surveyors allege in opposition to these that they do not find, as has been stated, the Sinaitic inscriptions more plentiful there than elsewhere, that the traces of early Christian occupancy do not point to it any more than early tradition and that it does not meet the topographical requirements in presenting a defined peak, convenient camping-ground, or a sufficient amount of pasturage.

"There only remains the long-established and venerated Jebel Musa—the orthodox Sinai, and this, in a remarkable and conspicuous manner, fulfills the required conditions, and illustrates the narrative itself in unexpected ways. This mountain has, however, two dominant peaks, that of Jebel Musa proper, 7,363 feet in height and Ras Sufsafeh, 6,937 feet. Of these, the explorers do not hesitate at once to prefer the latter. This peak or ridge is described as almost isolated, descending precipitously to the great plain of the district, Er Rahah, which is capable of accommodating two millions of persons in full view of the peak and has ample camping ground for the whole host in its tributary valleys. Further, it is so completely separated from the neighboring mountains that a short and quite intelligible description would define its limits, which could be easily marked out.

"Another remarkable feature is that we have here the brook descending out of the mount referred to in Exodus (Ch. 32:20), as well as five other perennial streams in addition to many good springs. The country is by no means desert, but supplies much pasturage; and when irrigated and attended to, forms good gardens, and is indeed one of the best and most fertile spots of the whole peninsula. The explorers show that the statements of some hasty travelers who have given a different view are quite incorrect and that there is reason to believe that there was greater rainfall and more vegetation in ancient times than at present in this part of the country. They further indicate the Wady Shreick, in which is the stream descending from the mount, as the probable place of the making and destruction of the golden calf, as well as a hill known as Jebel Moneijeh, the mount of conference, as the probable site of the Tabernacle. They think it not improbable that while Ras Sufsafeh was the Mount of the Law, the retirement of Moses during his sojourn on the mount may have been behind the peak, in the recesses of Jebel Musa, which thus might properly bear his name."

II. Shiloh—its ruins as recently investigated

Colonel Sir Charles Wilson thus describes the present ruins of Shiloh, in *"Exploration Fund Quarterly Statement"* for 1873, pp. 37, 38:

"The ruins of Seilûn (Shiloh) cover the surface of a 'tell,' or mound, on a spur which lies between two valleys that unite about a quarter of a mile above Khan Lubban and thence run to the sea. The existing remains are those of a *fellahin* village, with few earlier foundations, possibly of the date of the Crusades. The walls are built with old materials, but none of the fragments of columns mentioned by some travelers can now be seen. On the summit are a few heavy foundations, perhaps those of a keep, and on the southern side is a building with a heavy sloping buttress.

"The rock is exposed over nearly the whole surface, so that little can be expected from excavation. Northwards, the 'tell' slopes down to a broad shoulder across which a sort of level court, 77 feet wide and 412 feet long, has been cut out. The rock is in places scarped to a height of five feet, and along the sides are several excavations and a few small cisterns. The level portion of the rock is covered by a few inches of soil. It is not improbable that the place was thus prepared to receive the Tabernacle, which, according to Rabbinical traditions, was a structure of low stone walls, with the tent stretched over the top. At any rate, there is no other level space on the 'tell' sufficiently large to receive a tent of the dimensions of the Tabernacle.

"The spring of Seilûn is in a small valley which joins the main one a short distance northeast of the ruins. The supply, which is small, after running a few yards through a subterranean channel, was formerly led into a rock-hewn reservoir but now runs to waste."

To the above items Major Claude R. Conder, R. E., in his *"Tent Life in Palestine,"* Vol I, pp. 81, 82, adds as follows:

"There is no site in the country fixed with greater certainty than that of Shiloh. The modern name Seilûn preserves the most archaic form, which is found in the Bible in the ethnic Shilonite (1 Kings 11:29). The position of the ruins agrees exactly with the very definite description given in the Old Testament of the position of Shiloh, as 'on the north side of Bethel (now Beitin), on the east side of the highway that goes up from Bethel to Shechem, and on the south of Lebonah' (Lubbin) (Judges 21:19). It is here that Shiloh still stands in ruins. The scenery of the wild mountains is finer than that in Judea; the red color of the cliffs, which are of great height, is far more picturesque than the shapeless chalk mountains near Jerusalem; the fig gardens and olive groves are more luxuriant, but the crops are poor compared with the plain and around Bethlehem. A deep valley runs behind the town on the north, and in its sides are many rock-cut sepulchers.

"The vineyards of Shiloh have disappeared, though very possibly once surrounding the spring, and perhaps extending down the valley westwards, where water is also found. With the destruction of the village, desolation has spread over the barren hills around."

III. Nob—Site of the village identified

So thinks Rev. W. Shaw Caldecott. See his treatise on "*The Tabernacle, Its History and Structure*," pp. 53, 54:

"Four miles to the north of Jerusalem, and at the distance of a quarter of a mile to the east of the main road, is a curiously knobbed and double-topped hill, named by the Arabs *Tell* (or *Tuleil*) *el-Full*. The crown of this hill is thirty feet higher than Mount Zion, and Jerusalem can be plainly seen from it. On its top is a large pyramidal mound of unhewn stones, which Robinson supposes to have been originally a square tower of 40 or 50 feet, and to have been violently thrown down. No other foundations are to be seen. At the foot of the hill are ancient substructions that are built of large unhewn stones in low, massive walls. These are on the south side, and adjoin the great road.

"If we take the Scriptural indications as to the site of Nob (height), this hill and these ruins fulfill all the conditions of the case.

(a) Nob was so far regarded as belonging to Jerusalem as one of its villages (thus involving its proximity) that David's bringing Goliath's head and sword to the Tabernacle at Nob was regarded as bringing them to Jerusalem (1 Samuel 17:54).

(b) A clearer indication as to its situation is, however, gained by the record of the restoration towns and villages in which Nob is mentioned, the name occurring between those of Anathoth and Ananiah (Nehemiah 11:32). These two places still bear practically the same names and their sites are well known. In the narrow space between Anata and Hanina stands the hill Tell el-Full, which we take to be ancient Nob.

(c) Another indication is contained in Isaiah's account of Sennacherib's march on Jerusalem, the picturesque climax of which is, "This very day shall he halt at Nob; he shaketh his hand at the mount of the daughter of Zion, the hill of Jerusalem." (Isaiah 10:28–32) There are only two hills on the north from which the city can be seen, so as to give reality to the poet's words. One of these is *Neby Samwil*, and the other is *Tell el-Full*."

IV. Gibeon—identity of ancient city with El-Jib, also the "Great High Place," of 1 Kings 3:4, indicated

In Hastings' *Dictionary of the Bible*, Art. Gibeon, J. F. Stenning says the following:

> The identity of Gibeon with the village of *El-Jib*, which lies some six or seven miles northwest of Jerusalem is practically beyond dispute. The modern village still preserves the first part of the older name, while its situation agrees in every respect with the requirements of the history of the Old Testament. Just beyond Tell el-Full (Gibeah), the main road north from Jerusalem to Beitin (Bethel) is joined by a branch road leading up from the coast. The latter forms the continuation of the most southerly of three routes which connect the Jordan valley with the Maritime Plains. Now just before this road (coming up from the Jordan valley) leaves the higher ground and descends to the Shepheleh, it divides into two, the one branch leading down to the Wady Suleiman, the other running in a more southerly direction by way of the Bethhorons. Here, on this fertile, open plateau, slightly to the south of the main road, rises the hill on which the modern village of *El-Jib* is built, right on the frontier line which traverses the central range to the south of Bethel. It was the natural pass across Palestine, which in early times served as the political border between North and South Israel, and it was owing to its position that Gibeon acquired so much prominence in the reigns of David and Solomon. A short distance to the east of the village, at the foot of the hill, there is, further, a stone tank o reservoir of considerable size, supplied by a spring which rises in a cave higher up.

This spring, the explorers tell us, was probably the ancient "pool of Gibeon" mentioned in 2 Samuel 2:13. Also, respecting the "great high place," Smith's *Dictionary* has the following:

> The most natural position for the high place of Gibeon is the twin mountain immediately south of El-Jib, so close as to be all but a part of the town yet separate and distinct. In other words, the testimony of Epiphanius that the 'Mount of Gibeon' was the highest round Jerusalem, by which Dean Stanley supports his conjecture (that the present Neby Samwil was the great high place), should be received with caution, standing alone and belonging to an age which, though early, was marked by ignorance and by the most improbable conclusions.

Some additional facts, as given by Rev. W. Shaw Caldecott (ibid. pp. 60–62), are as follows:

> *El-Jib* is built upon an isolated oblong hill standing in a plain or basin of great fertility. The northern end of the hill is covered over with old massive ruins, which have fallen down in every direction, and in which the villagers now live. Across the plain to the south is the lofty range of Neby Samwil. Gibeon was one of the four towns in the division of Benjamin given as residences for the sons of Aaron (Joshua 21:17). It was thus already inhabited by priests, and this, added to its other advantages, made it, humanly speaking, a not unsuitable place for the capital of the new kingdom. No remains of (very ancient) buildings have been discovered, such as those of er-Ramah and Tell el-Full.

CHAPTER IX The Internal Evidence of the Fourth Gospel Canon

G. Osborne Troop

The whole Bible is stamped with the Divine "Hallmark" but the Gospel according to St. John is *primus inter pares*. Through it, as through a transparency, we gaze entranced into the very holy of holies, where shines in unearthly glory "the great vision of the face of Christ." Yet man's perversity has made it the "storm center" of New Testament criticism, doubtless for the very reason that it bears such unwavering testimony both to the deity of our Lord and Saviour, Jesus Christ and to His perfect humanity. The Christ of the fourth Gospel is no unhistoric, idealized vision of the later, dreaming church but is, as it practically claims to be, the picture drawn by "the disciple whom Jesus loved," an eye-witness of the blood and water that flowed from His pierced side. These may appear to be mere unsupported statements, and as such will at once be dismissed by a scientific reader. Nevertheless the appeal of this article is to the instinct of the "one flock" of the "one Shepherd." "They know His voice" and "a stranger will they not follow."

There is one passage in this Gospel that flashes like lightning—it dazzles our eyes by its very glory. To the broken-hearted Martha the Lord Jesus says with startling suddenness, "*I am* the resurrection and the life; he that believeth on Me, though he die, yet shall he live; and whosoever liveth and believeth in Me, shall never die."

It is humbly but confidently submitted that these words are utterly beyond the reach of human invention. It could never have entered the heart of man to say, "*I am* the resurrection and the life." "There is a resurrection and a life," would have been a great and notable saying, but *this Speaker* identifies *Himself* with the resurrection and with life eternal. The words can only be born from above, and He who utters them is worthy of the utmost adoration of the surrendered soul.

In an earlier chapter, John records a certain question addressed to and answered by our Lord in a manner that has no counterpart in the world's literature. "What shall we do," the eager people cry; "What shall we do that we might work the works of God?" "This is the work of God", our Lord replies, "that ye believe on Him whom He hath sent" (John 6:28, 29). I venture to say that such an answer to such a question has no parallel. This is the work of God that ye accept *Me*. I am the Root of the tree that bears the only fruit pleasing to God. Our Lord states the converse of this in chapter 6, when He says that the Holy Spirit will "convict the world of sin . . . because they believe not on *Me*." The root of all evil is unbelief in Christ. The condemning sin of the world lies in the rejection of the Redeemer. Here we have the root of righteousness and the root of sin in the acceptance or rejection of His wondrous personality. This is unique, and proclaims the Speaker to be "separate from sinners" though "the Lord hath laid on Him the iniquity of us all." Truly, "He is His own best evidence; His witness is within."

In John 14, listen to that Voice, which is as the voice of many waters, as it sounds in the ears of the troubled disciples: "Let not your heart be troubled; ye believe in God, believe *also* in *Me*. In My Father's house are many mansions: *if it were not so, I would have told you*. I go to prepare a place for you. And if I go and prepare a place for you, I will come again, and receive you unto Myself; that where I am, there ye may be also."

Who is he who dares to say: "Ye believe in *God*, believe *also* in Me"? He ventures thus to speak because He is the Father's Son. Man's son is man: can God's Son be anything less than God? Elsewhere in this Gospel He says: "I and the Father are one." The fourteenth chapter reveals the Lord Jesus as completely at home in the heavenly company. He speaks of His Father and of the Holy Spirit as Himself being one of the utterly holy Family. He knows all about His Father's house with its many mansions. He was familiar with it before the world was. Notice, too, the exquisite touch of transparent truthfulness: "If it were not so, I would have told you." An *ear*-witness alone could have caught and preserved that touching parenthesis, and who more likely than the disciple whom Jesus loved?

As we leave this famous chapter let us not forget to note the wondrous words in verse 23: "If a man love Me, he will keep My words; and My Father will love him, and We will come unto him and make our abode with him."

This saying can only be characterized as blasphemous, if it be not the true utterance of one equal with God. On the other hand, does any reasonable man seriously think that such words originated in the mind of a forger? "Every one that is of the truth heareth My voice", and surely that voice is here.

When we come to chapter 17, we pass indeed into the very inner chamber of the King of kings. It records the high-priestly prayer of our Lord, when He "lifted up His eyes to heaven and said, 'Father, the hour is come. Glorify Your Son that Your Son may also glorify You."

Let any man propose to himself the awful task of forging such a prayer and putting it into the mouth of an imaginary Christ. The brain reels at the very thought of it. It is, however, perfectly natural that John should record it. It must have fallen upon his and his fellow disciples' ears amid an awe-stricken silence in which they could hear the very throbbing of their listening hearts. For their hearts were listening through their ears as the Son poured out His soul unto the Father. It is a rare privilege, and one from which most men would sensitively shrink, to listen even to a fellow man alone with God. Yet the Lord Jesus in the midst of His disciples laid bare His soul before His Father, as really as if He had been alone with Him. He prayed with the cross and its awful death full in view, but in the prayer there is no hint of failure or regret, and there is no trace of confession of sin or need of forgiveness.

These are all indelible marks of genuineness. It would have been impossible for a sinful man to conceive such a prayer. But all is consistent with the character of Him who "spoke as never man spoke," and could challenge the world to convict Him of sin.

With such thoughts in mind let us now look more closely into the words of the prayer itself.

"Jesus spoke these things; and lifting up his eyes to heaven, He said, 'Father, the hour has come; glorify your Son, that the Son may glorify you, [1] just as you have given him authority over all flesh, so that he may give eternal life to all those whom you have given to him. This is eternal life, that they may know you, the only true God, and the one whom you sent, Jesus Christ."

Here we have again the calm placing of Himself on a level with the Father in connection with eternal life. And it is not out of place to recall the consistency of this utterance with that often-called "Johannine" saying recorded in Matthew 11:27: "All things are delivered unto Me of My Father: and no man knoweth the Son, but the Father; neither knoweth any man the Father, save the Son, and he to whomsoever the Son wills to reveal Him."

We read also in. John 14:6: "no one comes to the Father except through me." And as we reverently proceed further in the prayer, we find Him saying: "And now, Father, glorify me together with yourself, with the glory which I had with you before the world was" (John 17:5)

These words are natural to the Father's Son as we know and worship Him, but they are beyond the reach of an uninspired man, and who can imagine a forger inspired of the Holy Ghost? Such words would, however, be graven upon the very heart of an ear-witness such as the disciple whom Jesus loved.

We have in this prayer the fuller revelation of the "one flock" and "one Shepherd" pictured in John 17:20–23: "I do not ask for these only, but also for those who will believe in me through their word; that they may all be one, just as you, Father, are in me, and I in you, that they also may be in us, so that the world may believe that you have sent me. The glory that you have given me I have given to them, that they may be one even as we are one, I in them and you in me, that they may be perfected in unity, so that the world may know that you sent me, and loved them, even as you have loved me."

In these holy words there breathes a cry for such a unity as never entered into the heart of mortal man to dream of. It is no cold and formal ecclesiastical unity, such as that suggested by the curious and unhappy mistranslation of "one fold" for "one flock" in John 10:16. It is the living unity of the living flock with the living Shepherd of the living God. It is actually the same as the unity subsisting between the Father and the Son. And according to Paul in Romans 8:19, the creation is waiting for its revelation. The one Shepherd has from the beginning had His one flock in answer to His prayer, but the world has not yet seen it, and is therefore still unconvinced that our Jesus is indeed the Sent of God. The world has seen the Catholic Church and the Roman Catholic Church, but the Holy Catholic Church no eye as yet has seen but God's. For the Holy Catholic Church and the Shepherd's one flock are one and the same, and the world will not see either "till He come." The *Holy* Catholic Church is an object of faith and not of sight, and so is the one flock.

In spite of all attempts at elimination and organization, wheat and tares together grow, and sheep and wolves-in-sheep's-clothing are found together in the earthly pasture grounds. But when the Good Shepherd returns, He will bring His beautiful flock with Him, and eventually the world will see and believe. "O the depth of the riches both of the wisdom and knowledge of God! How unsearchable are His judgments, and His ways past finding out!"

The mystery of this spiritual unity lies hidden in the high-priestly prayer, but we may feel sure that no forger could ever discover it, for many of those who profess and call themselves Christians are blind to it even yet.

The "Christ before Pilate" of John 18:36–37 is also stamped with every mark of sincerity and truth. What mere human imagination could evolve the noble words: "my kingdom is not of this world. If my kingdom were of this world, then my servants would be fighting so that I would not be handed over to the Jews; but as it is, my kingdom is not of this world." Then Pilate said to him, "So you are a king?" Jesus answered, "You say that I am a king. For this purpose I was born and for this purpose I have come into the world, to testify to the truth. Everyone who is of the truth hears my voice"?

The whole wondrous story of the betrayal, the denial, the trial, the condemnation and crucifixion of the Lord Jesus, as given through John, breathes with the living sympathy of an eyewitness. The account, moreover, is as wonderful in the delicacy of its reserve as in the simplicity of its recital. It is entirely free from sensationalism and every form of exaggeration. It is calm and judicial in the highest degree. If it is written by the inspired disciple whom Jesus loved, all is natural and easily "understood of the people"; while on any other supposition, it is fraught with difficulties that cannot be explained away. "I am not credulous enough to be an unbeliever," is a wise saying in this as in many similar connections.

The Book of John opens and closes with surpassing grandeur. With Divine dignity, it links itself with the opening words of Genesis: "*In the beginning* was the Word, and the Word was with God, and the Word was *God.... And the Word became flesh and dwelt among us, and we have seen his glory, glory as of the only begotten one from the Father, full of grace and truth.*" What a lifelike contrast with this sublime description is found in the introduction of John the Baptist: "A man was sent from God, whose name was John.." In the incarnation, Christ did not become *a* man but *man.*

Moreover, in this, Paul and John are in agreement. "There is one God," says Paul to Timothy; "one Mediator also between God and man—*Himself Man*—Christ Jesus." The reality of the Divine Redeemer's human nature is beautifully manifested in the touching interview between the weary Savior and the guilty Samaritan woman at the well; as well as in His perfect human friendship with Mary and Martha and their brother Lazarus, culminating in the priceless words, "Jesus wept."

And so by the bitter way of the Cross, the grandeur of the incarnation passes into the glory of the resurrection. The last two chapters are alive with thrilling incident. If any one wishes to form a true conception of what those brief chapters contain, let him read *Jesus and the Resurrection* by the Bishop of Durham, Dr. Handley Moule, and his cup of holy joy will fill to overflowing. At the empty tomb, we breathe the air of the unseen kingdom, and presently we gaze enraptured on the face of the Crucified but risen and ever-living King. Mary Magdalene, standing in her broken-hearted despair, is unconscious of the wondrous fact that holy angels are right in front of her, and standing behind her is her living Lord and Master. Slowly but surely, the glad story spreads from lip to lip and heart to heart, until even the honest but stubborn Thomas is brought to his knees, crying in a burst of remorseful, adoring joy, "My Lord and my God!"

Then comes the lovely story of the fruitless all-night toil of the seven fishermen, the appearance at dawn of the Stranger on the beach, the miraculous draught of fishes, the glad cry of recognition, "It is the Lord!" and the never-to-be-forgotten breakfast with the risen Saviour or His searching interview with Peter, passing into the mystery of John's old age.

In all these swiftly-drawn outlines we feel ourselves instinctively in the presence of the truth. We are crowned with the Savior's beatitude: "Blessed are they that have not seen, and yet have believed." We are ready to yield a glad assent to the statement that closes chapter twenty: "Many other signs truly did Jesus in the presence of His disciples, which are not written in this book; but these are written that ye might believe that Jesus is the Christ, the Son of God; and that believing ye might have life in His Name."

CHAPTER X The Testimony of Christ to the Old Testament

William Caven

Both Jews and Christians receive the Old Testament as containing a revelation from God, while the latter regard it as standing in close and vital relationship to the New Testament. Everything connected with the Old Testament has, of recent years, been subjected to the closest scrutiny—the authorship of its several books, the time when they were written, their style, their historical value, their religious and ethical teachings. Apart from the veneration with which we regard the Old Testament writings on their own account, the intimate connection they have with the Christian Scriptures necessarily gives us the deepest interest in the conclusions that may be reached by Old Testament criticism. For us, the New Testament Dispensation presupposes and grows out of the Mosaic, so the books of the New Testament touch those of the Old at every point: *In vetere testamento novum latet, et in novo vetus patet.* (In the Old Testament the New is concealed, and in the New the Old is revealed.)

We propose to take a summary view of the testimony of our Lord to the Old Testament, as it is recorded by the Evangelists. The New Testament writers themselves largely quote and refer to the Old Testament, and the views they express regarding the old economy and its writings are in harmony with the statements of their Master. But, for various reasons, we confine ourselves to what is related of the Lord Himself.

Let us refer, first, to what is contained or necessarily implied in the Lord's testimony to the Old Testament Scriptures and to the critical value of His testimony.

The Lord's Testimony to the Old Testament

Our Lord's authority—though this is rather the *argumentum silentio*—may be cited in favor of the Old Testament canon as accepted by the Jews in His day. He never charges them with adding to or taking from the Scriptures, or in any way tampering with the text. Had they been guilty of so great a sin, it is hardly possible that among the charges brought against them this matter should not even be alluded to. The Lord reproaches His countrymen with ignorance of the Scriptures and with making the law void through their traditions, but He never hints that they have introduced an unwarranted book into the canon or rejected any deserved a place in it.

Now, the Old Testament canon of the first century is the same as our own. The evidence for this is complete, and the fact is hardly questioned. The New Testament contains, indeed, no catalogue of the Old Testament books, but the testimonies of Josephus, Melito of Sardis, Origen, Jerome, and of the Talmud, decisively show that the Old Testament canon, once fixed, has remained unaltered. Whether the steady Jewish tradition that the canon was finally determined by Ezra and the Great Synagogue is altogether correct or not, it is certain that the Septuagint agrees with the Hebrew as to the canon, thus showing that the subject was not in dispute two centuries before Christ. Nor is the testimony of the Septuagint weakened by the fact that the common Old Testament Apocrypha are appended to the canonical books; for "of no one among the Apocryphal books is it so much as hinted, either by the author, or by any other Jewish writer, that it was worthy of a place among the sacred books" (Kitto's Cyclo., art. *Canon*). The Lord, it is observed, never quotes any of the apocryphal books, nor refers to them.

No Part Assailed

If our Lord does not name the writers of the books of the Old Testament in detail, it may at least be said that He does not call into question the genuineness of any book and that he distinctly assigns several parts of Scripture to the writers whose names they pass under. The Law is ascribed to Moses; David's name is connected with the Psalms; the prophecies of Isaiah are attributed to Isaiah, and the prophecies of Daniel to Daniel. We shall afterward inquire whether these references are merely by way of accommodation or whether more importance should be attached to them.

In the meantime, we note that the Lord does not, in any instance, express dissent from the common opinion, and that, as to several parts of Scripture, He distinctly endorses it. He refers to Moses as legislator and writer several times: To the cleansed leper He says, "And Jesus said to him, "See that you tell no one, but go, show yourself to the priest and offer the gift that Moses commanded, for a testimony to them" (Matthew 8:4). "He said to them, "Because of your hardness of heart Moses permitted you to divorce your wives; but from the beginning it has not been this way" (Matthew 19:8). "But he said to him, 'If they do not listen to Moses and the prophets, neither will they be persuaded if someone rises from the dead" (Luke 16:31). "For Moses said, 'Honor your father and your mother'; and, 'He who speaks evil of father or mother, is to be put to death" (Mark 7:10). "And beginning from Moses and all the Prophets, he interpreted to them in all the Scriptures the things concerning himself" (Luke 24:27). "And he said to them, "These are my words that I spoke to you while I was still with you, that all things which are written about me in the law of Moses and the Prophets and the Psalms must be fulfilled" (Luke 24:44). "Do not think that I will accuse you to the Father. There is one who accuses you, Moses, in whom you have put your hope. For if you believed Moses, you would trust me; for that one wrote of me. But if you do not trust the writings of that one, how will you trust my words?" (John 5:45–47). "Has not Moses given you the law? Yet none of you keeps the law. Why are you seeking to kill me?" (John 7:19). "Moses has given you circumcision (not that it is from Moses, but from the forefathers), and you circumcise a man on the Sabbath. If on the Sabbath a man receives circumcision, so that the law of Moses may not be broken," etc. (John 7:22-23). The omitted parenthetical words—"not because it is of Moses, but of the fathers"—seem clearly to show, it may be remarked in passing, that the Lord is not unobservant of historical exactness.

The Psalms are quoted by our Lord more than once, but only once is a writer named. The 110th Psalm is ascribed to David; and the validity of the Lord's argument depends on its being Davidic. The reference, therefore, so far as it goes, confirms the inscriptions of the Psalms in relation to authorship.

Isaiah 6:9 is quoted thus: "In them is fulfilled the prophecy of Esaias, which saith, By hearing ye shall hear, and shall not understand" (Matthew 13:14, 15). Again, chapter 29:13 of Isaiah's prophecy is cited: "Well hath Esaias prophesied of you hypocrites. This people honoreth me with their lips, but their heart is far from me" (Mark 7:6).

In the beginning of His ministry, the Lord came to the synagogue in Nazareth, where "the scroll[35] of the prophet Isaiah was given to him. And he unrolled the scroll[36] and found the place where it was written, 'The Spirit of the Lord is upon me, because he has anointed me to proclaim good news[37] to the poor. He has sent me to proclaim release to the captives and recovering of sight to the blind, to set free those who are oppressed." (Luke 4:17–18). The passage read by our Lord is from the Isaiah 61, which belongs to the section of the book often ascribed to the second, or pseudo, Isaiah; but we do not press this point, as it may be said that the Evangelist, rather than Christ, ascribes the words to Isaiah.

In His great prophecy respecting the downfall of the Jewish state, the Lord refers to "the abomination of desolation, spoken of by Daniel the prophet:" As in Daniel 9:27, we read that "And he shall make a strong covenant with the many for one week, but in the middle of the week he shall cause the sacrifice and the offering to cease. And upon the wing of abominations shall come the one causing desolation, even until a complete destruction, one that is decreed, is poured out on the one causing desolation," and in chapter 12:11, that "that causes desolation is set up."

Narratives and Records Authentic

When Christ makes reference to Old Testament narratives and records, He accepts them as authentic, as historically true. He does not give or suggest in any case a mythical or allegorical interpretation. The accounts of the creation, of the flood, of the overthrow of Sodom and Gomorrah, as well as many incidents and events of later occurrence, are taken as authentic. It may, of course, be alleged that the Lord's references to the creation of man and woman, the flood, the cities of the plain, etc., equally serve His purpose of illustration, whether He regards them as historical or not. But on weighing His words, it will be seen that they lose much of their force and appropriateness unless the events had historical character.

Let us refer more particularly to this matter. When the Pharisees ask Christ whether it is lawful for a man to put away his wife for every cause, He answers them: "And he answered and said, 'Have you not read that he who created them from the beginning made them male and female,' 5 and said, 'For this reason a man shall leave his father and mother and be joined to his wife, and the two shall become one flesh'?" (Matthew 19:4-5). Again: "For as were the days of Noah, so will be the coming[38] of the Son of Man," [39] and "they knew not until the flood came, and took them all away; so will be the coming[39] of the Son of Man." (Matthew 24:37, 39). Again: "And you, Capernaum, will not be exalted to heaven? You will descend to Hades;[40] for if the mighty works had

---

[35] Or a *roll*

[36] Or a *roll*

[37] Or the gospel

[38] Or *presence* (Gr *parousia*), which denotes both an "arrival" and a consequent "presence with."

[39] Or *presence* (Gr *parousia*), which denotes both an "arrival" and a consequent "presence with.

[40] Everyone knows that Hades was "the underground abode of the dead in Greek mythology." (Elwell 1988, Volume 1, Page 912) However, as far as early Christianity, the Greek translation of the Old Testament, the Septuagint, uses the word Hades 73 times, employing it 60 times to translate the Hebrew word Sheol. In

occurred in Sodom which occurred in you, it would have remained to this day. ²⁴ Nevertheless I say to you that it will be more tolerable for the land of Sodom in the day of judgment, than for you." (Matthew 11:23, 24).

These utterances lose their weight and solemnity if there was no flood as described in Genesis and if the destruction of wicked Sodom is only a myth. Illustrations and parallels may, for certain purposes, be cited from fictitious literature, but when the Lord would warn men of the certainty of divine judgment, He will not confirm His teaching by instances of punishment that are fictitious. His argument that the Holy and Just God will do as He has done—will make bare His arm as in the days of old—is robbed, in this case, of all validity.

A present-day view is that, as with other nations, so with the Jews, the mythical period precedes the historical, and thus the earlier narratives of the Old Testament must be taken according to their true character. In later periods of the Old Testament, we have records that, on the whole, are historical; but in the very earliest times we must not look for authentic history at all. An adequate examination of this theory, which has, of course, momentous exegetical consequences, cannot be attempted here. We merely remark that our Lord's brief references to early Old Testament narrative would not suggest the distinction so often made between earlier and later Old Testament records on the score of trustworthiness.

The Old Testament from God

Suffice it to say that Christ accepts the Old Dispensation and its Scriptures as from God as having special, divine authority. Many who recognize no particular sacredness or authority in the religion of the Jews above other religions of the world would readily admit that it is from God. But their contention is that all religions (especially what they are pleased to call the *great religions*) have elements of truth in them, that they all furnish *media* through which devout souls have fellowship with the Power that rules the universe but that none of them should exalt its pretensions much above the others, far less claim exclusive divine sanction. All of them are the product of man's spiritual nature, as molded by his history and environment, in different nations and ages.

This is the view under which the study of comparative religion is prosecuted by many eminent scholars. A large and generous study of religions—their characteristics and history—tends, it is held, to bring them into closer fellowship with each other and only ignorance or prejudice (say these unbiased thinkers) can isolate the religion of the Old Testament or of the New and refuse to acknowledge in other religions the divine elements that entitle them to take rank with Judaism or Christianity.

Acts 2:27, Luke writes, "For you will not abandon my soul to Hades, or let your Holy One see corruption." Luke was quoting Psalm 16:10, which reads, "For you will not abandon my soul to Sheol, or let your holy one see corruption." Notice that Luke used Hades in place of Sheol. Therefore, Hades is the Greek equivalent of Sheol, as far as Christians and the Greek New Testament is concerned. In other words, Hades is also the abode of the dead in early Christian thought. Some translations choose to use a transliteration, Hades, as opposed to the English hell, ASV, AT, RSV, ESV, LEB, HCSB, and NAS.

The utterances of Jesus Christ on this question of the divinity of the Old Testament religion and cults are unmistakable. Not less clear and decided is His language respecting the writings in which this religion is delivered. God is the direct source of both the religion and the records of it. No man can claim Christ's authority for classing Judaism with Confucianism, Hinduism, Buddhism, and Parseeism. There is nothing, indeed, in the Lord's teaching that forbids us to recognize anything that is good in ethnic religions—any of those elements of spiritual truth which become the common property of the race and which were not completely lost in the night of heathenism.

On the other hand, it is abundantly evident that the Jewish faith is, to our Lord, the one true faith, and that the Jewish Scriptures have a place of their own—a place that cannot be shared with the sacred books of other peoples. Samaritanism, even though it had appropriated so largely from the religion of Israel, He will not recognize. "For salvation is of the Jews."

Almost any reference of our Lord to the Old Testament will support the statement that He regards the Dispensation and its Scriptures as from God. He shows, e.g., that Old Testament prophecy is fulfilled in Himself, or He vindicates His teaching and His claims by Scripture, or He enjoins obedience to the law (as in the case of the cleansed lepers). Again, He asserts the inviolability of the law till its complete fulfillment, or He accuses a blinded and self-righteous generation of superseding and vacating a law they were bound to observe.

A few instances of explicit recognition of the Old Testament Scriptures as proceeding from God and having divine authority, may be here cited. In His Sermon on the Mount, the Lord makes this strong and comprehensive statement: "For truly, I say to you, until heaven and earth pass away, not one iota[41] or one point shall pass from the Law until all is accomplished." (Matthew 5:18).

In the context, the law is distinguished from the prophets and, therefore, designates the Pentateuch; and surely the divine origin of this part of Scripture is unquestionably implied. No such inviolability could be claimed for any merely human institution or production. When the hypocritical and heartless son pretended to devote to God what should have gone to support his indigent parents, he quoted Exodus 21:17 and Leviticus 20:9: "For God said, 'Honor your father and your mother,' and 'The one who speaks evil of father or mother let him die the death.'"(Matt. 15:4). In purging the temple the Lord justifies His action in these words: "And he said to them, "And he said to them, "It is written, 'My house will be called a house of prayer,'[42] but you have made it a cave of robbers!" (Matt. 21:13). Again, "I am the God of Abraham, and the God of Isaac, and the God of Jacob'?[43] He is not God of the dead, but of the living" (Matt. 22:32). Again: "Abandoning the commandment of God, you hold fast to the tradition of men." (Mark 7:8).

---

[41] *one iota* is the smallest letter of the Greek alphabet and is akin to the Hebrew yodh, which is the smallest of the Hebrew letters, while *one point* is part of a letter of the alphabet, a small stroke attached to the letter.

[42] A quotation from Isa. 56:7

[43] A quotation from Ex. 3:6

So many passages of the Old Testament are quoted or alluded to by the Lord as having received, or as awaiting fulfillment, that it is scarcely necessary to make citations of this class. These all most certainly imply the divinity of Scripture; for no man, no creature, can tell what is hidden in the remote future. We are not forgetting that the Lord fully recognizes the imperfect and provisional character of the Mosaic Law and of the Old

Dispensation. Were the Old faultless, no place would have been found for the New. Had grace and truth come by Moses, the advent of Jesus Christ would have been unnecessary. So when the Pharisees put the question to Christ why Moses commanded to give to a wife who has found no favor with her husband a writing of divorcement and to put her away, He replied: "He said to them, "Because of your hardness of heart Moses permitted you to divorce your wives; but from the beginning it has not been this way." (Matt. 19:8).

The Mosaic legislation was not in every part absolutely the best that could be given, but it was such as the divine wisdom saw best for the time being and under the special circumstances of the[44] Hebrew people. Not only did the Old Testament set forth a typical economy, which must give place to another, but it embodied ethical elements of a provisional kind which must pass away when the incarnate Son had fully revealed the Father. The Old Testament is conscious of its own imperfections, for Jeremiah thus writes: "Behold, days are coming," declares Jehovah, "when I will make a new covenant with the house of Israel and with the house of Judah,not according to the covenant that I made with their fathers, in the day that I took them by the hand to bring them out of the land of Egypt" (Jeremiah 31:31).

But in all this there is nothing to modify the proposition that our Lord accepts the Old Testament economy and its Scriptures as from God, as stamped with divine authority and making known the divine mind and will. Marcion and the Gnostics did not receive any part of the Old Testament Scriptures, and the Old Dispensation itself they held to be of evil origin. So decided were they against the Old Testament that they would not admit into their New Testament canon the books that bear witness to the Old. But the Christian Church has followed its Master in regarding the Old Testament as the Word of God, as the Bible of the ages before the Advent, and as still part of the Bible for the Christian Church. Not until the days of developed rationalism was this position called in question, except among unbelievers. But it is obvious that the style of criticism which, in our own time, is frequently applied to the Old Testament (not to say anything about the New), touching its histories, its laws, its morality, is quite inconsistent with the recognition of any special divine characteristics or authority as belonging to it. The general consensus that criticism must deal with these writings precisely as it deals with other writings is a refusal to Scripture of the peculiar character it claims and that the Church has ever recognized in it. If a special divine authority can be vindicated for these books, or for any of them, clearely, it ought to be taken into account by the linguistic and historical critic.

Logically, we should begin our study of them by investigating their title to such authority and, should their claim prove credible, it should never be forgotten in the subsequent critical processes. The establishment of this high claim will imply in these writings moral characteristics (not to mention others) that should exempt them from a certain suspicion that the critic may not unjustifiably allow to be present when he begins to examine documents of an ordinary kind. Therefore, it is not correct to say that criticism, in commencing its inquiries, should know nothing of the alleged divine origin or sacred character of a book. If the book has no good vouchers for its claims to possess a sacred character, criticism must proceed unhindered; but correct conceptions of critical methods demand that every important fact already ascertained as to any writings should be kept faithfully before the mind in the examination of them.

Science must here unite with reverential feeling in requiring right treatment of a book that claims special divine sanction and is willing to have its claims duly investigated. The examination of a witness of established veracity and rectitude would not be conducted in precisely the same manner as that of a witness whose character is unknown or under suspicion. Wellhausen's style of treating the history of Israel can have no justification unless he should first show that the claim so often advanced in "Thus saith the Lord" is entirely baseless. So far from admitting the validity of the axiom referred to, we distinctly hold that it is unscientific.

A just and true criticism must have respect to everything already known and settled regarding the productions to which it is applied and assuredly so momentous a claim as that of divine authority demands careful preliminary examination. But criticism, it may be urged, is the very instrument by which we must test the pretensions of these writings to a special divine origin and character, and, hence, it cannot stand aside till this question has been considered. In requiring criticism to be silent till the verdict has been rendered, we are putting it under restrictions inconsistent with its functions and prerogatives. The reply, however, is that the principal external and internal evidences for the divine origin of the Scriptures can be weighed with sufficient accuracy to determine the general character and authority of these writings before criticism, either higher or lower, applies its hand.

"The heavenliness of the matter, the efficacy of the doctrine, the majesty of the style, the consent of all the parts, the scope of the whole (which is to give glory to God), the full discovery it makes of the only way of man's salvation, the many other incomparable excellences, and the entire perfection thereof, are arguments whereby it doth abundantly evince itself to be the word of God" (Conf. of Faith 1:5).

But all of these considerations can, in all that is material, be weighed and estimated before technical criticism begins its labors, as they have been estimated to the entire conviction of the divinity of Scripture on the part of thousands who had no acquaintance with criticism. Should the fair application of criticism, when its proper time comes, tend to beget doubt as to the general conclusion already reached regarding the Bible, it will doubtless be right to review carefully the evidence on which our conclusion depends. But the substantive and direct proofs of the Scriptures being from God should first be handled, and the decision arrived at should be kept in mind, while criticism is occupied with its proper task. This seems the true order of the procedure.

God Speaks

Our Lord certainly attributes to the Old Testament a far higher character than many have supposed. God speaks in it throughout, and while He will more perfectly reveal Himself in His Son, nothing contained in the older revelation shall fail of its end or be convicted of error. Christ does not use the term "inspiration" in speaking of the Old

Testament, but when we have cited His words regarding the origin and authority of these writings, it will be evident that, to Him, they are God-given in every part. It will be seen that His testimony falls not behind that of His apostles who say: "All Scripture is inspired by God " (2 Tim. 3:16), and "for no prophecy was ever produced by the will of man, but men carried along by the Holy Spirit spoke from God" (2 Peter 1:21).

Words and Commands of God

In speaking of Christ as teaching that the Old Testament is from God, we have referred to passages in which He says that its words and commands are the words and commands of God; e.g., "For God said, 'Honor your father and your mother,' and 'The one who speaks evil of father or mother let him die the death.'[45]

Again: "Now concerning the resurrection of the dead, have you not read what was spoken to you by God, saying, I am the God of Abraham, the God of Isaac, and the God of Jacob?" (Matthew 22:31).

In a comprehensive way, the laws of the Pentateuch, or of the Old Testament, are called "the commandments of God." "Abandoning the commandment of God, you hold fast to the tradition of men." He was also saying to them, "You skillfully disregard the commandment of God in order to keep your tradition" (Mark 7:8-9). In the context of this last quotation, the commandment of God is identified with what "Moses spoke," showing that the words of Moses are also the words of God.

Passages like these do more than prove that the Old Testament Scriptures express *on the whole* the mind of God, and, therefore, possess very high authority. If it can certainly be said that God spoke certain words, or that certain words and commandments are the words and commandments of God, we have more than a general endorsement, as when the editor of a periodical states that he is responsible for the general character and tendency of articles he submits but not for every sentiment or expression of opinion contained in them.

It needs, of course, no proof that the words quoted in the New Testament as spoken by God are not the only parts of the Old that have direct divine authority. The same thing may be said of other parts of the book.

Absolute Infallibility of Scripture

Attention may be specially called to three passages in which the Lord refers to the origin and the absolute infallibility of Scripture. Jesus asked the Pharisees, "What do you think about the Christ? Whose son is he?" They said to him, "The son of David." (Matthew 22:42). The reference is to Psalm 110, which the Lord says David spoke or wrote "in spirit;" i.e., David was completely under the Spirit's influence in the production of the psalm, so when he calls the Messiah his "Lord" the word has absolute authority. Such is clearly the Lord's meaning, and the Pharisees have no reply to His argument. The Lord does not say that the entire Old Testament was written "in the Spirit," nor even that all of

---

[45] A quotation from Ex. 21:17; Lev. 20:9

the psalms were so produced; He makes no direct statement of this nature, yet the plain reader would certainly regard this as implied. His hearers understood their Scriptures to have been all written by immediate inspiration of God and to be the word of God. He merely refers to Psalm 110 as having the character that belonged to Scripture at large.

In John 10:34-36, Christ vindicates Himself from the charge of blasphemy in claiming to be the Son of God: "Jesus answered them, 'Is it not written in your Law, "I said, you are gods"? If he called them gods to whom the word of God came, and Scripture cannot be broken, do you say of him whom the Father consecrated and sent into the world, "You are blaspheming," because I said, "I am the Son of God"?" The Scripture cannot be broken—*ou dunatai luthēnai*. The verb signifies to loose, unbind, dissolve, and as applied to Scripture means to subvert or deprive of authority. The authority of Scripture is then so complete—so pervasive—as to extend to its individual terms. "Gods" is the proper word because it is used to designate the Jewish rulers. If this is not verbal inspiration, it comes very near it. One may, of course, allege that the Lord's statement of inerrancy implies only that the principal words of Scripture must be taken precisely as they are, but that He does not claim the like authority for all its words. Without arguing this point, we merely say that it is not certain or obvious that the way is left open for this distinction. In face of Christ's utterances it devolves on those who hold that inspiration extends to the thought of Scripture only but not to the words or to the leading words but not to the words in general, to cite convincing arguments in support of their position. The burden of proof, it seems, is here made to rest on them.

The theory that inspiration may be affirmed only by the main views or positions of Scripture, not by the words or the development of the thoughts, cannot be harmonized with the Lord's teaching. Before turning to a third text, we may be allowed to set down these words of Augustine in writing to Jerome: "For I acknowledge with high esteem for thee, I have learned to ascribe such reverence and honor to those books of the Scriptures alone, which are now called canonical, that I believe most firmly that not one of their authors has made a mistake in writing them. And should I light upon anything in those writings that may seem opposed to truth, I shall contend for nothing else, than either that the manuscript was full of errors, or that the translator had not comprehended what was said, or that I had not understood it in the least degree."

In His sermon on the Mount, our Lord refers to His own relation to the Old Testament economy and its Scriptures: "Do not think that I have come to destroy the Law or the Prophets; I came not to destroy, but to fulfil. For truly, I say to you, until heaven and earth pass away, not one iota or one point[46] shall pass from the Law until all is accomplished" (Matt. 5:17, 18). No stronger words could be employed to affirm the divine authority of every part of the Old Testament; for the law and the prophets mean the entire Old Testament Scriptures.

If this declaration contemplates the *moral* element of these Scriptures, it means that no part of them shall be set aside by the New Dispensation, but "fulfilled"—i.e., filled up and completed by Jesus Christ as a sketch is filled up and completed by the painter. If, as others naturally interpret, the *typical* features of the Old Testament are included in the

---

[46] *one iota* is the smallest letter of the Greek alphabet and is akin to the Hebrew yodh, which is the smallest of the Hebrew letters, while *one point* is part of a letter of the alphabet, a small stroke attached to the letter.

statement, the term "fulfilled," as regards this element, will be taken in the more usual meaning. In either case the inviolability and, by implication, the divine origin of the Old Testament could not be more impressively declared. Note how comprehensive and absolute the words are: "One jot or one tittle." "Iota" (*iōta*) is *yod*, the smallest letter of the Hebrew alphabet; "*one point*" designates the little lines or projections by which Hebrew letters, similar in other respects, differ from each other. We have here, one might say, the inspiration of *letters* of the Old Testament. Everything contained in it has divine authority, and must, therefore, be divine in origin, for it is unnecessary to show that no such authority could be ascribed to writings merely human, or to writings in which the divine and the human interests could be separated analytically.

Should it be said that the "law," every iota of which must be fulfilled, means here the economy itself, the ordinances of Judaism, but not the record of them in writing; the reply is that we know nothing of these ordinances except through the record so that what is affirmed must apply to the Scriptures as well as to the Dispensation.

The only questions that can be raised are, first, whether the "law and the prophets" designate the entire Scriptures or two great divisions of them only; and, secondly, whether the words of Jesus can be taken at their full meaning, or, for some other reason, must be discounted. The first question is hardly worthwhile to discuss, for, if neither not one iota of the "law and the prophets" shall fail, it will hardly be contended that the Psalms, or whatever parts of the Old Testament are not included, have a less stable character. The latter question, of momentous importance, we shall consider presently.

Fulfillment of Prophecy

The inspiration of the Old Testament Scriptures is clearly implied in the many declarations of our Lord, respecting the fulfillment of prophecies contained in them. It is God's prerogative to know, and to make known, the future. Human presage cannot go beyond what is foreshadowed in events that have transpired, or is wrapped up in causes which we plainly see in operation. If, therefore, the Old Testament reveals, hundreds of years in advance, what is coming to pass, omniscience must have directed the pen of the writer; i.e., these Scriptures, or at least their predictive parts, must be inspired.

The passage already quoted from the Sermon on the Mount may be noticed for its bearing on prophecy: "Do not think that I have come to destroy the Law or the Prophets; I came not to destroy, but to fulfill." While *plērōsai*, as referring to the *law*, has the special meaning above pointed out; as referring to the *prophets*, it has its more common import. We have here, then, a general statement as to the Old Testament containing prophecies which were fulfilled by Christ and in Him. Here are examples. The rejection of Messiah by the Jewish authorities, as well as the ultimate triumph of His cause, is announced in Psalm 118, in words that Christ applies to Himself: "The stone which the builders rejected is become the head of the corner." The desertion of Jesus by His disciples when He was apprehended fulfills the prediction of Zechariah: "Then Jesus said to them, "You will all fall away because of me this night. For it is written, 'I will strike the shepherd, and the sheep of the flock will be scattered.'[47] (Matthew 26:31). Should angelic intervention rescue

---

[47] A quotation from Zech 13:7

Jesus from death, "How then should the Scriptures be fulfilled, that it must be so?" (Matthew 26:54). All that related to His betrayal, apprehension, and death took place, "that the Scriptures of the prophets might be fulfilled" (Matthew 26:56). "For if you believed Moses, you would trust me; for that one wrote of me" (John 5:46).

Psalm 41:9 preannounces the treachery of Judas in these words: "Even my close friend in whom I trusted, who ate my bread, has lifted his heel against me," and the defection of the son of perdition takes place, "that the Scriptures may be fulfilled" (John 17:12). The persistent and malignant opposition of His enemies fulfills that which is written: "They hated Me without a cause" (John 15:25). Finally, in discoursing to the two disciples on the way to Emmaus, the Lord, "And beginning from Moses and all the Prophets, he interpreted to them in all the Scriptures the things concerning himself." (Luke 24:27). And he said to them, "These are my words that I spoke to you while I was still with you, that all things which are written about me in the law of Moses and the Prophets and the Psalms must be fulfilled." **45** Then he opened their minds to understand the Scriptures, **46** and said to them, "Thus it is written, that the Christ should suffer and rise again from the dead the third day. (Luke 24:44–46).

It is not denied that in some instances the word "fulfill" is used in the New Testament merely as signifying that some event or condition of things corresponds with or realizes something that is written in the Old Testament; as when the words in Isaiah, "Keep on listening, but do not understand; keep on looking but do not perceive." are said to be fulfilled in the blind obduracy of the Pharisees. Nor, again, is it denied that "fulfill" has the meaning of filling, or expanding, or completing. But clearly our Lord, in the passages here cited, employs the term in another acceptation. He means nothing less than this: that the Scriptures to which He says were "fulfilled" were intended by the Spirit of God to have the very application He makes of them; they were predictions in the sense ordinarily meant by that term.

If the Messiah of the Old Testament were merely an ideal personage, there would be little force in saying that the Lord "opened the understanding" of the disciples that they might see His death and resurrection to be set forth in the prophecies. But to teach that the Old Testament contains authentic predictions is, as we have said, to teach that it is inspired. The challenge to heathen deities is, "Tell us what is to come hereafter, that we may know that you are gods; do good, or do harm, that we may be dismayed and terrified" (Isaiah 41:23).

We thus find that our Lord recognizes the same Old Testament canon as we have, that so far as He makes reference to particular books of the canon He ascribes them to the writers whose names they bear, that He regards the Jewish religion and its sacred books as in a special sense—a sense not to be affirmed of any other religion—from God, that the writers of Scripture, in His view, spake in the Spirit, that their words are so properly chosen that an argument may rest on the exactness of a term, that no part of Scripture shall fail of its end or be convicted of error, and that the predictions of Scripture are genuine predictions, which must all in their time receive fulfillment.

We cannot discuss the doctrine of inspiration; but on the ground of the Lord's testimony to the Old Testament, as above summarized, we may surely affirm that He claims for it throughout all that is meant by inspiration when we use that term in the most definite sense. No higher authority could well be ascribed to apostolic teaching, or to any part of the New Testament Scriptures, than the Lord attributes to the more ancient

Scriptures when He declares that "not one iota shall pass from them till all be fulfilled," and that if men "If they do not listen to Moses and the prophets, neither will they be persuaded if someone rises from the dead" (Luke 16:31).

The Value of Christ's Testimony

It remains that we should briefly advert to the value, for the scientific student of the Bible, of Christ's testimony to the Old Testament. The very announcement of such a topic may not be heard without pain, but in view of theories with which Biblical students are familiar, it becomes necessary to look into the question. Can we, then, accept the utterances of Christ on the matters referred to as having value—as of authority—in relation to the Biblical scholarship? Can we take them at their face value, or must they be discounted? Or again, are these words of Jesus valid for criticism on some questions, but not on others? There are two ways in which it is sought to invalidate Christ's testimony to the Old Testament.

Ignorance of Jesus Alleged

It is alleged that Jesus had no knowledge beyond that of His contemporaries as to the origin and literary characteristics of the Scriptures. The Jews believed that Moses wrote the Pentateuch, that the narratives of the Old Testament are all authentic history and that the words of Scripture are all inspired. Christ shared the opinions of His countrymen on these topics, even when they were in error. To hold this view, it is maintained, does not detract from the Lord's qualifications for His proper work, which was religious and spiritual, not literary; for in relation to the religious value of the Old Testament and its spiritual uses and applications He may confidently be accepted as our guide. His knowledge was adequate to the delivery of the doctrines of His kingdom but did not necessarily extend to questions of scholarship and criticism. Of these He speaks as any other man; and to seek to arrest, or direct, criticism by appeal to His authority, is procedure which can only recoil upon those who adopt it. This view is advanced not only by critics who reject the divinity of Christ but also by many who profess to believe that doctrine.

In the preface to his first volume on the Pentateuch and Joshua, Colenso thus writes: "It is perfectly consistent with the most entire and sincere belief in our Lord's divinity to hold, as many do, that when He disclosed Himself to become the 'Son of man,' He took our nature fully and voluntarily entered into all the conditions of humanity, and, among others, into that which makes our growth in all ordinary knowledge gradual and limited.

It is not supposed that, in His human nature, He was acquainted more than any Jew of His age with the mysteries of all modern sciences, nor can it be seriously maintained that, as an infant or young child, He possessed a knowledge surpassing that of the most pious and learned adults of His nation, upon the subject of the authorship and age of the different portions of the Pentateuch. At what period, then, of His life on earth, is it to be supposed that He had granted to Him as the Son of man, supernaturally, full and accurate information on these points?" etc. (vol. i., p. 32). "It should also be observed," says Dr. S. Davidson, "that historical and critical questions could only belong to His human culture, a culture stamped with the characteristics of His age and country."

The doctrine of the *Kenosis* is invoked to explain the imperfection of our Lord's knowledge on critical questions, as evidenced by the way in which He speaks of the

Pentateuch and of various Old Testament problems. The general subject of the limitation of Christ's knowledge during His life on earth is, of course, a very difficult one, but we do not need here to consider it. The Gospel of Mark does speak of the day and hour when the heaven and earth shall pass away as being known to the Father only, and not to the Son; but without venturing any opinion on a subject so mysterious, we may affirm that the Lord's knowledge was entirely adequate to the perfect discharge of His prophetical office. To impute imperfection to Him as the Teacher of the Church were indeed impious. Now the case stands thus: By a certain class of critics we are assured that, in the interests of truth, in order to an apologetic such as the present time absolutely requires, the traditional opinions regarding the authorship of the Old Testament books and the degree of authority which attaches to several, if not all of them, must be revised. In order to save the ship, we must throw overboard this cumbrous and antiquated tackling. We are assured that much more than points of scholarship are involved; for intelligent and truth-loving men cannot retain their confidence in the Bible and its religion unless we discard the opinions which have prevailed as to the Old Testament, even though these opinions can apparently plead in their favor the authority of Jesus Christ.

Now mark the position in which the Lord, as our Teacher, is thus placed. We have followed Him in holding opinions that turn out to be unscientific, untrue, and so it is necessary to relinquish these opinions that neither the Jewish nor the Christian faith can be satisfactorily defended if we cling to them. Is it not, therefore, quite clear that the Lord's teaching is, in something material, found in error—that His prophetical office is assailed? For the allegation is that, in holding fast to what He is freely allowed to have taught, we are imperiling the interests of religion. The critics whom we have in view must admit either that the points in question are of no importance or that the Lord was imperfectly qualified for His prophetical work.

Those who have reverence for the Bible will not admit either position. For why should scholarship so magnify the necessity to apologetics of correcting the traditional opinion as to the age and authorship of the Pentateuch, and other questions of Old Testament criticism, unless it means to show that the Old Testament requires more exact, more enlightened, handling than the Lord gave it? Should it be replied that the Lord, had He been on earth *now*, would have spoken otherwise on the topics concerned? The obvious answer is that the Lord's teaching is for all ages and that His word "cannot be broken."

Theory of Accommadation

The theory of accommodation is brought forward in explanation of those references of Christ to the Old Testament that endorse what are regarded as inaccuracies or popular errors. He spoke, it is said, regarding the Old Testament after the current opinion or belief. This belief would be sometimes right and sometimes wrong. Where no interest of religion or morality was affected—where spiritual truth was not involved—He allowed Himself, even where the common belief was erroneous, to speak in accordance with it. Some extend the principle of accommodation to the *interpretation* of the Old Testament as well as to questions of canon and authorship; and in following it the Lord is declared to have acted prudently, for no good end could have been served, it is alleged, by crossing the opinion upon matters of little importance, and awakening or strengthening suspicion as to His teaching in general.

As to the accommodation supposed to have been practiced by our Lord, we observe that if it implies, as the propriety of the term requires, a more accurate knowledge on His part than His language reveals, it becomes difficult to vindicate His perfect integrity. In some cases where accommodation is alleged, it might be innocent enough, but in others it would be inconsistent with due regard to truth. Most of the statements of the Lord touching the Old Testament to which attention has been directed in this discussion seem to be of this latter kind.

Davidson himself says: "Agreeing as we do in the sentiment that our Savior and His Apostles accommodated their mode of reasoning to the habitual notions of the Jews, no authority can be attributed to that reasoning *except when it takes the form of an independent declaration or statement* and so rests on the speaker's credit." Now the statements of Christ respecting the Old Testament Scriptures to which we specially direct attention are precisely of this nature. Are not these "independent declarations"? "One iota or one point shall not pass," etc; "The Scripture cannot be broken;" "David in spirit calls him Lord;" "All things must be fulfilled which are written in the Law of Moses, and in the prophets, and in the psalms concerning Me."

Further, we may say as before, that if our Lord's statements—His *obiter dicta*, if you will—about the authorship of parts of Scripture give a measure of countenance to opinions standing in the way of both genuine scholarship and of faith, it is hard to see how they can be regarded as instances of a justifiable accommodation. It seems to us (may we reverently use the words) that in this case you cannot vindicate the Lord's absolute truthfulness except by imputing to Him a degree of ignorance that would unfit Him for His office as permanent Teacher of the Church.

Here is the dilemma for the radical critic—either he is agitating the Church about trifles, or, if his views have the apologetical importance that he usually attributes to them, he is censuring the Lord's discharge of His prophetic office; for the allegation is that Christ's words prove perplexing and misleading in regard to weighty issues that the progress of knowledge has obliged us to face. Surely, we should be apprehensive of danger if we discover that views which claim our adhesion, on any grounds whatever, tend to depreciate the wisdom of Him whom we call "Lord and Master," upon whom the Spirit was bestowed "without measure," and who "spake as never man spake." It is a great thing in this controversy to have the Lord on our side.

Are, then, the Lord's references to Moses and the law to be regarded as evidence that He believed the Pentateuch to be written by Moses, or should they be classed as instances of accommodation? When we take *in cumulo* all the passages in which the legislation of the Pentateuch and the writing of it are connected with Moses, a very strong case is made out against mere accommodation. The obvious accuracy of speech observed in some of these references cannot be overlooked; e.g., "Moses, therefore, gave you circumcision *(not because it is of Moses, but of the fathers)*." Again, "There is one who accuses you, Moses, in whom you have put your hope. For if you believed Moses, you would trust me; for that one wrote of me. But if you do not trust the writings of that one, how will you trust my words?" (John 5:45–47). This is not the style of one who does not wish his words to be taken strictly!

Two Positions Clear

Two positions may, I think, be affirmed: First, the legislation of the Pentateuch is actually ascribed to Moses by the Lord. If this legislation is, in the main, long subsequent to Moses, and a good deal of it later than the exile, the Lord's language is positively misleading, and endorses an error that vitiates the entire construction of Old Testament history and the development of religion in Israel. Second, Moses is to such extent the writer of the law that it may, with propriety, be spoken of as "his writings." All admit that there are passages in the Books of Moses that were written by another hand or other hands, and should even additions other than certain brief explanatory interpolations and the last chapter of Deuteronomy have to be recognized, which has not yet been demonstrated, the Pentateuch would remain Mosaic. Should Moses have dictated much of his writings, as Paul did, they would, it is unnecessary to say, be not the less his. The words of Jesus we consider as evidence that He regarded Moses as, substantially, the writer of the books that bear his name. Less than this robs several of our Lord's statements of their point and propriety.

It is hardly necessary to say that we have no desire to see a true and reverent criticism of the Old Testament, and of the New as well, arrested or hindered in its progress. Criticism must accomplish its task, and every lover of truth is more than willing that it should do so. Reluctance to see truth fully investigated, fully ascertained and established, in any department of thought and inquiry, and most of all in the highest departments, is lamentable evidence of moral weakness and imperfect confidence in Him who is the God of truth. But criticism must proceed by legitimate methods and in a true spirit. It must steadfastly keep before it all the facts essential to be taken into account. In the case of its application to the Bible and religion, it is most reasonable to demand that full weight should be allowed to all the teachings, all the words of Him who only knows the Father, who came to reveal Him to the world, and who is Himself the Truth. If all Scripture bears testimony to Christ, we cannot refuse to hear Him when He speaks of its characteristics. It is folly, it is unutterable impiety, to decide differently from the Lord any question regarding the Bible on which we have His verdict; nor does it improve the case to say that we shall listen to Him when He speaks of spiritual truth, but shall count ourselves free when the question is one of scholarship.

Alas, for our scholarship when it brings us into controversy with Him who is the Prophet, as He is the Priest and King of the Church and by whose Spirit both prophets and apostles spoke!

Nothing has been said in this paper respecting the proper method of *interpreting* the different books and parts of the Old Testament, nor the way of dealing with specific difficulties.Our object has been to show that the Lord regards the entire book, or collection of books, as divine, authoritative, and infallible. But in the wide variety of these writings there are many forms of composition, and every part, it is obvious to say, must be understood and explained in accordance with the rules of interpretation that apply to literature of its kind. We have not been trying in advance to bind up the interpreter to an unintelligent literalism in exegesis, which should take no account of what is peculiar to different species of writing, treating poetry and prose, history and allegory, the symbolical and the literal, as if all were the same. The consideration of this most important subject of interpretation with which apologetical interests are, indeed, closely connected, has not been before us. But nothing which we could be called upon to advance regarding the interpretation of the Old Testament could modify the results here reached in relation to the subject of which we have spoken. Our Lord's testimony to the character of the Old Testament must remain unimpaired.

CHAPTER XI The Early Narrative of Genesis

James Orr

By the early narratives of Genesis are to be understood the first eleven chapters of the book—those that precede the times of Abraham. These chapters present peculiarities of their own, and I confine attention to them, although the critical treatment applied to them is not confined to these chapters but extends throughout the Book of Genesis and Exodus and the later history with much the same result in reducing them to legend.

We may begin by looking at the matter covered by these eleven chapters with which we have to deal. See what they contain. First, we have the sublime preface to the Book of Genesis, and to the Bible as a whole, in the account of the Creation in Genesis 1. However it got there, this chapter manifestly stands in its fit place as the introduction to all that follows. Where is there anything like it in all literature? There is nothing anywhere, in Babylonian legend or anywhere else.

You ask what interest has religious faith in the doctrine of creation—in any theory or speculation on how the world came to be? I answer, it has the very deepest interest. The interest of religion in the doctrine of creation is that this doctrine is our guarantee for the dependence of all things on God—the ground of our assurance that everything in nature and Providence is at His disposal. "My help comes from the Lord who made heaven and earth." Suppose there was anything in the universe that was not created by God—that existed independently of Him—how could we be sure that that element might not thwart, defeat, destroy the fulfillment of God's purposes? The Biblical doctrine of creation forever excludes that supposition.

Following on this primary account of creation is a second narrative in a different style—from chapter 2 to 4—but closely connected with the first by the words, "In the day that the Lord God made earth and heaven." This is sometimes spoken of as a second narrative of creation and is often said to contradict the first. But this is a mistake. As the critic Dillmann points out, this second narrative is not a history of creation in the sense of the first at all. It has nothing to say of the creation of either heaven or earth, of the heavenly bodies, of the general world of vegetation. It deals simply with man and God's dealings with man when first created, and everything in the narrative is regarded and grouped from this point of view. The heart of the narrative is the story of the temptation and the fall of man. It is sometimes said that the Fall is not alluded to in later Old Testament Scripture, and therefore cannot be regarded as an essential part of revelation.

It would be truer to say that the story of the Fall, standing there at the commencement of the Bible, furnishes the key to all that follows. What is the picture given in the whole Bible—Old Testament and New? Is it not that of a world turned aside from God—living in rebellion and defiance to Him—disobedient to His calls and resisting His grace? What is the explanation of this universal apostasy and transgression if it is not that man has fallen from his first estate? For certainly this is not the state in which God made man, or wishes him to be. The truth is, if this story of the Fall were not there at the beginning of the Bible, we would require to put it there for ourselves in order to explain the moral state of the world as the Bible pictures it to us and as we know it to be. In Chapter 4, as an appendage to these narratives, there follows the story of Cain and Abel, with brief notices of the beginning of civilization in the line of Cain, and of the start of a holier line in Seth.

Next, returning to the style of Genesis 1—what is called the "Elohistic" style—we have the genealogical line of Seth extending from Adam to Noah. You are struck with the longevity ascribed to those patriarchal figures in the dawn of time, but not less with the constant mournful refrain which ends each notice, Enoch's alone excepted, "and he died." This chapter connects directly with the account of creation in Genesis 1, but presupposes equally the narrative of the Fall in the intervening chapters. We often read in critical books assertions to the contrary of this. The "priestly writer," we are told, "knows nothing" of a Fall. Put that is not so. Wellhausen, that master-critic, is on any side here. Speaking of the so-called "priestly" sections in the story of the flood, he says, "The flood is well led up to; in Q. [that is his name for the priestly writing] we should be inclined to ask in surprise how the earth has come all at once to be so corrupted after being in the best of order. Did we not know it from J. E.? [that is, the *Fall Narrative*]." Another leading critical authority, Dr. Carpenter, writes in the same strain.

Then you come to the flood story in Genesis 6:9, in which two narratives are held to be interblended. There are two writers here, criticism says—the Elohistic and the Jehovistic—yet criticism must own that these two stories fit wonderfully into one another, and the one is incomplete without the other. If one, for instance, gives the command to Noah and his house to enter the Ark, it is the other that narrates the building of the Ark. If one tells of Noah's "house," it is the other that gives the names of Noah's sons. What is still more striking when you compare these Bible stories with the Babylonian story of the deluge, you find that it takes both of these so-called "narratives" in Genesis to make up the one complete story of the tablets. Then, following on the flood and the covenant with Noah, the race of mankind spreads out again as depicted in the table of nations in chapter 10. In verse 25 it is noted that in the days of Peleg was the earth divided; then in chapter 11 you have the story of the divine judgment at Babel confusing human speech. This is followed by a new genealogy extending to Abraham.

Such is a brief survey of the material and on the face of it, it must be acknowledged that this is a wonderfully well-knit piece of history of its own kind that we have before us, not in the least resembling the loose, incoherent, confused mythologies of other nations. There is nothing resembling it in any other history or religious book, and when we come to speak of the great ideas which pervade it and give it its unity, our wonder is still increased.

Ah, yes, our critical friends will tell us, the great ideas are there, but they were not originally there. They were put in later by the prophets. The prophets took the old legends and put these grand ideas into them, and made them religiously profitable. If that was the way in which God chose to give us His revelation, we would be bound gratefully to accept it, but I must be pardoned if I prefer to believe that the great ideas did not need to be put into these narratives; they were there in the things themselves from the very first.

The truth is, a great deal here depends on your method of approach to these old narratives. There is a saying, "Everything can be laid hold of by two handles," and that is true of these ancient stories. Approach them in one way and you make them out to be a bundle of fables, legends, myths, without historical basis of any kind. Then wonderful feats can be performed in the handling of the myths. Professor Gunkel, for example, that very capable Old Testament scholar, is not content with the analysis of books, chapters, and verses, but adds to it the analysis of personalities. He will show you, for instance, that Cain is composed originally out of three distinct figures, blended together, Noah out of another three, and so on.

I have ventured to describe Gunkel's theory as the explanation of the patriarchal history on the ancient principle of a fortuitous concourse of atoms. Only that does not quite answer to the kind of history we have in these narratives, which stand in such organic connection with the rest of revelation. Approach these narratives in another way and they are the oldest and most precious traditions of our race—worthy in their intrinsic merit of standing where they do at the commencement of the Word of God, and capable of vindicating their right to be there, not merely vehicles of great ideas, but presenting in their own archaic way—for archaic they are in form—the memory of great historic truths. The story of the Fall, for example, is not a myth, but enshrines the shuddering memory of an actual moral catastrophe in the beginning of our race that brought death into the world and all our woe.

Coming now to deal a little more closely with these narratives, I suppose I ought to say something on the critical aspect of the question. But this I must pass over briefly, for I want to get to more important matters. In two points only, I would desire to indicate my decided break with current critical theory. The one is the carrying down of the whole Levitical system and history connected with it to the post-exilian age. That, I believe, is not a sound result of criticism, but one which in a very short time will have to be abandoned, as indeed it is already being abandoned or greatly modified in influential quarters. This applies specifically to the date of Genesis 1. Professor Delitzsh, a commentator often cited as having come round practically to the newer critical view, takes a firm stand here. In his new commentary on the chapter, he tells us, "The essential matters in the account of the creation are among the most ancient foundations of the religion of Israel—there are no marks of style which constrain us to relegate the Elohistic account of the creation to the exile—it is in any case a tradition reaching back to the Mosaic period."

The other point on which I dissent is the idea that the Israelites began their religious history without the idea of the one true God, Maker of heaven and earth; that they began with a tribal god, the storm god of Sinai or some other local deity, and gradually clothed him from their own minds with the attributes which belong to Jehovah. This, which is the product of the evolutionary theory of religion, and not a fair deduction from any evidence we possess, I entirely disbelieve, and I am glad to say that this view also is being greatly modified or parted with. It is this theory, however, which lies behind a great deal of the criticism of these early narratives of Genesis. Those things, it is said, could not be; those great ideas could not be there; for man at that early stage could not have evolved them. Even God, it appears, could not have given them to him. Our "could be's," however, will have to be ruled by facts, and my contention is that the facts are adverse to the theory as currently set forth.

I come now to the question: Is there any external corroboration or confirmation of these early narratives in Genesis? In relation of these narratives to Babylonia, everyone has heard something of the wonderful discoveries in Babylonia, and it would be difficult to exaggerate the brilliance and importance of these marvelous discoveries. The point that concerns us chiefly is the extraordinary light thrown on the high culture of this early civilization. Here, long before the time of Abraham, we find ourselves in the midst of cities, arts, letters, books, libraries, and Abraham's own age—that of Hammurabi—was the bloomtime of this civilization. Instead of Israel being a people just emerging from the dim dawn of barbarism, we find in the light of these discoveries that it was a people on whom from its own standpoint the ends of the earth had come—heir to the riches of a civilization extending millenniums into the past. If you say this creates a difficulty in representing the chronology (I may touch on this later), I answer that it gives much greater help by showing how the knowledge of very ancient things could be safely handed down.

For us, the chief interest of these discoveries is the help they give us in answering how far do the narratives in Genesis embody the oldest traditions of our race? There are two reasons that lead us to look with some confidence to Babylonia for the answer to this question. For one thing, in early Babylonia we are already far back into the times to which many of these traditions relate. For another, the Bible itself points to Babylonia as the original city of those traditions. Eden was in Babylonia, as shown by its rivers, the Euphrates and Tigris. It was in Babylonia the Ark was built; and on a mountain in the neighborhood of Babylonia the Ark rested. It was from the plain of Shinar, in Babylonia, that the new distribution of the race took place. To Babylonia, therefore, if anywhere, we are entitled to look for light on these ancient traditions; and do we not find it? I read sometimes with astonishment of the statement that Babylonian discovery has done little or nothing for the confirmation of these old parts of Genesis, but has rather proved that they belong to the region of the mythical.

Take only one or two examples. I leave over meanwhile the Babylonian story of the creation and the flood, and take the tenth chapter of Genesis, the "Table of Nations." Professor Kautzsch, of Halle, a critic of note, says of that old table, "The so-called Table of Nations remains, according to all results of monumental exploration, an ethnographic original document of the first rank that nothing can replace."

In Genesis 10:8–10, we have certain statements about the origin of Babylonian civilization. We learn (1) that Babylonia is the oldest of civilizations; (2) that Assyrian civilization was derived from Babylonia; and (3) strangest of all, that the founders of Babylonian civilization were not Semites, but Hamites—descendants of Cush. Each of these statements was in contradiction to old classical notices and to what was believed until recently about those ancient people. Yet it will not be disputed that exploration has justified the Bible on each of these points. Assyria, undoubtedly, was younger than Babylonia; it derived its civilization, arts, religion, institutions, all that it had, from Babylonia. Strangest of all, the originators of Babylonia civilization, the Accadians, or Sumerians, were a people not of Semitic but Turanian ,or what the Bible would call Hamitic stock. Take another instance: in verse 22, Elam appears as the son of Shem; but here was a difficulty. The Elamites of history were not a Semitic but an Aryan people, and their language was Aryan. Even Professor Hommel, in defending the ancient Hebrew tradition, thought he had to admit an error here. But was there? A French expedition went out to excavate Susa, the capital of Elam, and below the ruins of the historical Elam discovered bricks and other remains of an older civilization, with Babylonian inscriptions showing the people to be of Semitic stock; so Elam was, after all, the son of Shem. In the story of the Tower of Babel in chapter 11, again, is it not interesting to find the Bible deriving all the streams of mankind from the Plain of Shinar and to find archaeology bringing corroborative proof that it is likely all the greater streams of civilization do take their origin from this region? For that is the view to which the opinions of scholars now tend.

Glance now at the stories of Creation, of Paradise, and of the Deluge. The story of Paradise and the Fall we may dismiss in this connection, for, except in the case of the picture on an ancient seal which does bear some relation to the story of the temptation in Eden, there has yet been no proper parallel to the Bible story of the fall. On the other hand, from the ruins of Assyrian libraries have been disinterred fragments of an account of creation, and the Babylonian version of the story of the deluge, both of which have been brought into comparison with the narratives of the Bible. Little need be said of the Babylonian creation story. It is a debased, polytheistic, drawn-out, mythical affair without order; only here and there suggesting analogies to the divine works in Genesis. The flood story has much more resemblance, but also is debased and mythical and lacks wholly in the higher ideas that give its character to the Biblical account. Yet this is the quarry from which our critical friends would have us derive the narratives in the Bible. The Israelites borrowed them, it is thought, and purified these confused polytheistic legends and made them the vehicles of nobler teaching.

We need not discuss the time and manner of this borrowing, for I cannot see my way to accept this version of events at all. There is not only no proof that these stories were borrowed in their crude form from the Babylonians, but the contrast in spirit and character between the Babylonians' products and the Bible's seems to me to forbid any such derivation. The debased form may conceivably arise from corruption of the higher, but not vice versa. Much rather may we hold with scholars like Delitzsch and Kittel, that the relation is one of cognateness, not of derivation. These traditions came down from a much older source, and are preserved by the Hebrews in their purer form. This appears to me to explain the phenomena as no theory of derivation can do, and it is in accordance with the Bible's own representation of the line of revelation from the beginning along which the sacred tradition can be transmitted.

Leaving Babylonia, I must now say a few words on the scientific and historical aspects of these narratives. Science is invoked to prove that the narratives of creation in Genesis 1, the story of man's origin and fall in chapters 2 and 3, the account of patriarchal longevity in chapters 5 and 11, the story of the deluge, and other matters, must all be rejected because in patent contradiction to the facts of modern knowledge. I would ask you, however, to suspend judgment until we have looked at the relation in which these two things, science and the Bible, stand to each other. When science is said to contradict the Bible, I should like to ask first, What is meant by contradiction here? The Bible was never given us in order to anticipate or forestall the discoveries of modern twentieth century science. The Bible, as every sensible interpreter of Scripture has always held, takes the world as it is, not as it is seen through the eyes of twentieth century specialists, but as it lies spread out before the eyes of original men, and uses the popular every-day language appropriate to this standpoint. As Calvin in his commentary on Genesis 1 says "Moses wrote in the popular style, which, without instruction, all ordinary persons endowed with common sense are able to understand. He does not call us up to heaven; he only proposes things that lie open before our eyes."

It does not follow that because the Bible does not teach modern science, we are justified in saying that it contradicts it. What I see in these narratives of Genesis is that, so true is the standpoint of the author, so divine the illumination with which he is endowed, so unerring his insight into the order of nature, that there is little in his description that even yet, with our advanced knowledge, we need to change. You say there is the "six days" and the question whether those days are meant to be measured by the twenty-four hours of the sun's revolution around the earth—I speak of these things popularly. It is difficult to see how they should be so measured when the sun that is to measure them is not introduced until the fourth day. Do not think that this larger reading of the days is a new speculation. In early times, Augustine declared that it is hard or altogether impossible to say of what fashion these days are. Thomas Aquinas, in the middle ages, leaves the matter an open question. To my mind these narratives in Genesis stand out as a marvel, not for its discordance with science but for *its agreement with it*.

Time does not permit me to enter into the details of the story of man's origin in Genesis, but I have already indicated the general point of view from which I think this narrative is to be regarded. It would be well if those who speak of disagreement with science would look to the great truths embedded in these narratives that science may be called upon to confirm. There is, for example,

the truth that man is the last of God's created works—the crown and summit of God's creation. Does science contradict that?

There is the great truth of the unity of the human race. No ancient people believed in such unity of the race, and even science until recently cast doubts upon it. How strange to find this great truth of the unity of the mankind confirmed in the pages of the Bible from the very beginning. This truth holds in it already the doctrine of monotheism, for if God is the Creator of the beings from whom the whole race sprang, He is the God of the whole race that sprang from them.

Also, there is the declaration that man was made in God's image—that God breathed into man a spirit akin to His ow. Does the science of man's nature contradict that, or does it not rather show that in his personal, spiritual-nature man stands alone as bearing the image of God on earth, and founds a new kingdom in the world that can only be carried back in its origin to the divine creative cause?

Additionally, science increasingly points to this very region in Babylonia as the seat of man's origin. Is it then the picture of the condition in which man was created, pure and unfallen, and the idea that man, when introduced into the world, was not left as an orphaned being.God's divine care was about him—God spoke with him and made known His will to him in such forms as he was able to apprehend. Is it this that is in contradiction with history? It lies outside the sphere of science to contradict this. Personally, I do not know of any worthier conception than that which supposes God to have placed Himself in communication with man, in living relations with His moral creatures, from the very first.

Certainly there would be contradiction if Darwinian theory had its way and we had to conceive of man as a slow, gradual ascent from the bestial stage, but I am convinced, and have elsewhere sought to show, that genuine science teaches no such doctrine. Evolution is not to be identified offhand with Darwinianism. Later evolutionary theory may rather be described as a revolt against Darwinianism and leaves the story open to a conception of man quite in harmony with that of the Bible. Of the fall, I have already said that if the story of it were not in the Bible we should require to put it there for ourselves in order to explain the condition of the world as it is.

On the question of patriarchal longevity, I would only say that there is here on the one hand the question of interpretation, for, as the most conservative theologians have come gradually to see, the names in these genealogies are not necessarily to be construed as only individuals. But I would add that I am not disposed to question the tradition of the extraordinary longevity in those olden times. Death, as I understand it, is not a necessary part of man's lot at all. Had man not sinned, he would never have died. Death—the separation of soul and body, the two integral parts of his nature—is something for him abnormal, unnatural. It is not strange, then, that in the earliest period life should have been much longer than it became afterward. Even a physiologist like Weissmann tells us that the problem for science today is not why organisms live so long, but why they ever die.

I have referred to Babylonian story of the flood, and can only add a word on the alleged contradiction of science on this subject. Very confident statements are often made as to the impossibility of such a submergence of the inhabited world, and destruction of human and animal life as the Bible represents. It would be well if those who speak thus confidently would study the accumulated evidence, which distinguished scientific men have brought forward that such a catastrophe as Genesis describes is not only possible, but has actually taken place since the advent of man. My attention was first drawn to this subject by an interesting lecture by the late Duke of Argyle given in Glasgow, and the same view has been advocated by other eminent geological specialists on glacial and post-glacial times, as Prestwich, Dawson, Howorth, Dr. Wright, etc. The universal terms employed need not be read as extending beyond the regions inhabited by man. There seems to be no substantial reason for doubting that in the flood of Noah we have an actual historical occurrence of which traditions appear to have survived in most regions of the world.

In conclusion, it is clear that the narratives of Creation, the Fall, the Flood, are not myths but narratives enshrining the knowledge or memory of real transactions. The creation of the world was certainly not a myth but a fact, and the representation of the stages of creation dealt likewise with facts. The language used was not that of modern science, but, under divine guidance, the sacred writer gives a broad, general picture that conveys a true idea of the order of the divine working in creation. Man's fall was likewise a tremendous fact, with universal consequences in sin and death to the race. Man's origin can only be explained through an exercise of direct creative activity, whatever subordinate factors evolution may have contributed. The flood was an historical fact, and the preservation of Noah and his family is one of the best and most widely attested of human traditions. In these narratives in Genesis and the facts they embody laid the foundation of all else in the Bible. The unity of revelation binds them up with the Christian Gospel.

CHAPTER XII One Isaiah

George L. Robinson

"For about twenty-five centuries no one doubted that Isaiah, the son of Amoz, was the author of every part of the book that goes under his name. Those who still maintain the unity of authorship are accustomed to pointvto the unanimity of the Christian Church on the matter until a few German scholars arose, about a century ago, and called in question the unity of this book." Thus wrote the late Dr. A. B. Davidson, Professor of Hebrew in New College, Edinburgh, (*Old Testament Prophecy*, p. 244, 1903).

The History of Criticism

The critical disintegration of the Book of Isaiah began with Koppe, who in 1780 first doubted the genuineness of chapter 50. Nine years later, Doederlein suspected chapters 40–66. He was followed by Rosenmueller, who was the first to deny the prophecy against Babylon in chapters 13:1–14:23. Eichhorn, at the beginning of the last century, further eliminated the oracle against Tyre in chapter 23, and, with Gesenius and Ewald, also denied the Isaianic origin of chapters 24–27. Gesenius also ascribed to some unknown prophet chapters 15 and 16. Rosenmueller went further, and pronounced against chapters 34 and 35; not long afterwards (1840), Ewald questioned chapters 12 and 33. Thus by the middle of the nineteenth century, some thirty-seven or thirty-eight chapters were rejected as no part of Isaiah's actual writings.

In 1879–80, the celebrated Leipzig professor, Franz Delitzsch, who for years previous had defended the genuineness of the entire book, finally yielded to the modern critical position, and in the new edition of his commentary published in 1889, interpreted chapters 40–66, though with considerable hesitation, as coming from the close of the period of Babylonian exile. About the same time (1888–90), Canon Driver and Dr. George Adam Smith gave popular impetus to similar views in Great Britain.

Since 1890, the criticism of Isaiah has been even more trenchant and microscopic than before. Duhm, Stade, Guthe, Hackmann, Cornill and Marti on the Continent, and Cheyne, Whitehouse, Box, Glazebrook, Kennett and others in Great Britain and America, have questioned portions which were supposed to be genuine.

The Disintegration of "Deutero-Isalar"

Even the unity of chapters 40–66, which were supposed to be the work of the Second, or "Deutero-Isaiah," is given up. What prior to 1890 was supposed to be the unique product of some celebrated but anonymous sage who lived in Babylonia (about 550 B. C.), is now commonly divided and subdivided and in large part distributed among various writers from Cyrus to Simon.

At first it was thought sufficient to separate chapters 63–66 as a later addition to "Deutero-Isaiah's" prophecies; more recently it has become the fashion to distinguish between chapters 40–55, which are alleged to have been written in Babylonia about 549–538 B. C., and chapters 56–66, which are now claimed to have been composed about

460–445 B. C. Some carry disintegration farther even than this, especially in the case of chapters 56–66, which are subdivided into various fragments and said to be the product of a school of writers rather than of a single pen. Opinions also conflict as to the place of their composition, whether in Babylonia, Palestine, Phoenicia, or Egypt.

Recent Views

Among the latest to investigate the problem is the Rev. Robert H. Kennett, D. D., Regius Professor of Hebrew and Fellow of Queen's College, Cambridge, whose Schweich Lectures (1909) have been published for the British Academy by the Oxford University Press, 1910. The volume is entitled, "The Composition of the Book of Isaiah in the Light of History and Archaeology" and is a professed "attempt to tell in a simple way the story of the book of Isaiah." The results of his investigations he sums up as follows (pp. 84–85):

(1) All of chapters 3, 5, 6, 7, 20 and 31, and portions of chapters 1, 2, 4, 8, 9, 10, 14, 17, 22 and 23, may be assigned to Isaiah, the son of Amoz.

(2) All of chapters 13, 40 and 47, and portions of chapters 14, 21, 41, 43, 44, 45, 46 and 48, may be assigned to the time of Cyrus.

(3) All of chapters 15, 36, 37 and 39, and portions of chapters 16 and 38, may be assigned to the period between Nebuchadnezzar and Alexander the Great, but cannot be dated precisely.

(4) Chapter 23:1–14 may be assigned to the time of Alexander the Great (332 B. C.).

(5) All of chapters 11, 12, 19, 24–27, 29, 30, 32–35, 42, 49–66, and portions of chapters 1, 2, 4, 8, 9, 10, 16, 17, 18, 23, 41, 44, 45 and 48, may be assigned to the second century B. C. Dr. Kennett thus assigns more than one-half of the book of Isaiah to the Maccabean Age.

Prof. C. F. Kent, also, in his "Sermons, Epistles and Apocalypses of Israel's Prophets," 1910, makes the following noteworthy observations on the prophecies of the so-called "Deutero-Isaiah." He says, "The prophecies of Haggai and Zechariah...afford by far the best approach for the study of the difficult problems presented by Isaiah 40–66 . . . Chapters 56–66 are generally recognized as post-exilic . . . In Isaiah 56 and the following chapters there are repeated references to the temple and its service, indicating that it had already been restored. Moreover, these references are not confined to the latter part of the book. The fact, on the one hand, that there are few, if any, allusions to contemporary events in these chapters, and that little or nothing is known of the condition and hopes of the Jews during this period (the closing years of the Babylonian exile) makes the dating of these prophecies possible although far from certain. Also the assumption that the author of these chapters lived in the Babylonian exile is not supported by a close examination of the prophecies themselves.

Possibly, their author was one of the few who, like Zerubbabel, had been born in Babylon and later returned to Palestine. He was also dealing with such broad and universal problems that he gives few indications of his date and place of abode; but all the evidence that is found points to Jerusalem as the place where he lived and wrote. The prophet's interest and point of view center throughout in Jerusalem, and he shows himself far more familiar with conditions in Palestine than in distant Babylon. Most of his illustrations are drawn from the agricultural life of Palestine. His vocabulary is also that of a man dwelling in Palestine, and in this respect is in marked contrast with the synonyms employed by Ezekiel, the prophet of the Babylonian exile" (pp. 27, 28).

That is to say, the two most recent investigators of the Book of Isaiah reach conclusions quite at variance with the opinions advocated in 1890, when Delitzsch so reluctantly allowed that chapters 40–66 may have sprung from the period of Babylonian exile. These last twenty-seven chapters are now found to have been written most probably in Palestine rather than in Babylonia and are no longer claimed to speak primarily to the suffering exiles in captivity as was formerly supposed.

The Present State of the Question

The present state of the Isaiah question is, to say the least, complex, if not chaotic. Those who deny the integrity of the book may be divided into two groups that we may call moderates and radicals. Among the moderates may be included Drs. Driver, G. A. Smith, Skinner, Kirkpatrick, Koenig, A. B. Davidson, and Whitehouse. These all practically agree that the following chapters and verses are not Isaiah's: 11:10–16; 12:1–6; 13:1–14:23; 15:1–16:12; 21:1–10; 24–27; 34–66. That is to say, some forty-four chapters out of the whole number, sixty-six, were not written by Isaiah; or, approximately 800 out of 1,292 verses are not genuine.

Among the radicals are Drs. Cheyne, Duhm, Hackmann, Guthe, Marti and Kennett. These all reject approximately 1,030 verses out of the total 1,292, retaining the following only as the genuine product of Isaiah and his age: 1:2–26, 29–31; 2:6–19; 3:1, 5, 8, 9, 12–17, 24; 4:1; 5:1–14, 17–29; 6:1–13; 7:1–8:22; 9:8–10:9; 10:13, 14, 27–32; 14:24–32; 17:1–14; 18:1–6; 20:1–6; 22:1–22; 28:1–4, 7–22; 29:1–6, 9, 10, 13–15; 30:1–17; 31:1–4. That is, only about 262 verses out of the total 1,292 are allowed to be genuine.

This is, we believe, a fair statement of the Isaiah question as it exists today.

On the other hand, there are those who still defend the unity of Isaiah's book, e.g., Strachey (1874), Naegelsbach (1877), Bredenkamp (1887), Douglas (1895), W. H. Cobb (1883–1908), W. H. Green (1892), Vos (1898–99), Thirtle (1907) and Margoliouth (1910).[48]

The Prime Reason for Disecting Isaiah

The fundamental axiom of criticism is the dictum that a prophet always spoke out of a definite historical situation to the present needs of the people among whom he lived, and that a definite historical situation shall be pointed out for each prophecy. This fundamental postulate underlies all modern criticism of Old Testament prophecy.

This principle on the whole is sound, but it can easily be overworked. Certain cautions are necessary, for example:

---

[48] Compare also the writer's *"The Book of Isaiah,"* Y. M. C. A. Press, N. Y., 1910.

(1). It is impossible to trace each separate section of prophecy, independently of its context, to a definite historical situation. Besides, the prophets often speak in poetry, and poetry ought not as a rule to be taken literally.

(2). It is not necessarily the greatest event in a nation's history or the event about which we happen to know the most that may actually have given birth, humanly speaking, to a particular prophecy. Israel's history is full of crises and events, any one of which may easily be claimed to furnish an appropriate, or at least a possible, background for a given prophecy.

(3). The prophets usually spoke directly to the needs of their own generation, but they spoke also to the generations yet to come. Isaiah, for example, commanded, "Bind up the testimony; seal the teaching among my disciples." (8:16); that is, preserve My teachings for the future. Again in 30:8, he says, "Now, go, write it before them on a tablet and inscribe it in a scroll that it may be for the time to come as a witness forever and ever." And also in 42:23, "Who among you will give ear to this, will attend and listen for the time to come?"

Alleged External Evidence Against Unity

Recently, certain writers have appealed to the author of 2 Chronicles to prove that chapters 40–66 existed as a separate collection in his age. Whitehouse in the New Century Bible (*Isaiah*, Vol. I, p. 70), says: "This is clear from 2 Chronicles 36:22 ff, in which the passage Isaiah 44:28 (that Cyrus would cause the temple to be built) is treated as the word of Jeremiah. The so-called 'Deutero-Isaiah' (chs. 40–66) must at that time (c. 300 B. C.) have been regarded as a body of literature standing quite apart from the Isaianic collection or collections which then existed." But the evidence obtained from this source is so doubtful that it is valueless. For it is not the prediction concerning Cyrus to which the chronicler points as "the word of Jehovah by the mouth of Jeremiah," but "the three-score-and-ten years" spoken of in verse 21 of the same context which Jeremiah did predict. On the other hand, the *order* of the prophets among the Jews of antiquity was (1) Jeremiah, (2) Ezekiel, (3) Isaiah, and (4) The Twelve; accordingly, any portion of any of these prophecies might be cited as belonging to Jeremiah, because his book stood first.

In any case, to seek for external evidence in behalf of the dissection of the book is indicative!

The Literary History of the Book

When or how the Book of Isaiah was edited and brought into its present form is unknown. Jesus ben-Sirach, the author of Ecclesiasticus, writing c. 180 B.C., cites Isaiah as one of the notable worthies of Hebrew antiquity, in whose days "the sun went backward and he added life to the king" (Ecclus. 48:20–25; cf. Isa. 38:4–8). He adds, "who saw by an excellent spirit that which should come to pass at the last and comforted them that mourned in Zion." Evidently, therefore, at the beginning of the second century B. C., at the latest, the Book of Isaiah had reached its present form, and the last twenty-seven chapters were already ascribed to the son of Amoz.

Furthermore, there is absolutely no proof that chapters 1–39, or any other considerable section of Isaiah's prophecies ever existed by themselves as an independent collection; or is there any ground for thinking that the promissory and Messianic portions have been systematically interpolated by editors long subsequent to Isaiah's own time. It is quite arbitrary to suppose that the earlier prophets only threatened.

Certain False Presumptions

Certain false presuppositions govern critics in their disintegration of the Book of Isaiah. Only a few examples need be given by way of illustration.

(1). To one, "the conversion of the heathen" lay quite beyond the horizon of any eighth-century prophet, and consequently Isaiah 2:2–4 and all similar passages should be relegated to a subsequent age.

(2). To another, "the picture of universal peace" in Isaiah 11:1–9 is a symptom of late date, and therefore this section and kindred ones must be deleted.

(3). To another, the thought of "universal judgment" upon "the whole earth" in chapter 14:26 quite transcends Isaiah's range of thought.

(4). To still another, the apocalyptic character of chapters 24–27 represents a phase of Hebrew thought that prevailed in Israel only after Ezekiel.

(5). Even to those who are considered moderates, the poetic character of a passage like chapter 12 and the references to a *return* from captivity as in 11:11–16, and the promises and consolations such as are found in chapter 33, are cited as grounds for assigning these and kindred passages to a much later age.

Radicals deny the existence of Messianic passages among Isaiah's own predictions. But, to deny to Isaiah of the eighth century all catholicity of grace, all universalism of salvation or judgment, every highly developed Messianic ideal, every rich note of promise and comfort, all sublime faith in the sacrosanct character of Zion, as some do, is unwarrantably to create a new Isaiah of greatly reduced proportions, a mere preacher of righteousness, a statesman of not very optimistic vein, and the exponent of a cold, ethical religion without the warmth and glow of the messages that are actually ascribed to the prophet of the eighth century.

The Writer's Personal Attitude

More and more, the writer is persuaded that the fundamental postulates of much criticism are unsound and that broad facts must decide the unity or collective character of Isaiah's book. To determine the exact historical background of each individual section is simply impossible, as the history of criticism plainly shows. Verbal exegesis may do more harm than good. Greater regard must be paid to the structure of the book. When treated as an organic whole, the book is a grand masterpiece. One great purpose dominates the author throughout, which, as he proceeds, is brought to a climax in a picture of Israel's redemption and the glorification of Zion. Failure to recognize this unity incapacitates a man to do it exegetical justice. The prophecies of the Book of Isaiah simply cannot be properly understood without some comprehension of the author's scheme of thought as a whole. There is an obvious, though it may be to some extent an editorial, unity to Isaiah's prophecies. But there is as true a unity in the Book of Isaiah as is usually found in a volume of sermons. To regard them as a heterogeneous mass of miscellaneous prophecies, which were written at widely separated times and under varied circumstances from Isaiah's own period down to the Maccabean age, and freely interpolated throughout the intervening centuries, is to lose sight of the great historic realities and perspective of the prophet. In short, the whole problem of how much or how little Isaiah wrote would become immensely simplified if critics would only divest themselves of a mass of unwarranted presuppositions and arbitrary restrictions that fix hard and fast what each century can think and say.

Accordingly, the writer's attitude is that of those who, while welcoming all ascertained results of investigation, decline to accept any mere conjectures or theories as final conclusions. And while he acknowledges his very great debt to critics of all latitudes, he nevertheless believes that the Book of Isaiah, practically as we have it, may have been, and probably was, all written by Isaiah, the son of Amoz, in the later half of the eighth century B. C.

Arguments for Isaiah

It is as unreasonable to expect to be able to prove the unity of Isaiah as to suppose that it has been disproven. Internal evidence is indecisive in either case. There are arguments, however, which corroborate a belief that there was but one Isaiah. Here are some of those which might be mentioned:

1. *The Circle of Ideas* is strikingly the same throughout. For example, take the name for God which is almost peculiar to the Book of Isaiah, "the Holy One of Israel." This title for Jehovah occurs in the Book of Isaiah a total of twenty-five times and only six times elsewhere in the Old Testament (one of which is in a parallel passage). It interlocks all the various portions with one another and stamps them with the personal imprimatur of him who saw the vision of the majestic God seated upon His throne, high and lifted up, and heard the angelic choirs singing: "Holy, Holy, Holy is Jehovah of hosts: the whole earth is full of Thy glory" (Chapter 6). The presence of this Divine name in all the different sections of the book is of more value in identifying Isaiah as the author of all these prophecies than though his name had been inscribed at the beginning of every chapter, for the reason that his theology is woven into the very fiber and texture of the whole book.

The title occurs twelve times in chapters 1-39, and thirteen times in chapters 40-66; and it is simply unscientific to say that the various alleged authors of the disputed portions all employed the same title through imitation. (Isa. 1:4; 5:19, 24; 10:20; 12:6; 17:7; 29:19; 30:11, 12, 15; 31:1; 37:23. Also, 41:14, 16, 20; 43:3, 14; 45:11; 47:4; 48:17; 49:7; 54:5; 55:5; 60:9, 14. Compare 2 Kings 19:22; Psa. 71:22; 78:41; 89:18; Jer. 50:29; 51:5.)

Another unique idea which occurs with considerable repetition in the Book of Isaiah is the thought of a "highway". Cf. 11:16; 35:8; 40:3; 43:19; 49:11; 57:14; 62:10.

Still another is the idea of a "remnant". Cf. 1:9; 6:13; 10:20, 21, 22; 11:11, 12, 16; 14:22, 30; 15:9; 16:14; 17:3, 6; 21:17; 28:5; 37:31; 46:3; 65:8, 9.

Additionally, there is the position occupied by "Zion" in the prophet's thoughts. Cf. 2:3; 4:5; 18:7; 24:23; 27:13; 28:16; 29:8; 30:19; 31:9; 33:5, 20; 34:8; 46:13; 49:14; 51:3; 11; 52:1; 57:13; 59:20; 60:14; 62:1; 11; 65:11; 25; 66:8.

Finally, another is the expression, "pangs of a woman in travail." Cf. 13:8; 21:3; 26:17, 18; 42:14; 54:1; 66:7.

All these, and many others which are less distinctive, stamp psychologically the book with an individuality that is difficult to account for if it be broken up into various sections and distributed, as some do, over the centuries.

2. *Literary Style*. As negative evidence, literary style is not a very safe argument, for as Professor McCurdy says, "In the case of a writer of Isaiah's endowments, style is not a sure criterion of authorship" ("History, Prophecy and the Monuments," II, p. 317 n.). Yet it is remarkable that the clause, "for the mouth of Jehovah hath spoken it" should be found three times in the Book of Isaiah, and nowhere else in the Old Testament. Cf. 1:20; 40:5; 58:14.

It is also singular that the Divine title, "the Mighty One of Israel," should occur three times in Isaiah and nowhere else in the Old Testament. Cf. 1:24; 49:26; 60:16. And it is noteworthy that the phrase, "streams of water," should occur twice in Isaiah and nowhere else. Cf. 30:25; 44:4. Most peculiar is the tendency on the part of the author to emphatic reduplication. Cf. 2:7, 8; 6:3; 8:9; 24:16, 19; 40:1; 43:11, 25; 48:15; 51:12; 57:19; 62:10.

Isaiah's style differs widely from that of every other Old Testament prophet and is as far removed as possible from that of Ezekiel and the post-exilic prophets.

3. *Historical References*. Take for example, first, the prophet's constant reference to Judah and Jerusalem, 1:7–9; 3:8; 5:13; 24:19; 25:2; 40:2, 9; 62:4, as well as to the temple and its ritual of worship and sacrifice. In chapter 1:11–15, when all was prosperous, the prophet complained that the people are profuse and formal in their ceremonies and sacrifices; in chapter 43:23, 24, on the contrary, when the country had been overrun by the Assyrians and Sennacherib had besieged the city, the prophet complains that they had not brought to Jehovah the sheep of their burnt offerings, nor honored Him with their sacrifices. In chapter 66:1–3, 6, 20, not only is the existence of the temple and the observance of the temple ritual presupposed, but those are sentenced who place their trust in the material temple, and the outward ceremonials of temple worship.

As for the "exile", the prophet's attitude to it throughout is that of both anticipation and realization. Thus in chapter 57:1, judgment is only threatened, not yet inflicted: "The righteous is taken away *from the evil to come*." That is to say, the exile is described as still future. On the other hand, in chapter 3:8, "Jerusalem is ruined, and Judah is fallen," while in chapter 11:11, 12, "the Lord will set His hand again the second time to recover the remnant ... from the four corners of the earth." To interpret such statements literally without regard to Isaiah's manifest attitude to the exile, leads only to confusion. No prophet realized so keenly or described so vividly the destiny of the Hebrews.

4. *The Predictive Element*. This is the strongest proof of the unity of the Book of Isaiah. Prediction is the very essence of prophecy. Isaiah was preeminently a *prophet of the future*. With unparalleled suddenness he repeatedly leaps from despair to hope, from threat to promise, from the actual to the ideal. What Kent says of "Deutero-Isaiah" may with equal justice be said of Isaiah himself: "While in touch with his own age, the great unknown prophet lives in the atmosphere of the past and the future" (Cf. "Sermons, Epistles and Apocalypses of Israel's Prophets", p. 28).

Isaiah spoke to his own age, but he also addressed himself to the ages to come. His verb tenses are characteristically futures and prophetic perfects. Of him A. B. Davidson's words are particularly true: "If any prophetic book be examined ... it will appear that the ethical and religious teaching is always secondary, and that the essential thing in the book or discourse is the prophet's outlook into the future" (Hastings' *Dictionary of the Bible*, article, "Prophecy and Prophets").

Isaiah was exceptionally given to predicting: thus,

(1). *Before the Syro-Ephraimitic war (734 B. C.)*, he predicted that within sixty-five years Ephraim should be broken in pieces (7:8); and that before the child Maher-shalal-hash-baz should have knowledge to cry, "My father" or "My mother," the riches of Damascus and the spoil of Samaria should be carried away (8:4; cf. 7:16). There are numerous other predictions among his earlier prophecies. (Cf. 1:27, 28; 2:2–4; 6:13; 10:20–23; 11:6–16; 17:14.)

(2). *Shortly before the downfall of Samaria in 722 B. C.* Isaiah predicted that Tyre shall be forgotten seventy years, and that after the end of seventy years her merchandise shall be holiness of Jehovah. (Cf. Isaiah 23:15.)

(3). *Likewise prior to the siege of Ashdod in 711 B. C.*, he proclaimed that within three years Moab should be brought into contempt (Isaiah 16:14), and that within a year all the glory of Kedar should fail (Isaiah 21:16).

(4). *And not long prior to the siege of Jerusalem by Sennacherib in 701 B. C.*, he predicted that in an instant, suddenly, a multitude of Jerusalem's foes should be as dust (Isaiah 29:5); that yet a very little while and Lebanon should be turned into a fruitful field (Isaiah 29:17); that Assyria should be dismayed and fall by the sword but not of men (Isaiah 30:17, 31; 31:8). Furthermore, that for days beyond a year, the careless women of Jerusalem should be troubled (Isaiah 32:10, 16–20); and that the righteous in Zion should see Jerusalem a quiet habitation, and return and come with singing (Isaiah 33:17–24; 35:4, 10); but that Sennacherib on the contrary should hear tidings and return without shooting an arrow into the city (Isaiah 37:7, 26–29, 33–35).

In like manner *after* the siege of Jerusalem by Sennacherib, 701 B. C., the prophet continued to predict; and, in order to demonstrate to the suffering remnant about him the deity of Jehovah and the folly of idolatry, pointed to the predictions which he had already made in the earlier years of his ministry, and to the fact that they had been fulfilled. For example, he says:

In chapter 41:26: "Who declared it from the beginning, that we might know, and beforehand, that we might say, "He is right"? There was none who declared it, none who proclaimed, none who heard your words."

In chapter 42:9, 23: "Behold, the former things have come to pass, and new things I now declar; before they spring forth I tell you of them" . . . Who among you will give ear to this, will attend and listen for the time to come?"

In chapter 43:9, 12: "Who among them can declare this, and show us the former things? . . . I am the One who declared and saved and proclaimed, when there was no strange god among you; and you are my witnesses," declares Jehovah, "and I am God."

In chapter 44:7–8, 27–28: "Who is like me? Let him proclaim it. Let him declare and set it before me, since I appointed an ancient people. Let them declare what is to come, and what will happen. Fear not, nor be afraid; have I not told you from of old and declared it? And you are my witnesses! Is there a God besides me? There is no Rock; I know not any." . . . "who says to the deep, 'Be dry; I will dry up your rivers'; who says of Cyrus, 'He is my shepherd, and he shall fulfill all my purpose'; saying of Jerusalem, 'She shall be built,' and of the temple, 'Your foundation shall be laid.'"

In chapter 45:1–4, 11, 21: "Thus says Jehovah to his anointed, to Cyrus, whose right hand I have grasped, to subdue nations before him and to ungird the loins of kings, to open doors before him that gates may not be closed. "I will go before you and level the mountains,[49] I will break in pieces the doors of bronze and cut through the bars of iron, I will give you the treasures of darkness and the hoards in secret places, that you may know that it is I, Jehovah, the God of Israel, who call you by your name. For the sake of my servant Jacob, and Israel my chosen, I call you by your name, I name you, though you do not know me. . . Thus says Jehovah, the Holy One of Israel, and the one who formed him. "Ask me of things to come; will you command me concerning my children and the work of my hands? . . . Declare and present your case; let them take counsel together!"

In chapter 46:10–11: "declaring the end from the beginning and from ancient times things not yet done, saying, 'My counsel shall stand, and I will accomplish all my purpose,' calling a bird of prey from the east, the man of my counsel from a far country. I have spoken, and I will bring it to pass; I have purposed, and I will do it."

In chapter 48:3, 5: "The former things I declared of old; they went out from my mouth, and I announced them then suddenly I did them, and they came to pass. I declared them to you from of old, before they came to pass I announced them to you, lest you should say, 'My idol did them, my carved image and my metal image commanded them.'"

And again in chapter 48:6–8, 14–16: "You have heard; now see all this; and will you not declare it. From this time forth I announce to you new things, hidden things that you have not known. They are created now, not long ago; before today you have never heard of them, lest you should say, 'Behold, I knew them.' You have never heard, you have never known, from of old your ear has not been opened. For I knew that you would surely deal treacherously, and that from before birth you were called a rebel. . . ."Assemble, all of you, and listen! Who among them has declared these things! Jehovah loves him; he shall perform his purpose on Babylon, and his arm shall be against the Chaldeans.
I, even I, have spoken and called him; I have brought him, and he will prosper in his way. Draw near to me, hear this: from the beginning I have not spoken in secret, from the time it came to be I have been there."And now Jehovah God has sent me, and his Spirit." To which long list of predictions the prophet adds by way of lamentation: "Oh that you had paid attention to my commandments! Then your peace would have been like a river, and your righteousness like the waves of the sea . . ." (48:18).

Cyrus a Subject of Predictions

From all these numerous explicit and oft-repeated predictions one thing is obvious, namely, that great emphasis is laid on prediction throughout the Book of Isaiah. "Cyrus"

---

[49] Or level the exalted places

138

must be considered as predicted from any point of view. The only question is: Does the prophet emphasize the fact that he is himself predicting the coming of Cyrus? Or are the former predictions concerning Cyrus now in his time coming to pass?

Canon Cheyne's remark upon this point is apropos. He says: "The editor, who doubtless held the later Jewish theory of prophecy, may have inferred from a number of passages; especially 41:26; 48:3, 6, 14, that the first appearance of Cyrus had been predicted by an ancient prophet, and observing certain Isaianic elements in the phraseology of these chapters may have identified the prophet with Isaiah" ("*Introduction to the Book of Isaiah*," p. 238). Why not regard "the editor's" inference legitimate?

Dr. George Adam Smith likewise allows that Cyrus is the fulfillment of *former predictions*. He says: "Nor is it possible to argue as some have tried to do, that the prophet is predicting these things as if they had already happened. For as part of an argument for the unique divinity of the God of Israel, Cyrus, alive and irresistible, and already accredited with success, is pointed out as the unmistakable proof that *former* prophecies of a deliverance for Israel are already coming to pass. Cyrus, in short, is not presented as a prediction but as a proof *that a prediction is being fulfilled*" (Hastings' Dictionary of the Bible, art. Isaiah, p. 493). Further, he says: "The chief claim, therefore, which chapters 40 ff. make for the God of Jehovah is His power to direct the history of the world in conformity to a long predicted and faithfully followed purpose. This claim starts from the proof *that Jehovah has long before predicted events now happening* or about to happen, with Cyrus as their center" (Idem, p. 496).*

Hence in any case it must be allowed that Cyrus is the subject of prediction. It really makes little difference at which end of history one stands, whether in the eighth century B. C. or in the sixth, *Cyrus, to the author of chapters 40–48, is the subject of prediction.* Whether, indeed, he is really predicting Cyrus in advance of all fulfillment, or whether Cyrus to him is the fulfillment of some ancient prediction does not alter the fact that Cyrus was the subject of prediction on the part of somebody. As was stated above, the whole question is, which does the prophet emphasize, (1) the fact that he is predicting? or, (2) that former predictions are now before his eyes coming to pass? The truth is, the prophet seems to live in the atmosphere of both the past and the future. This is true of Isaiah, who in his inaugural vision (ch. 6) paints a scene which Delitzsch describes as "like a prediction in the process of being fulfilled." The same is presumably true of chapters 24–27. There the prophet repeatedly projects himself into the future, and speaks from the standpoint of the fulfillment of his prediction. This was an outstanding characteristic of Isaiah. At one time he emphasizes the fact that he is predicting, and a little later he seems to emphasize that his predictions are coming to pass. Accordingly, if a decision must be made as to when Cyrus was actually predicted, it is obviously necessary to assume that he was predicted *long before his actual appearance*.

This is in keeping with the Deuteronomic test of prophecy, which says: "When a prophet speaketh in the name of Jehovah, if the thing follow not, nor come to pass, that is the thing which Jehovah hath not spoken; the prophet hath spoken it presumptuously, thou shalt not be afraid of him" (Deuteronomy 18:22).

---

* The italics are ours.

There is a similar prediction in the Old Testament: King Josiah was predicted by name two centuries before he came. (1 Kings 13:2; cf. 2 Kings 23:15, 16.)

Dr. W. H. Cobb, in the "Journal of Biblical Literature and Exegesis", 1901 (p. 79), pleads for a "shrinkage of Cyrus", because Cyrus figures only in chapters 40–48, and is then dismissed. Dr. Thirtle in his volume entitled, "*Old Testament Problems*" (pp. 244–264), argues that the name "Cyrus" is a mere appellative, being originally not *Koresh* (Cyrus), but *Horesh* (workman, artificer, image-breaker), and that chapter 44:27, 28 is therefore a gloss. But in opposition to these views the present writer prefers to write Cyrus large, and to allow frankly that he is the subject of prediction; for, the very point of the author's argument is, that he is predicting events that Jehovah alone is capable of foretelling or bringing to pass; in other words, that prescience is the proof of Jehovah's deity.

Isaiah lived in an age when prediction was needed; cf. Amos 3:9. Political events were kaleidoscopic and there was every incentive to predict. But Jehovah's predictions alone were trustworthy. That Isaiah's prophecies contain wonderful predictions is attested both by Jesus ben-Sirach in Ecclus. 48:20–25, which was written about 180 B. C., and by Josephus in his "Antiquities" XI, I, 1, 2, dating from about 100 A. D.

Why should men object to prediction on so large a scale? Unless there is definiteness about any given prediction, unless it transcends ordinary prognostication there is no extra special value in it. The only possible objection is that prediction of so minute a character is "abhorrent to reason." But the answer to such an objection is already at hand; it may be abhorrent to reason, but it is certainly a handmaid to faith. Faith has to do with the future even as prediction has to do with the future; and the Old Testament is preeminently a book that encourages faith.

The one outstanding differentiating characteristic of Israel's religion is predictive prophecy. Only the Hebrews ever predicted the coming of the Messiah of the kingdom of God. Accordingly, to predict the coming of a Cyrus as the *human* agent of Israel's salvation is but the reverse side of the same prophet's picture of the *Divine agent*, the obedient, suffering Servant of Jehovah, who would redeem Israel from their sin.

Deny to Isaiah the son of Amoz the predictions concerning Cyrus, and the prophecy is robbed of its essential character and unique perspective; emasculate these latter chapters of Isaiah of their predictive feature, and they are reduced to a mere *vaticinium ex eventu* (already aware of information being foretold), and their religious value is largely lost.

CHAPTER XIII The Book of Daniel

Joseph D. Wilson

Modern objections to the Book of Daniel were started by German scholars who were prejudiced against the supernatural. Daniel foretells events that have occurred in history. Therefore, argue these scholars, the alleged predictions must have been written after the events.

However, the supernatural is not impossible, nor is it improbable, if sufficient reason for it exists. It is not impossible, for instance, that an event as marvelous as the coming of the Divine into humanity in the person of Jesus Christ should be predicted. So far from being impossible, it seems exceedingly probable and not unreasonable that a prophet predicting a great and distant event, like that indicated above, should give some evidence to his contemporaries or immediate successors that he was a true prophet. Jeremiah foretold the seventy years captivity. Could his hearers be warranted in believing that? Certainly; for he also foretold that all those lands would be subjected to the king of Babylon. A few years showed this latter prophecy to be true, and reasonable men believed the prediction about the seventy years.

But the attacks of the German scholars would have been innocuous had it not been for their copyists. The German scholars—even theological professors—are not necessarily Christians. Religion is with them an interesting psychological phenomenon. Their performances are not taken too seriously by their peers. But outside of their learned circles a considerable number of writers and professors in schools, anxious to be in the forefront, have taken the German theories for proven facts, and by saying "all scholars are agreed," etc., have spread an opinion that the Book of Daniel is a pious fraud.

There is another class of impugners of Daniel—good men, who do not deny the ability of God to interpose in human affairs and foretell to His servants what shall be hereafter. These men, accepting as true what they hear asserted as the judgment of "all scholars" and regretfully supposing that Daniel is a fiction, have endeavored to save something from the wreck of a book which has been the stay of suffering saints through the ages, by expatiating on its moral and religious teaching. It is probable that these apologists—victims themselves of a delusion they did not create but hastily and foolishly accepted—have done more harm than the mistaken scholars or the hasty copyists. They have fostered the notion that a frand may be used for holy ends, and that a forger is a proper teacher of religious truth, and that the Son of God approved a lie.

The scholars find that in chapter 8 of Daniel, under the figure of a very little horn, Antiochus Epiphanes is predicted as doing much hurt to the Jews. The vision is of the ram and male goat, which represent Persia and Greece, so specified by name. A notable horn of the goat, Alexander the Great, was broken, and in its place came four horns, the four kingdoms into which the Greek empire was divided. From one of these four sprang the little horn. That this refers primarily to Antiochus Epiphanes there is no doubt. He died about 163 B. C. The theory of the rationalistic critics is that some "pious and learned Jew" wrote the Book of Daniel at that time to encourage the Maccabees in their revolt against this bad king; that the book pretends to have been written in Babylon, 370 years before, in order to make it pass current as a revelation from God. This theory has been supported by numerous arguments, mostly conjectural, all worthless, and, in a recent publication, a few designedly delusive.

The imaginary Jew is termed "pious" because lofty religious ideas mark the book, and "learned" because he exhibits so intimate an acquaintance with the conditions and environments of the Babylonian court four centuries before his date. But as no man, however educated, can write an extended history out of his own imagination without some inaccuracies, the critics have searched diligently for mistakes. The chief of these supposed mistakes will be considered below.

We meet a difficulty at the threshold of the critics' hypothesis. Daniel 9:26 predicts the destruction of Jerusalem and the temple—a calamity so frightful to the Jewish mind that the Septuagint shrank from translating the Hebrew. What sort of encouragement was this? The hypothesis limps at the threshold.

Having Antiochus Epiphanes in chapter 8, the rationalistic critics try to force him into chapter 7. They find a "little horn" in chapter 7 and struggle to identify him with the "very little horn" of chapter 8. There is no resemblance between them. The words translated "little horn" are different in the different chapters. The little horn of chapter 7 springs up as an eleventh horn among *ten* kings. He is diverse from other kings. He continues till the Son of Man comes in the clouds of heaven and the kingdom that will never be destroyed is set up. Antiochus Epiphanes, the little horn of chapter 8, comes out of one of the *four* horns into which Alexander's kingdom resolved itself. He was not diverse from other kings but was like scores of other bad monarchs, and he did not continue till the Son of Man.

These divergences render the attempted identification absurd, but an examination of the two sets of prophecies in their entirety shows this clearly. Chapters 2 and 7 are a prophecy of the world's history to the end. Chapters 8 and 11 refer to a crisis in Jewish history, a crisis now long past.

Chapter 2, the "Image," or large statue, with its head of gold, breast of silver, belly of brass, legs of iron, feet and toes of mingled iron and clay, tells of four world kingdoms, to be succeeded by a number of sovereignties, some strong, some weak, which would continue till the God of heaven should set up a kingdom never to be destroyed. Chapter 7, the Four Beasts, is parallel to the Image. The same four world empires are described: the fourth beast, strong and terrible, to be succeeded by ten kings, who should continue till the coming of the Son of Man, who should set up an everlasting kingdom.

These four world empires were Babylon, Persia, Greece, and Rome. There have been no other world empires since. Efforts have been made to unite the divided sovereignties of Europe by royal intermarriages and by conquest, but the iron and clay would not cleave together. The rapidity of the Greek conquest is symbolized by the swift leopard with four wings; its division by four heads. The Roman empire is diverse from the others—it was a republic, and its iron strength is dissipated among the nations that followed it and still exist today, still iron and clay.

These prophecies illustrated by history to the present moment stand in the way of the unbelieving theory. The Roman empire, the greatest of all, must be eliminated to get rid of prediction, and any shift promising that end has been welcomed. One set of critics makes the kingdom of the Seleticidae, which was one of the parts of the Greek empire, the fourth world kingdom, but it never was. It was part of the Greek empire—one of the four heads upon the leopard. Another set creates an imaginary Median empire between Babylon and Persia. There was no such empire. The Medo-Persian empire was one. Cyrus, the Persian, conquered Babylon. All history says so and the excavations prove it.

Among the nations that were to take the place of the fallen Roman empire, another power was to rise—a "little horn," shrewd and arrogant. It was to wear out the saints of the Most High, to be diverse from the other ten sovereignties, to have the other sovereignties given into its hand, and to keep its dominion till the coming of the Son of Man.

Whatever this dread power is, or is to be, it was to follow the fall of the Roman empire and to rise among the nations which, ever since, in some form or other have existed where Rome once held sway. Whether that power, differing from civil governments and holding dominance over them, exists now and has existed for more than a thousand years, or is to be developed in the future, it was to arise in the Christian era. The words are so descriptive, that no reader would ever have doubted were it not that the prophecy involves prediction.

The attempt of the "very little horn" of chapter 8, Antiochus Epiphanes, to destroy the truth, failed. Yet it was well-nigh successful. The majority of the nation was brought to abandon Jehovah and to serve Diana. The high priest in Jerusalem sent the treasurers of the temple to Antioch as an offering to Hercules. Jews out-bade each other in their subservience to Antiochus. His cruelties were great but his persuasions were more effective for his purpose; "by peace he destroyed many." Idolatrous sacrifices were offered throughout Judea. Judaism was all but dead, and with its death, the worship of the one God would have found no place in all the earth.

This prophecy encouraged the few faithful ones to resist the Greek and their own faithless fellow countrymen. God foresaw and forewarned. The warning went unheeded by the mass of the Jews. Sadduceeism then did not believe in the supernatural and it has repeated its disbelief. Fortunately, there was a believing remnant and true religion was saved from extinction.

The Seventy Weeks. (Daniel 9:24–27.) "Weeks" in this prophecy are not weeks of days but "sevens," probably years, but whether astronomical years of 365 1/4 days or prophetic years of 360 days does not appear. Our Lord's saying when referring to the prophecy of Daniel (Matthew 24:15), "let the reader understand," seems to indicate a peculiarity about the period foretold.

From the issuance of a commandment to restore and rebuild Jerusalem unto Messiah there would be sixty-nine sevens, i.e., 483 years. Messiah would be cut off and have nothing, and the people of a prince would destroy Jerusalem and the temple.

It came to pass in the procuratorship of Pontius Pilate. Messiah appeared; He was cut off; He had nothing, no place to lay His head, nothing except a cross. And before the generation that crucified Him passed away, the soldiers of the Roman emperor destroyed the city and sanctuary, slew all the priests and ended Jewish church and nation.

Unto Messiah the Prince there were to be 483 years from an edict to rebuild Jerusalem. That edict was issued in the twentieth year of Artaxerxes Longimanus. Somewhere between 454 B. C. and 444 B. C. is the date, with the prominent opinion in favor of the later date. Four hundred and eighty-three years brings us to 29–39 A. D. Or, if prophetic years are meant, the *terminus ad quem* is 22–32 A. D. Pontius Pilate was procurator of Judea from 26 A. D. to 36 A. D.

All this is plain enough, and if the words of Daniel had been written after the death of our Saviour and the fall of Jerusalem, no one could fail to see that Jesus Christ is indicated. But if written in the exile, this would be supernatural prediction, and hence the struggles of the critics to evade somehow the implications of the passage. To find some prominent person who was "cut-off" prior to 163 B. C. was the first need. The high priest Onias, who was murdered through the intrigues of rival candidates for his office, was the most suitable person. He was in no respect the Messiah, but having been anointed he might be made to serve. He died 171 B. C. The next step was to find an edict to restore and rebuild Jerusalem, 483 years before 171 B. C. That date was 654 B. C., during the reign of Manasseh, son of Hezekiah. No edict could be looked for there. But by deducting 49 years, the date was brought to 605 B. C., and as in that year Jeremiah (25:9) had foretold the destruction of Jerusalem, perhaps this would do.

There were two objections to this hypothesis; one, that a prophecy of desolation and ruin to a city and sanctuary then in existence was not a commandment to restore and rebuild; the other objection was that this also was a supernatural prediction, and as such, offensive to the critical mind. Accordingly, recourse was had to the decree of Cyrus (Ezra 1:1–4) made in 536 B. C. But the decree of Cyrus authorized not the building of Jerusalem but the building of the temple. It is argued that forts and other defenses, including a city wall, must have been intended by Cyrus, and this would be rebuilding Jerusalem. But the terms of the edict are given and no such defences are mentioned. Nor is it likely that a wise man like Cyrus would have intended or permitted a fortified city to be built in a remote corner of his empire close to his enemy, Egypt, with which enemy the Jews had frequently toyed with in previous years.

At all events, the city was not restored until the twentieth year of Artaxerxes, as appears from Nehemiah 2:3, 8, 13, etc., where Nehemiah laments the defenseless condition of Jerusalem. Permission to build could safely be given then, for Egypt had been conquered and the loyalty of the Jews to Persia had been tested. Moreover, the date of Cyrus' decree does not meet the conditions. From 536 B. C. to 171 B. C. is 365 years and not 483. A "learned and pious Jew" would not have made such a blunder in arithmetic in foisting a forgery upon his countrymen.

There were four decrees concerning Jerusalem issued by the Persian court. The first under Cyrus, alluded to above, the second under Darius Hystaspis. (Ezra 6.) The third in the seventh year of Artaxerxes. (Ezra 7:12–26.) All of these concern the temple. The fourth in the twentieth year of Artaxerxes was the only one to restore and rebuild a walled town.

The Book of Daniel was translated into Greek about 123 B.C., forty years after the death of Antiochus Epiphanes. This prophecy of the seventy weeks troubled the Jewish translators. It foretold disaster to Jerusalem. City and sanctuary would be destroyed. They had been destroyed 464 years before by Nebuchadnezzar. Would they be destroyed again? The translators were unwilling to believe that such a calamity would occur again. Could they not make out that the words referred to the troubles under Antiochus? It was true that he had not destroyed a temple, but he had polluted the temple. Perhaps that was equivalent to destruction. At all events they did not dare to say that another destruction of Jerusalem lay in the future.

But there stood the words. From the going forth of commandment to restore Jerusalem unto Messiah the Prince would be seven weeks and three score and two weeks, 483 years. They could do nothing with those words. They left them out, and mangled the rest of the passage to give obscurely the impression that the foretold disasters were a thing of the past. This mistranslation of a Divine oracle to make it say what they wished was a high-handed proceeding, but it did not prevent its fulfillment. At the time appointed, Messiah came and was crucified, and Jerusalem fell. The critics' efforts to force some meaning other than a prediction of Christ into this prophecy is not without precedent.

Supposed Inaccuracies

But the rationalistic interpretations of the aforementioned great prophecies are so unnatural, so evidently forced in order to sustain a preconceived theory, that they would have deceived none except those predisposed to be deceived. Accordingly, attempts have been made to discredit the Book of Daniel to show that it could not have been written in Babylon, to expose historical inaccuracies, and so forth. The scholars discovered some supposed inaccuracies, and, the fashion having been set, the imitation scholars eagerly sought for more, and, with the help of imagination, have compiled a considerable number. In every case, they are instances of the inaccuracy of the critics.

First, as the only one ever having had any weight, is the fact that no historian mentions Belshazzar. It was therefore assumed that "the learned and pious Jew," whom the critics imagined, had invented the name. Since 1854, this "inaccuracy" has disappeared from the rationalistic dictionaries and other productions. The excavations have answered that.

Second, disappointed at the discovery of the truth, the critics now find fault with the title "king," which Daniel gives to Belshazzar, and assert that no tablets have been found dated in his reign. It is not probable that any such tablets will be found, for his father outlived him, and even though Belshazzar was co-king, his father's name would be in the dates. The tablets, however, show that Belshazzar was the commander of the troops, that he was the man of action—his father being a studious recluse—and that he was the darling of the people and actual administration was in his hands. He was the heir to the throne and, even if not formally invested, was the virtual king in the eyes of the people.

Next, it is objected that Belshazzar was not the son of Nebuchadnezzar as told by the queen mother in Daniel 5:11. If he were the grandson through his mother, the same language would be used, and the undisturbed reign of Nabonidus in turbulent Babylon is accounted for in this way.

Additionally, the quibble that the monuments do not say that Belshazzar was slain at the taking of Babylon is unworthy of the scholar who makes it. It is admitted that Belshazzar was a prominent figure before the city was captured, that "the son of the king died," and that he then "disappeared from history." He was heir to the kingdom. He was a soldier. His dynasty was overthrown. He disappeared from history. Common sense can make its inference.

However, it is hard for the impugners of Daniel to let the Belshazzar argument go. To have him appear prominently in the inscriptions, after criticism had decided that he never existed, is awkward. Accordingly, we have a long dissertation (Sayce's *Higher Criticism and Monuments*, p. 497–531) showing that the claim of Cyrus to have captured

Babylon without fighting is inconsistent with the accounts of the secular historians, which dwell upon the long siege, the desperate fighting, the turning of the river, the surprise at night, etc.

The two accounts are inconsistent. But what has this to do with Daniel? His account is as follows: "In that night was Belshazzar the Chaldean king slain, and Darius the Mede received the kingdom" (Daniel 5:31). Not a word about a siege or more—an account entirely consistent with the inscription of Cyrus. And yet the critic has the audacity to say that "the monumental evidence has here pronounced against the historical accuracy of the Scripture narrative" (*Higher Criticism and Monuments*, p. 531). This is not criticism; it is misrepresentation.

Next, Daniel mentions the "Chaldeans" as a guild of wise men. This has been made a ground of attack. "In the time of the exile", they tell us, "the Chaldeans were an imperial nation. Four centuries afterward the term signified a guild; therefore, Daniel was written four centuries afterward." It is strange that none of the critics consulted Herodotus, the historian nearest to Daniel in time. He visited Babylon in the same century with Daniel and uses the word in the same sense as Daniel and in no other. (Herodotus 1:181, 185.)

The Book of Daniel spells Nebuchadnezzar with an "n" in instead of an "r." Therefore, the critics argue, it must have been written 370 years later. But Ezra spells it with an "n." So do 2 Kings, 1 & 2 Chronicles, and so does Jeremiah seven times out of sixteen. Jeremiah preceded Daniel, and if either Kings or Chronicles was written in Babylon, we have the same spelling in the same country and about the same time.

As for the Greek words in Daniel, relied on by Driver to prove a late date, when we discover that these are the names of musical instruments and that the Babylonians knew the Greeks in commerce and in war and realize that musical instruments carry their native names with them, this argument vanishes like the rest.

But, it is urged, Daniel gives the beginning of the captivity (1:1) in the third year of Jehoiakim, 606 B. C., whereas Jerusalem was not destroyed till 587 B. C., therefore, Daniel dates the captivity from the time that he and the other youths were carried away. A glance at the history will suggest when that was. Pharaoh Necho came out of Egypt against Babylon in 609 B. C. He met and defeated Josiah at Megiddo. He then marched on northward. In three months he marched back to Egypt, having accomplished nothing against Babylon. The interval, 609 to 605 B. C., was the opportunity for Nebuchadnezzar. He secured as allies or as subjects the various tribes in Palestine, as appears from Berosus.

Among the rest "Jehoiakim (2 Kings 24:1) became his servant three years." During that time he took as guests, or hostages, the noble youths. At the end of the three years, in 605, Necho reappeared on his way to fatal Carchemish. Jehoiakim renounced Nebuchadnezzar, and sided with Necho. A merciful Providence counted the seventy years captivity from the very first deportation, and Daniel tells us when that was. The captivity ended in 536 B. C.

Finally, there is the Aramaic. One critic said Aramaic was not spoken in Babylon. Others, not so self-confident, said the Aramaic in Babylon was different from Daniel's Aramaic. None of them knew what Aramaic was spoken in Babylon. There was Ezra's Aramaic. It was like Daniel's, and Ezra was a native of Babylon. To save their argument, they post-dated Ezra, too.

In 1906 and 1908, there were unearthed papyrus rolls in Aramaic written in the fifth century, B. C. It is impossible to suggest redactors and other imaginary persons in this case, and so the Aramaic argument goes the way of all the rest. Before these recent finds, the Aramaic weapon had begun to lose its potency. The clay tablets, thousands of which have been found in Babylonia, are legal documents and are written in Babylonian. Upon the backs of some of them was Aramaic filing marks stating the contents. These filings were for ready reference and evidently in the common language of the people, the same language that the frightened Chaldeans used when the angry monarch threatened them. (Daniel 2:4.)

There are some other alleged inaccuracies more frivolous than the above. Lack of space forbids their consideration here.

Two new objections to the genuineness of Daniel appear in a dictionary of the Bible, edited by three American clergymen. The article on Daniel states that "the BABA BATHRA[50] ascribes the writing not to Daniel but along with that of some other books to the men of the Great Synagogue." This statement is correct in words but by concealment conveys a false impression. The trick lies in the phrase, "some other books." What are those other books? They are Ezekiel, Hosea, Amos—all the minor prophets—and Esther. The statement itself is nonsensical, like many other things in the Talmud, but whatever its meaning, it places Daniel on the same footing as Ezekiel and the rest.

The other objection is "Chapter 11 (of Daniel) with its four world kingdoms is wonderfully cleared when viewed from this standpoint, i.e. as a Maccabean production. The third of these kingdoms is explicitly named as the Persian (11:2). The fourth to follow is evidently the Greek."

Every phrase in this is false. The chapter says nothing about four world kingdoms, nor does 11:2 say that the Persian was the third or that the Greek was the fourth. No explanation or modification of these astonishing statements is offered. How could the writer expect to escape detection? True, the Baba Bathra is inaccessible to most people, but Daniel 11 is in everybody's hands.

Daniel was a wise and well-known man in the time of Ezekiel, else all point in the irony of Ezekiel 28:3 is lost. He was also eminent for goodness and must have been esteemed an especial recipient of God's favor and to have had intercourse with the Most High like Noah and Job. Ezekiel 14:15, 20: "even if Noah, Daniel, and Job were in it, as surely as I am alive,' declares the Sovereign Lord Jehovah, 'they would save neither their sons nor their daughters; they would save only their soul[51] because of their righteousness.'" A striking collocation: Noah the second father of the race, Job the Gentile and Daniel the Jew.

Daniel is better attested than any other book of the Old Testament. Ezekiel mentions the man. Zechariah appears to have read the book. The bungling attempt of the Septuagint to alter a prediction of disaster to one of promise; our Savior's recognition of Daniel as a prophet. Compare Ezekiel; there is not a word in the Bible to show that he

---

[50] The passage is found in the Talmud Babylon, Tract Baba Bathra, fol. 15a., and reads, "The men of the Great Synagogue have written Ezekiel, the Twelve Minor Prophets, Daniel and Esther."—Editor.

[51] i.e. *save only themselves*

ever existed, but as he does not plainly predict the Savior, no voice is raised or pen wagged against him.

CHAPTER XIV Inspiration – Or to What Extent Is The Bible Inspired of God?

R. A. Torrey

"For no prophecy was ever produced by the will of man, but men carried along by the Holy Spirit spoke from God." (2 Peter 1:21).

"All Scripture is inspired by God and profitable for teaching, for reproof, for correction, for training in righteousness; [17] so that the man of God may be fully competent, equipped for every good work." (2 Tim. 3:16, 17).

Our subject is "The Inspiration of the Bible or to What Extent Is the Bible Inspired of God?" The subject is of vital and fundamental importance. If we can make it clear that the writers of the various books of the Bible were inspired of God in a sense that no other men were ever inspired of God, that they were so gifted and taught and led and governed by the Holy Spirit in their utterances as recorded in the Bible, that they taught the truth and nothing but the truth, that their teachings were absolutely without error, then we have in the Bible a court of final appeal and of infallible wisdom to which we can go to settle every question of doctrine or duty. But if the writers of the Bible were "inspired" only in the vague and uncertain sense that Shakespeare, Browning, or many other men of genius were inspired to the extent that their minds were made more keen to see the truth than ordinary men but still made mistakes, then we are all at sea in hopeless confusion, and each generation must settle for itself through the blundering reporters what the Holy Spirit meant to say.

There is great need of crystal clear teaching on this subject, because our colleges, seminaries, pulpits, Sunday schools, and religious papers are full of teaching that is vague, inaccurate, misleading, unscriptural, and oftentimes grossly false. There are many in these days who say "I believe that the Bible is inspired" when by "inspired" they do not mean what the mighty men of faith in the past meant by "inspired." They often say that they "believe the Bible is the Word of God," when at the same time they believe it is full of errors.

Now the Bible is as clear as crystal in its teachings and claims regarding itself, and either those claims are true, or the Bible is the biggest fraud in all the literature of the human race. The position held by so many today, that the Bible is a good book, perhaps the best book in the world, but at the same time it is full of errors that must be corrected by the higher wisdom of our day, is utterly illogical and absolutely ridiculous. If the Bible is not what it claims to be, it is a fraud—an outrageous fraud.

What does the Bible teach and claim concerning itself? What does it teach and claim regarding the fact and extent of its own inspiration?

I. The Work of the Holy Spirit in Apostles and Prophets Is Different in Character from His Work in All Other Persons

The first thing that the Bible teaches and claims for itself is *that the work of the Holy Spirit in apostles, prophets, and the various authors of different books of the Bible, differs from His work in other men, even in other believers in Christ*. It teaches that the Holy Spirit imparts to apostles and prophets a special gift for a special purpose. We find this clearly taught in 1 Corinthians 12:4, 8–11, 28, 29, where we read, "**4** Now there are different gifts, but there is the same Spirit; **5** and there are different ministries, and yet there is the same Lord; **6** and there are varieties of effects, but the same God who works all things in all persons. **7** But the manifestation of the Spirit is given to each one for a beneficial purpose. **8** For to one is given speech of wisdom through the Spirit, to another speech of knowledge according to the same Spirit, **9** to another faith by the same Spirit, to another gifts of healing by that one Spirit, **10** to yet another operations of miraculous powers, to another prophesying, to another the distinguishing of spirits, to another different tongues, and to another interpretation of tongues. **11** But all these operations are performed by the very same Spirit, distributing to each one respectively just as it wills.

28 And God has set some in the congregation,[52] first apostles, second prophets, third teachers, then powerful works,[53] then gifts of healings, helps, administrations, various kinds of tongues. **29** Not all are apostles, are they? Not all are prophets, are they? Not all are teachers, are they? Not all are workers of powerful works,[54] are they?

This chapter is the fullest and clearest chapter in the Bible on the subject of the various gifts of the Holy Spirit. It is the classic chapter on the subject, and it states in terms the meaning of which is unmistakable, that the gift bestowed on apostles and prophets *differed in kind* from the gifts bestowed on other believers, even though those believers were filled with the Holy Spirit. Not only did the work of the Holy Spirit in the apostles and prophets differ from His work in men of genius, but even from His work in other believers.

These verses make it as plain as day that the work of the Holy Spirit in preachers and teachers and in ordinary believers, illuminating them and guiding them into the truth and into the understanding of the Word of God, is the same in kind and differs only in degree from the work of the Holy Spirit in apostles and prophets is thoroughly unscriptural and untrue. This doctrine overlooks what is here so clearly stated and so carefully elucidated, that while there is "the same Spirit" "there are different gifts" "different ministries," "varieties of effects" (1 Corinthians 12:4–6) and that not all are prophets or apostles (1 Corinthians 12:29).

Those who desire to minimize the difference between the work of the Holy Spirit in apostles and prophets and His work in other men often refer to the fact that the Bible itself says that Bezaleel, the architect of the tabernacle, was to be "filled him with the Spirit of God in wisdom, in understanding, in knowledge, and in all kinds of craftsmanship," "to devise artistic designs" (Ex. 31:1–11), as a proof that the inspiration of the prophet does not differ in kind from the inspiration of the artist or the architect. This argument at first glance seems plausible, but when we bear in mind the facts about the tabernacle, especially the fact that the tabernacle was to be built after the pattern shown to Moses in the mount (Exodus 25:8–9, 40) and that therefore it was itself a revelation from God—a prophecy, a

---

[52] Gr *ekklesia* ("assembly;" "congregation, i.e., of Christians")

[53] Or *miracles*

[54] Or *workers of miracles*

setting forth of the truth of God—the argument loses all its force. The tabernacle was the Word of God done into wood, gold, silver, brass, cloth, skin, etc., just as truly the Word of God and the revealing of God's truth as if the truth were printed on a page. So, of course, Bezaleel needed to be inspired, he was a prophet, a prophet who uttered his prophecies in the details of the tabernacle. There is much reasoning about inspiration today that appear at first sight very learned, but that will not bear much scrutiny or candid comparison with the teachings of the Word of God. There is nothing in the Bible more inspired than the tabernacle, and if the destructive critics would study the tabernacle more carefully and thoroughly they would be led to give up their ingenious but untenable theories, not only about the construction of the tabernacle, but about many other things as well. I have never heard or known of a single destructive critic who had ever given a thorough study to the real meaning of the tabernacle in all its parts, or who had any considerable understanding of the types of Scripture. I have challenged the critics in the University centres of England, Ireland, and Scotland to name one single destructive critic who had ever made any thorough study of the types, and no one has ever attempted to even suggest one.

II. Truth Hidden from Men for Ages that They Had Not Discovered and Could Not Discover by the Unaided Processes of Human Reasoning Has Been Revealed to Apostles and Prophets in the Spirit

The second thing taught in the Bible regarding the inspiration of the apostles and prophets, the inspiration of the various authors of the books of the Bible, is that *truth hidden from men for ages, and which they had not discovered, and could not discove, by the unaided processes of human reasoning, even human reasoning at its very best and highest, has been revealed to apostles and Prophets in the Holy Spirit*. We find this very clearly taught in Ephesians 3:2–5 if indeed you have heard of the stewardship of God's grace which was given to me for you; that by revelation there was made known to me the mystery,[55] as I wrote before in brief. When you read this, you can understand my insight into the mystery[56] of Christ, which in other generations was not made known to the sons of men, as it has now been revealed to his holy apostles and prophets in the Spirit . . ."

The meaning of these words is unmistakable. Paul here declares in words the meaning of which is perfectly plain, that God "in the Spirit" had revealed "unto His holy apostles and prophets" "the mystery of Christ," which in former generations had not been made known unto the sons of men, that they had not discovered and could not discover except by revelation from God; Paul and the other apostles and prophets knew it by direct revelation from God himself through the Holy Ghost.

The teaching is inescapable that the Bible contains truth that men never had discovered and never could have discovered if left to themselves, but truth which the Father in great grace has revealed to His children through His servants the prophets and apostles. We see in this the folly, a folly so common in our day, of seeking to test the statements of Scripture by the conclusions of human reasoning,or by the intuitions of the "Christian consciousness." The revelation of God transcends human reasoning, and

---

[55] *i.e., secret plan*
[56] *i.e., secret plan*

therefore human reasoning cannot be its test. Furthermore, a consciousness that is truly and fully Christian is *the product* of the study and absorption of Bible truth. It is not *the test* of the truth of the Bible,—it is *the product* of meditation on the Bible. If our "consciousness" differs from the statements of the Bible, it is not as yet a fully "Christian consciousness," and the thing for us to do is not to try to pull God's revelation down to the level of our consciousness but to tone our consciousness up to the level of God's Word.

III. The Revelation Made to the Prophets by the Holy Spirit Was Independent of Their Own Thinking

The third thing that the Bible makes perfectly clear as to the inspiration of the prophets and apostles is that *the revelation made by God through His Holy Spirit to the prophets was independent of the prophets' own thinking, that it was made to them by the Spirit of Christ, which was in them, and that they themselves oftentimes did not thoroughly understand the full meaning of what the Spirit was saying through them and that what they said was a subject of diligent search and inquiry to their own mind as to its meaning.* This comes out very plainly in 1 Pet. 1:10–12, "Concerning this salvation the prophets sought and searched diligently, who prophesied of the grace that should come to you, searching for what time or what particular time the spirit of Christ which was in them did point to as it testified beforehand about the sufferings of Christ and the glories after these things. To whom it was revealed that they were not serving themselves, but you, in these things which now have been announced to you through those who preached the gospel to you by the Holy Spirit sent from heaven, things into which angels desire to look."

Here again the meaning is clear and inescapable. We are told that the prophets had a revelation made to them by the Holy Spirit, the meaning of which they did not thoroughly comprehend, and that they themselves "sought and searched diligently" as to the meaning of this revelation that was made to them and they recorded. The Spirit through them testified beforehand the sufferings of Christ (e. g. in Isaiah 53:3, Psalm 22) and the glories that should follow them. They recorded what the Spirit testified, but what it meant they did not thoroughly understand. It was not merely that their minds were made keen to see things they would not otherwise see and were therefore more or less accurately recorded. No, there was a very definite revelation, arising *not from their own minds at all*, but from the Spirit of God, Who made the revelation to them and this they recorded. But it was not of themselves to that extent that they themselves wondered as to what its meaning might be. What they recorded was not at all their own thought; it was the thought of the Holy Spirit who spoke through them. How utterly different this conception is from that which is so persistently taught in many of our colleges and theological seminaries and pulpits—how utterly different it is from the conception that was taught a week ago today in one of the pulpits of our own city.

IV. No Prophetic Utterance Was of the Prophet's Own Will, But the Prophetic Spoke from God and the Prophet Was Carried Along by the Holy Spirit and Not by His Own Impulse or Reasoning in What He Said

The fourth thing that the Bible makes perfectly clear is, that *not one single prophetic utterance was of the prophet's own will (i. e., it was not in any sense merely what he wished to say), but in every instance the prophet spoke from God, and the prophet was carried along in the prophetic utterance by the Holy Spirit, regardless of his own will or thought.* We find this stated practically in so many words in 2 Peter 1:21 where we read:

"for no prophecy was ever produced by the will of man, but men carried along by the Holy Spirit spoke from God."

There can be no honest mistaking of the meaning of this language. The prophet never thought that there was something that needed to be said and therefore said it, but God took possession of the prophet, *carried him along* in his utterance, by the power of the Holy Spirit, and he spoke, not from his own consciousness or reasoning, nor from his own intuition, but *"from God."* As God's messenger he spoke what God told him to say.

V. The Holy Spirit Was the Real Speaker Who Spoke in the Prophetic Utterances

The fifth thing that the Bible teaches regarding the inspiration of the prophets and the apostles and their utterances is that the Holy Spirit was the real speaker in the prophetic utterances, that what was said or written was the Holy Spirit's Word that was upon the apostle's tongu, and not the word of the prophet or apostle. This is said in the Bible in so many words, over and over again. For example, in Hebrews 3:7 we read: "Therefore, just as the Holy Spirit says, 'Today, if you hear his voice . . .'"

The author of the epistle to the Hebrews is quoting Psalm 95:7–8 and says that what the Psalmist is recorded as saying "the Holy Spirit saith." Again in Hebrews 10:15–16, we read: "And the Holy Spirit also testifies to us; for after saying, "This is the covenant that I will make with them after those days, declares the Lord: I will put my laws on their hearts, and write them on their minds."

Now the author of the Epistle to the Hebrews is quoting Jeremiah 31:33, and he does not hesitate to say that the testimony that Jeremiah is the testimony of the Holy Ghost, that the Holy Ghost was the real speaker.

Again we read in Acts 28:25–26 that Paul said, "And when they did not agree with one another, they began leaving after Paul had spoken one parting word, "The Holy Spirit rightly spoke through Isaiah the prophet to your fathers, "'Go to this people, and say, "You will keep on hearing but never understand, and you will keep on seeing but never perceive."

Here Paul is quoting Isaiah's words as recorded in Isaiah 6:9–10, and he distinctly says that the real speaker was not Isaiah but "the Holy Spirit" who spoke "through Isaiah the prophet."

Turning now to the old Testament, we read in 2 Samuel 23:2 this assertion by David regarding the things that he said and wrote: "The Spirit of Jehovah speaks by me; his word is on my tongue."

There can be no mistaking the meaning of these words on the part of any one who goes to the Bible to find out what it really claims and teaches. The Holy Spirit was the real speaker in the prophetic utterance. It was the Holy Spirit's utterance that was upon the prophet's tongue. The prophet was simply the mouth by which the Holy Spirit spoke. Merely as a man, except as the Holy Spirit taught him and used him, the prophet was fallible as other men are fallible, but when the Spirit was upon him, when he was taken up and borne along by the Holy Spirit, then he became infallible in his teachings; his teachings were not his, but the teachings of the Holy Spirit. It was God who was then speaking, not the prophet. For example, Paul merely as a man, even as a Christian man, doubtless had many mistaken notions on many things, and was more or less subject to the ideas and opinions of his time. But when he taught as an apostle, under the power of the Holy Spirit he was infallible, or rather the Spirit who taught through him was infallible, and the teachings that resulted from the Spirit's teaching through him, were infallible, as infallible as God.

Common sense demands of us that we carefully distinguish between what Paul may have thought as a man, and what he actually taught as an apostle. In the Bible we have the record of what he taught as an apostle. Someone may cite as a possible exception to this statement 1 Corinthians 7:6, 25, where he says: "But this I say by way of concession, not of command . . . Now concerning virgins I do not have a command from the Lord, but I am giving an opinion as one shown mercy by the Lord to be trustworthy." There are those who think that Paul does not seem to have been sure here that he had the word of the Lord in this particular matter, but that is not the meaning of the passage. The meaning of verse 6 is that the teaching he had just given was by way of concession to their weakness and not a commandment as to what they must do. And the teaching of verse 25 is that the Lord, during His earthly life, had given no commandment on this subject but that Paul was giving his judgment; but he says distinctly that he was giving it as one who had obtained mercy of the Lord to be trustworthy. Furthermore, in the verse 40, he distinctly says that in his judgment he had the Spirit of God. But even allowing that the other interpretation of this passage is the correct one and that Paul was not absolutely sure in this case that he had the Word of the Lord and the mind of the Lord, that would only show that where Paul was not absolutely sure that he was teaching in the Holy Ghost he was careful to note the fact, and this would only give additional certainty to all other passages that he wrote.

It is sometimes said that Paul taught in his earlier epistles that the Lord would return during his lifetime and that in this matter he certainly was mistaken. But Paul never taught in his earlier epistles, or any epistles, or anywhere that the Lord would return during his lifetime. This assertion is contrary to fact. He does say in 1 Thessalonians 4:17: "Then we who are alive, who remain will be caught up together with them in the clouds to meet the Lord in the air, and so we shall always be with the Lord."

He does put himself in the same class with those who were still alive when he wrote the words. He naturally and necessarily did not include himself with those who had already fallen asleep. In speaking of the Lord's return, Paul does not say nor hint that he will be still alive when the Lord returns. It is quite probable that Paul did believe at this time that he might be alive when the Lord returned but he never taught that he would be alive.

The attitude of expectancy is the true attitude in all ages for every believer. This was the attitude that Paul took until it was distinctly revealed to him that he would depart before the Lord came. I think it very probable that Paul in the earlier part of his ministry was inclined to believe that he would live until the coming of the Lord, but the Holy Ghost kept him from so teaching, and also kept him from all other errors in his teachings.

VI. The Holy Spirit in the Apostles Gave Not Only the Thought, But the Words in Which the Thought Was to Be Expressed

The sixth thing that the Bible makes clear as to the inspiration of the apostle and prophets is that, the Holy Spirit in the prophets and apostles gave not only the thought but also gave the words in which the thought was to be expressed. We find this very clearly stated in 1 Corinthians 2:13: "which things we also speak, not in words taught by human wisdom, but in those taught by the Spirit, combining spiritual thoughts with spiritual words."

One of the most popular of the false theories of inspiration in our day is that the Holy Spirit was the author of the thought but that the apostles were left to their own choice of words in the expression of the thought; therefore, in studying the Bible we cannot emphasise the exact meaning of the words but must try to find the thought of God that was back of the words and what the writer has more or less inaccurately expressed. There are many teachers in our theological seminaries and pulpits today who speak very arrogantly of those who believe in verbal inspiration, i. e., those who believe that the Holy Spirit chose the very words in which the thought he was teaching was to be expressed, but certainly the Bible claims that it was verbally inspired. The passage above makes it as plain as language can possibly make it that the "words" in which the apostle spoke were not words that man's wisdom teaches but that the of the Spirit.

Now if this is not the fact, if only the *thought* that was given to Paul was the thought of God, and he clothed the thought in his own words, then Paul was a thoroughly deceived man on a fundamental point, in which case no dependence at all can be placed in his teachings on any point, or else he was a deliberate fraud. There is no possibility of finding any middle ground, and the attempts to find a middle ground have landed those who have tried it in all kinds of absurdities. If you have an exact and logical mind, you must take your choice between verbal inspiration and bald infidelity.

Paul distinctly states that the words he conveyed to others the truth that was revealed to him were the words the Holy Spirit taught him. The Holy Spirit himself has anticipated all these modern ingenious, but wholly unbiblical and utterly illogical and entirely false theories regarding his own work in the apostles. The theory that "the concept" was inspired but the words in which the concept was expressed were not was anticipated by the Holy Spirit Himself and exploded 1,800 years before our supposedly wise 19th century theological teachers conceived it and attempted to foist it upon an unsuspecting public. It was exploded eighteen centuries before it was exploited. Furthermore, the theory is absurd in itself. As the only way in which thought can be conveyed from one mind to another, from one man's mind to another man's mind, or from the mind of God to the mind of man is by words, therefore if the words are imperfect the thought expressed in those words is necessarily imperfect.

The theory is an absurdity on its very face, and it is difficult to see how intelligent men could have ever deceived themselves into believing such a thoroughly illogical theory. If the words are not inspired the Bible is not inspired. Let us not deceive ourselves; let us face facts.

Furthermore, the more carefully one studies the *wording* of the statements of this wonderful book—the Bible—the more he will become convinced of the marvellous accuracy of *the very words* used to express the thought. To a superficial thinker the doctrine of verbal inspiration may appear questionable or even absurd, but any regenerate and Spirit-taught man who *ponders the words* of the Scripture day by day, and year after year, will become thoroughly and immovably convinced that the wisdom of God is in *the very words* used as well as in the thought expressed in the words.

It is a significant and deeply impressive fact that our difficulties with the Bible rapidly disappear as we note *the precise language* used. The changing of a word or letter, or of a tense, case or number, would oftentimes land us in contradiction or untruth, but taking the *words exactly as written*, difficulties disappear and truth shines forth. Countless times people have come to me with apparent difficulties and supposed contradictions in the Bible and asked a solution, and I have pointed them to the exact words used and the solution was found in taking the words exactly as written. It was because they changed in a slight degree the very words that God spoke that a difficulty had seemed to arise. The Divine origin of nature shines forth more and more clearly the more closely we examine it under the microscope. As by the use of a powerful microscope we see the perfection of form and the adaptation of means to end in the minutest particles of matter, we are overwhelmingly convinced that God, a God of infinite wisdom and power, a wisdom extending down to the minutest parts of matter, is the author of the material universe: so likewise the divine origin of the Bible shines forth more and more clearly under the microscope. The more minutely we study the Bible the more we note the perfection with which the turn of a word reveals the absolute thought of God.

There is an important question, and a question that has puzzled many writers at this point: If the Holy Spirit is the author of the very words of Scripture, how do we account for the variations in style and diction? How is it, for example, that Paul always used Pauline language, and John used Johannean language, and Peter used language that was characteristic of himself? The answer to this question is very simple and is twofold: First, even though we could not account at all for this fact, it would have little weight against the explicit statement of God's Word with any one who is humble enough and wise enough to recognise that there are a great many things which he cannot account for at all which could be easily accounted for if he knew a little more. It is only the man of amazing conceit that thinks he knows as much as God, that he is infinite in wisdom and give up an explicit statement of God's Word simply because he sees a difficulty in the way of the acceptance of that statement, which he in his limited knowledge cannot solve.

But there is a second answer, and an all-sufficient one, and that is this: these variations in style and diction are easily accounted for. The Holy Spirit is infinitely wise. He Himself is the Creator of Man and of man's power of speech, and therefore he is wise enough and has enough facility in the use of language in revealing truth to and through any individual to use words, phrases, and forms of expression that are in that person's ordinary vocabulary and forms of thought. He is also wise enough to make use of that person's peculiar individuality in revealing the truth through him. It is one of the marks of the Divine wisdom of this book that the same Divine truth is expressed with absolute accuracy in such widely variant forms of expression.

VII. All Scripture is Inspired of God

The seventh thing that the Bible makes plain regarding the work of the Holy Spirit in the various writers of Scripture is that *all Scripture, that is everything contained in all the books of the Old and New Testament, is inspired of God*. We are distinctly taught this in 2 Timothy 3:16–17. Here we read, "All Scripture is inspired by God and profitable for teaching, for reproof, for correction, for training in righteousness; so that the man of God may be fully competent, equipped for every good work."

An attempt has been made to obscure the full force of these words by a revised translation given in both the English Revision and American Standard Version. In this revised translation, the words are rendered as follows: "Every Scripture inspired of God is also profitable for teaching, for reproof, for correction, for instruction which is in righteousness; that the man of God may be complete, furnished completely unto every good work." There is absolutely no warrant in the Greek text for changing "Every Scripture is given by inspiration of God and is profitable for doctrine, etc.," into "Every Scripture inspired of God *is also* profitable for teaching, etc." "Every" is in the Greek. There is no "*is*" in the Greek. It must be supplied, as is often the case in translating from Greek into English. "Is" must be supplied somewhere, either before "given by inspiration" (or God-breathed), or else supplied after it, in the latter case necessitating the change of "and" into "also" (a change which is possible, but very uncommon. There is not a single instance in the New Testament outside of this in which two adjectives coupled by the simplest copulative "and (kai)" are ripped apart and the "is" placed between them and an "and" changed into "also."

The other construction, that of the Authorised Version, is not at all uncommon. The translation of the revisers does violence to all customary usage of the Greek language. But we do not need to dwell upon that, for, even accepting the changes given in the Revision, the thought is not essentially changed; for if Paul had said what the revisers make him say that "Every Scripture inspired of God is also profitable for teaching, etc.," there can be no question but by "every scripture inspired of God" he referred to every Scripture contained in the Old Testament. Here, then, taking whichever translation you will, we have the plain teaching that every Scripture of the Old Testament is "God-breathed" or "inspired of God." Certainly if we can believe this about the Old Testament there is no difficulty in believing it about the New, and there can be no question that Paul claimed for his own teaching an equal authority with the Old Testament teaching. This we shall see clearly under the next head. And not only did Paul so claim, but the apostle Peter also classes the teaching of Paul with the Old Testament teaching as being "Scripture." Peter says in 2 Peter 3:15–16, " and regard the patience of our Lord as salvation; just as also our beloved brother Paul, according to the wisdom given him, wrote to you, [16] as also in all his letters, speaking in them of these things, in which are some things hard to understand, which the untaught and unstable distort, as they do also the rest of the Scriptures, to their own destruction."

Here, Peter clearly speaks of Paul's epistles as being "Scripture."

VIII. The Bible is the Word of God

Next, the Bible teaches concerning the extent of the inspiration of its writings is that because of this inspiration of prophets and apostles, the writers of the Bible, the whole Bible as originally given becomes the absolutely inerrant Word of God. In 2 Samuel 23:2, David says of his own writings, "The Spirit of Jehovah speaks by me; his word is on my tongue."

In Mark 7:13, our Lord Jesus Himself calls the law of Moses "the Word of God." He says "thus making void the word of God by your tradition that you have handed down. And many such things you do."

In the verses immediately preceding, e has been drawing a contrast between the teachings of the Mosaic law (not only the teachings of the Ten Commandments but also other parts of the Mosaic law as well) and the traditions of the scribes and Pharisees, and has shown how the traditions of the scribes and Pharisees flatly contradicted the requirements of the law as given through Moses. Summing up the matter, he says in the verse just quoted that the Scribes and Pharisees made void "the Word of God" by their traditions, thus calling the law of Moses "the Word of God." When I was in England a high dignitary and scholar in the Church of England in a private correspondence tried to call me down by saying that the Bible nowhere claimed to be "the Word of God," but I replied to him by showing him that not only did the Bible claim it, but that the Lord Jesus Himself said in so many words that the law given through Moses was "the Word of God."

In 1 Thessalonians 2:13 the Apostle Paul claims that his own epistles and teachings are "the Word of God." He says: "For this reason we also constantly thank God that when you received the word of God which you heard from us, you accepted it not as the word of men, but for what it really is, the word of God, which also is at work in you who believe." Paul claims for his own teaching in the most absolute way that the message that he gave was "the Word of God." When we read the words that Jeremiah, Isaiah, Paul, John, James, and Jude and the other Bible writers wrote, we are reading what God says. We are not listening to the voice of man, but we are listening to the voice of God. "The Word of God," which we have in the Old and New Testaments, as originally given, is absolutely inerrant down to the smallest word and smallest letter or part of a letter. Our Lord Jesus Himself says of the Pentateuch in Matthew 5:18: "For verily I say unto you, till heaven and earth pass away, one jot or one tittle shall in no wise pass away from the law till all things be accomplished."

Now a "jot" is the Hebrew character "yodh," the smallest character in the Hebrew alphabet, less than half the size of any other letter in the Hebrew alphabet, and a "tittle" is a part of a letter, the little horn put on some of the Hebrew consonants, less than the cross we put on a "t." Here our Lord says that the law given through Moses was absolutely inerrant, down to its smallest letter or part of a letter. That certainly is verbal inspiration with a vengeance.

Again he said, as recorded in John 10:35, after having quoted from Psalm 82:6 as conclusive proof of a point, "The Scripture cannot be broken," thus asserting the absolute irrefragability or inerrancy and finality of the Scriptures. If the Scriptures as originally given were not the inerrant Word of God, then not only is the Bible a fraud, but Jesus Christ Himself was utterly misled and is therefore utterly unreliable as a teacher. I have said that the Scriptures of the Old and New Testaments as originally given were absolutely inerrant, and the question of course arises to what extent is the Authorized Version or the Revised Version, the inerrant Word of God. The answer is simple; they are the inerrant Word of God just to that extent that they are an accurate rendering of the Scriptures of the Old and New Testaments as originally given, and to all practical intents and purposes they are a thoroughly accurate rendering of the Scriptures of the Old and New Testaments as originally given. There are, it is true, many variations in the many manuscripts we possess, thousands of variations, but by a careful study of these very variations, we are able to find with marvellous accuracy what the original manuscripts said.

A very large share of the variations are of no value whatever, as it is evident from a comparison of different manuscripts that they are mistakes of a transcriber. Many other variations simply concern the order of the words used, and in translating into English, in which the order of words is often different from what it is in the Greek, the variation is not translatable. Many other variations are of small Greek particles, many of which are not translatable into English any way. When all the variations of any significance have been reduced to the minimum to which it is possible to reduce them by a careful study of manuscripts, there is not one single variation left that affects any doctrine held by the evangelical churches, and the Scriptures as we have them today translated into our English language in the ASV (1901), RSV (1952), NASB (1995), UASV (2016), are to all practical intents and purposes the inerrant Word of God.

CHAPTER XV Three Peculiarities of the Pentateuch that Are Incompatible with the Graf-Wellhausen Theories of Its Composition

Andrew Craig Robinson

There are three remarkable peculiarities in the Pentateuch that seem to be incompatible with modern theories of its composition and call for explanation from the critics. The first of these peculiarities is:

The absence of the name "Jerusalem" from the Pentateuch

The first occurrence of the name "Jerusalem" in the Bible is in the Book of Joshua (10:1): "And it happened that when Adoni-Zedek king of Jerusalem. . ." In the Pentateuch, the city is only once named (Genesis 14) and then it is called "Salem"—an abbreviation of its cuneiform name "Uru-salem." Now on the traditional view of the Pentateuch, the absence of the name Jerusalem presents no difficulty; the fact that Bethel, Hebron, and other shrines are named, while Jerusalem is not, would merely mean that at these other shrines the patriarchs had built their altars, while at Jerusalem they had not.

But from the point of view of modern critics who hold that the Pentateuch was in great part composed to glorify the priesthood at Jerusalem, and that the Book of Deuteronomy in particular was produced to establish Jerusalem as the central and only acceptable shrine for the worship of Israel—this omission to name the great city, then of historic and sacred fame that they wished to exalt and glorify, seems very strange indeed. According to the theories of the critics, the composers of the Pentateuch had a very free hand to write whatsoever they wished, and they are held to have freely exercised it. It seems strange then to find the "Yahvist" supposed to have been written in the southern kingdom, and to have been imbued with all its prejudices, consecrating Bethel by a notable theophany (Genesis 28:16, 19), while in all that he is supposed to have written in the Pentateuch, he never once names his own Jerusalem. And so the "priestly writer" also, to whom a shrine like Bethel ought to be an anathema, is found nevertheless consecrating Bethel with another theophany: "Jacob called the name of the place where God spoke with him Bethel" (Genesis 35:14–15), and he never even names Jerusalem.

What is the explanation of all this? What is the inner meaning of this absence of the name Jerusalem from the Pentateuch? Is it not this: that at the time the Pentateuch was written, Jerusalem, with all her sacred glories, *had not entered yet into the life of Israel?*

The second remarkable peculiarity is:

The Absence of an mention of sacred song from the ritual of the Pentateuch

This is in glaring contrast to the ritual of the second temple, in which timbrels, harps, and Levite singers bore a conspicuous part. Yet it was just in the very time of the second temple that the critics allege that a great portion of the Pentateuch was composed. How is it then that none of these things occur in the Mosaic ritual? It might have been expected that the priests in post-exilic times would have sought to establish the highest possible sanction for this musical ritual, by representing it as having been ordained by Moses. But no such ordinance in point of fact occurs, and the Pentateuch stands in its primitive simplicity, destitute of any ordinance of music in connection with the ritual, except those passages in which the blowing of the trumpets is enjoined at the Feast of Trumpets, which is the blowing of the trumpet throughout the land in the year of Jubilee. Also was the command contained in a single passage (Numbers 10:10), that in the day of gladness, and in the beginnings of the months, over the burnt offerings and over the sacrifices of the peace offerings the silver trumpets were to sound. No mention in connection with the ritual of cymbals, harps, timbrels, or psalteries; no mention of sacred song, or Levite singers. No music proper entered into the ritual, only the crude and warlike blare of trumpets. No ordinance of sacred song, no band of Levite singers. The duties of the Levites, in the Book of Numbers, are specially defined. The sons of Gershom were to bear the tabernacle and its hangings on the march; the sons of Kohath bore the altars and the sacred vessels; the sons of Merari were to bear the boards and bands and pillars of the sanctuary. No mention whatsoever of any ministry of sacred song. A strange omission this would be, if the "Priestly Code" (so-called), which thus defines the duties of the Levites, had been composed in post-exilic times, when Levite singers—sons of Asaph—cymbals, harp, and song of praise formed leading features in the ritual. Does it not seem that the Mosaic Code, enjoining no music but the simple sounding of the trumpet-blast, stands far behind these niceties of music and of song, seeming to know nothing of them all?

The third remarkable peculiarity to which attention is called is:

The absence of the Divine title "Lord of Hosts" from the Pentateuch

The first occurrence of this Divine title in the Bible is in 1 Samuel 1:3: "Now this man used to go up from his town year by year[57] to worship and to sacrifice to Jehovah of hosts in Shiloh, and there the two sons of Eli, Hophni and Phinehas, were priests to Jehovah." After this it occurs in a number of the remaining books of the Bible, with increasing frequency. The pre-Samuelitic period of the history of Israel is thus differentiated from the post-Samuelitic period by this circumstance, that in connection with the former period this title is never used, whilst in connection with the latter it is used, and with growing frequency—at all stages of the history, even down to the end of the Book of Malachi; occurring altogether 281 times.

Now the theory of the criticism of the present day is that the Pentateuch was composed, edited, and manipulated, during a period of more than four hundred years, by motley groups and series of writers, of differing views, and various tendencies. One writer composed one part and one composed another; these parts were united by a different hand. Another composed a further part, and this by yet another was united to the two that went before. After this another portion was composed by yet another scribe and afterwards was joined on to the three. Matter was absorbed, interpolated, harmonized, smoothed over, colored, edited from various points of view and with different—not to

---

[57] Lit *from days to days*

say opposing—motives. And yet when the completed product—the Pentateuch—coming out of this curious literary seething pot is examined, it is found to have this remarkable characteristic, that not one of the manifold manipulators—neither "J", nor "E", nor "JE", nor "D", nor "RD", nor "P", nor "P2", nor "P3", nor "P4", nor any one of the "Redactors of P", who were innumerable—would appear to have allowed himself to be betrayed even by accident into using this title, "Lord of Hosts" so much in vogue in the days in which he is supposed to have written. The Pentateuch, devoid as it is of this expression, shows an unmistakable mark that it could not possibly have been composed in the way asserted by the criticism, because it would have been a literary impossibility for such a number of writers, extending over hundreds of years, to have one and all, never even by accident, slipped into the use of this Divine title for Jehovah, "Lord of Hosts" so much in vogue during those centuries. In point of fact, the Pentateuch *was written before the title was invented*.

These three peculiarities of the Pentateuch are absolutely undeniable. No one can say that the name "Jerusalem" *does* occur in the Pentateuch; no one can say that any mention of sacred song *does* occur in the ritual of the Pentateuch; and no one can say that the Divine title "Lord of Hosts" *does* occur in the Pentateuch.

CHAPTER XVI The Testimony of the Monuments to the Truth of the Scriptures

George Frederick Wright

All history is fragmentary. Each particular fact is the center of an infinite complex of circumstances. No man has intelligence enough to insert a disingenuous fact into circumstances not belonging to it and make it exactly fit. Only infinite intelligence could do this. A successful forgery, therefore, is impossible if only we have a sufficient number of the original circumstances with which to compare it. It is this principle that gives such importance to the cross-examination of witnesses. If the witness is truthful, the more he is questioned the more perfectly will his testimony be seen to accord with the framework of circumstances into which it is fitted. If false, the more will his falsehood become apparent.

Remarkable opportunities for cross-examining the Old Testament Scriptures have been afforded by the recent uncovering of long-buried monuments in Bible lands and by deciphering the inscriptions upon them. It is the object of this essay to give the results of a sufficient portion of this cross-examination to afford a reasonable test of the competence and honesty of the historians of the Old Testament and of the faithfulness with which their record has been transmitted to us. But the prescribed limits will not permit the half to be told, while room is left for an entire essay on the discoveries of the last five years to be treated by another hand, specifically competent for the task.

Passing by the monumental evidence that has removed objections to the historical statements of the New Testament, as less needing support, attention will be given first to one of the Old Testament narratives nearest to us in time and against which the harshest judgments of modern critics have been hurled. We refer to the statements in the Book of Daniel concerning the personality and fate of Belshazzar.

The Identification of Belshazzar

In the fifth chapter of Daniel, Belshazzar is called the "son of Nebuchadnezzar," and is said to have been "king" of Babylon and to have been slain on the night in which the city was taken. But according to the other historians, he was the son of Nabonidus, who was then king, and who is known to have been out of the city when it was captured, and to have lived sometime afterwards.

Here, certainly, there is about as glaring an apparent discrepancy as could be imagined. Indeed, there would seem to be a contradiction between profane and sacred historians. But in 1854 while excavating in the ruins of Mugheir (identified as the site of the city of Ur, from which Abraham emigrated), Sir Henry Rawlinson found inscriptions that stated when Nabonidus was near the end of his reign, he associated with him on the throne his eldest son, Bil-shar-uzzur. The inscriptions also report that Nabonidus allowed Bil-shar-uzzur the royal title, thus making it perfectly credible that Belshazzar should have been in Babylon, as he is said to have been in the Bible, that he should have been called king, and that he should have perished in the city while Nabonidus survived outside.

That he should have been called king while his father was still living is no more strange than that Jehoram should have been appointed by his father, Jehoshaphat, king of

Judah, seven years before his father's death (see 2 Kings 1:17 and 8:16), or that Jotham should have been made king before his father, Uzziah, died of leprosy, though Uzziah is still called king in some of the references to him.

That Belshazzar should have been called son of Nebuchadnezzar is readily accounted for on the supposition that he was his grandson and there are many things to indicate that Nabonidus married Nebuchadnezzar's daughter, while there is nothing known to the contrary. But if this theory is rejected, there is the natural supposition that in the loose use of terms of relationship common among Oriental people "son" might be applied to one who was simply a successor. In the inscriptions on the monuments of Shalmaneser II, referred to below, Jehu, the *extirpator* of the house of Omri, is called the "son of Omri."

The status of Belshazzar implied in this explanation is confirmed incidentally by the fact that Daniel is promised in verse 6 the "third" place in the kingdom, and in verse 29 is given that place, all of which implies that Belshazzar was second only.

Thus, what was formerly thought to be an insuperable objection to the historical accuracy of the Book of Daniel proves to be, in all reasonable probability, a mark of accuracy. The coincidences are all the more remarkable for being so evidently undesigned.

The Black Obelisk of Shalmaneser

From various inscriptions in widely separated places we are now able to trace the movements of Shalmaneser H. through nearly all of his career. In B. C. 842, he crossed the Euphrates for the sixteenth time and carried his conquests to the shores of the Mediterranean. Being opposed by Hazael of Damascus, he overthrew the Syrian army and pursued it to the royal city and shut it up there, while he devastated the territory surrounding. But while there is no mention of his fighting with the Tyrians, Sidonians, and Israelites, he is said to have received tribute from them and "from Jehu, the son of Omri." This inscription occurs on the celebrated Black Obelisk discovered many years ago by Sir Henry Rawlinson in the ruins of Nimroud. On it are represented strings of captives with evident Jewish features, in the act of bringing their tribute to the Assyrian king. Now, though there is no mention in the sacred records of any defeat of Jehu by the Assyrians, nor of the paying of tribute by him, it is most natural that tribute should have been paid under the circumstances, for in the period subsequent to the battle of Karkar, Damascus had turned against Israel so that Israel's most likely method of getting even with Hazael would have been to make terms with his enemy and pay tribute, as she is said to have done to Shalmaneser.

The Moabite Stone

One of the most important discoveries, giving reality to Old Testament history is that of the Moabite Stone, discovered at Dibon, east of the Jordan in 1868, which was set up by King Mesha (about 850 B. C.) to signalize his deliverance from the yoke of Omri, king of Israel. The inscription is valuable for its witness to the civilized condition of the Moabites at that time and to the close similarity of their language to that of the Hebrews. From this inscription we learn that Omri, king of Israel, was compelled by the rebellion of Mesha to resubjugate Moab. After doing so, he and his son occupied the cities of Moab for a period of forty years, but after a series of battles, it was restored to Moab in the days of Mesha. Whereupon the cities and fortresses retaken were strengthened and the country repopulated, while the methods of warfare were similar to those practiced by Israel. On comparing this with 2 Kings 3:4–27, we find a parallel account that dovetails in with this in a most remarkable manner, although the biblical narrative treats lightly of the reconquest by Mesha, simply stating that, on account of the horror created by the idolatrous sacrifice of his eldest son upon the walls before them, the Israelites departed from the land and returned to their own country.

The Expedition of Shishak

In 1 Kings 14, we have a brief account of an expedition of Shishak, king of Egypt, against Jerusalem in the fifth year of Rehoboam. To the humiliation of Judah, it is told that Shishak succeeded in taking away the treasures of the house of Jehovah and of the king's house, among them the shields of gold which Solomon had made; so that Rehoboam made shields of brass in their stead. To this simple, unadorned account there is given a wonderful air of reality as one gazes on the southern wall of the court of the temple of Amen at Karnak and beholds the great expanse of sculptures and hieroglyphics that are there inscribed to represent this campaign of Shishak. One hundred and fifty-six places are enumerated among those that were captured, the northernmost being Megiddo. Among the places are Gaza, Adullam, Beth-Horon, Aijalon, Gibeon, and Juda-Malech, in which Dr. Birch is probably correct in recognizing the sacred city of Jerusalem—*Malech* being the word for royalty.

Israel in Egypt

The city of Tahpanhes in Egypt, mentioned by Jeremiah as the place to which the refugees fled to escape from Nebuchadnezzar, was discovered in 1886 in the mound known as Tel Defenneh in the northeastern portion of the delta where Mr. Flinders Petrie found not only evidences of the destruction of the palace caused by Nebuchadnezzar but apparently the very "brick work or pavement" spoken of in Jeremiah 43:8: "Take in your hands large stones and hide them in the mortar in the brickwork[58] that is at the entrance to Pharaoh's palace[59] in Tahpanhes, in the sight of the men of Judah, [10] and say to them, 'Thus says Jehovah of hosts, the God of Israel: Behold, I will send and take Nebuchadnezzar the king of Babylon, my servant, and I will set his throne above these stones that I have hidden, and he will spread his royal canopy over them."

A brick platform in partial ruins, corresponding to this description, was found by Mr. Petrie adjoining the fort "upon the northwest." In every respect, the arrangement corresponded to that indicated in the Book of Jeremiah.

Farther to the north, not far from Tahpanhes on the Tanitic branch of the Nile at the modern village of San, excavations revealed the ancient Egyptian capital Tanis, which went under the earlier name of Zoan, where the Pharaoh of the oppression frequently made his headquarters. According to the Psalmist, it was in the field of "Zoan" that Moses and Aaron wrought their wonders before Pharaoh, and, according to the Book of

---

[58] Or *brick pavement*
[59] Lit *house*

Numbers, "Hebron" was built only seven years before Zoan. As Hebron was a place of importance before Abraham's time, it is a matter of much significance that Zoan appears to have been an ancient city which was a favorite dwelling-place of the Hyksos, or Shepherd Kings, who preceded the period of the Exodus and were likely to be friendly to the Hebrews, thus giving greater credibility to the precise statements made in Numbers and to the whole narrative of the reception of the patriarchs in Egypt.

The Pharaoh of the oppression, "who knew not Joseph," is generally supposed to be Rameses II, the third king of the nineteenth dynasty, known among the Greeks as Sesostris, one of the greatest of the Egyptian monarchs. Among his most important expeditions was one directed against the tribes of Palestine and Syria, where, at the battle of Kadesh, east of the Lebanon Mountains, he encountered the Hittites. The encounter ended practically in a drawn battle, after which a treaty of peace was made. But the whole state of things revealed by this campaign and subsequent events shows that Palestine was in substantially the same condition of affairs which was found by the children of Israel when they occupied it shortly after, thus confirming the Scripture account.

This Rameses during his reign of sixty-seven years was among the greatest builders of the Egyptian monarchs. It is estimated that nearly half of the extant temples were built in his reign, among which are those at Karnak, Luxor, Abydos, Memphis, and Bubastis. The great Ramesseum at Thebes is also his work, and his name is found carved on almost every monument in Egypt. His oppression of the children of Israel was but an incident in his remarkable career. While engaged in his Asiatic campaigns, he naturally made his headquarters at Bubastis, in the land of Goshen, near where the old canal and the present railroad turn off from the delta toward the Bitter Lakes and the Gulf of Suez. Here the ruins of the temple referred to are of immense extent and include the fragments of innumerable statues and monuments that bear the impress of the great oppressor. At length, also, his mummy has been identified so that now we have a photograph of it that illustrates in all its lineaments the strong features of his character.

The Store Cities of Pithom and Rameses

But most interesting of all, in 1883, there were uncovered, a short distance east of Bubastis, the remains of vast vaults, which had evidently served as receptacles for storing grain preparatory to supplying military and other expeditions setting out for Palestine and the far East. Unwittingly, the engineers of the railroad had named the station Rameses. But from the inscriptions that were found, it is seen that its original name was Pithom, and its founder was none other than Rameses II, proving it to be the very place where it is said in the Bible that the children of Israel "built for Pharaoh store-cities, Pithom and Raamses" (Exodus 1:11), when the Egyptians "So they appointed taskmasters over them to afflict them with hard labor.[60] And they built for Pharaoh storage cities, Pithom and Raamses." It was in connection with the building of these cities that the oppression of the children of Israel reached its climax, when they were compelled (after the failure of the straw holding the brick together) to gather for themselves stubble that should serve the purpose of straw, and finally, when even the stubble failed, to make brick without straw (Exodus 5).

---

[60]Lit *their burdens*

Now, as these store pits at Pithom were uncovered by Mr. Petrie, they were found (unlike anything else in Egypt) to be built with *mortar*. Moreover, the lower layers were built of brick which contained straw, while the middle layers were made of brick in which stubble, instead of straw, had been used in their formation, and the upper layers were of brick made without straw. A more perfect circumstantial confirmation of the Bible account could not be imagined. Every point in the confirmation consists of unexpected discoveries. The use of mortar is elsewhere unknown in Ancient Egypt, as is the peculiar succession in the quality of the brick used in the construction of the walls.

Thus have all Egyptian explorations shown that the writer of the Pentateuch had such familiarity with the country, the civilization, and the history of Egypt as could have been obtained only by intimate, personal experience. The leaf that is here given is in its right place. It could not have been inserted except by a participant in the events or by direct Divine revelation.

The Hittites

In Joshua 1:4, the country between Lebanon and the Euphrates is called the land of the Hittites. In 2 Samuel 24:6, according to the reading of the Septuagint, the limit of Joab's conquests was that of "the Hittites of Kadesh," which is in Coele, Syria, some distance north of the present Baalbeck. Solomon is also said to have imported horses from "the kings of the Hittites," and when the Syrians were besieging Samaria, according to 2 Kings 7:6, they were alarmed from fear that the king of Israel had hired against them "the kings of the Hittites." These references imply the existence of a strong nation widely spread over the northern part of Syria and the regions beyond. At the same time frequent mention is made of Hittite families in Palestine itself. It was of a Hittite (Genesis 23:10) that Abraham bought his burying-place at Hebron. Bathsheba, the mother of Solomon, had been the wife of Uriah the Hittite, and Esau had two Hittite wives. Hittites are also mentioned as dwelling with the Jebusites and Amorites in the mountain region of Canaan.

Until the decipherment of the inscriptions on the monuments of Egypt and Assyria, the numerous references in the Bible to this mysterious people were unconfirmed by any other historical authorities, so many regarded the biblical statements as mythical and an indication of the general untrustworthiness of biblical history. A prominent English biblical critic declared not many years ago that an alliance between Egypt and the Hittites was as improbable as would be one at the present time between England and the Choctaws. But, alas for the over-confident critic, recent investigations have shown not only that such an alliance was natural but also that it actually occurred.

From the monuments of Egypt we learn that Thothmes III of the eighteenth dynasty in 1470 B. C. marched to the banks of the Euphrates and received tribute from "the Greater Hittites" to the amount of 3,200 pounds of silver and a "great piece of crystal." Seven years later, tribute was again sent from "the king of the Greater Hittite land." Later, Amenophis III and IV are said in the Tel el-Amarna tablets to have been constantly called upon to aid in repelling the attacks of the Hittite king, who came down from the north and made plans with the disaffected Canaanitish tribes in Palestine, while in B. C. 1343, Rameses the Great attempted to capture the Hittite capital at Kadesh, but was unsuccessful and came near losing his life in the attempt, extricating himself from an ambush only by most heroic deeds of valor. Four years later, a treaty of peace was signed between the

Hittites and the Egyptians, and a daughter of the Hittite king was given in marriage to Rameses.

The Assyrian monuments also bear abundant testimony to the prominence of the Hittites north and west of the Euphrates, of which the most prominent state was that with its capital at Carchemish in the time of Tiglath-pileser I, about 1100 B. C. In 854 B. C. Shalmaneser II included the kings of Israel, of Ammon, and of the Arabs among the "Hittite" princes whom he had subdued, thus bearing most emphatic testimony to the prominence they assumed in his estimation. The cuneiform inscriptions of Armenia also speak of numerous wars with the Hittites and describe "the land of the Hittites" as extending far westward from the banks of the Euphrates.

Hittite sculptures and inscriptions are now traced in abundance from Kadesh, in Coele Syria, westward to Lydia, in Asia Minor, and northward to the Black Sea beyond Marsovan. Indeed, the extensive ruins of Boghaz-Keui, seventy-five miles southwest of Marsovan, seem to mark the principal capital of the Hittites. Here, partial excavations have already revealed sculptures of high artistic order, representing deities, warriors and amazons, together with many hieroglyphs, which have not yet been translated. The inscriptions are written in both directions, from left to right, and then below back from right to left. Similar inscriptions are found in numerous other places. No clue to their meaning has yet been found, and even the class of languages to which they belong has not been discovered. But enough is known to show that the Hittites exerted considerable influence upon the later civilization that sprung up in Greece and on the western coasts of Asia Minor. It was through them that the emblem of the winged horse made its way into Europe.

The mural crown carved upon the head of some of the goddesses at Boghaz-Keui also passed into Grecian sculpture; while the remarkable lions sculptured over the gate at Mycenae are thought to represent Hittite, rather than Babylonian art.

It is impossible to overestimate the value of this testimony in confirmation of the correctness of biblical history. It shows conclusively that the silence of profane historians regarding facts stated by the biblical writers is of small account, in face of direct statements made by the biblical historians. All the doubts entertained in former times concerning the accuracy of the numerous biblical statements concerning the Hittites is now seen to be due to our ignorance. It was pure ignorance, not superior knowledge, that led so many to discredit these representations. When shall we learn the inconclusiveness of negative testimony?

The Tel el-Armana Tablets

In 1887 some Arabs discovered a wonderful collection of tablets at Tel el-Amarna, an obscure settlement on the east bank of the Nile about two hundred miles above Cairo and about as far below Thebes. The clay tablets had been written over with cuneiform inscriptions, such as are found in Babylonia, and then burned, so as to be indestructible. When the inscriptions were deciphered, it appeared that they were a collection of official letters that had been sent shortly before 1300 B. C. to the last kings of the eighteenth dynasty.

There were in all about three hundred letters, most of which were from officers of the Egyptian army scattered over Palestine to maintain the Egyptian rule that had been established by the preceding kings, most prominent of whom was Tahutimes III, who reigned about one hundred years earlier. But many of the letters were from the kings and princes of Babylonia. What surprised the world most, however, was that this correspondence was carried on, not in the hieroglyphic script of Egypt, but in the cuneiform script of Babylonia.

All this was partly explained when more became known about the character of the Egyptian king to whom the letters were addressed. His original title was Amenhotep IV, indicating that he was a priest of the sun god who is worshiped at Thebes. But in his anxiety to introduce religious reform, he changed his name to Aken-Aten,—Aten being the name of the deity worshiped at Heliopolis, near Cairo, where Joseph got his wife. The efforts of Aken-Aten to transform the religious worship of Egypt were prodigious. To accomplish it, he removed his capital from Thebes to Tel el-Amarna and there collected literary men, artists, and architects in great numbers and erected temples and palaces, which, after being buried in the sand with all their treasures for more than three thousand years, were discovered by some wandering Arabs twenty-two years ago.

A number of the longest and most interesting of the letters are those that passed between the courts of Egypt and those of Babylonia. It appears that not only did Aken-Aten marry a daughter of the Babylonian king but also his mother and grandmother were members of the royal family in Babylonia, and one of the daughters of the king of Egypt had been sent to Babylonia to become the wife of the king. All this comes out in the letters that passed back and forth relating to the dowry to be bestowed upon these daughters and relating to their health and welfare.

From these letters we learn that, although the king of Babylon had sent his sister to be the wife of the king of Egypt, that was not sufficient. The king of Egypt requested also the daughter of the king of Babylon. This led the king of Babylon to say that he did not know how his sister was treated; in fact, he did not know whether she was alive, for he could not tell whether or not to believe the evidence he received. In response, the king of Egypt wrote, "Why don't you send someone who knows your sister that you can trust?" Whereupon the royal correspondents break off into discussions concerning the gifts that are to pass between the two in consideration of their friendship and intimate relations.

Syria and Palestine were at this time also, as at the present day, infested by robbers, and the messengers passing between these royal houses were occasionally delayed. Whereupon the one who suffered loss would claim damages from the other if it was in his territory, because he had not properly protected the road. An interesting thing in connection with one of these robberies is that it took place at "Hannathon," one of the border towns mentioned in Joshua 19:14, but of which nothing else was ever known until it appeared in this unexpected manner.

Most of the Tel el-Amarna letters, however, consist of those which were addressed to the king of Egypt (Amenhotep IV) by his officers who were attempting to hold the Egyptian fortresses in Syria and Palestine against various enemies who were pressing hard upon them. Among these were the Hittites, of whom we hear so much in later times, and who, coming down from the far north, were gradually extending their colonies into Palestine and usurping control over the northern part of the country.

About sixty of the letters are from an officer named Rib-addi, who is most profuse in his expressions of humility and loyalty, addressing the king as "his lord" and "sun," and calling himself the "footstool of the king's feet," and saying that he "prostrates himself seven times seven times at his feet." He complains, however, that he is not properly supported in his efforts to defend the provinces of the king and is constantly wanting more soldiers, more cavalry, more money, more provisions, and more everything. So frequent are his importunities that the king finally tells him that if he will write less and fight more he would be better pleased, and that there would be more hopes of his maintaining his power. But Rib-addi says that he is being betrayed by the "curs" that are surrounding him, who represent the other countries that pretend to be friendly to Egypt but are not.

From this correspondence and letters from the south of Palestine, it is made plain that the Egyptian power was fast losing its hold of the country, thus preparing the way for the condition of things which prevailed a century or two later, when Joshua took possession of the promised land and found no resistance except from a number of disorganized tribes then in possession.

In this varied correspondence a large number of places are mentioned with which we are familiar in Bible history, among them Damascus, Sidon, Lachish, Ashkelon, Gaza, Joppa, and Jerusalem. Indeed, several of the letters are written from Jerusalem by one Abd-hiba, who complains that someone is slandering him to the king, charging that he was in revolt against his lord. This, he says, the king ought to know is absurd, from the fact that "neither my father nor my mother appointed me to this place. The strong arm of the king inaugurated me in my father's territory. Why should I commit an offense against my lord, the king?" The argument being that, as his office is not hereditary but one which is held by the king's favor and appointment, his loyalty should be above question.

A single one of these Jerusalem letters may suffice for an illustration: "To My Lord the King:—Abd-hiba, your servant. At the feet of my lord the king, seven and seven times I fall. Behold the deed which Milki-il and Suardata have done against the land of my lord the king—they have hired the soldiers of Gazri, of Gimti and of Kilti, and have taken the territory of Rubuti. The territory of the king is lost to Habiri. And now, indeed, a city of the territory of Jerusalem, called Bit-Ninib, one of the cities of the king, has been lost to the people of Kilti. Let the king listen to Abd-hiba, his servant, and send troops that I may bring back the king's land to the king. For if there are no troops, the land of the king will be lost to the Habiri. This is the deed of Suardata and Milki-il * * * [defective], and let the king take care of his land."

The discovery of these Tel el-Amarna letters came like a flash of lightning upon the scholarly world. In this case the overturning of a few spadefuls of earth let in a flood of light upon the darkest portion of ancient history and in every way confirmed the Bible story.

As an official letter-writer, Rib-addi has had few equals, and he wrote on material that the more it was burned the longer it lasted. Those who think that a history of Israel could not have been written in Moses' time, and that, if written, it could not have been preserved, are reasoning without due knowledge of the facts. Considering the habits of the time, it would have been well nigh a miracle if Moses and his band of associates coming out of Egypt had not left upon imperishable clay tablets a record of the striking events through which they passed.

Accuracy of Geographical Details

Many persons doubtless wonder why it is that the Bible so abounds in "uninteresting" lists of names both of persons and places that seem to have no relation to modern times or current events. Such, however, will cease to wonder when they come to see the relation these lists sustain to our confidence in the trustworthiness of the records containing them. They are like the watermarks in paper that bear indelible evidence of the time and place of manufacture. If, furthermore, one should contemplate personal explorations in Egypt, Canaan, or Babylonia, he would find that for his purposes the most interesting and important portions of the Bible would be these very lists of the names of persons and places, which seemed to encumber the historical books of the Old Testament.

One of the most striking peculiarities of the Bible is the "long look" toward the permanent wants of mankind that is everywhere manifested in its preparation; so that it circulates best in its entirety. No man knows enough to abridge the Bible without impairing its usefulness. The parts that the reviser would cut out as superfluous are sure, very soon, to be found to be "the more necessary." If we find that we have not any use for any portion of the Bible, the reason doubtless is that we have not lived long enough or have not had sufficiently wide experience to test its merits in all particulars.

Gezer was an important place in Joshua's time, but it afterward became a heap of ruins, and its location was unknown until 1870, when M. Clermont-Ganneau discovered the site in Tel Jezer and, on excavating it, found three inscriptions that, after interpretation, read "Boundary of Gezer."

Among the places conquered by Joshua one of the most important and difficult to capture was Lachish (Joshua 10:31). This has but recently been identified in Tel el-Hesy, about eighteen miles northeast of Gaza. Extensive excavations, first in 1890 by Dr. Flinders Petrie, and finally by Dr. Bliss, found a succession of ruins, one below the other, the lower foundations of which extended back to about 1700 B. C.—some time before the period of conquest, showing at that time a walled city of great strength. In the debris somewhat higher than this there was found a tablet with cuneiform inscriptions corresponding to the Tel el-Amarna tablets, which are known to have been sent to Egypt from this region about 1400 B. C. At a later period, in the time of Sennacherib, Lachish was assaulted and taken by the Assyrian army, and the account of the siege forms one of the most conspicuous scenes on the walls of Sennacherib's palace in Nineveh. These sculptures are now in the British Museum.

Among the places mentioned in the Tel el-Amarna correspondence from which letters were sent to Egypt about 1400 B. C., are Gebal, Beirut, Tyre, Accho (Acre), Hazor, Joppha, Ashkelon, Makkadah, Lachish, Gezer, Jerusalem; while mention is also made of Rabbah, Sarepta, Ashtaroth, Gaza, Gath, Bethshemesh, all of which are familiar names, showing that the Palestine of Joshua is the Palestine known to Egypt in the preceding century. Two hundred years before this (about 1600 B. C.) Thothmes III conquered Palestine and gives in an inscription the names of more than fifty towns that can be confidently identified with those in the Book of Joshua.

Finally, the forty-two stations named in Numbers 33 as camping places for the children of Israel on their way to Palestine, while they cannot all of them be identified, can be determined in sufficient numbers to show that it is not a fictitious list nor a mere pilgrim's diary, since the scenes of greatest interest, like the region immediately about

Mount Sinai, are specially adapted to the great transactions recorded as taking place. Besides, it is incredible that a writer of fiction should have encumbered his pages with such a barren catalogue of places. But as part of the great historical movement they are perfectly appropriate.

This conformity of newly discovered facts to the narrative of Sacred Scripture confirms our confidence in the main testimony; just as the consistency of a witness in a cross-examination upon minor and incidental points establishes confidence in his general testimony. The late Sir Walter Besant, in addition to his other literary and philanthropic labors, was for many years secretary of the Palestine Exploration Fund. In reply to the inquiry whether the work of the survey under his direction sustained the historical character of the Old Testament, he says: "To my mind, absolute truth in local details, a thing which cannot possibly be invented, when it is spread over a history covering many centuries, is proof almost absolute as to the truth of the things related." Such proof we have for every part of the Bible.

Genesis 14

The fourteenth chapter of Genesis relates that "In the days of Amraphel, king of Shinar, Arioch, king of Ellasar, Chedorlaomer, king of Elam, and Tidal, king of Goiim (nations), they made war with Bera, king of Sodom, and with Bersha, king of Gomorrah, and Shinab, king of Admah, and Shemeber, king of Zeboim, and the king of Bela (the same is Zoar)." The Babylonian kings were successful and the region about the Dead Sea was subject to them for twelve years, when a rebellion was instigated and in the following year Chedorlaomer and the kings that were with him appeared on the scene and, after capturing numerous surrounding cities, joined battle with the rebellious allies in the vale of Siddim, which was full of slime pits. The victory of Chedorlaomer was complete, and after capturing Lot and his goods in Sodom, he started homeward by way of Damascus, near the place Abraham overtook him, and by a successful stratagem scattered his forces by night and recovered Lot and his goods. This story, told with so many details that its refutation, would be easy if it were not true to the facts and if there were contemporary records with which to compare it, has been a point of ridicule of the higher critics of the Wellhausen school, Professor Nöldeke confidently declaring as late as 1869 that criticism had forever disproved its claim to be historical. But here again the inscriptions on the monuments of Babylonia have come to the rescue of the sacred historian, if, indeed, he were in need of rescue. For where general ignorance was so profound forty years ago, true modesty should have suggested caution in the expression of positive opinions in contradiction to such a detailed historical statement as this is.

From the inscriptions already discovered and deciphered in the Valley of the Euphrates, it is now shown beyond reasonable doubt that the four kings mentioned in the Bible as joining in this expedition are not, as was freely said, "etymological inventions," but real historical persons. Amraphel is identified as the Hammurabi whose marvelous code of laws was so recently discovered by De Morgan at Susa. The "H" in the latter word simply expresses the rough breathing so well known in Hebrew. The "p" in the biblical name has taken the place of "b" by a well-recognized law of phonetic change. "Amrap" is equivalent to "Hamrab." The addition of "il" in the biblical name is probably the suffix of the divine name, like "el" in Israel.

Hammurabi is now known to have had his capital at Babylon at the time of Abraham. Until recently, this chronology was disputed so that the editors and contributors of the *New Schaff-Herzog Cyclopedia* dogmatically asserted that as Abraham lived nearly 300 years later than Hammurabi, the biblical story must be unhistorical. Hardly had these statements been printed, however, when Dr. King of the British Museum discovered indisputable evidence that two of the dynasties that formerly had been reckoned as consecutive were, in fact, contemporaneous, thus making it easy to bring Hammurabi's time down exactly to that of Abraham.

Chedorlaomer is pretty certainly identified as Kudur-Lagamar (servant of Lagamar, one of the principal Elamite gods). Kudur-Lagamar was king of Elam, and was either the father or the brother of Kudur-Mabug, whose son, Eri-Aku (Arioch), reigned over Larsa and Ur, and other cities of southern Babylonia. He speaks of Kudur-Mabug "as the father of the land of the Amorites," *i.e.*, of Palestine and Syria.

Tidal, "king of nations," was supposed by Dr. Pinches to be referred to on a late tablet in connection with Chedorlaomer and Arioch under the name Tudghula, who are said, together, to have "attacked and spoiled Babylon."

However much doubt there may be about the identification of some of these names, the main points are established, revealing a condition of things just such as is implied by the biblical narrative. Arioch styles himself king of Shumer and Accad, which embraced Babylon, where Amraphel (Hammurabi) was in his early years subject to him. This furnishes a reason for the association of Chedorlaomer and Amraphel in a campaign against the rebellious subjects in Palestine. Again, Kudur-Mabug, the father of Arioch, styles himself "Prince of the land of Amurru," *i.e.*, of Palestine and Syria. Moreover, for a long period before, kings from Babylonia had claimed possession of the whole eastern shore of the Mediterranean, including the Sinaitic Peninsula.

In light of these well-attested facts, one reads with astonishment the following words of Wellhausen, written no longer ago than 1889: "That four kings from the Persian Gulf should, 'in the time of Abraham,' have made an incursion into the Sinaitic Peninsula, that they should on this occasion have attacked five kinglets on the Dead Sea Littoral and have carried them off prisoners, and finally that Abraham should have set out in pursuit of the retreating victors, accompanied by 318 men servants, and have forced them to disgorge their prey,—all these incidents are sheer impossibilities gain nothing in credibility from the fact that they are placed in a world that had passed away."

And we can have little respect for the logic of a later scholar (George Adam Smith), who can write the following: "We must admit that while archæology has richly illustrated the possibility of the main outlines of the Book of Genesis from Abraham to Joseph, it has not one whit of proof to offer for the personal existence or the characters of the patriarchs themselves. This is the whole change archæology has wrought; it has given us a background and an atmosphere for the stories of Genesis; it is unable to recall or certify their heroes."

But the name Abraham does appear in tablets of the age of Hammurabi. (See Professor George Barton in *Journal of Biblical Literature*, Vol. 28, 1909, p. 153.) It is true that this evidently is not the Abraham of the Bible but that of a small farmer who had rented land of a well-to-do land owner. The preservation of his name is due to the fact that the most of the tablets preserved contain contracts relating to the business of the times. There is little reason to expect that we should find a definite reference to the Abraham who in early life migrated from his native land. But it is of a good deal of significance that his name appears to have been a common one in the time and place of his nativity.

In considering the arguments in the case, it is important to keep in mind that where so few facts are known, and general ignorance is so great, negative evidence is of small account, while every scrap of positive evidence has great weight. The burden of proof in such cases falls upon those who dispute the positive evidence. For example, in the article above referred to, Professor Barton argues that it is not "quite certain" that Arioch (Eri-Agu) was a real Babylonian king. But he admits that our ignorance is such that we must admit its "possibility." Dr. Barton further argues that "we have as yet no evidence from the inscriptions that Arad-Sin, even if he were called Iri-Agu, ever had anything to do with Hammurabi." He adds, "Of course, it is possible that he may have had, as their reigns must have overlapped, but that remains to be proved."

All such reasoning (and there is any amount of it in the critics of the prevalent school) reveals a lamentable lack in their logical training. When we have a reputable document containing positive historical statements which are shown by circumstantial evidence to be possible, that is all we need to accept them as true. When, further, we find a great amount of circumstantial evidence positively showing that the statements conform to the conditions of time and place, so far as we know them, this adds immensely to the weight of the testimony. We never can fill in all the background of any historical fact. But if the statement of it fits into the background so far as we can fill it in, we should accept the fact until positive contrary evidence is produced.

No supposition can be more extravagant than that which Professor Barton seems to accept (which is that of the German critic, Meyer) that a Jew, more than 1,000 years after the event, obtained in Babylon the amount of exact information concerning the conditions in Babylonia in Abraham's time, found in Genesis 14 and interpolated the story of Chedorlaomer's expedition into the background thus furnished. To entertain such a supposition discredits the prevalent critical scholarship rather than the Sacred Scriptures.

Present space forbids further enumeration of particulars. It is sufficient to say that while many more positive confirmations of the seemingly improbable statements of the sacred historians can be adduced, there have been no discoveries which necessarily contravene their statements. The cases already enumerated relate to such widely separated times and places and furnish explanations so unexpected, yet natural, to difficulties that have been thought insuperable, that their testimony cannot be ignored or rejected. That this history should be confirmed in so many cases and in such a remarkable manner by monuments uncovered 3,000 years after their erection can be nothing else than providential.

Surely, God has seen to it that the failing faith of these later days should not be left to grope in darkness. When the faith of many was waning and many heralds of truth were tempted to speak with uncertain sound, the very stones have cried out with a voice that only the deaf could fail to hear. Both in the writing and in the preservation of the Bible, we behold the handiwork of God.

CHAPTER XVII My Personal Experience with Higher Criticism

J. J. Reeve

The purpose of this chapter is to state in a very brief way the influences that led me to accept certain views of the "Higher Criticism," and after further consideration, to reject them. Necessarily the reasons for rejecting will be given at greater length than those for accepting. Space will not permit me to mention names of persons, books, articles and various other influences that produce these results. I confine myself to an outline of the mental processes, which resulted from my contact with the Critical Movement.

In outlining this change of view, I shall deal with:

I. The Presuppositions of the Higher Criticism

These presuppositions and assumptions are the determining elements in the entire movement. Once they are understood, it is not difficult to understand the higher critics. It is their philosophy or worldview that is responsible for all their speculations and theories. Their mental attitude toward the world and its phenomena is the same as their attitude toward the Bible and the religion therein revealed. These presuppositions appealed to me very strongly. Having spent some time at one of the great American universities, thus coming in contact with some of the leading minds of the country, I was presented ably and attractively with the critical view. Though resisted for a time, the forcefulness of the teaching and influence of the university atmosphere largely won my assent. The critics seemed to have the logic of things on their side. The results to which they had arrived seemed inevitable.

But upon closer thinking, I saw that the whole movement with its conclusions was the result of the adoption of the hypothesis of evolution. My professors had accepted this view and were thoroughly convinced of its correctness as a working hypothesis. Thus, I was made to feel the power of this hypothesis and to adopt it. This worldview is wonderfully fascinating and almost compelling. The vision of a cosmos developing from the lowest types and stages upward through beast and man to higher and better man is enchanting and almost overwhelming. That there is a grain of truth in all this most thinkers will concede. One can hardly refuse to believe that through the ages "An increasing purpose runs," that there is "One God, one law, one element, and one far-off divine event to which the whole creation moves." This worldview had at first a charm and witchery that was almost intoxicating. It created more of a *revolution* than an *evolution*, in my thinking. But more careful consideration convinced me that the little truth in it served to sugar-coat and give plausibility to some deadly errors that lurked within. I saw that the hypothesis did not apply to a great part of the world's phenomena.

That this theory of evolution underlies and is the inspiration of the higher criticism goes without saying. That there is a grain of truth in it we may admit or not, as we see fit, but the whole question is, what kind of evolution is it that has given rise to this criticism. There are many varieties of the theory. There is the Idealism of Hegel, and the Materialism of Haeckel; a theistic evolution and an antitheistic; the view that it is God's only method, and the view that it is only one of God's methods; the theory that includes a Creator and the theory that excludes Him; the deistic evolution, which starts the world with God, who then withdraws and leaves it a closed system of cause and effect, antecedent and consequent, which admits of no break or change in the natural process. There is also the theory that on the whole there is progress, but allowance must be made for retrogression and degeneration. This admits of the direct action of God in arresting the downward process and reversing the current; that is, there is an evolution through revelation, etc., rather than a revelation by evolution.

On examining the evolution of the leaders of the Critical School, I found that it was of a naturalistic or practically deistic kind. All natural and mental phenomena are in a closed system of cause and effect, and the hypothesis applies universally to religion and revelation as well as to mechanisms.

This type of evolution may not be accepted by all adherents of the Critical School, but it is substantially the view of the leaders, Reuss, Graf, Vatke, Kuenen and Wellhausen. To them all nature and history are a product of forces within and in process of development. There has not been and could not be any direct action of God upon man, there could be no break in the chain of cause and effect, of antecedent and consequent. Hence there can be no miracle or anything of what is known as the supernatural. There could be no "interference" in any way with the natural course of events or "injection" of any power into the cosmic process from without; God is shut up to the one method of bringing things to pass. He is thus little more than a prisoner in His own cosmos.

Thus I discovered that the Critical Movement was essentially and fundamentally anti-supernatural and anti-miraculous. According to it all religious movements are human developments along natural and materialistic lines. The religion of Israel and the Bible is no exception, as there can be no exception to this principle. The revelation contained in the Bible is, strictly speaking, no *revelation*; it is a natural development with God in the cosmic process behind it, but yet a steady, straight-lined, mechanical development such as can be traced step by step as a flight of stairs may be measured by a foot-rule. There could have been no epoch-making revelation, no revivals and lapses, no marvelous exhibitions of divine power, no real redemption. With these foregone conclusions fixed in their minds, the entire question is practically settled beforehand. As it is transparently clear that the Bible on the face of it does not correspond to this view, it must be rearranged so as to correspond to it. To do this, they must deny point-blank the claims and statements of most of the Bible writers.

Now, if the Bible claims to be anything, it claims to be a revelation from God—a miraculous or supernatural book, recording the numerous direct acts of God in nature and history, and His interference with the natural course of events. Are the writers of the Bible correct, or are the critics? It is impossible that both should be right.

Reasoning thus, it became perfectly clear to me that the presuppositions and beliefs of the Bible writers and of the critics were absolutely contradictory. To maintain that the modern view is a development and advance upon the Biblical view, is absurd. No presupposition can develop a presupposition that contradicts and nullifies it. To say that the critical position and the Biblical position, or the traditional evangelical view which is the same as the Biblical, are reconcilable is the most foolish delusion. Kuenen and others have recognized this contradiction and have acknowledged it, not hesitating to set aside the Biblical view. Many of their disciples have failed to see as clearly as their masters. They think the two can be combined. I was of the same opinion myself, but further reflection showed this to be an impossibility. I thought it possible to accept the results of the higher criticism without accepting its presuppositions. This is saying that one can accept as valid and true the results of a process and at the same time deny the validity of the process itself. But doesn't this involve an inner contradiction and absurdity? If I accept the results of the Kuenen-Wellhausen hypothesis as correct, then I accept as correct the methods and processes that led to these results, and if I accept these methods, I also accept the presuppositions which give rise to these methods.

If the "assured results" of which the critics are so fond of boasting are true, then the naturalistic evolution hypothesis that produced these results is correct. Then it is impossible to accept the miraculous or supernatural; the Bible as an authoritative record of supernatural revelation is completely upset, and its claims regarding itself are false and misleading. I can see no way of escaping these conclusions. There is no possible middle ground as I once fondly imagined there was. Thus, I was compelled to conclude that although there is some truth in the evolutionary view of the world, yet as an explanation of history and revelation it is utterly inadequate, so inadequate as to be erroneous and false. A worldview must be broad enough to admit of all the facts of history and experience. Even then it is only a human point of view and necessarily imperfect. Will any one dare to say that the evolutionary hypothesis is divine? Then we would have a Bible and a philosophy both claiming to be divine and absolutely contradicting each other. To attempt to eliminate the miraculous and supernatural from the Bible and accept the remainder as divine is impossible, for they are all one and inextricably woven together. In either case the Bible is robbed of its claims to authority. Some critics do not hesitate to deny its authority and cut themselves loose from historical Christianity.

However, in spite of the serious faults of the higher criticism, it has given rise to what is known as the scientific and historical method in the study of the Old Testament. This method is destined to stay and render invaluable aid. To the scholarly mind its appeal is irresistible. Only in the light of the historical occasion upon which it was produced, can the Old Testament be properly understood. A flood of light has already been poured in upon these writings. The scientific spirit which gave rise to it is one of the noblest instincts in the intellectual life of man. It is a thirst for the real and the true, that will be satisfied with nothing else.

But, noble as is this scientific spirit, and invaluable as is the historical method, there are subtle dangers in connection with them. Everything depends upon the presuppositions with which we use the method. A certain mental attitude must be in place. What shall it be? A materialistic evolution such as Kuenen and his confreres or a theistic evolution that admits the supernatural? Investigating in the mental attitude of the first of these, the scholar will inevitably arrive at or accept the results of the critics. Another, working at the same problem with Christian presuppositions will arrive at very different conclusions.

Shall we have the point of view of the Christian or the critic? I found that the critics' claim to possess the only really scientific method was slightly true but largely false. Their results were scientific because they fitted the hypothesis. The Christan scholar with his broader presuppositions was peremptorily ruled out of court. Anything savoring of the miraculous, etc., could not be scientific to the critic, and hence it could not be true, therefore, it must be discarded or branded as myth, legend, poesy, saga, etc. Such narrowness of view is scarcely credible on the part of scholars who claim to be so broad and liberal.

Another question confronted me. How can so many Christian scholars and preachers accept the views of the critics and still adhere to evangelical Christianity with intense devotion? As we have seen, to accept the results of higher criticism is to accept the methods and presuppositions that produced these results. To accept their assumptions is to accept a naturalistic evolution, which is fundamentally contradictory to the biblical and Christian point of view. Therefore, it is essentially contradictory to Christianity, for what is the latter if it is not a supernaturally revealed knowledge of the plan of salvation, with supernatural power to effectuate that salvation? All who have experienced the power of Christianity will assent to this definition. How then can Christians who are higher critics escape endorsing the presuppositions of the critics? There is an inner contradiction between the assumptions of their scientific reason and the assumptions of their religious faith. A careful study of the attitude of these mediating critics, as they are called, has revealed a sense of contradiction somewhere of which they are vaguely conscious. They maintain their attitude by an inconsistency. Thus, they have many difficulties they cannot explain. This inner contradiction runs through much of their exegesis, and they wonder that evangelical Christians do not accept their views. Already many of them are not quite so sure of their "assured results" as they were. Many evangelical Christians do not accept these views because they can "see through" them.

The second line of thinking that led me to reject the critics' view was a consideration of the following.

II. Their Methods

At first, I was enthusiastic over the method. At last, we had the correct method that will in time solve all difficulties. Let it be readily granted that the historical method has settled many difficulties and will continue to do so. Yet the whole question lies in the attitude of mind a man brings to the task. Among the critics, their hypothesis is absolute and dominates every attempt to understand the record, shapes every conclusion, arranges and rearranges the facts in its own order, discards what does not fit or reshapes it to fit. The critics may deny this but their treatment of the Old Testament is too well known to need any proof of it. The use of the redactor is a case in point. This purely imaginary being, unhistorical and unscientific, is brought into requisition at almost every difficulty. It is acknowledged that at times he acts in a manner wholly inexplicable. To assume such a person interjecting names of God, changing names and making explanations to suit the purposes of their hypothesis and imagination is the very negation of science, notwithstanding their boast of a scientific method. Their minds seem to be in abject slavery to their theory. No reason is more impervious to facts than one preoccupied with a theory that does not agree with these facts. Their mental attitude being biased and partial, their methods are partial and the results very one-sided and untrustworthy. They give more credence to the guesses of some so-called scholar, a clay tablet, a heathen king's boast, or a rude drawing in stone, than to the Scripture record. They feel instinctively that to accept the Bible statements would be the ruin of their hypothesis, and what they call their hard-won historical method. In this, their instinct is true. The Bible and their hypothesis are irreconcilable. As their theory must not be interfered with, since it is identical with the truth itself, the Bible must stand aside in the interests of truth.

For this reason they deny all historicity to Genesis 1–11, the stories of Creation, the Fall, the Flood, etc. No theory of naturalistic evolution can possibly admit the truth of these chapters. Likewise, there is but a substratum of truth in the stories of Abraham, Isaac, Jacob, Joseph, and Moses. Nearly all legislation is denied to the latter, because it represents too rapid an advance or a stage too advanced. But is such the case? Centuries before Moses, laws, government, civilization, culture, art, education, religion, temples, ritual, and priesthood had flourished in Babylonia and Egypt and were a chief factor in the education of Moses.

With all this previous development upon which to build, what objections to ascribing these laws to Moses, who, during the forty years under divine guidance, selected, purified, heightened, and adopted such laws as best served the needs of the people. The development of external laws and customs had preceded Moses, and there is no need to suppose a development afterward in the history of the people; that history records the fitful attempts at the assimilation of these laws. To maintain that they were at first put in the exact form in which they have come down to us is wholly unnecessary and contrary to certain facts in the records themselves. But to my mind one of the greatest weaknesses of the critical position is that because there is little or no mention of the laws in the history that follows the death of Moses, therefore these laws could not have existed. To the critic this is one of the strongest arguments in his favor. Now he has found out how to make the history and the laws correspond. But does the non-mention or non-observance of a law prove its non-existence? All history shows that such is not the case. Moreover, the books of Joshua, Judges, and Samuel make no pretence at giving a complete detailed history. If non-mention or non-observance were proof of non-existence, then the Book of the Covenant and Deuteronomy could not have existed until the return from Exile; for the laws against idolatry were not carried out until then. Apply this same method of reasoning to laws in general and the most absurd results will follow. The Decalogue could never have existed, for all of its laws are constantly being broken. No New Testament could have existed through the Dark Ages, for almost every precept in it was violated during that period. The facts of life plainly show that men with the law of God in their hands will continually violate them. But why didn't Joshua and those succeeding him for several centuries carry out the law of Moses? The answer is obvious. The circumstances did not permit it, and no one, not even Moses, had any idea of the law being fully observed at once. He looked forward to a time when they should be settled and should have a capital and central sanctuary.

Moreover, a large portion of the laws was intended for the priest alone and may have been observed. The laws were flexible and to be fulfilled as the circumstances permitted. If the Book of Deuteronomy could not be observed, the Book of the Covenant could be followed. Changes and modifications were purposely made by Moses to meet the demands of the changing circumstances. If the non-fulfillment of these laws proved their non-existence, then the Book of the Covenant and Deuteronomy were not in existence in the time of Jehoiakim, for idolatry was then rampant.

By its arbitrary methods, modern criticism does wholesale violence to the record of the discovery of the Law Book as recorded in 2 Kings 22:8–20. It denies any real discovery, distinctly implies fraud upon the part of the writers, assumes a far too easy deception of the king, the prophetess, the king's counsellors, Jeremiah and the people. It implies a marvelous success in perpetrating this forged document on the people. The writers did evil that good might come, and God seems to have been behind it all and endorsed it. Such a transaction is utterly incredible. "The people would not hear Moses and the prophet, yet they were easily persuaded by a forged Mosaic document." The critics disagree among themselves regarding the authorship of the Book of Deuteronomy. Some maintain it was by the priestly class and some by the prophetic class, but there are insuperable objections to each. They have failed to show why there were so many laws incorporated in it which absolutely contradict a later date and why the Mosaic dress succeeded so well although contradictory to some of the genuinely Mosaic laws.

According to the critics also, Ezra perpetrated a tremendous fraud when he pawned off his completed Code as a Mosaic origin. That the people should accept it as genuinely Mosaic, although it increased their burdens and contradicted many laws previously known as Mosaic, is incredible. That such a people at such a time and under such circumstances could be so easily imposed upon and deceived, and that such a man as Ezra could perform such a colossal fraud and have it all succeed so well, seems inconceivable except by a person whose moral consciousness is numbed by some philosophical theory. According to the critics, the authors of Deuteronomy and the Levitical code not only produced such intensely religious books and laws but also were deliberate inventors and falsifiers of history, as well as deceivers of the people. What such views imply regarding the character of God, who is behind it all, we shall consider later.

Space does not permit me to more than refer to the J. E. P. analysis. That certain documents existed and were ultimately combined to make up the five books of Moses no one need doubt. It in no way detracts from their inspiration or authenticity to do so, nor does it in any way deny the essentially Mosaic origin of the legislation. But the J. E. P. analysis on the basis of the different names for God, I found to require such an arbitrary handling and artificial manipulation of the text, to need the help of so many redactors whose methods and motives are wholly inexplicable, with a multitude of exceptions to account for, that I was convinced the analysis could not be maintained. Astruc's clue in Exodus 6:3, which was the starting point for the analysis, cannot be made to decide the time of the use of the names of God, for the text is not perfectly certain. There is considerable difference between the two readings, "was known," and "made myself known." Even if God had not previously revealed Himself by the name Jehovah, that does not prove the name unknown or that God was not known by that name. And even if he had so revealed Himself, the earlier record would not be less authentic, for they were either written or rewritten and edited after the revelation to Moses in the light of a fuller revelation. Thus it was made perfectly clear that El, Elohim, El-Elyon, El-Shaddai, were identical with Jehovah.

The methods of the critics in regarding the earlier histories as little more than fiction and invention, to palm off certain laws as genuinely Mosaic, found some lodgment in my mind for a time. But the more I considered it, the more I was convinced that it was the critics who were the inventors and falsifiers. They were the ones who had such a superficial imagination, they could "manufacture" history at their "green tables" to suit their theories and were doing so fast and loose. They could create nations and empires out of a desert, and like the alchemists of the Middle Ages with their magic wand, transform all things into their own special and favorite metal. To charge the Scripture writers with this invention and falsification is grossly to malign them and slander the God that wrought through them. The quality of their products does not lend countenance to such a view, and it is abhorrent to the Christian consciousness. Such a conception cannot be long held by any whose moral and religious natures have not been dulled by their philosophical presuppositions.

The habit of discarding the Books of Chronicles, because they give no history of northern Israel, lay considerable emphasis upon the temple and priesthood, pass over the faults and sins of the kings, etc., and are therefore a biased, untrustworthy history. When the compiler of Chronicles covers the same history of Kings, he agrees with these histories substantially, though varying in some minor details. If he is reliable in this material, why not in the other material not found in Kings? The real reason is that he records many facts about the temple and its services that do not fit in with the critics' hypothesis, and therefore something must be done to discredit the Chronicler and get rid of his testimony.

But my third reason for rejecting the critical standpoint is:

III. The Spirit of the Movement

Grant that there is a genuine scientific interest underlying it all, the real question is, what is the standpoint of the scientific mind which investigates. What is authoritative with him? His philosophical theory and working hypothesis, or his religious faith? In other words, does his *religion* or *philosophy* control his thinking? Is it reason or faith that is supreme? Is his authority human or divine? There is no question here of having one without the other, that is, having faith without reason, for that is impossible. The question is, which is supreme? For some time I thought one could hold these views of the Old Testament and still retain his faith in evangelical Christianity. I found, however, that this could be done only by holding my philosophy in check and within certain limits. It could not be rigorously applied to all things. Two supreme things could not exist in the mind at the same time. If my theories were supreme, then I was following human reason, not faith, and was a rationalist to that extent. If the presuppositions of my religious faith were supreme and in accordance with the Biblical presuppositions and beliefs, then my philosophy must be held in abeyance.

The fundamentals of our religious faith, as known in the Bible and history, are a belief in divine revelation, the miraculous birth, the life and resurrection of Jesus Christ, the God-Man. Inseparable from these, there is also the fact of a supernatural power in regeneration. The philosophy of the critics cannot consistently make room for these. Thus the real question becomes one of authority; in other words, shall the scientific hypothesis be supreme in my thinking, or the presuppositions of the Christian faith? If I make my philosophical viewpoint supreme, then I am compelled to construe the Bible and Christianity through my theory and everything that may not fit into that theory must be rejected. This is the actual standpoint of the critic. His is a philosophical rather than a religious spirit. Such was Gnosticism in the early centuries. It construed Christ and Christianity through the categories of a Graeco-Oriental philosophy and thus was compelled to reject some of the essentials of Christianity. Such was the Scholasticism of the Middle Ages, which construed Christianity through the categories of the Aristotelian Logic and the Neo-platonic Philosophy. Such is the higher criticism, which construes everything through the hypothesis of evolution. The spirit of the movement is thus essentially scholastic and rationalistic.

It became more and more obvious to me that the movement was entirely intellectual, an attempt in reality to intellectualize all religious phenomena. I saw also that it was a partial and one-sided intellectualism, with a strong bias against the fundamental tenets of biblical Christianity. Such a movement does not produce the intellectual humility that belongs to the Christian mind. On the contrary, it is responsible for a vast amount of intellectual pride, an aristocracy of intellect with all the snobbery that usually accompanies that term. Do they not exactly correspond to Paul's word, "vainly puffed up in his fleshly mind and not holding fast the head . . .?" They have a splendid scorn for all opinions that do not agree with theirs. Under the spell of this sublime contempt, they think they can ignore anything that does not square with their evolutionary hypothesis.

The center of gravity of their thinking is in the theoretical not in the religious, in reason, not in faith. Supremely satisfied with its self-constituted authority, the mind thinks itself competent to criticise the Bible, the thinking of all the centuries, and even Jesus Christ Himself. The followers of this cult have their full share of the frailties of human nature. Rarely, if ever, can a thorough critic be an evangelist or even evangelistic; he is educational. How is it possible for a preacher to be a power for God, whose source of authority is his own reason and convictions? The Bible can scarcely contain more than good advice for such a man.

I was much impressed with their boast of having all scholarship on their side. It is very gratifying to feel oneself abreast with the times and in the front rank of thought. But some investigation and consideration led me to see that the boast of scholarship is tremendously overdone. Many leading scholars are with them, but a majority of the most reverent and judicious scholars are not. The arrogant boasts of these people would be very amusing, if they were not so influential. Certainly, most of the books put forth of late by Old Testament scholars are on their side, but there is a formidable list on the other side, and it is growing larger every day. Conservative scholarship is rapidly awakening, and, while it will retain the legitimate use of the invaluable historical method, will sweep from the field most of the speculations of the critics. A striking characteristic of these people is a persistent ignoring of what is written on the other side. They think to kill their antagonist by either ignoring or despising him. They treat their opponents something as Goliath treated David, and in the end the result will be similar. They have made no attempt to answer Robertson's *The Early Religion of Israel;* Orr's *The Problem of the Old Testament;* Wiener's *Studies in Biblical Law,* and *Studies in Pentateuchical Criticism,* etc. They still treat these books, which have undermined the very foundations of their theories, with the same magnificent scorn. There is a nemesis in such an attitude.

But the spirit of the critical movement manifests some very doubtful aspects in its practical working out among the pastors and churches. Adherents of this movement accept the spiritual oversight of churches which hold fast to the Biblical view of the Bible, while they know that their own views will undermine many of the most cherished beliefs of the churches. Many try to be critics and conservative at the same time. They would "run with the hare and hunt with the hounds," professing to be in full sympathy with evangelical Christianity while abiding their opportunity to inculcate their own views, which, as we have seen, is really to forsake the Christian standpoint. The morality of such conduct is, to say the least, very doubtful. It has led to much mischief among the churches and injury to the work. A preacher who has thoroughly imbibed these beliefs has no proper place in an evangelical Christian pulpit. Such a spirit is not according to the spirit of the religion they profess to believe.

But another weighty reason for rejecting the higher criticism is:

IV. A Consideration of Its Results

Ten or twenty years ago these scholars believed their views would immensely advance the cause of Christianity and true religion. They are by no means so sure of that now. It is not meeting with the universal acceptance they anticipated. Making a mere hypothesis the supreme thing in our thinking, we are forced to construe everything accordingly. Thus the Bible, the Christ and the religious experiences of men are subjected to the same scientific analysis. Carry this out to its logical conclusion and what would be the result? There would be all science and no religion. In the array of scientific facts all religion would be evaporated. God, Christ, the Bible, and all else would be reduced to a mathematical or chemical formula. This is the ideal and goal of the evolutionary hypothesis. The rationalist would rejoice at it, but the Christian mind shrinks with horror from it. The Christian consciousness perceives that a hypothesis that leads to such results is one of its deadliest foes.

Another danger also arises here. When one makes his philosophy his authority, it is not a long step until he makes himself his own god. His own reason becomes supreme in his thinking and this reason becomes his lord. This is the inevitable logic of the hypothesis mentioned, and some adherents of the school have taken this step. They recognize no authority but their own moral instincts and philosophical reason. Now, as the evolution theory makes all things exist only in a state of flux, or of becoming, God is therefore changing and developing, the Bible and Christ will be outgrown, Christianity itself will be left behind. Hence, there is no *absolute* truth, nothing in the moral religious world is fixed or certain. All truth is in solution; there is no cause upon which we can rely. There is no *absolute* standard of ethics, no *authority* in religion, every one is practically his own god. Jesus Christ is politely thanked for His services in the past, gallantly conducted to the confines of His world and bowed out as He is no longer needed, and His presence might be very troublesome to some people.

Such a religion is the very negation of Christianity, is a distinct reversion to heathenism. It may be a cultured and refined heathenism with a Christian veneer, but yet a genuine heathenism.

I am far from saying that all adherents of this school go to such lengths, but why do they not? Most of them had an early training under the best conservative influences which inculcated a wholesome reverence for the Bible as an authority in religion and morals. This training they can never fully outgrow. Many of them are of a good, sturdy religious ancestry, of rigid, conservative training and genuine religious experience. Under these influences they have acquired a strong hold upon Christianity and can never be removed from it. They hold a theoretical standpoint and a religious experience together, failing, I believe, to see the fundamental contradiction between them.

Slowly the Christian consciousness and scholarship are asserting themselves. Men are beginning to see how irreconcilable the two positions are, and there will be the inevitable split in the future. Churches are none too soon or too seriously alarmed. Christianity is beginning to see that its very existence is at stake in this subtle attempt to do away with the supernatural. I have seen the Unitarian, the Jew, the free thinker, and the Christian who has imbibed critical views, in thorough agreement on the Old Testament and its teachings. They can readily hobnob together, for the religious element becomes a lost quantity; the Bible itself becomes a plaything for the intellect, a merry-go-round for the mind partially intoxicated with its theory.

As has been already intimated, one of the results of the critical processes has been to rearrange the Bible according to its own point of view. This means that it has to a large extent set it aside as an authority. Such a result is serious enough, but a much more serious result follows. This is the reflection such a Bible casts upon the character and methods of God in His revelation of Himself to men. It will scarcely be doubted by even a radical critic, that the Bible is the most uplifting book in the world, that its religious teachings are the best the world has known.

If such be the case, it must reflect more of God's character and methods than any other book. The writers themselves must exemplify many of the traits of the God they write about. What then must be the methods of a holy and loving God? If He teaches men truth by parable or history or illustration, the one essential thing about these parables or histories is that they be true to life or history or nature. Can a God who is absolutely just and holy teach men truths about Himself by means of that which is false? Men may have taught truth by means of falsehoods and other instruments and perhaps succeeded, but God can hardly be legitimately conceived of as using any such means.

Jesus Christ taught the greatest of truths by means of parables, illustrations, etc., but every one was true to life or nature or history. The Christian consciousness, which is the highest expression of the religious life of mankind, can never conceive of Jesus as using that which was in itself untrue, as a vehicle to convey that which is true. In like manner, if God had anything to do with the Old Testament, would He make use of mere myths, legends, or falsified history that have no foundation in fact? Will God seek to uplift mankind by means of falsehood? Will He sanction the use of such dishonest means and pious frauds, such as a large part of the Pentateuch is, if the critics are right? Could He make use of such means for such a holy purpose and let His people feed on falsehood for centuries and centuries and deceive them into righteousness? Falsehood will not do God's will; only truth can do that. Is there nothing in the story of creation, of the fall, the flood, the call and promise to Abraham, the life of Jacob and Joseph and the great work of Moses? If all these things are not true to fact or to life, then God has been an arch-deceiver. This would apply to the finding of the Law in Josiah's time, and the giving of the law under Ezra. That such a lot of deceptive history should achieve such a success is most astonishing.

Is it possible that a holy God should be behind all this and promote righteousness thereby? This surely is conniving at evil and using methods unworthy of the name of God. To say that God was shut up to such a method is preposterous. Such a conception of God as is implied in the critical position is abhorrent to one who believes in a God of truth.

Perhaps the Book of Daniel at the hands of the critic best illustrates this point. No one can deny the religious quality of the book. It has sublime heights and depths and has had a mighty influence in the world. No one can read the book carefully and reverently without feeling its power. Yet according to the modern view, the first six or seven chapters have but a grain of truth in them. They picture in a wonderfully vivid manner the supernatural help of God in giving Daniel power to interpret dreams, in delivering from the fiery furnace, in saving from the lion's mouth, smiting King Nebuchadnezzar, etc., All this is high religious teaching, has had a great influence for good and was intended for a message from God to encourage faith. Yet, according to the critics these events had no foundation in fact; the supernatural did not take place, the supposed facts upon which these sublime religious lessons are based could never have occurred. Yet the God of truth has used such a book with such teaching to do great good in the world. He thus made abundant use of fiction and falsehood.

According to this view, He has also been deceiving the best people of the world for millenniums, using the false as though true. Such a God may be believed in by a critic, but the Christian consciousness revolts at it. It is worthy of a Zeus or perhaps the Demiurge of Marcion, but He is not the God of Israel, not the God and Father of Jesus Christ. "But," says the critic, "the religious lessons are great and good." Are they? Can a story or illustration or parable teach good religious lessons when it is in itself essentially untrue to nature, history and life? To assert such a thing would seem to imply a moral and religious blindness that is scarcely credible. It is true there are many grave difficulties in the book of Daniel, but are they as great as the moral difficulty implied in the critical view?

The foregoing embody my chief reasons for rejecting the position of the critical school with which I was once in sympathy. Their positions are not merely vagaries, they are essentially attempts to undermine revelation, the Bible and evangelical Christianity. If these views should ultimately prevail, Christianity will be set aside for what is known as the New Religion, which is not religion but a philosophy. All critics believe that traditional Christianity will largely, if not altogether, give place to the modern view, as it is called. But we maintain that traditional Christianity has the right of way. It must and will be somewhat modified by the conception of a developing revelation and the application of the historical method, but must prevail in all its essential features.

The Bible has a noble ancestry and a glorious history. Its writers are all on its side; the bulk of Jewish scholars of the past are in the procession; it has Jesus, the Son of God, in its ranks, with the apostles, prophets, the martyrs, the reformers, the theologians, the missionaries, and the great preachers and evangelists. The great mass of God's people are with it. I prefer to belong to that goodly company rather than with the heathen Porphyry, the pantheistic Spinoza, the immoral Astruc, the rationalistic Reuss, Vatke, Graf, Kuenen, and Wellhausen, with a multitude of their disciples of all grades. Theirs is a new traditionalism begun by those men and handed down to others in England and America. Most of these disciples owe their religious life and training almost entirely to the traditional view. The movement has quickened study of the Old Testament, has given a valuable method, a great many facts, a fresh point of view, but its extravagancies, its false assumptions and immoralities will in time be sloughed by the Christian consciousness as in the past it has sloughed off Gnosticism, Pantheism, Scholasticism and a host of other philosophical or scientific fads and fancies.

CHAPTER XVIII Bible Difficulties Explained

Edward D. Andrews

It seems that the charge that the Bible contradicts itself has increased more in the last 20 years. Generally, those making such claims are merely repeating what they have heard, because most have not even read the Bible, let alone done an in-depth study of it. I do not wish, however, to set aside all concerns as though they have no merit. There are many who raise legitimate questions that seem on the surface to be about well-founded contradiction. Sadly, these issues have caused many to lose their faith in God's Word. The purpose of this books is to assist its readers defend the Bible against Bible critics (1 Peter 3:15), to contend for the faith (Jude 1:3), and help those, who have begun to doubt (Jude 1:22-23).

Before we begin explaining things, let us jump right in, getting our feet wet, and deal with two major Bible difficulties, so we can see that there are reasonable, logical answers. After that, we will delve deeper into explaining Bible difficulties.

Is God permitting Human Sacrifice in Judges 11:30-31?

Judges 11:29-34, 37-41 English Standard Version (ESV) reads, "Then the Spirit of the Lord was upon Jephthah, and he passed through Gilead and Manasseh and passed on to Mizpah of Gilead, and from Mizpah of Gilead he passed on to the Ammonites. And Jephthah **made a vow** to the Lord and said, 'If you will give the Ammonites into my hand, then **whatever**[61] comes out from the doors of my house to meet me when I return in peace from the Ammonites shall be the Lord's, and I will offer it up for a burnt offering.' So Jephthah crossed over to the Ammonites to fight against them, and the Lord gave them into his hand. And he struck them from Aroer to the neighborhood of Minnith, twenty cities, and as far as Abel-keramim, with a great blow. So the Ammonites were subdued before the people of Israel.

Then Jephthah came to his home at Mizpah. And behold, **his daughter came out** to meet him with tambourines and with dances. She was his only child; besides her he had neither son nor daughter.

"So she said to her father, 'Let this thing be done for me: leave me alone two months, that I may go up and down on the mountains and weep for my virginity, I and my companions.' So he said, 'Go.' Then he sent her away for two months, and she departed, **she and her companions, and wept for her virginity** on the mountains. And at the end of two months, she returned to her father, who **did with her according to his vow that he had made**. She had never known a man [been intimate with a man], and it became a custom in Israel that the daughters of Israel went year by year to **lament [or commemorate] the daughter** of Jephthah the Gileadite four days in the year."

It is true; to infer that having the idea of an animal sacrifice would not have been an impressive vow, which the context requires. Human sacrifice would be repugnant, if we

---

[61] Whoever

are talking about taking a life. Jephthah had no sons, so he likely knew it was the daughter who would come to greet him.

First, the text does not say he killed his daughter. The idea of some that he did kill her is concluded only by an inference. While it is not good policy to interpret backward, using Paul on Judges, he does say humans are to be **"as a living sacrifice."** Therefore, Jephthah could have offered his daughter at the temple, "as a living sacrifice" in service, like Samuel.

This is not to be taken dismissively, because under Jewish backgrounds, it is no small thing to offer a **perpetual virginity** as a sacrifice. This would mean Jephthah's lineage would not be carried on; the family name was no more. Second, the context says she went out to weep for two months, not mourn her death. It says, "she left with her friends and **mourned her virginity**." If she was facing impending death, she could have married and spent that last two months as a married woman. There would be absolutely no reason for her to mourn her virginity, if she were not facing perpetual virginity (Exodus 38:8; 1 Samuel 2:22). Third, it was completely forbidden to offer a human sacrifice (Leviticus 18:21; 20:2-5; Deuteronomy 12:31; 18:10).

Imagine an Israelite believing that he could please God with a human sacrifice. To do so would have been a rejection of Jehovah's Sovereignty (the very person you are asking for help), and a rejection of the Law that made them a special people. Worse still, this interpretation would have us believe that Jehovah knew this was coming, allowed the vow, and then aided this type of man to succeed over his enemies. If such a man who would make such a vow, in gross violation of the law, and then carry it out, there is no way he would be mentioned by Paul in Hebrews chapter 11.

There is no way God would have granted and helped in Jephthah's initial success knowing the vow that was coming, because both Jehovah and Jephthah would be as bad as the Canaanites. There is no way that God would accept such a vow and then go on to help Jephthah with his enemies yet again, let alone put Jephthah on the wall of star witnesses for God in Hebrews chapter 11.

Does Isaiah 45:7 mean that God Is the Author of Evil?

Isaiah 45:7 King James Version (KJV) "I form the light and create darkness: I make peace, and **create evil**: I the LORD do all these things."

Isaiah 45:7 (ESV) "I form light and create darkness, I make well-being and **create calamity**, I am the Lord, who does all these things."[62]

Encarta Dictionary: (Evil) (1) morally bad: profoundly immoral or wrong (2) deliberately causing great harm, pain, or upset

Question: Is this view of evil always the case? No, as you will see below.

Some apologetic authors may say that we are not understanding Isaiah 45:7 correctly, because there are other verses that say God is not evil (1 John 1:5), cannot look approvingly on evil (Habakkuk 1:13), and cannot be tempted by evil. (James 1:13). While

---

[62] See Jeremiah 18:11, Lamentations 3:18, and Amos 3:6

all of these things are scripturally true, the question at hand is not: Is God evil, can God approvingly look on evil, or can God be tempted with evil? Those questions are not relevant to the one at hand, as God cannot be those things, and at the same time, he can be the yes to our question. The question is: Is God the author, the creator of evil?

We would hardly argue that God was **not just** in his bringing "calamity" or "evil" down on Adam and Eve. Thus, we have Isaiah 45:7 saying that God is the creator of "calamity" or "evil."

Let us begin simple, without trying to be philosophical. When God removed Adam and Eve from the Garden of Eden, he sentenced them and humanity to sickness, old age, and death. (Romans 5:8; i.e., enforce penalty for sin), which was to bring "calamity" or "evil" upon humankind. Therefore, "evil" does not always mean wrongdoing. Other examples of God bringing "calamity" or "evil" are Noah and the flood, the Ten Plagues of Egypt, and the destruction of the Canaanites. These acts of evil were not acts of wrongdoing. Rather, they were righteous and just, because God, the Creator of all things, was administering justice to wrongdoers, to sinners. He warned the perfect first couple what the penalty was for sin. He warned the people for a hundred years by Noah's preaching. He warned the Canaanites centuries before.

Nevertheless, there are times when God extends mercy, refraining from the execution of his righteous judgment to one worthy of calamity. For example, he warned Nineveh, the city of blood, and they repented, so he pardoned them (Jonah 3:10). God has made it a practice to warn persons of the results of sin, giving them undeservedly many opportunities to change their ways (Ezekiel 33:11).

God cannot sin; to do so is impossible for him. So, when did he create evil? Without getting into the eternity of his knowing what he was going to do and when, let us just say evil did not exist when he was the only person in existence. We might say the idea of evil existed because he knew what he was going to do. However, the moment he created creatures (spirit and human), the potential for evil came into existence because both have a free will to sin. Evil became a reality the moment Satan entertained the idea of causing Adam to sin, to get humanity for himself, and then acted on it.

God has the right and is just to bring calamity or evil down on anyone that is an unrepentant sinner. God did not even have to give us the underserved kindness of offering us his Son. God is the author or agent of evil regardless of the source books that claim otherwise. If he had never created free will beings, evil would have never gone from the idea of evil to the potential of evil, to the existence of evil. However, God felt that it was better to get the sinful state out of angel and human existence, recover, and then any who would sin thereafter, he would be justified in handing out evil or calamity to just that person or angel alone.

Who among us would argue that he should have created humans and angels like robots, automatons with no free will? The moment he chose the free will, he moved evil from an idea to a potential, and Satan moved it to a reality. God has a moral nature that does not bring about evil and sin when he is the only person in existence. However, the moment he created beings in his image who had the potential to sin, he brought about evil. The moment we have a moral code of good and evil that is placed upon one's with free will, then, we have evil.

In English, the very comprehensive Hebrew word ra' is variously translated as "bad," "downcast (sad, NASB)," "ugly," "evil," "grievous (distressing, NASB)," "sore," "selfish (stingy, HCSB)," and "envious," depending upon the context (Genesis 2:9; 40:7; 41:3; Exodus 33:4; Deuteronomy 6:22; 28:35; Proverbs 23:6; 28:22).

Evil as an adjective **describes** the **quality of** a class of people, places, or things, or of a specific person, place, or thing

Evil as a noun, **defines** the **nature** of a class of people, places, or things or of a specific person, place, or thing (e.g., the evil one, evil eye).

We can agree that "evil" is a thing. Create means to bring something into existence, be it people, places, or things, as well something abstract, for lack of a better word at the moment. We would agree that when God was alone evil was not a reality, it did not exist? We would agree that the moment that God created free will creatures (angels and humans), creating humans in his image, with his moral nature, he also brought the potential for evil into existence, and it was realized by Satan.

Inerrancy: Can the Bible Be Trusted?

If the Bible is the Word of God, it should be in complete agreement throughout; there should be no contradictions. Yet, the rational mind must ask, why is it that some passages appear to be contradictions when compared with others? For example, Numbers 25:9 tells us that 24,000 died from the scourge, whereas in 1 Corinthians 10:8, the apostle Paul says it was 23,000. This would seem to be a clear error. Before addressing such matters, let us first look at some background information.

Full inerrancy in this book means that the original writings are fully without error in all that they state, as are the words. The words were not dictated (automaton), but the intended meaning is inspired, as are the words that convey that meaning. The Author allowed the writer to use his style of writing yet controlled the meaning to the extent of not allowing the writer to choose a wrong word, which would not convey the intended meaning. Other more liberal-minded persons hold with *partial inerrancy*, which claims that as far as faith is concerned, this portion of God's Word is without error, but that there are historical, geographical, and scientific errors.

There are several different levels of inerrancy. *Absolute Inerrancy* is the belief that the Bible is fully true and exact in every way; including not only relationships and doctrine, but also science and history. In other words, all information is completely exact. *Full Inerrancy* is the belief that the Bible was not written as a science or historical textbook but is phenomenological, in that it is written from the human perspective. In other words, speaking of such things as the sun rising, the four corners of the earth, or the rounding off of number approximations are all from a human perspective. *Limited Inerrancy* is the belief that the Bible is meant only as a reflection of God's purposes and will, so the science and history is the understanding of the author's day and is limited. Thus, the Bible is susceptible to errors in these areas. *Inerrancy of Purpose* is the belief that it is only inerrant in the purpose of bringing its readers to a saving faith. The Bible is not about facts but about persons and relationships and subject to error. *Inspired: Not Inerrant* is the belief that its authors are human and thus subject to human error. It should be noted that this author holds the position of full inerrancy.

For many today, the Bible is nothing more than a book written by men. The Bible critic believes the Bible to be full of myths and legends, contradictions, and geographical, historical, and scientific errors. University professor Gerald A. Larue said, "The views of the writers as expressed in the Bible reflect the ideas, beliefs, and concepts current in their own times and are limited by the extent of knowledge in those times."[63] On the other hand, the Bible's authors claim that their writings were inspired of God, as the Holy Spirit moved them along. We will discover shortly that the Bible critics have much to say, but it is inflated or empty.

2 Timothy 3:16-17 Updated American Standard Version (UASV)

[16] All Scripture is inspired by God and profitable for teaching, for reproof, for correction, for training in righteousness; [17] so that the man of God may be fully competent, equipped for every good work.

2 Peter 1:21 Updated American Standard Version (UASV)

[21] for no prophecy was ever produced by the will of man, but men carried along by the Holy Spirit spoke from God.

The question remains as to whether the Bible is a book written by imperfect men and full of errors, or is written by imperfect men, but inspired of God. If the Bible is just another book by imperfect man, there is no hope for humankind. If it is inspired of God and without error, although penned by imperfect men, we have the hope of everything that it offers: a rich happy life now by applying counsel that lies within and the real life that is to come, everlasting life. This author contends that the Bible is inspired of God and free of human error, although written by imperfect humans.

Before we take on the critics who seem to sift the Scriptures looking for problematic verses, let us take a moment to reflect on how we should approach these alleged problem texts. The critic's argument goes something like this: "If God does not err and the Bible is the Word of God, then the Bible should not have one single error or contradiction, yet it is full of errors and contradictions." If the Bible is riddled with nothing but contradictions and errors as the critics would have us believe, why, out of 31,173 verses in the Bible, should there be only 2-3 thousand Bible difficulties that are called into question, this being less than ten percent of the whole?

First, let it be said that it is every Christian's obligation to get a deeper understanding of God's Word, just as the apostle Paul told Timothy, "Practice these things, be absorbed in them, so that your progress will be evident to all. Pay close attention to yourself and to your teaching; persevere in these things, for as you do this you will ensure salvation both for yourself and for those who hear you (1 Timothy 4:15-16).

In 2 Corinthians Paul also said, 10:4-5 "For the weapons of our warfare are not of the flesh but powerful to God for destroying strongholds.[64] We are destroying speculations and every lofty thing raised up against the knowledge of God, and we are taking every thought captive to the obedience of Christ."

---

[63] Gerald Larue, "The Bible as a Political Weapon," *Free Inquiry* (Summer 1983): 39.

[64] That is *tearing down false arguments*

Paul also told the Philippians (1:7), "It is right for me to feel thus about you all, because I hold you in my heart, for you are all partakers with me of grace, both in my imprisonment and in the defense and confirmation of the gospel."

In being able to defend against the modern-day critic, one has to be able to reason from the Scriptures and overturn the critic's argument(s) with mildness. If someone were to approach us about an alleged error or contradiction, what should we do? We should be frank and honest. If we do not have an answer, we should admit it. If the text in question gives the appearance of difficulty, we should admit this as well. If we are unsure as to how we should answer, we can simply say that we will look into it and get back with them, returning with a reasonable answer.

However, do not express disbelief and doubt to your critics, because they will be emboldened in their disbelief. It will put them on the offense and you on the defense. With great confidence, you can express that there is an answer. The Bible has withstood the test of 2,000 years of persecution and is the most printed book of all time, currently being translated into 2,287 languages. If these critical questions were so threatening, the Bible would not be the book that it is.

When you are pursuing the text in question, be unwavering in purpose or resolved to find an answer. In some cases, it may take hours of digging to find the solution. Consider this: as you resolve these difficulties, you are also building your faith that God's Word is inerrant. Moreover, you will want to do preventative maintenance in your personal study. As you are doing your Bible reading, take note of these surface discrepancies and resolve them as you work your way through the Bible. Make this a part of your prayers as well. I recommend the following program.

At the end of this chapter, I list several books that deal with difficult passages. As you read your Bible from Genesis to Revelation, do not attempt it in one year; make it a four-year program. Use a good exegetical commentary like *The New International Commentary of the Old and New Testament* (NICOT/NICNT) or *The New American Commentary* set, and *The Big Book of Bible Difficulties* by Norman L. Geisler, as well as *The Encyclopedia of Bible Difficulties* by Gleason Archer.

You should be aware that the originally written books were penned by men under inspiration. In fact, we do not have those originals—what textual scholars call autographs—but we do have thousands of copies. The copyists, however, were not inspired; therefore, as one might expect, throughout the first 1,400 years of copying, thousands of errors were transmitted into the texts that were being copied by imperfect hands that were not under inspiration when copying. Yet, the next 450 years saw a restoration of the text by textual scholars from around the world. Therefore, while many of our best literal translations today may not be inspired, they are a mirror-like reflection of the autographs by way of textual criticism.[65] Therefore, the fallacy could be with the copyist error that has simply not been weeded out. In addition, you must keep in mind that God's Word is without error, but our interpretation and understanding of that Word is not.

---

[65] Textual criticism is the study of copies of any written work of which the autograph (original) is unknown, with the purpose of ascertaining the original text. Harold J. Green, *Introduction to New Testament Textual Criticism* (Peabody, MA: Hendrickson, 1995), 1.

In this chapter, we are not going to take the space that we will in later chapters that are dedicated to one difficulty. Here, in short, we will address a number of them. Before looking at a few examples, it should be noted that the Bible is made up of 66 smaller books that were handwritten over a period of 1,600 years, having some 40 writers of various trades such as shepherd, king, priest, tax collector, governor, physician, copyist, fisherman, and tentmaker. Therefore, it should not surprise us that some difficulties are encountered as we casually read through the Bible. Yet, if one were to take a deeper look, one would find that these difficulties are easily explained. Let us take a few pages to examine some passages that have been under attack.

Again, our objective here is not to be exhaustive but to cover a few alleged contradictions and mistakes. This is to give the reader a small sampling of the reasonable answers that you will find in the recommended books at the end of the chapter. Remember, your Bible is a sword that you must use both offensively and defensively. One must wonder how long a warrior of ancient times would last who was not expertly trained in the use of his weapon. Let us look at a few scriptures that support our need to learn our Bible well so will be able to defend what we believe to be true.

When "false apostles, deceitful workmen, disguising themselves as apostles of Christ" were causing trouble in the congregation in Corinth, the apostle Paul wrote that under such circumstances, we are to *tear down their arguments* and *take every thought captive*. (2 Corinthians 10:4, 5; 11:13–15) All who present critical arguments against God's Word, or contrary to it, can have their arguments overturned by the Christian who is able and ready to defend that Word in mildness (2 Timothy 2:24–26).

1 Peter 3:15: ". . . but sanctify Christ as Lord in your hearts, always being prepared to make a defense[66] to anyone who asks you for a reason for the hope that is in you; yet do it with gentleness and respect."

Peter says that we need to be prepared to make a *defense*. The Greek word behind the English 'defense' is *apologia*, which is actually a legal term that refers to the defense of a defendant in court. Our English apologetics is just what Peter spoke of, having the ability to give a reason to any who may challenge us, or to answer those who are not challenging us but who have honest questions that deserve to be answered.

2 Timothy 2:24-25: "For a slave of the Lord does not need to fight, but needs to be kind to all, qualified to teach, showing restraint when wronged with gentleness, correcting those who are in opposition, if perhaps God may grant them repentance leading to accurate knowledge[67] of the truth."

Look at the Greek word (*epignosis*) behind the English "knowledge" in the above. "It is more intensive than *gnosis* (1108), knowledge, because it expresses a more thorough participation in the acquiring of knowledge on the part of the learner."[68] The requirement of all of the Lord's servants is that they be able to teach, but not in a quarrelsome way, and in a way to correct his opponents with mildness. Why? Because the purpose of it all is

---

[66] Or *argument*; or *explanation*

[67] *Epignosis* is a strengthened or intensified form of *gnosis* (*epi*, meaning "additional"), meaning, "true," "real," "full," "complete" or "accurate," depending upon the context. Paul and Peter alone use *epignosis*.

[68] Spiros Zodhiates, *The Complete Word Study Dictionary: New Testament*, Electronic ed. (Chattanooga, TN: AMG Publishers, 2000, c1992, c1993), S. G1922.

that by God, and through the Christian teacher, one may come to repentance and begin taking in an accurate knowledge of the truth.

Inerrancy: Practical Principles to Overcoming Bible Difficulties

Below are several ways of looking at the Bible that enable readers to see they are not dealing with an error or a contradiction but rather a Bible difficulty.

Different Points of View

At times, you may have two different writers who are writing from two different points of view.

Numbers 35:14: New International Version (NIV) "Give three on this side of the Jordan and three in Canaan as cities of refuge."

Joshua 22:4: (NIV) "Now that the Lord your God has given them rest as he promised, return to your homes in the land that Moses the servant of the Lord gave you on the other side of the Jordan."

Here we see that Moses is speaking about the east side of the Jordan when he says "on this side of the Jordan." Joshua, on the other hand, is also speaking about the east side of the Jordan when he says "on the other side of the Jordan." So, who is correct? Both are. When Moses was penning Numbers, the Israelites had not yet crossed the Jordan River, so the east side was "this side," the side he was on. On the other hand, when Joshua penned his book, the Israelites had crossed the Jordan, so the east side was just as he had said, "on the other side of the Jordan." Thus, we should not assume that two different writers are writing from the same perspective.

A Careful Reading

At times, it may simply be a case of needing to slow down and carefully read the account, considering exactly what is being said.

Joshua 18:28: New American Standard Bible (NASB)

" . . . and Zelah, Haeleph and the Jebusite (that is, Jerusalem), Gibeah, Kiriath; fourteen cities with their villages. This is the inheritance of the sons of Benjamin according to their families."

Judges 1:21: (NIV) "The Benjamites, however, did not drive out the Jebusites, who were living in Jerusalem; to this day the Jebusites live there with the Benjamites."

Joshua 15:63: (NIV) "Judah could not dislodge the Jebusites, who were living in Jerusalem; to this day the Jebusites live there with the people of Judah."

Judges 1:8-9" (NASB) "Then the sons of Judah fought against Jerusalem and captured it and struck it with the edge of the sword and set the city on fire. Afterward the sons of Judah went down to fight against the Canaanites living in the hill country and in the Negev and in the lowland."

2 Samuel 5:5-9: (NASB) "At Hebron he reigned over Judah seven years and six months, and in Jerusalem he reigned thirty-three years over all Israel and Judah. Now the

king and his men went to Jerusalem against the Jebusites, the inhabitants of the land, and they said to David, 'You shall not come in here, but the blind and lame shall turn you away; thinking, "David cannot enter here." Nevertheless, David captured the stronghold of Zion, that is the city of David. David said on that day, 'Whoever would strike the Jebusites, let him reach the lame and the blind, who are hated by David's soul, through the water tunnel.' Therefore they say, 'The blind or the lame shall not come into the house.' So David lived in the stronghold and called it the city of David. And David built all around from the Millo and inward."

There is no doubt that even the advanced Bible reader of many years can come away confused because the above accounts seem to be contradictory. In Joshua 18:28 and Judges 1:21, we see that Jerusalem was an inheritance of the tribe of Benjamin, yet the Benjamites were unable to conquer Jerusalem. But in Joshua 15:63 we see that the tribe of Judah could not conquer them either, with the reading giving the impression that it was a part of their inheritance. In Judges 1:8, however, Judah was eventually able to conquer Jerusalem and burn it with fire. Yet, to add even more to the confusion, we find at 2 Samuel 5:5–8 that David is said to have conquered Jerusalem hundreds of years later.

Now that we have the particulars, let us look at it more clearly. The boundary between Benjamin's inheritances ran right through the middle of Jerusalem. Joshua 8:28 is correct, in that what would later be called the "city of David" was in the territory of Benjamin, but it also, in part, crossed over the line into the territory of Judah, causing both tribes to go to war against this Jebusite city. It is also true that the tribe of Benjamin was unable to conquer the city and that the tribe of Judah eventually did. However, if you look at Judges 1:9 again, you will see that Judah did not finish the job entirely and moved on to conquer other areas. This allowed the remaining ones to regroup and form a resistance that neither Benjamin nor Judah could overcome, so these Jebusites remained until the time of David, hundreds of years later.

Intended Meaning of Writer

First, the Bible student needs to understand the level that the Bible intends to be exact in what is written. If Jim told a friend that 650 graduated with him from high school in 1984, it is not challenged, because it is all too clear that he is using rounded numbers and is not meaning to be exactly precise. This is how God's Word operates as well. Sometimes it means to be exact, at other times, it is simply rounding numbers, in other cases, the intention of the writer is a general reference, to give readers of that time and succeeding generations some perspective. Did Samuel, the author of judges, intend to pen a book on the chronology of Judges, or was his focus on the falling away, oppression, and the rescue by a judge, repeatedly. Now, it would seem that Jeremiah, the author of 1 Kings was more interested in giving his readers an exact number of years.

Acts 2:41 English Standard Version (ESV) "So those who received his word were baptized, and there were added that day about three thousand souls."

As you can see here, numbers within the Bible are often used with approximations. This is a frequent practice even today, in both written works and verbal conversation.

Acts 7:2-3: (ESV) "And Stephen said: 'Brothers and fathers, hear me. The God of glory appeared to our father Abraham when he was in Mesopotamia, before he lived in

Haran, and said to him, "Go out from your land and from your kindred and go into the land that I will show you."'"

If you were to check the Hebrew scriptures at Genesis 12:1, you would find that what is claimed to have been said by God to Abraham is not quoted word for word; it is simply a paraphrase. This is a normal practice within Scripture and in writing in general.

Numbers 34:15: (ESV) "The two tribes and the half-tribe have received their inheritance beyond the Jordan east of Jericho, toward the sunrise."

Just as you would read in today's local newspaper, the Bible writer has written from the human standpoint, how it appeared to him. The Bible also speaks of "to the end of the earth" (Psalm 46:9), "from the four corners of the earth" (Isaiah 11:12), and "the four winds of the earth" (Revelation 7:1). These phrases are still used today.

Unexplained Does Not Mean Unexplainable

Considering that there are 31,173 verses in the Bible, encompassing 66 books written by about 40 writers, ranging from shepherds, to kings, an army general, fishermen, a tax collector, a physician, and on and on over a 1,600 year period, one does find a few hundred Bible difficulties (about one percent). However, 99 percent of those are explainable. Yet no one wants to be so arrogant to say that he can explain them all. It has nothing to do with the inadequacy of God's Word but is based on human understanding. In many cases, science or archaeology and the field of custom and culture of ancient peoples has helped explain difficulties in hundreds of passages. Therefore, there may be less than one percent left to be answered, yet our knowledge of God's Word continues to grow.

Guilty Until Proven Innocent

This is exactly the perception that the critic has of God's Word. The legal principle of being "innocent until proven guilty" afforded mankind in courts of justice is withheld from the very Word of God. What is ironic here is that this policy has contributed to these Bible critics looking foolish over and over again when something comes to light that vindicates the portion of Scripture they are challenging.

Daniel 5:1: (ESV) "King Belshazzar made a great feast for a thousand of his lords and drank wine in front of the thousand."

Bible critics had long claimed that Belshazzar was not known outside of the book Daniel; therefore, they argue that Daniel was mistaken. Yet it hardly seems prudent to argue error from absence of outside evidence. Just because archaeology had not discovered such a person did not mean that Daniel was wrong or that such a person did not exist. In 1854, some small clay cylinders were discovered in modern-day southern Iraq, which would have been the city of Ur in ancient Babylonia. The cuneiform documents were a prayer of King Nabonidus for "Bel-sar-ussur, my eldest son." These tablets also showed that this "Bel-sar-ussur" had secretaries as well as a household staff. Other tablets were discovered a short time later that showed that the kingship was entrusted to this eldest son as a coregent while his father was away.

He entrusted the 'Camp' to his oldest (son), the firstborn [Belshazzar], the troops everywhere in the country he ordered under his (command). He let (everything) go, entrusted the kingship to him and, himself, he [Nabonidus] started out for a long journey, the (military) forces of Akkad marching with him; he turned towards Tema (deep) in the west."[69]

Ignoring Literary Styles

The Bible is a diverse book when it comes to literary styles: narrative, poetic, prophetic, and apocalyptic; also containing parables, metaphors, similes, hyperbole, and other figures of speech. Too often, these alleged errors are the result of a reader taking a figure of speech as literal, or reading a parable as though it is a narrative.

Matthew 24:35 (ESV): "Heaven and earth will pass away, but my words will not pass away."

If some do not recognize that they are dealing with a figure of speech, they are bound to come away with the wrong meaning. Some have concluded from Matthew 24:35 that Jesus was speaking of an eventual destruction of the earth. This is hardly the case, as his listeners would not have understood it that way based on their understanding of the Old Testament. They would have understood that he was simply being emphatic about the words he spoke, using hyperbole. What he was conveying is that his words are more enduring than heaven and earth, and with heaven and earth being understood as eternal, this merely conveyed even more so that Jesus' words could be trusted.

Two Accounts of the Same Incident

If you were to speak to officers that take accident reports for their police department, you would find that there is cohesion in the accounts, but each person has merely witnessed aspects that have stood out to them. We will see that this is the case as well with the examples below, which is the same account in two different gospels:

Matthew 8:5 (ESV): "When he had entered Capernaum, a centurion came forward to him, appealing to him . . ."

Luke 7:3 (ESV): "When the centurion heard about Jesus, he sent to him elders of the Jews, asking him to come and heal his servant."

Immediately, we see the problem of whether the centurion or the elders of the Jews spoke with Jesus. The solution is not really hidden from us. Which of the two accounts is the more detailed account? You are correct if you said Luke. The centurion sent the elders of the Jews to represent him to Jesus, so; that whatever response Jesus might give, it would be as though he were addressing the centurion. Therefore, Matthew gave his readers the basic thought, not seeing the need of mentioning the elders of the Jews aspect. This is how a representative was viewed in the first century, just as some countries see ambassadors today as being the very person they represent. Therefore, both Matthew and Luke are correct.

---

[69] J. Pritchard, ed., *Ancient Near Eastern Texts* (1974), 313.

Man's Fallible Interpretations

Inspiration by God is infallible, without error. Imperfect man and his interpretations over the centuries, as bad as many of them have been, should not cast a shadow over God's inspired Word. The entire Word of God has one meaning and one meaning only for every penned word, which is what God willed to be conveyed by the human writer he chose to use.

The Autograph Alone Is Inspired and Inerrant

It has been argued by conservative scholars that only the autograph manuscripts were inspired and inerrant, not the copying of those manuscripts over the next 3,000 years for the Old Testament and 1,500 years for the New Testament. While I would agree with this position as well, it should be noted that we do not possess the autographs, so to argue that they are inerrant is to speak of nonexistent documents. However, it should be further understood that through the science of textual criticism, we can establish a mirror reflection of the autograph manuscripts. B. F. Westcott, F. J. A. Hort, F. F. Bruce, and many other textual scholars would agree with Norman L Geisler's assessment: "The New Testament, then, has not only survived in more manuscripts than any other book from antiquity, but it has survived in a purer form than any other great book—*a form that is 99.5 percent pure.*"[70]

An example of a copyist error can be found in Luke's genealogy of Jesus at Luke 3:35–37. In verse 37 you will find a Cainan, and in verse 36 you will find a second Cainan between Arphaxad (Arpachshad) and Shelah. As one can see from most footnotes in different study Bibles, the Cainan in verse 36 is seen as a scribal error, and is not found in the Hebrew Old Testament, the Samaritan Pentateuch, or the Aramaic Targums, but is found in the Greek Septuagint. (Genesis 10:24; 11:12, 13; 1 Chronicles 1:18, but not 1 Chronicles 1:24) It seems quite unlikely that it was in the earlier copies of the Septuagint, because the first-century Jewish historian Josephus lists Shelah next as the son of Arphaxad, and Josephus normally followed the Septuagint.[71] So one might ask why this second Cainan is found in the translations at all if this is the case? The manuscripts that do contain this second Cainan are some of the best manuscripts that are used in establishing the original text: 01 B L A^1 33 (Kainam); A 038 044 0102 A^{13} (Kainan).

Look at the Context

Many alleged inconsistencies disappear by simply looking at the context. Taking words out of context can distort their meaning. *Merriam-Webster's Collegiate Dictionary* defines context as "the parts of a discourse that surround a word or passage and can throw light on its meaning."[72] Context can also be "the circumstances or events that form the environment within which something exists or takes place." If we were to look in a

---

[70] Norman L. Geisler and William E. Nix: *A General Introduction to the Bible* (Chicago, Moody Press, 1980), 367. (Emphasis is mine.)

[71] *Jewish Antiquities*, I, 146 [vi, 4].

[72] Merriam-Webster, Inc: *Merriam-Webster's Collegiate Dictionary*. Eleventh ed. (Springfield, Mass.: Merriam-Webster, Inc. 2003).

thesaurus for a synonym, we would find "background" for this second meaning. At 2 Timothy 2:15, the apostle Paul brings home the point of why context is so important: "Do your best to present yourself to God as one approved, a worker who has no need to be ashamed, rightly handling the word of truth."

Ephesians 2:8-9 (ESV): "For by grace you have been saved through faith. And this is not your own doing; it is the gift of God, not a result of works, so that no one may boast."

James 2:26 (ESV): "For as the body apart from the spirit is dead, so also faith apart from works is dead."

So, which is it? Is salvation possible by faith alone as Paul wrote to the Ephesians, or is faith dead without works as James wrote to his readers? As our subtitle brings out, let us look at the context. In the letter to the Ephesians, the apostle Paul is speaking to the Jewish Christians who were looking to the works of the Mosaic Law as a means to salvation, a righteous standing before God. Paul was telling these legalistic Jewish Christians that this is not so. In fact, this would invalidate Christ's ransom, because there would have been no need for it if one could achieve salvation by meticulously keeping the Mosaic Law (Romans 5:18).

But James was writing to those in a congregation who were concerned with their status before other men, who were looking for prominent positions within the congregation, and not taking care of those that were in need (James 2:14–17), so, James is merely addressing those who call themselves Christian in name only. No person could truly be a Christian and not possess some good works, such as feeding the poor or helping the elderly. This type of work was an evident demonstration of one's Christian personality. Paul was in perfect harmony with James on this (Romans 10:10; 1 Corinthians 15:58; Ephesians 5:15, 21–33; 6:15; 1 Timothy 4:16; 2 Timothy 4:5; Hebrews 10:23-25).

Inerrancy: Are There Contradictions?

Below I will follow this pattern. I will list the critic's argument first, followed by the text of difficulty, and conclude with an answer to the critic. What should be kept at the forefront of our mind is this: one is simply looking for the best answer, not absoluteness. If there is a reasonable answer to a Bible difficulty, why are the critics able to set them aside with ease? Because they start with the premise that this is not the Word of God, but only a book by imperfect men and full of contradictions; thus, the bias toward errors has blinded their judgment.

Critic: The critic would argue that there was an Adam and Eve, and an Abel who was now dead, so, where did Cain get his wife? This is one of the most common questions by Bible critics.

Genesis 4:17 New English Translation (NET): "Cain had marital relations with his wife, and she became pregnant and gave birth to Enoch. Cain was building a city, and he named the city after his son Enoch."

Answer: If one were to read a little further along, they would come to the realization that Adam had a son named Seth; it further adds that Adam "became father to *sons and daughters.*" (Genesis 5:4) Adam lived for a total of 800 years after fathering Seth, giving him ample opportunity to father many more sons and daughters. So it could be that

Cain married one of his sisters. If he waited until one of his brothers and sisters had a daughter, he could have married one of his nieces once she was old enough. In the beginning, humans were closer to perfection; this explains why they lived longer and why at that time there was little health risk of genetic defects in the case of children born to closely related parents, in contrast to how it is today.

As time passed, genetic defects increased and life spans decreased. Adam lived to see 930 years. Yet Shem, who lived after the Flood, died at 600 years, while Shem's son Arpachshad only lived 438 years, dying before his father died. Abraham saw an even greater decrease in that he only lived 175 years, while his grandson Jacob was 147 years when he died. Thus, due to increasing imperfection, God prohibited the marriage of closely related people under the Mosaic Law because of the likelihood of genetic defects (Leviticus 18:9).

Critic: If God is here hardening Pharaoh's heart, what exactly makes Pharaoh responsible for the decisions he makes?

Exodus 4:21 (RSV): "And the Lord said to Moses, 'When you go back to Egypt, see that you do before Pharaoh all the miracles which I have put in your power; but I will harden his heart, so that he will not let the people go.'"

Answer: This is actually a prophecy. God knew that what he was about to do would contribute to a stubborn and obstinate Pharaoh, who was going to be unwilling to change or give up the Israelites so they could go off to worship their God. Therefore, this is not stating what God is going to do; it is prophesying that Pharaoh's heart will harden because of the actions of God. The fact is, Pharaoh allowed his own heart to harden because he was determined not to agree with Moses' wishes or accept Jehovah's request to let the people go. Moses tells us at Exodus 7:13 (ESV) that "Pharaoh's heart was hardened, and he would not listen to them, as the Lord had said." Again, at 8:15 we read, "When Pharaoh saw that there was a respite, he hardened his heart and would not listen to them, as the Lord had said."

Critic: The Israelites had just received the Ten Commandments, with one commandment being: "You shall not make for yourself a carved image, or any likeness of anything that is in heaven above, or that is in the earth beneath, or that is in the water under the earth." Therefore, how is the bronze serpent not a violation of this commandment?

Numbers 21:9 (ESV): "So Moses made a bronze serpent and set it on a pole. And if a serpent bit anyone, he would look at the bronze serpent and live."

Answer: First, an idol is "a representation or symbol of an object of worship; *broadly*: a false god."[73] Second, it should be noted that not all images are idols. The bronze serpent was not made for the purpose of worship or for some passionate devotion or veneration. There were times, however, when images were created with absolutely no intention of it receiving devotion, veneration, or worship yet were later made into objects of veneration. That is exactly what happened with the copper serpent that Moses had formed in the wilderness. Many centuries later, "in the third year of Hoshea son of Elah,

---

[73] Merriam-Webster, Inc: *Merriam-Webster's Collegiate Dictionary*. Eleventh ed. (Springfield, Mass.: Merriam-Webster, Inc., 2003).

king of Israel, Hezekiah the son of Ahaz, king of Judah, began to reign. He removed the high places and broke the pillars and cut down the Asherah. And he broke in pieces the bronze serpent that Moses had made; for until those days the people of Israel had made offerings to it (it was called Nehushtan)" (2 Kings 18:1, 4).

Critic: Deuteronomy 15:11 (NET) says: "There will never cease to be some poor people in the land; therefore, I am commanding you to make sure you open your hand to your fellow Israelites who are needy and poor in your land." Is this not a contradiction of Deuteronomy 15:4? Will there be no poor among the Israelites, or will there be poor among them? Which is it?

Deuteronomy 15:4 (NET): "However, there should not be any poor among you, for the Lord will surely bless you in the land that he is giving you as an inheritance . . ."

Answer: If you look at the context, Deuteronomy 15:4 is stating that if the Israelites obey Jehovah's command to take care of the poor, "there should not be any poor among" them. Thus, for every poor person, there will be one to take care of that need. If an Israelite fell on hard times, there was to be a fellow Israelite ready to step in to help him through those hard times. Verse 11 stresses the truth of the imperfect world since the rebellion of Adam and inherited sin: there will always be poor among mankind, the Israelites being no different. However, the difference with God's people is that those who were well off were to offset conditions for those who fell on difficult times. This is not to be confused with the socialistic welfare systems in the world today. Those Jews were hard-working men, who labored from sunup to sundown to take care of their families. But if disease overtook their herd or unseasonal weather brought about failed crops, an Israelite could sell himself into the service of a fellow Israelite for a period of time; thereafter, he would be back on his feet. And many years down the road, he may very well do the same for another Israelite who fell on difficult times.

Critic: Joshua 11:23 says that Joshua took the land according to what God had spoken to Moses and handed it on to the nation of Israel as planned. However, in Joshua 13:1, God is telling Joshua that he has grown old and much of the Promised Land has yet to be taken possession of. How can both be true? Is this not a contradiction?

Joshua 11:23 (ESV): "So Joshua took the whole land, according to all that the Lord had spoken to Moses. And Joshua gave it for an inheritance to Israel according to their tribal allotments. And the land had rest from war."

Joshua 13:1 (ESV): "Now Joshua was old and advanced in years, and the Lord said to him, "You are old and advanced in years, and there remains yet very much land to possess."

Answer: No, it is not a contradiction. When the Israelites were to take the land, it was to take place in two different stages: the nation as a whole was to go to war and defeat the 31 kings of this land; thereafter, each Israelite tribe was to take their part of the land based on their individual actions (Joshua 17:14–18; 18:3). Joshua fulfilled his role, which is expressed in 11:23, while the individual tribes did not complete their campaigns, which is expressed in 13:1. Even though the individual tribes failed to live up to taking their portion, the remaining Canaanites posed no real threat. Joshua 21:44, UASV, reads: "Jehovah gave them rest round about."

Critic: The critic would point out that John 1:18 clearly says that "no one has ever seen God," while Exodus 24:10 explicitly states that Moses and Aaron, Nadab and Abihu, and seventy of the elders of Israel "saw the God of Israel." Worse still, God informs them in Exodus 33:20: "You cannot see my face, for man shall not see me and live." The critic with his knowing smile says, "This is a blatant contradiction."

John 1:18 ble (NASB): "No one has seen God at any time; the only begotten God who is in the bosom of the Father, He has explained *Him*."

Exodus 24:10 (NASB): ". . . and they saw the God of Israel; and under His feet there appeared to be a pavement of sapphire, as clear as the sky itself."

Exodus 33:20 (ESV): "But," he [God] said, "you cannot see my face, for man shall not see me and live."

Answer: Exodus 33:20 is one-hundred percent correct: No human could see Jehovah God and live. The apostle Paul at Colossians 1:15 tell us that Christ is the image of the invisible God, and the writer informs us at Hebrews 1:3 that Jesus is the "exact representation of His nature." Yet if you were to read the account of Saul of Tarsus (the apostle Paul), you would see that a mere partial manifestation of Christ's glory blinded Saul (Acts 9:1–18).

When the Bible says that Moses and others have seen God, it is not speaking of *literally* seeing Him, because, first of all, He is an invisible spirit person. It is a *manifestation* of his glory, which is an act of showing or demonstrating His presence, making Himself perceptible to the human mind. In fact, it is generally an angelic representative that stands in His place and not Him personally. Exodus 24:16 informs us that "the glory of the Lord dwelt on Mount Sinai," not the Lord himself personally. When texts such as Exodus 24:10 explicitly state that Moses and Aaron, Nadab and Abihu, and seventy of the elders of Israel "saw the God of Israel," it is this "glory of the Lord," an angelic representative. This is shown to be the case at Luke 2:9, which reads: "And an angel of the Lord" appeared to them, and the glory of the Lord shone around them [the shepherds], and they were filled with fear."

Many Bible difficulties are cleared up elsewhere in Scripture; for example, in the New Testament you will find a text clarifying a difficulty from the Old Testament, such as Acts 7:53, which refers to those "who received the law *as delivered by angels* and did not keep it." Support comes from Paul at Galatians 3:19: "Why then the law? It was added because of transgressions, until the offspring should come to whom the promise had been made, and it was put in place through angels by an intermediary." The writer of Hebrews chimes in at 2:2 with "For since the message *declared by angels* proved to be reliable, and every transgression or disobedience received a just retribution. . . ."

As we travel back to Exodus again, to 19:19 specifically, we find support that it was not God's own voice, which Moses heard; no, it was an angelic representative, for it reads: "Moses was speaking and God was answering him with a voice." Exodus 33:22–23 also helps us to appreciate that it was the back of these angelic representatives of Jehovah that Moses saw: "While my glory passes by . . . Then I will take away my hand, and you shall see my back, but my face shall not be seen."

Exodus 3:4 states: "God called to him out of the bush, 'Moses, Moses!' And he said, 'Here I am.'" Verse 6 informs us: "I am the God of your father, the God of Abraham, the

God of Isaac, and the God of Jacob." Yet, in verse 2 we read: "And the angel of the Lord appeared to him in a flame of fire out of the midst of a bush." Here is another example of using God's Word to clear up what seems to be unclear or difficult to understand at first glance. Thus, while it speaks of the Lord making a direct appearance, it is really an angelic representative. Even today, we hear such comments, as 'the president of the United States is to visit the Middle East later this week.' However, later in the article it is made clear that he is not going personally, but it is one of his high-ranking representatives. Let us close with two examples, starting with:

Genesis 32:24-30 (ESV): "And Jacob was left alone. And a man wrestled with him until the breaking of the day. When the man saw that he did not prevail against Jacob, he touched his hip socket, and Jacob's hip was put out of joint as he wrestled with him. Then he said, 'Let me go, for the day has broken.' But Jacob said, 'I will not let you go unless you bless me.' And he said to him, 'What is your name?' And he said, 'Jacob.' Then he said, 'Your name shall no longer be called Jacob, but Israel, for you have striven with God and with men, and have prevailed.' Then Jacob asked him, 'Please tell me your name.' But he said, 'Why is it that you ask my name?' And there he blessed him. So Jacob called the name of the place Peniel, saying, 'For I have seen God face to face, and yet my life has been delivered.'"

It is all too obvious here that this man is simply a materialized angel in the form of a man, another angelic representative of Jehovah God. Moreover, the reader of this book should have taken in that the Israelites as a whole saw these angelic representatives and spoke of them as though they were dealing directly with Jehovah God himself.

This proved to be the case in the second example found in the Book of Judges, where an angelic representative visited Manoah and his wife. Like the above mentioned account, Manoah and his wife treated this angelic representative as if he were Jehovah God himself: "And Manoah said to the angel of the Lord, 'What is your name, so that, when your words come true, we may honor you?' And the angel of the Lord said to him, 'Why do you ask my name, seeing it is wonderful?' Then Manoah knew that he was the angel of the Lord. And Manoah said to his wife, "We shall surely die, *for we have seen God*" (Judges 13:3–22).

Inerrancy: Are There Mistakes?

I have addressed the alleged contradictions, so it would seem that our job is finished, right? Not hardly. Yes, there are just as many who claim that the Bible is full of mistakes.

Critic: Matthew 27:5 states that Judas hanged himself, whereas Acts 1:18 says that "falling headlong he burst open in the middle and all his bowels gushed out."

Matthew 27:5 (ESV): "And throwing down the pieces of silver into the temple, he departed, and he went and hanged himself."

Acts 1:18 (ESV): "(Now this man acquired a field with the reward of his wickedness, and falling headlong he burst open in the middle and all his bowels gushed out.)"

Answer: Neither Matthew nor Luke made a mistake. What you have is Matthew giving the reader the manner in which Judas committed suicide. On the other hand, Luke is giving the reader of Acts the result of that suicide. Therefore, instead of a mistake, we have two texts that complement each other, really giving the reader the full picture. Judas came to a tree alongside a cliff that had rocks below. He tied the rope to a branch and the other end around his neck and jumped over the edge of the cliff in an attempt at hanging himself. One of two things could have happened: either the limb broke plunging him to the rocks below, or the rope broke with the same result, and he burst open onto the rocks below.

Critic: The apostle Paul made a mistake when he quotes how many people died.

Numbers 25:9 (ESV): "Nevertheless, those who died by the plague were twenty-four thousand."

1 Corinthians 10:8 (ESV): "We must not indulge in sexual immorality as some of them did, and twenty-three thousand fell in a single day."

Answer: We must keep in mind the above principle that we spoke of, the *intended meaning of the writer*. We live in a far more precise age today, where specificity is highly important. However, we round large numbers off (even estimate) all the time: "There were 237,000 people in Time Square last night." The simplest answer is that the number of people slain was in between 23,000 and 24,000, and both writers rounded the number off. However, there is even another possibility, because the Book of Numbers specifically speaks of "all the chiefs of the people" (25:4-5), which could account for the extra 1,000, which is mentioned in Numbers' 24,000. Thus, you have the people killing the chiefs of the people and the plague killing the people. Therefore, both books are correct.

Critic: After 215 years in Egypt, the descendants of Jacob arrived at the Promised Land. As you recall, they sinned against God and were sentenced to forty years in the wilderness. But once they entered the Promised Land, they buried Joseph's bones "at Shechem, in the piece of land that Jacob bought from the sons of Hamor the father of Shechem," as stated at Joshua 24:32. Yet, when Stephen had to defend himself before the Jewish religious leaders, he said that Joseph was buried "in the tomb that Abraham had bought for a sum of silver from the sons of Hamor." Therefore, it appears that we have a mistake on the part of Stephen.

Acts 7:15-16 (ESV): "And Jacob went down into Egypt, and he died, he and our fathers, and they were carried back to Shechem and laid in the tomb that Abraham had bought for a sum of silver from the sons of Hamor in Shechem."

Genesis 23:17-18 (ESV): "So the field of Ephron in Machpelah, which was to the east of Mamre, the field with the cave that was in it and all the trees that were in the field, throughout its whole area, was made over to Abraham as a possession in the presence of the Hittites, before all who went in at the gate of his city."

Genesis 33:19 (ESV): "And from the sons of Hamor, Shechem's father, he [Jacob] bought for a hundred pieces of money the piece of land on which he had pitched his tent."

Joshua 24:32 (ESV): "As for the bones of Joseph, which the people of Israel brought up from Egypt, they buried them at Shechem, in the piece of land that Jacob bought from the sons of Hamor the father of Shechem for a hundred pieces of money. It became an inheritance of the descendants of Joseph."

Answer: If we look back to Genesis 12:6-7, we will find that Abraham's first stop after entering Canaan from Haran was Shechem. It is here that Jehovah told Abraham:

"To your offspring I will give this land." At this point Abraham built an altar to Jehovah. It seems reasonable that Abraham would need to purchase this land that had not yet been given to his offspring. While it is true that the Old Testament does not mention this purchase, it is likely that Stephen would be aware of such by way of oral tradition. As Acts chapter 7 demonstrates, Stephen had a wide-ranging knowledge of Old Testament history.

Later, Jacob would have had difficulty laying claim to the tract of land that his grandfather Abraham had purchased, because there would have been a new generation of inhabitants of Shechem. This would have been many years after Abraham moved further south and Isaac moved to Beersheba, and including Jacob's twenty years in Paddan-aram (Genesis 28:6–7). The simplest answer is that this land was not in use for about 120 years because of Abraham's extensive travels and Isaac's having moved away, leaving it unused; likely it was put to use by others. So, Jacob simply repurchased what Abraham had bought over a hundred years earlier. This is very similar to the time Isaac had to repurchase the well at Beersheba that Abraham had already purchased earlier (Genesis 21:27–30; 26:26–32).

Genesis 33:18–20 tells us that 'Jacob bought this land for a hundred pieces of money, from the sons of Hamor.' This same transaction is also mentioned at Joshua 24:32, in reference to transporting Joseph's bones from Egypt, to be buried in Shechem.

We should also address the cave of Machpelah that Abraham had purchased in Hebron from Ephron the Hittite. The word "tomb" is not mentioned until Joshua 24:32 and is in reference to the tract of land in Shechem. Nowhere in the Old Testament does it say that Abraham bought a "tomb." The cave of Machpelah obtained by Abraham would eventually become a family tomb, receiving Sarah's body and, eventually, his own and those of Isaac, Rebekah, Jacob, and Leah. (Genesis 23:14–19; 25:9; 49:30, 31; 50:13)

Gleason L. Archer, Jr., concludes this Bible difficulty, saying, "The reference to a *mnema* ("tomb") in connection with Shechem must either have been proleptic [to anticipate] for the later use of that Shechemite tract for Joseph's tomb (i.e., "the tomb that Abraham bought" was intended to imply "the tomb location that Abraham bought") or else conceivably the dative relative pronoun *ho* was intended elliptically [omission] for *en to topo ho onesato Abraam* ("in the place that Abraham bought") as describing the location of the *mnema* near the Oak of Moreh right outside Shechem. Normally Greek would have used the relative-locative adverb *hou* to express 'in which' or 'where'; but this would have left *onesato* ("bought") without an object in its own clause, and so *ho* was much more suitable in this context. (Archer 1982, 379–81).

Another solution could be that Jacob is being viewed as a representative of Abraham, for he is the grandson of Abraham. This was quite appropriate in Biblical times, to attribute the purchase to Abraham as the Patriarchal family head.

Critic: 2 Samuel 24:1 says that God moved David to count the Israelites, while in 1 Chronicles 21:1, Satan or a resister did. This would seem to be a clear mistake on the part of one of these authors.

2 Samuel 24:1 (ESV): "Again the anger of the Lord was kindled against Israel, and he incited David against them, saying, 'Go, number Israel and Judah.'"

1 Chronicles 21:1 (ESV): "Then Satan stood against Israel and incited David to number Israel."

Answer: In this period of David's reign, Jehovah was very displeased with Israel, and therefore he did not prevent Satan from bringing this sin on them. Often in Scripture, it is spoken of as though God did something when he allowed an event to take place. For example, it is said that God 'hardened Pharaoh's heart' (Exodus 4:21), when he actually allowed the Pharaoh's heart to harden.

Inerrancy: Are There Scientific Errors?

Many truths about God are beyond the scope of science. Science and the Bible are not at odds. In fact, we can thank modern day science, as it has helped us to better understand the creation of God, from our solar system, to the universes, to the human body and mind. What we find is a level of order, precision, design, and sophistication, which points the eyes of many Christians to a Designer—an Almighty God with infinite intelligence and power. The apostle Paul makes this all too clear, when he writes, "For his invisible attributes, namely, his eternal power and divine nature, have been clearly perceived, ever since the creation of the world, in the things that have been made. So they are without excuse" (Romans 1:20).

In the seventeenth century, the world-renowned scientist Galileo proved beyond any doubt that the earth was not the center of the universe, nor did the sun orbit the earth. In fact, he proved the opposite, with the earth revolving around the sun. However, he was brought up on charges of heresy by the Catholic Church and ordered to recant his position. Why? From the viewpoint of the Catholic Church, Galileo was contradicting God's Word, the Bible. As it turned out, Galileo and science were correct and the Church was wrong, for which it issued a formal apology in 1992. However, the point we wish to make here is that in all the controversy, the Bible was never in the wrong. It was a misinterpretation on the part of the Catholic Church, and not a fault with the Bible. One will find no place in the Bible that claims the sun orbits the earth. So where would the Church get such an idea? The Church got such an idea from Ptolemy (b. about 85 C.E.), an ancient astronomer, who argued for such an idea.

As it usually turns out, the so-called contradiction between science and God's Word lies at the feet of those who are interpreting Scripture incorrectly. Galileo expressed the same sentiments when writing to a pupil: "Even though Scripture cannot err, its interpreters and expositors can in various ways. One of these, very serious and very frequent, would be when they always want to stop at the purely literal sense."[74]

I believe that today's scholars, in hindsight, would have no problem agreeing. While the Bible is not a science textbook, it is scientifically accurate when it touches on matters of science.

The Circle of the Earth Hangs on Nothing

Isaiah 40:22 (ESV): "It is he who sits above **the circle of the earth**, and its inhabitants are like grasshoppers; who stretches out the heavens like a curtain, and spreads them like a tent to dwell in."

---

[74] Letter from Galileo to Benedetto Castelli, December 21, 1613.

More than 2,500 years ago, the prophet Isaiah wrote that the earth is a circle or sphere. First, how would it be possible for Isaiah to know the earth is a circle or sphere, if not from inspiration? Scientific America writes, "As countless photos from space can attest, Earth is round—the "Blue Marble," as astronauts have affectionately dubbed it. Appearances, however, can be deceiving. Planet Earth is not, in fact, perfectly round."[75] Scientifically speaking, the sun is not perfectly, absolutely 100 percent round but in everyday speech, this verse is both acceptable and accurate, when we keep in mind it is written from a human perspective, not from a scientific perspective. Moreover, Isaiah was not discussing astronomy; he was simply making an inspired observation that man came to realize once he was in space, looking back at the earth, it is round. See the section about title, "Intended Meaning of Writer."

Job 26:7 Updated American standard Version (UASV)

⁷ "He stretches out the north over empty space
and hangs the earth on nothing.

Here the author describes the earth as hanging upon nothing. Many have never heard of the Greek mathematician and astronomer Eratosthenes. He was born in about 276 B.C.E. and received some of his education in Athens, Greece. In 240 B.C., the "Greek astronomer, geographer, mathematician and librarian Eratosthenes calculates the Earth's circumference. His data was rough, but he wasn't far off."[76] While man very early on used God given intelligence to arrive at some outstanding conclusion that was actually accurate, we learn two points here: Eratosthenes was a very astute scientist, while Isaiah, who wrote some 500 years earlier, was no scientist at all. Moreover, Moses, who wrote the Book of Job over 1,230 years before Eratosthenes, knew that the earth hung upon nothing.

How Is the Sun Standing Still Possible?

Joshua 10:13 (ESV): "And the sun stood still, and the moon stopped, until the nation took vengeance on their enemies."

The Canaanites had besieged the Gibeonites, a group of people who gained Jehovah God's backing because they had faith in Him. In this battle, Jehovah helped the Israelites continue their attack by causing "the sun [to stand] still, and the moon stopped, until the nation took vengeance on their enemies" (Joshua 10:1-14). Those who accept God as the Creator of the universe and life can accept that He would know a way of stopping the earth from rotating. However, there are other ways of understanding this account. We must keep in mind that the Bible speaks from an earthly observer point of view, so it need not be that He stopped the rotation. It could have been a refraction of solar and lunar light rays, which would have produced the same effect.

Psalm 136:6 (ESV): "to him who spread out the earth above the waters, for his steadfast love endures forever . . ."

---

[75] Charles Q. Choi (April 12, 2007). Scientific America. Strange but True: Earth Is Not Round. Retrieved Monday, August 03, 2015.

http://www.scientificamerican.com/article/earth-is-not-round/

[76] Alfred, Randy (June 19, 2008). "June 19, 240 B.C.E: The Earth Is Round, and It's This Big". Wired. Retrieved Monday, August 03, 2015.

Hebrews 3:4 (ESV): "(For every house is built by someone, but the builder of all things is God.)

2 Kings 20:8-11 (ESV): "And Hezekiah said to Isaiah, 'What shall be the sign that the LORD will heal me, and that I shall go up to the house of the LORD on the third day?' And Isaiah said, 'This shall be the sign to you from the LORD, that the LORD will do the thing that he has promised: shall the shadow go forward ten steps, or go back ten steps?' And Hezekiah answered, 'It is an easy thing for the shadow to lengthen ten steps. Rather let the shadow go back ten steps.' And Isaiah the prophet called to the LORD, and he brought the shadow back ten steps, by which it had gone down on the steps of Ahaz."

How Did the Stars Fight on behalf of Barak?

Judges 5:20 (ESV): "From heaven the stars fought, from their courses they fought against Sisera."

Judges 4:15 (ESV): "And the LORD routed Sisera and all his chariots and all his army before Barak by the edge of the sword. And Sisera got down from his chariot and fled away on foot."

In the Bible, you have biblical prose and biblical poetry.

Prose: language that is not poetry: (1) writing or speech in its normal continuous form, without the rhythmic or visual line structure of poetry **(2)** ordinary style of expression: writing or speech that is ordinary or matter-of-fact, without embellishment.

Poetry: literature in verse: (1) literary works written in verse, in particular verse writing of high quality, great beauty, emotional sincerity or intensity, or profound insight **(2) beauty or grace:** something that resembles poetry in its beauty, rhythmic grace, or imaginative, elevated, or decorative style.

We have a beautiful example of both of these forms of writing-communication in the Book of Judges, chapters 4 and 5. Judges 4 is a prose account of Deborah and Barak, while Judges 5 is a poetic account. As we have learned from the above, poetry is less concerned with accuracy than evoking emotions. Poetry has a license to say things like what we find in of 5:20, which is in the poetry chapter: "from heaven the stars fought." This can be said, and the reader is expected to not take the language literally. What we can surmise from it is that God was acting against Sisera in some way; there was divine intervention.

Procedures for Handling Biblical Difficulties

1. Be completely convinced a reason or understanding exists.

2. Have total trust and conviction in the inerrancy of the Scripture as originally written down.

3. Study the context and framework of the verse carefully, to establish what the author meant by the words he used. In other words, find the beginning and the end of the context that your passage falls within.

4. Understand exegesis: find the historical setting, determine author intent, study key words, and note parallel passages. You need carefully read the account, considering exactly what is being said

5. Find a reasonable harmonization of parallel passages.

6. Consider a variety of trusted Bible commentaries, dictionaries, lexical sources, encyclopedias, as well as books on Bible difficulties.

7. Investigate as to whether the difficulty is a transmissional error in the original text.

8. Keep in mind that the historical accuracy of the biblical text is unmatched; that thousands of extant manuscripts some of which date back to the second century B.C. support the transmitted text of Scripture.

9. Remember that the Bible is a diverse book when it comes to literary styles: narrative, poetic, prophetic, and apocalyptic; also containing parables, metaphors, similes, hyperbole, and other figures of speech. Too often, these alleged errors are the result of a reader taking a figure of speech as literal or reading a parable as though it is a narrative.

10. Understand what level that the Bible intends to be exact in what is written. If Jim told a friend that 650 graduated with him from high school in 1984, it is not challenged, because it is all too clear that he is using rounded numbers and is not meaning to be precise.

CHAPTER XIX The Documentary Hypothesis

Edward D. Andrews

It was in the latter half of the nineteenth century that higher criticism began to be taken seriously. These critics rejected Moses as the writer of the Pentateuch, arguing instead that the accounts in Genesis, Exodus, Leviticus, Numbers, and Deuteronomy were based on four other sources [writers] written between the 10th and the 6th centuries B.C.E. To differentiate these sources one from the other, they are simply known as the "J," "E," "D," and "P" sources. The letters are the initial to the name of these alleged sources, also known as the Documentary Hypothesis.

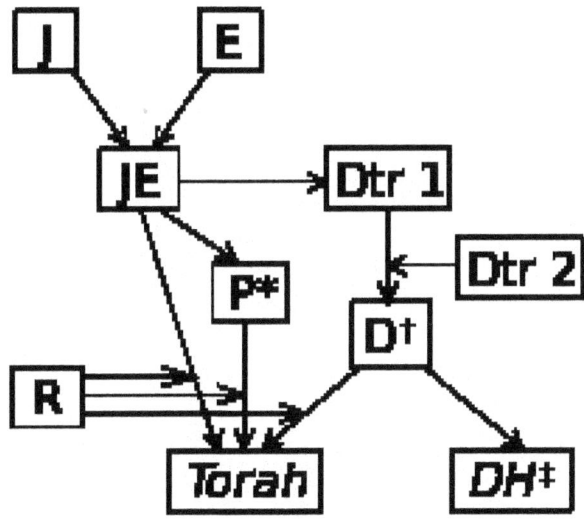

Image 1 Diagram of the Documentary Hypothesis.

*   includes most of Leviticus

†   includes most of Deuteronomy

‡   "Deuteronomic history": Joshua, Judges, 1 & 2 Samuel, 1 & 2 Kings – Wikipedia

Source Criticism, a sub-discipline of Higher Criticism, is an attempt by liberal Bible scholars to discover the original sources that the Bible writer(s) [not Moses] used to pen these five books. It should be noted that most scholars who engage in higher criticism start with liberal presuppositions. Dr. Gleason L. Archer, Jr., identifies many flaws in the reasoning of those who support the Documentary Hypothesis; however, this one flaw being quoted herein is indeed the most grievous and lays the foundation for other irrational reasoning in their thinking. Identifying their problem, Archer writes, "The Wellhausen school started with the pure assumption (which they have hardly bothered to demonstrate) that Israel's religion was of merely human origin like any other, and that it was to be explained as a mere product of evolution."[77] In other words, Wellhausen and those who followed him begin with the presupposition that God's Word is *not* that at all, the Word of God, but is the word of mere man, and then they reason **into** the Scripture not **out of** the Scriptures based on that premise. As to the effect, this has on God's Word and those who hold it as such; it is comparable to having a natural disaster wash the foundation right out from under our home.

Liberal Christianity says that Moses did not pen every word from Genesis through Deuteronomy. They conclude that this is nothing more than a tradition that originated in the times that the Jews returned from their exile in Babylon in 537 B.C.E. and the destruction of Jerusalem in 70 C.E. These source critics reason that there was and is a misunderstanding of Deuteronomy 31:9, which says that Moses "[wrote] this law, and delivered it unto the priests the sons of Levi, that bare the ark of the covenant of Jehovah, and unto all the elders of Israel." They argue that Deuteronomy only implies that Moses wrote the laws of Deuteronomy chapters 12–28; moreover, this was extended into a tradition that encompassed the belief that the entire Pentateuch was *not* written by Moses.

In addition, these source critics put forth that the language of Deuteronomy chapters 12–18, as well as the historical and theological context, places the writing and completion of these five books centuries after Moses died. According to these critics, this alleged tradition of Moses being the author of the first five books of our Bible was completely accepted as fact by the time Jesus Christ arrived on the scene in the first-century C.E. These critics further argue that Jesus, the Son of God, was also duped by this tradition and simply perpetuated it when he referred to "the book of Moses" (Mark 12:26), which to the Jews at that time counted Genesis, Exodus, Leviticus, Numbers, and Deuteronomy as a book by Moses. In addition, at John 17:23, Jesus spoke of "the law of Moses," which he and all others Jews had long held to be the Pentateuch. Thus, for the critic, Jesus simply handed this misunderstood tradition off to first-century Christianity.

We have read much in previous chapters thus far about these critical scholars, but it will not hurt to review, before delving into discrediting their hypothesis. How has such extreme thinking as this Documentary Hypothesis come down to us, going from being a hypothesis to being accepted as *law* in secular universities and most seminaries? What is the relationship between a hypothesis, theory, and law? In the physical sciences, there are several steps before a description of a phenomenon becomes law.

(1) **Observation:** "I noticed that objects fall to the earth."

(2) **Hypothesis:** "I think something must be pulling these objects to the earth. Let me call it gravity."

(3) **Experimentation:** "Let me put this to the test by releasing different objects from that cliff. Umm, it seems that everything I let go falls. My hypothesis seems to be right."

(4) **Theory:** "I have noticed that every time I release an object, and wherever I do it, over the sidewalk, from the 32nd floor of that office building and even from the

---

[77] 77. Gleason L. Archer, A Survey of Old Testament Introduction (Moody Publishers, Chicago, 2007), 98.

cruise ship—they fall to the earth as if pulled by something. It happens often enough to be called a theory."

(5) **Law:** "Well, this has consistently been occurring over the years. It must be absolutely true and therefore a Law."

Where does the "Documentary Hypothesis" fit into this scheme? Wellhausen *et al.* made certain **Observations** and then produced a **Hypothesis** to explain what they saw. I would argue that is as far as they made it in following the formula for the scientific method.

The Forefathers of Source Criticisms

Abraham Ibn Ezra (1089–1164) Ibn Ezra was, by far, the most famous Bible scholar of medieval times. True enough, he may have questioned the idea that Moses wrote the entire Torah; however, he chose not to do this in an outward way; he chose to be more subtle in presenting such an idea. For Ibn Ezra, several verses seemed not to have come from Moses, but one verse stood out above the others. Deuteronomy 1:1 reads: "These are the words that Moses spoke to all of Israel beyond the Jordan." The east side of the Jordan would be "this" side with the west side being the "other side." (Numbers 35:14; Joshua 22:4) The point of his contention here being the fact that Moses was never on the other side of the Jordan, the west side, with the Israelite nation. Therefore, the question begs to be asked, Why would Moses pen "beyond," a seeming reference to the west side? This will be answered soon enough.

Thomas Hobbes (1588–1679) writes, "It is therefore sufficiently evident that the five books of Moses were written after his time, though how long after it be not so manifest." Is Hobbes a friend or foe of Christianity? Like Francis Bacon before him, he deepened the crack in the acceptance of the Bible being a source of divine authority.[78]

Benedict Spinoza (1632–1677) writes, "It is thus clearer than the sun at noon the Pentateuch was not written by Moses but by someone who lived long after Moses." Spinoza lays the groundwork for higher criticism based on logical or reasonable deduction, believing that thought and actions should be governed by reason, deductive rationalism.[79] He writes that because "There are many passages in the Pentateuch which Moses could not have written, it follows that the belief that Moses was the author of the Pentateuch is ungrounded and irrational."[80] Moses was not the only Biblical author to lose his writership at the chopping block of Spinoza. "I pass on, then, to the prophetic books ... An examination of these assures me that the prophecies therein contained have been compiled from other books ... but are only such as were collected here and there, so that they are fragmentary." Daniel did not fare so well either, he is only credited with the last five chapters of his book. Spinoza presents the notion that the 39 books of the Hebrew

---

[78] Garrett, Don, *The Cambridge companion to Spinoza* (Cambridge: Cambridge University Press, 1996), 389.

[79] Richard Elliot Friedman, *Who Wrote The Bible* (San Francisco: Harper Collins, 1997), 21.

[80] R. H. M. Elwes, *A Theologico-political Treatise, and a Political Treatise* (New York, NY: Cosimo Classics, 2005), 126.

Old Testament were set down by none other than the Pharisees. Moreover, the prophets spoke not by God, being inspired, but of their own accord. As to the apostles, Spinoza wrote, "The mode of expression and discourse adopted by [them] in the Epistles show very clearly that the latter are not written by revelation and divine command, but merely by the natural powers and judgment of the authors." Did Matthew, Mark, Luke, and John, fare any better? Hardly! Spinoza states: "It is scarcely credible that God can have designated to narrate the life of Christ four times over, and to communicate it thus to mankind."

Spinoza had no respect for those he deemed fools because of their belief in miracles. He writes, "Anyone who seeks for the true causes of miracles and strives to understand natural phenomena as an intelligent being, and not gaze upon them like a fool, is set down and denounced as an impious heretic by those, whom the masses adore as the interpreters of nature and the gods. Such a person knows that, with the removal of ignorance, the wonder which forms their only available means for proving and preserving their authority would vanish also. . . . A miracle, whether a contravention to, or beyond nature is a mere absurdity."[81] Such a dogmatic disbelief in miracles is a contributing factor to Spinoza being the father of modern-day higher criticism.

Richard Simon (1638–1712). This French Catholic priest accepted Moses as the author for most of the Pentateuch, but he is the first to notice repetition with certain portions that would come to be known as doublets.

- two different creation stories
- two stories of the Abrahamic covenant
- two stories where Abraham names his son, Isaac
- two stories where Abraham claims Sarah as his sister
- two stories of Jacob's journey to Haran
- two stories where God revealed himself to Jacob at Bethel
- two stories where God changes Jacob's name to Israel
- two stories of when Moses got water from a rock at Meribah

Jean Astruc (1684–1766) This French physician and professor of medicine would, by a rather naïve observation, get the Documentary Hypothesis underway. While Astruc never denied Mosaic writership, he had observed that there seemed to be two sources for Moses' penning the early chapters of Genesis: one that favored the title God (Elohim), and another that favored the personal name of God (Jehovah). This theory seemed to carry even more support by duplicate material, as Astruc viewed Genesis chapter one as one creation account and Genesis chapter two as another. It should be kept in mind that Astruc credited Moses as the writer, but was simply looking for what Moses may have drawn on in penning the Pentateuch.[82]

---

[81] Norman L. Geisler, *Inerrancy* (Grand Rapids, MI: Zondervan, 1980), 318.

[82] Norman L. Geisler and William E. Nix, *A General Introduction to the Bible. Rev. and Expanded* (Chicago, IL: Moody Press, c.1986, 1996), 156.

David Hume (1711–1776) was an eighteenth-century Scottish philosopher whose influence on the denial of divine authority, miracles, and prophecy has had a major impact that has reached down to the twenty-first century! Hume has three major pillars that hold up his refutation of divine authority. First, he writes, "A miracle is a violation of the laws of nature."[83] The laws of nature have been with man since his start. If a person falls from a high place, he will hit the ground. If a rock is dropped into the sea, it will sink. Each morning our sun comes over the horizon and each night it goes down, and so on. Without a doubt, there are laws of nature that never fail to follow their purpose. Therefore, for Hume, there is nothing that would ever violate the laws of nature. This 'conclusive evidence,' Hume felt, "is as entire as any argument from experience" that there could never be miracles.

Hume's second pillar is based on his belief that humankind is gullible. Moreover, he reasons that the masses of 'religious persons' want to believe in miracles. In addition, there have been many who have lied about so-called miracles, which have been nothing but a sham. For his third pillar, Hume argues that miracles have occurred only in the time periods of ignorance; as the enlightenment of man grew the miraculous diminished. Hume reported, "Such prodigious events never happen in our days." Hume rejected the inspiration of Scripture on two grounds: (1) he denied the possibility of miracles and prophecy, and (2) he rejected the Bible's divine authority as a whole because, to him, it was based upon perception or feeling, rather than upon fact, nor could it be proved by observation and experiment. Thus, for Hume, the result is that the Bible "contains nothing but sophistry and illusion."[84] As we can see, Hume's conclusion is obvious: Because the Bible is, in fact, not inspired, it could never be a true source of knowledge that it claims, and it is certainly not God's Word for humankind.

Johann Gottfried Eichhorn (1752–1827) took Jean Astruc's conjectures beyond Genesis to other books of the Pentateuch, arguing that the Pentateuch contained three primary sources that were distinct by vocabulary, style, and theological features. He also borrowed the phrase "higher criticism" from Presbyterian minister and scientist Joseph Priestly, and he was the first to name these alleged sources "E" (for Elohim) and "J" for Jehovah.[85]

Karl Heinrich Graf (1815–1869), aside from Julius Wellhausen, was the person we look to most for the modern documentary hypothesis. For Graf the "J" source was the earliest, composed in the ninth century B.C.E.;[86] the "E" source was written shortly thereafter. The author of Deuteronomy wrote shortly before Josiah's clearing away false worship in the seventh century B.C.E., and finally, the "P" source was written in the sixth century after the exile.

---

[83] David Hume, *An Enquiry Concerning Human Understanding* (Boston, MA: Digireads.com, 2006), 65.

[84] Ibid., 90.

[85] Norman L. Geisler and William E. Nix, *A General Introduction to the Bible. Rev. and Expanded* (Chicago, IL: Moody Press, c.1986, 1996), 157.

[86] B.C.E. means "before the Common Era," which is more accurate than B.C. ("before Christ"). C.E. denotes "Common Era," often called A.D., for anno Domini, meaning "in the year of our Lord."

In 1878, the German Bible critic **Julius Wellhausen (1844–1918),** writing in *Prolegomena zur Geschichte Israels (Prolegomena to the History of Israel),* popularized the ideas of the above scholars that the first five books of the Bible, as well as Joshua, were written from the 9th century into the 5th century B.C.E., over a millennium [1,000 years] after the events described.[87]

The capital letter "J" is used to represent an alleged writer. In this case it stands for any place God's personal name, Jehovah, is used. It is argued that this author is perhaps a woman as it is the only one of their presented authors who is not a priest. (Harold Bloom, *The Book of "J"*) They date the portion set out to "J" to c.850 B.C.E. Some scholars place this author in the southern portion of the Promised Land, Judah.[88]

Another writer is put forth as "E," for it stands for the portion that has Jehovah's title Elohim, God. Most higher critics place this author c.750–700 B.C.E. Unlike "J," this author "E" is said to reside in the northern kingdom of Israel. As stated earlier, this author is reckoned a priest, with his lineage going back to Moses. It is also proffered that he bought this office. In addition, it is argued that an editor combined "J" and "E" after the destruction of Israel by the Assyrians but before the destruction of Jerusalem by the Babylonians, which they date to about 722 BC.E.[89]

These same critics hold out that the language and theological content of "D," Deuteronomy, is different from Genesis, Exodus, Leviticus, and Numbers. Thus they have another author. They argue that the priests living in the northern kingdom of Israel gathered "D" over several hundred years; however, it was not until much later that "D" was combined with the earlier works. It is also said that the "D" writer (source) was also behind Joshua, Judges, 1 and 2 Samuel and 1 and 2 Kings (Dtr). It is suggested strongly that, in fact, this is the book found in the temple by Hilkiah the high priest and given to King Josiah. (2 Kings 22:8) It is further put forth that J/E/D were fused together as one document in about 586 B.C.E.[90]

The source critics use the capital letter "P" for Priestly. This is because this portion of the Pentateuch usually relates to the priesthood. For instance, things like the sacrifices would be tagged as belonging to this author. Many scholars suggest that "P" was written before the destruction of Jerusalem, which they date at 586 B.C.E. Others put forth that it was written during the exile of seventy years, the Priest(s) composing this holy portion for the people who would return from exile, while others say it was written after the exile, about 450 B.C.E. These liberal scholars find no consensus on when this supposed author "P" wrote this portion of the first five books. The critics tell us that the final form of J/E/D/P was composed into one document about 400 B.C.E.[91]

---

[87] Ernest Nicholson, *The Pentateuch in the Twentieth Century: The Legacy of Julius Wellhausen* (New York: Oxford University Press, 1998), 36–47.

[88] Mark F. Rooker, *Leviticus: The New American Commentary* (Nashville: Broadman & Holman, 2001), 23.

[89] Ibid., 23.

[90] Ibid., 23.

[91] Ibid., 23–24.

The capital "R" represents the editor(s) who put it together and may have altered some portions to facilitate their social-circumstances of their day. The "R" comes from the German word *Redakteur* (Redactor), which is an editor or reviser of a work.

With all the focus on Wellhausen and the impetus he has given to the Documentary Hypothesis, one would conclude that he had made an enormous, critical investigation of the text, which, in essence, moved him to cosign with his predecessors. If that is your conclusion, you will have to regroup, for it was simply a feeling that something was not quite right that moved Wellhausen to accept a system of understanding without any evidence whatsoever. In his book *Prolegomena to the History of Israel*, first published in 1878, Wellhausen helps his readers to appreciate just how he came about his expressed interest in the Documentary Hypothesis:

> In my early student days I was attracted by the stories of Saul and David, Ahab and Elijah; the discourses of Amos and Isaiah laid strong hold on me, and I read myself well into the prophetic and historical books of the Old Testament. Thanks to such aids as were accessible to me, I even considered that I understood them tolerably, but at the same time was troubled with a bad conscience, as if I were beginning with the roof instead of the foundation; for I had no thorough acquaintance with the Law, of which I was accustomed to be told that it was the basis and postulate of the whole literature. At last I took courage and made my way through Exodus, Leviticus, Numbers, and even through Knobel's Commentary to these books. But it was in vain that I looked for the light which was to be shed from this source on the historical and prophetical books. On the contrary, my enjoyment of the latter was marred by the Law; it did not bring them any nearer me, but intruded itself uneasily, like a ghost that makes a noise indeed, but is not visible and really effects nothing. Even where there were points of contact between it and them, differences also made themselves felt, and I found it impossible to give a candid decision in favour of the priority of the Law. Dimly I began to perceive that throughout there was between them all the difference that separates two wholly distinct worlds. Yet, so far from attaining clear conceptions, I only fell into deeper confusion, which was worse confounded by the explanations of Ewald in the second volume of history of Israel. At last, in the course of a casual visit in Göttingen in the summer of 1867, I learned through Ritschl that Karl Heinrich Graf placed the law later than the Prophets, and, almost without knowing his reasons for the hypothesis, I was prepared to accept it; I readily acknowledged to myself the possibility of understanding Hebrew antiquity without the book of the Torah.[92]

Martin Noth (1902–1968) A liberal twentieth-century German scholar who specialized in the pre-Exilic history of the Jewish people. Noth presented what he called the "Deuteronomic Historian." He argued that the language and theological outlook of Joshua, Judges, 1 and 2 Samuel and 1 and 2 Kings was the same as the book of Deuteronomy. Noth believed this writer lived during the exile because of a reference from 2 Kings to the exile. Modern critics, however, believed this writer lived before the exile, with 2 Kings 25:27 being a later addition.

---

[92] Julius Wellhausen, *Prolegomena to the History of Israel* (1878), 3–4

Frank M. Cross, Jr., Hebrew and Biblical scholar' muddies the water even more with his proposition that there was not one Deuteronomistic history, but two. The first he proposed to be written during the reign of the Judean King Josiah to aid him in cleaning up the false worship going on within Judah. After the destruction of Jerusalem, Cross said the same writer or possibly another goes back to edit this work, to add in the destruction of Jerusalem and the exile to Babylon.

Redaction Criticism

I briefly address the Redaction Theory here because of its relationship to the Documentary Hypothesis. As stated above in our alphabet soup of alleged authors ("J," "E," "D," "P," and "R"), a redactor is an editor or reviser of a work. Redaction Criticism is another form of Biblical criticism that intends to investigate the Scriptures and draw conclusions concerning their authorship, historicity, and time of writing. This form of criticism as well as the others has really done nothing more than tear down God's Word. R. E. Friedman, the Documentary Hypothesis' biggest advocate, asserts that the "J" document was composed between 922–722 B.C.E. in the southern kingdom of Judah, while the northern kingdom of Israel was composing the "E" document during these same years. Friedman contends that sometime thereafter a compiler of history put these two sources together, resulting in "J/E," with the compiler being known as "RJE." Friedman states that shortly thereafter, the priesthood in Jerusalem put out yet another document, known today as "P," this being another story to be added to the above "J/E." Going back to their authors for the first five books of the Bible, Friedman and these critics claim a redactor, or editor put the whole Pentateuch together using "D," "P," and the combination of "J/E." For them this editor (Deuteronomist) used the written sources he had available to make his additions for dealing with the social conditions of his day. They claim this editor's express purpose was to alter Scripture to bring comfort and hope to those who were in exile in Babylon. Wellhausen's theories, with some adjustments, have spread like a contagious disease, until they have consumed the body of Christendom. However, the real question is, Do these higher critics have any serious evidence to overturn thousands of years of belief by three major religious groups (Jews, Christians, and Muslims) that the Pentateuch was written by Moses?

What these critics have are pebbles, each representing minute inferences and implications [circumstantial evidence at best] that they place on one side of a scale. These are weighed out against the conservative evidence of Moses' authorship of the Pentateuch. As unsuspecting readers work their way through the books and articles written by these critics, the scales seem to be tilted all to one side, as if there were no evidence for the other side. Thus, like a jury, many uninformed readers; conclude that there is no alternative but to accept the idea that there are multiple authors for the Pentateuch instead of Moses, who is traditionally held to be the sole author.

Just what impact has the Documentary Hypothesis had on academia? Let us allow R. Rendtorf, professor Emeritus of the University of Heidelberg, to answer:

> Current international study of the Pentateuch presents at first glance a picture of complete unanimity. The overwhelming majority of scholars in almost all countries where scholarly study of Old Testament is pursued, take the documentary hypothesis as the virtually uncontested point of departure for their

work; and their interest in the most precise understanding of the nature and theological purposes of the individual written sources seems undisturbed.[93]

Let us take a moment to look at many of these pebbles and see which side of the scale they are to be placed on. As stated at the outset, we will address the major arguments as a case against the whole. Some of these pebbles are major obstacles for honest-hearted Christians.

Arguments of Higher Critics for the Documentary Hypothesis

We will address four areas of argumentation from the higher critics: (1) the divine names, (2) discrepancies, (3) repetition, known as "doublets," and (4) differences in language and style. We will give at least one example of each and address at least one example under the evidence for Moses' writership.

Divine Names

The higher critics argue that every Bible verse that contains the Hebrew word for God, ('Elohim'), set off by itself has its own writer, designated by the capital "E" ("Elohist"). On the other hand, any verse that contains the Tetragrammaton, (Jehovah, Yahweh), God's personal name, is attributed to yet another writer, "J" ("Jawist"). (Cassuto, 18-21) Let us see how they explain this. The critics argue that "God" ('Elohim') is restricted in use exclusively in the first chapter of Genesis (1:1–31) in relation to God's creation activity, and that starting in Genesis 2:4 through the end of the second chapter we find God's personal name.

R. E. Friedman speaks of a discovery by three men: "One was a minister, one was a physician, and one was a professor. The discovery that they made ultimately came down to the combination of two pieces of evidence: doublets and the names of God. They saw that there were apparently two versions each of a large number of Biblical stories: two accounts of the creation, two accounts each of several stories about the patriarchs Abraham and Jacob, and so on. Then, they noticed that, quite often, one of the two versions of a story would refer to God by one name and the other version would refer to God by a different name." (R. E. Friedman, 50)

Different settings, however, require different uses. This principle holds true throughout the whole of the entire Old Testament. Moses may choose to use ('Elohim') in a setting in which he wants to show a particular quality clearly, like power, creative activity, and so on. On the other hand, Moses may choose to use God's personal name (Jehovah, Yahweh) when the setting begs for that personal relationship between the Father and his children, the Israelites, or even more personable, a one-on-one conversation between Jehovah God and a faithful servant.

The Divine Names: The weakness of claiming multiple authors because of the different names used for God is quite evident when we look at just one small portion of the book of Genesis in the *American Standard Version* (1901). God is called "God Most

---

[93] R. Rendtorff, "The Problem of the Process of Transmission in the Pentateuch," *JSOT* (1990): 101.

High," "possessor (or maker) of heaven and earth," "O Lord Jehovah," "a God that seeth," "God Almighty," "God," "[the] God,"[94] and "the Judge of all the earth." (Genesis 14:18, 19; 15:2; 16:13; 17:1, 3; 18:25) It is difficult to believe that different authors wrote these verses. Moreover, let us look at Genesis 28:13, which says, "And, behold, Jehovah stood above it, and said, I am Jehovah, the God ["Elohim"] of Abraham thy father, and the God of Isaac: the land whereon thou liest, to thee will I give it, and to thy seed." Another scripture, Psalm 47:5, says, "God is gone up with a shout, Jehovah with the sound of a trumpet."[95] In applying their documentary analysis, we would have to accept the idea that two authors worked together on each of these two verses.

Many conservative scholars have come to realize that in a narrative format one will often find a ruler being referred to not only by name but also by a title, such as "king." M. H. Segal observes: "Just as those interchanges of human proper names and their respective appellative common nouns cannot by any stretch of the imagination be ascribed to a change of author or source of document, so also the corresponding interchanges of the divine names in the Pentateuch must not be attributed to such a literary cause."[96] If one were to look up "Adolf Hitler" using Academic American Encyclopedia, within three paragraphs he will find the terms "Führer," "Adolf Hitler," and simply "Hitler." Who is so bold as to suggest that there are three different authors for these three paragraphs?

Dr. John J. Davis[97] helps us to appreciate that there is "no other religious document from the ancient Near East [that] was compiled in such a manner; a documentary analysis of the Gilgameš Epic or Enūma Eliš would be complete folly. The author of Genesis may have selected divine names on the basis of theological emphasis rather than dogmatic preference. Many divine names were probably interchangeable; Baal and Hadad were used interchangeably in the Hadad Tablet from Ugarit,[98] and similar examples could be cited from Egyptian texts."[99]

In fact, we now know that there were many deities in the ancient Near East that had multiple names. As stated above with the Babylonian Creation account, the Enuma Elish, the god Marduk (Merodach), chief deity of Babylon, also had some 50 different names.[100] It would not even be thinkable to apply any of the Documentary Hypothesis analysis to any of these works. Why? Not only because we can see that ancient writers are no different than modern writers and are able to use different names and titles interchangeably within their work, but they were written on stone, so to speak. If one has one clay tablet that has both a personal name and two different titles for the same king, it would be difficult to argue that there were two or three different authors for the one

---

[94] The title 'Elo·him´ preceded by the definite article ha, giving the expression ha·'Elo·him´.

[95] See also Psalm 46:11; 48:1, 8.

[96] See also Psalm 46:11; 48:1, 8.

[97] John J. Davis, *Paradise to Prison: Studies in Genesis* (Salem: Sheffield, 1975), 22–23.

[98] G. R. Driver, *Canaanite Myths and Legends* (New York: T. & T. Clark, 1971), 70-72.

[99] For example, see the "Stele of Ikhernofret" in James B. Pritchard, ed., *Ancient Near Eastern Texts*, 2nd ed. Princeton: Princeton University Press, 1955, pp. 329-30.

[100] K. A. Kitchen, *On the Reliability of the Old Testament* (Grand Rapids: Eerdmans, 2003), 424–5.

tablet. Bible scholar Mark F. Rooker has the following to say about the use of Elohim and Yahweh in the Old Testament:

> Moreover, it is clear that throughout the Old Testament that the occurrence of the names of God as Elohim or Yahweh is to be attributed to contextual and semantic issues, not the existence of sources. This conclusion is borne out by the fact that the names consistently occur in predictable genre. In the legal and prophetic texts the name Yahweh always appears, while in wisdom literature the name for God is invariably Elohim. In narrative literature, which includes much of the Pentateuch, both Yahweh and Elohim are used.[101] Yet consistently the names do not indicate different sources but were chosen by design. The name Elohim was used in passages to express the abstract idea of Deity as evident in God's role as Creator of the universe and the Ruler of nature. Yahweh, on the other hand, is the special covenant name of God who has entered into a relationship with the Israelites since the name reflects God's ethical character. (Cassuto, 31) Given the understanding of the meaning of these names for God, it is no wonder that the source which contains the name Yahweh would appear to reflect a different theology from a selected group of texts which contained the name Elohim."[102]

Let us, on a small scale, do our own analysis of the divine names in the first two chapters of Genesis. The Hebrew word ('*elohim*´) is most often agreed upon to be from a root meaning "be strong," "mighty," or "power."[103] It should be said too that by far, most Hebrew scholars recognize the plural form (*im*) of this title '*elo·him*´ to be used as a plural of "majesty," "greatness," or "excellence." The Hebrew word ('*elo·him*´) is used for the Creator 35 times from Genesis 1:1 to 2:4a. Exactly what is the context of this use? It is used in a setting that deals with God's power, his greatness, his excellence, his creation activity, all of which seems appropriate, does it not?

Moving on to Genesis 2:4b–25, we find God now being referred to by his personal name, the Tetragrammaton (YHWH, JHVH), which is translated "Jehovah" (KJV, ASV, NW, NEB, etc.) or "Yahweh" (AT, NAB, JB, HCSB, etc.). It is found in verses 4b–25 eleven times; however, it comes before his title ('*elo·him*´).[104] Why the switch, and what is the context of this use? This personal name of God is used in a setting that deals with his personal relationship with man and woman. This is not a second creation account; it is a more detailed account of the creation of man, which was only briefly mentioned in chapter one in passing, as each feature of creation was ticked off. In chapter two, the Creator becomes a person as he speaks to his intelligent creation, giving them the prospect of an perfect eternal life in a paradise garden, which is to be cultivated earth wide, to be filled with perfect offspring. Therefore, we see a personal interchange between God and man as He lays out His plans to Adam, which seems very appropriate, does it not when

---

[101] Similarly, Livingston has pointed out that the cognate West Semitic divine names il and ya(w) appear to be interchangeable in the Eblaite tablets. (*The Pentateuch in Its Cultural Environment*, 224.)

[102] Mark F. Rooker, *Leviticus: The New American Commentary* (Nashville: Broadman & Holman, 2001), 26–27.

[103] Ibid., 27.

[104] "Jehovah God." Heb., Yehwah´ 'Elohim´.

switching from using a title in chapter one to using a personal name in chapter two? In chapter two, we have the coupling of the personal name "Jehovah" with the title "God," to show that we are still talking about this 'great,' 'majestic,' 'all powerful' Creator, but personalized as he introduces himself to his new earthly creation.

Thus, there is no reason to assume that we are talking about two different writers. No, it is two different settings in which a skilled writer would make the transition just as Moses did. It would be no different than if a modern-day news commentator was giving as a report about the United States President visiting Russia to meet with Dmitry Anatolyevich Medvedev, in which he used the title President predominately. The following week the same news commentator may be covering the President visiting a hospital with injured children who had survived a tornado, and refer to the President as President Obama. It isn't difficult to see that one is an official setting where the President needs to be portrayed as powerful, while in the other setting; he needs to be portrayed as personable. The same principles used herein apply to the rest of the Pentateuch and the Old Testament as a whole.

Discrepancies

Discrepancies, or should I say "perceived" discrepancies, are the critic's favorite pebble. These perceived discrepancies set off an alarm for the critic, and then he rushes off with his pebble like a child to add it to the multiple-authors side of the scale. To differentiate between the supposed different sources texts, I will lay them out as follows:

> **("J")** will be used to represent an alleged writer. In this case, it stands for any place God's name Jehovah is used.
>
> **("E")** will be for the portion that has Jehovah's title, *Elohim*, God.
>
> **("P")** will be for the portion of priestly activities.
>
> **("D")** Deuteronomy is different from Genesis, Exodus, Leviticus, and Numbers. Thus, it has another author.
>
> **("RJE")** will represent the compiler who put "J" and "E" together.
>
> **("R")** will represent the editor(s), who put it all together and may have altered some portions to express their social circumstances of their day.
>
> **("U")** will represent the alleged "unknown independent texts."

"Narrative Discrepancy" (Genesis 12:1, ASV) Now Jehovah said unto Abram, Get thee out of thy country, and from thy kindred, and from thy father's house, unto the land that I will show thee: ("J") (after Terah, Abram's father, died, Abram is commanded to leave Haran)

> **(Genesis 11:26, ESV)** When Terah had lived 70 years, he fathered Abram, Nahor, and Haran ("U"). (When Terah was 70, Abram was born.)

(Genesis 11:32, ESV) The days of Terah were 205 years ("U"): and Terah died in Haran ("R"). (Terah died at the age of 205, which would make Abraham 135 when he left Ur.)

(Genesis 12:4, ASV) So Abram went, as Jehovah had spoken unto him; and Lot went with him ("J"): and Abram was seventy and five years old when he departed out ("P") of Haran ("R"). (12:4 has Abram being only 75 when he leaves Haran.)

Discrepancy: According to 11:32, Terah died at the age of 205; hence, Abram must have been 135 when he was called to leave Haran. However, 12:4 says that he was only 75 when he left Haran. The Source Critic informs us that this seeming contradiction is resolved if Genesis chapter 12 is of a different source from the genealogy of Genesis chapter 11.

The above need not be a contradiction at all. True enough, it was at the age of 70 that Terah began having children (Genesis 11:26), but does Abraham have to be the firstborn child simply because he is listed first? Consider, what weight does the names Nahor and Haran play in the Bible account? Now consider, what about the name Abraham? He is considered the father and founder of three of the greatest religions on this planet: Judaism, Christianity, and Islam. He is the third most prominent person named in God's Word. This practice, that of placing the most prominent son first in a list of sons even though they are not the firstborn is followed elsewhere in God's Word with other prominent men of great faith, for example, Shem and Isaac. (Genesis 5:32; 11:10; 1 Chronicles 1:28) Therefore, let us keep it simple. Genesis 11:26 does not say that Abram was the firstborn; it simply says that Terah began fathering children, and then it goes on to list his three sons, listing the most prominent one first. Thus, it is obvious that Terah fathered Abram at the age of 130. (Genesis 11:26, 32; 12:4) In addition, it is true that Sarah was Abram's half-sister, not by the same mother, but by having Terah as the same father. (Genesis 20:12) Therefore, in all likelihood, it is Haran who is the firstborn of Terah, whose daughter was old enough to marry Nahor, another of Terah's three sons. – Genesis 11:29.

"Narrative Discrepancy" (Genesis 37:25-28, 36; 38:1; 39:1, YLT)

(Genesis 37:25-28, YLT) And they sit down to eat bread ("E"), and they lift up their eyes, and look, and lo, a company of Ishmaelites coming from Gilead, and their camels bearing spices, and balm, and myrrh, going to take [them] down to Egypt. 26 And Judah saith unto his brethren, 'What gain when we slay our brother, and have concealed his blood? 27 Come, and we sell him to the Ishmaelites, and our hands are not on him, for he [is] our brother—our flesh;' and his brethren hearken ("J"). 28 And Midianite merchantmen pass by and they draw out and bring up Joseph out of the pit ("E"), and sold him to the Ishmaelites for twenty shekels of silver. They took Joseph to Egypt ("J"). (Genesis 37:36) And the Medanites have sold him unto Egypt, to Potiphar, a eunuch of Pharaoh, head of the executioners ("E"). (Genesis 38:1) And it cometh to pass, at that time, that Judah goeth down from his brethren, and turneth aside unto a man, an Adullamite, whose name [is] Hirah ("J"). (Genesis 39:1) And Joseph hath been brought down to Egypt, and Potiphar, a eunuch of Pharaoh, head of the executioners, an Egyptian man, buyeth him out of the hands of the Ishmaelites who have brought him thither ("J").

Discrepancy: In Genesis 37:25 the Ishmaelites are passing by at the opportune time mentioned in verses 26 and 27, with Judah suggesting that instead of killing Joseph they sell him to the Ishmaelites. Yet, verse 28 switches in midstride to the Midianites, as they drew Joseph from the pit, selling him to the Ishmaelites. In verse 36, the Medanites (likely a scribal error; almost every translation has Midianites, so we will accept that as so) are selling Joseph to Potiphar in Egypt. Yet, the discrepancy pushes the envelope even further, for Genesis 39:1 says, it was the Ishmaelites who delivered and sold Joseph to Potiphar in Egypt. Was Joseph sold to Ishmaelites or to Midianites? In addition, who delivered and sold Joseph to Potiphar in Egypt? It seems that the higher critics are bent on using ambiguous passages (ambiguous at first glance to the casual reader) to facilitate their Documentary Hypothesis. You might say that these discrepancies are fuel for the engine that drives their Documentary Hypothesis locomotive. E. A. Speiser writes:

> The narrative is broken up into two originally independent versions. One of these (J) used the name Israel, featured Judah as Joseph's protector, and identified the Ishmaelites as the traders who bought Joseph from his brothers. The other (E) spoke of Jacob as the father and named Reuben as Joseph's friend; the slave traders in that version were Midianites who discovered Joseph by accident and sold him in Egypt to Potiphar.[105]

For Speiser, it is time to slice up the text and divide it up between our alleged "J"-Text and "E"-Text writers. It is also hypothesized that our "R"-Redactor edits the two and slips in some additional information as well, suggesting that the Midianites are the ones who were actually passing by, selling Joseph later to the Ishmaelites. Thus, it would be the Ishmaelites, who would deliver and sell Joseph to Potiphar in Egypt. Yes, at first glimpse, this would appear to make it all well, but we still have a problem: Genesis 37:36 states that it was the Midianites, who sold Joseph to Potiphar in Egypt.

Actually, when one looks below the surface reading, there is no discrepancy here at all. Ishmael (son of Hagar and Abraham) and Midian (son of Keturah and Abraham) were half-brothers. It is highly likely that there was intermarriage between the descendants of these two, allowing for an interchangeable use of the expression "Ishmaelites" and "Midianites." (Genesis 25:1–4; 37:25–28; 39:1) We see this in the days of Judge Gideon when Israel was being attacked, with both terms "Ishmaelites" and "Midianites" being used to describe the attackers. (Judges 8:24; 7:25; 8:22, 26) Alternatively, even still we could have an Ishmaelite caravan encompassing Midianite merchants that were passing by, with the Midianites brokering the deal and delivering Joseph from the pit to the Ishmaelite caravan, where Joseph would be under the Ishmaelites' custody even if he was being *detained* by the Midianites. Once they arrived at Potiphar's place in Egypt, it would be the Midianites to broker the deal with Potiphar. Thus, it can be stated either way, the Ishmaelites or the Midianites delivered and sold Joseph to Potiphar in Egypt.

---

[105] E. A. Speiser, *Genesis*, Anchor Bible (Garden City, N.Y.: Doubleday, 1964), 293–4.

Repetitions (Doublets)

What are doublets? It is the telling of the same story twice, making the same events appear to happen more than once. For example,

(1) there are two stories of the creation account,

(2) two stories of God's covenant with Abraham,

(3) two stories where Abraham names his son Isaac,

(4) two stories where Abraham claims Sarah is his sister, two stories of Jacob's journey to Haran,

(5) two stories where God revealed himself to Jacob at Bethel,

(6) two stories where God changes Jacob's name to Israel,

(7) two stories of when Moses got water from the rock at Meribah, and a detailed description in Exodus 24–29 of how to build the tabernacle, then within five chapters a retelling of how they did it, repeating the details again in chapters 34–40.

The critic goes on to point out that, there is more to this "doublet" story than meets the eye; they argue that one of the doublets will contain the title for the Creator, God (*Elohim*); while the other doublet of the same story will contain the personal name for the Creator, Jehovah. Moreover, they argue that there are other defining features that are only within one side or the other.

(Genesis 1:27, ESV) So God created man in his own image, in the image of God he created him; male and female he created them.

(Genesis 2:7, ASV) And Jehovah God formed man of the dust of the ground, and breathed into his nostrils the breath of life; and man became a living soul.

Within two chapters, we have two verses where the writer, if one person, informs us of the creation of man twice, the second as though the first was never mentioned at all. Again, the source critic will argue that there were two sources of the same information on the creation of man and the compiler allowed both to remain. What the source critic fails to tell his reader is that there are sense breaks within the various accounts in these first three chapters. Genesis 1:1–2:3 is the basic creation account. Genesis 2:4–25 is the restating of day three (verses 5, 6) and the subsequent preparation of the earth for the settling of man and woman in the Garden of Eden. Genesis 3:1–24 is specifically about the temptation, the entry of sin and death into the world, the promise of a seed to save humankind, a description of the conditions of imperfection and of man's loss of the Garden of Eden.

Bible scholar Leon Kass, who supports the Documentary Hypothesis, had this to say about the creation account of Genesis chapters 1 and 2:

Once we recognize the independence of the two creation stories, we are compelled to adopt a critical principle of reading if we mean to understand each story on its own terms. We must scrupulously avoid reading into the second story any facts or notions taken from the first, and vice versa. Thus, in reading about the origin of man in the story of the Garden of Eden, we must not say or even think that man is here created in God's image or that man is to be the ruler over the animals. Neither, when we try to understand the relation of man and woman in the Garden, are we to think about or make use of the first story's account of the coequal coeval creation of man and woman. Only after we have read and interpreted each story entirely on its own should we try to integrate the two disparate teachings. By proceeding in this way, we will discover why these two separate and divergent accounts have been juxtaposed and how they function to convey a coherent, noncontradictory teaching about human life.[106]

Let us look at another example in which the critic has argued that one source says forty days while the other speaks of 150 days:

(Gen 7:12, NET) And the rain fell on the earth forty days and forty nights.

(Gen 7:24, NET) The waters prevailed over the earth for 150 days.

Genesis 7:24 and 8:3 say the floodwaters lasted for 150 days, yet; Genesis 7:4, 12 and 17 say it was only forty days. Once again, the difference is solved with a simple explanation. Each is referring to two different time periods. Let us look at these verses again (italics mine):

(Gen 7:12, NET) And the rain fell on the earth forty days and forty nights. [Notice that the 40-days refer to how long the rain fell—"the rain fell."]

(Gen 7:24, NET) The waters prevailed over the earth for 150 days. [Notice that the 150-days refer to how long the flood lasted—"waters prevailed."]

(Gen 8:3, NET) The waters kept receding steadily from the earth, so that they had gone down by the end of the 150 days.

(Gen 8:4, NET) On the seventeenth day of the seventh month, the ark came to rest on one of the mountains of Ararat.

(Gen 7:11; 8:13, 14, NET) In the *six hundredth year of Noah's life, in the second month*, on the seventeenth day of the month, on that day all the fountains of the great deep burst open and the floodgates of the heavens were opened. *In Noah's six hundred and first year, in the first day of the first month, the waters had dried up* from the earth, and Noah removed the covering from the ark and saw that *the surface of the ground was dry. And by the twenty-seventh day of the second month the earth was dry.*

By the end of the 150 days, the water had gone down [Gen 8:3]. Five months from the beginning of the rain, the ark comes to rest on Mount Ararat [8:4]. Eleven months later the waters dried up [7:11; 8:13]. Exactly 370 days from the start (lunar months), Noah and his family left the ark and were on dry ground.

Yet another example is found in 2 Kings 24:10-16. Verses 10-14 say, "At that time the servants of Nebuchadnezzar king of Babylon came up to Jerusalem, and the city was

---

[106] Leon R. Kass, *The Beginning of Wisdom: Reading Genesis* (New York: Free Press, 2003), 56.

besieged. And Nebuchadnezzar king of Babylon came to the city while his servants were besieging it, and Jehoiachin the king of Judah gave himself up to the king of Babylon, himself and his mother and his servants and his officials and his palace officials. The king of Babylon took him prisoner in the eighth year of his reign and carried off all the treasures of the house of the LORD and the treasures of the king's house, and cut in pieces all the vessels of gold in the temple of the LORD, which Solomon king of Israel had made, as the LORD had foretold. He carried away all Jerusalem and all the officials and all the mighty men of valor, 10,000 captives, and all the craftsmen and the smiths. None remained, except the poorest people of the land."

Verses 15-16 say, "And he carried away Jehoiachin to Babylon. The king's mother, the king's wives, his officials, and the chief men of the land he took into captivity from Jerusalem to Babylon. And the king of Babylon brought captive to Babylon all the men of valor, 7,000, and the craftsmen and the metal workers, 1,000, all of them strong and fit for war."

Here we have a repetition of the same events back-to-back. Why? Is it multiple sources and the redactor simply keeping both? In an attempt to stave off the conservative view of Moses' writership, scholar, and critic Richard Elliot Friedman writes:

> Those who defended the traditional belief in Mosaic authorship argued that the doublets were always complementary, not repetitive, and that they did not contradict each other, but came to teach us a lesson by their 'apparent' contradiction. But another clue was discovered that undermined this traditional response. Investigators found that in most cases one of the two versions of a doublet story would refer to the deity by the divine name, Yahweh . . . , and the other version of the story would refer to the deity simply as 'God.' That is, the doublets lined up into two groups of parallel versions of stories. Each group was almost always consistent with the name it used. Moreover, the investigators found that it was not only the names of the deity that lined up. They found various other terms and characteristics that regularly appeared in one of the other group. This tended to support the hypothesis that someone had taken two different old source documents, cut them up, and woven them together to form the continuous story in the Five Books of Moses.[107]

Ancient Semitic literature has other similar examples of repetition. Moreover, the use of Elohim in one instance and Jehovah in another is due to context and semantic issues. Notice Friedman's use of the phrases "in most cases" and "almost always." Which is it? And as we will see, he is overstating his case to the point of exaggeration. Let us look at the most popular example in the "Matriarch in Danger." It has three occurrences in Genesis: Sarah in Egypt with Pharaoh (Genesis 12:10–20), Sarah in Gerar with Abimelech (Genesis 20:1–18), and Rebekah in Gerar with Abimelech (Genesis 26:7–11). Friedman would argue that we simply have one story with three different sources that had been maintained over time. The personal name of God, Jehovah, is used in the account of Sarah in Egypt with Pharaoh (vs. 17). The title Elohim is used in the account about Sarah in Gerar with Abimelech (vs. 3), but so is Jehovah (vs. 18). In the account of Rebekah in Gerar with Abimelech, neither Elohim nor Jehovah is used. Therefore, Friedman's case is

---

[107] Richard Elliot Friedman, *Who Wrote The Bible* (San Francisco: Harper Collins, 1997), 22.

really no case at all, because both Jehovah and Elohim appear in one account with Sarah in Gerar with Abimelech and neither Jehovah nor Elohim appear in the account with Rebekah in Gerar with Abimelech. It should be noted that all three occurrences are in reference to Abimelech and Pharaoh, but both times that the name Jehovah is used, it is in reference to Jehovah executing a punishment of these rulers. If their best example does not even come close to their claims, then what are we to think of the others? Before moving on to the differences in language and style, we should close with one last point about the literature of the Ancient Near East (ANE). One of the features of ANE literature, which includes Hebrew, is its parallelism, repetition, the telling of stories that are similar to stress patterns that are important. Even in the book of Acts, you have three different accounts of Paul's conversion (Ac 9:3-8; 22:6-11; 26:12-18). It is repetition for emphasis. At the outset of this section, we mentioned that chapters 24-29 of Exodus give a detailed description of how the tabernacle was built, and chapters 34-40 repeat the very same information. Chapters 24-29 contain the directions, and chapters 34-40 show how they did it; thus, the repetition is emphasizing that they did exactly what Jehovah had asked them to do.

Differences in Language and Style

Supporters of the Documentary Hypothesis would argue that within the Pentateuch we see such things as preferences for certain words, differences in vocabulary, reoccurring expressions in Deuteronomy that are not found in Genesis, Exodus, Leviticus, and Numbers, all evidence for the higher critics and their multiple source theory. Also, there are individual characteristics in grammar and syntax. Further, the critic describes "P" as being very boring, completely lacking in interest or excitement, dry; while the writers of "J" and "E" are very vivid and lively, holding the reader's interest in their storytelling. Additionally, "D" uses expressions like 'with all your heart and all your soul,' which the rest of the Pentateuch lacks in those types of expressions. Their conclusion is that there is no alternative but to have multiple writers as the differences in language and style dictate.

If the alleged writers of the Pentateuch were so narrow in their vocabulary and writing abilities that they would use only one given word for a given idea and never use another when dealing with that idea, it would be easy to suggest a division of actual sources. Yet this is not the case at all. The writers of the Hebrew Scriptures throughout ancient Israel actually expressed a great variety of words in their work. Douglas K. Stuart (Ph.D., Harvard University), Professor of Old Testament at Gordon–Conwell Theological Seminary, is of the same opinion:

> In fact, the contrary situation appears to be true. In ancient Israel there were four demonstrable indications of a preference for variety in written expression rather than for desire for stylistic consistency. (1) If there were two different ways of spelling a word the Israelites chose to preserve both spellings as valid and to include both of them frequently in any document. Thus with regard to spelling (orthography), ancient Israelites had no commitment to consistency to style, but the free use of alternative spellings was regarded as not only proper, but desirable. (2) In the case of common expressions, a similar phenomenon can be observed. Where variation was possible, it apparently was not avoided, but preferred. Alternative ways of forming a given multiword expression were employed commonly so that both alternatives were preserved. Thus, in the case of repeated phraseology in prose contexts, there was no

commitment to consistency of style, but rather the alternative formulation was regarded not only proper, but desirable. (3) With regard to variation in grammatical forms, a similar phenomenon is observed. If there existed two different ways of saying something, even in the case of a common verb form, both ways were used so as to preserve both in the common discourse. Again, the preference appears to have been for inclusion of variety rather than for consistency of one form if two existed. (4) The Masoretic system of *Kethib-Qere* represents a fourth indicator of the tendency in past times to preserve variance rather than to select one option and to employ it consistently, a tendency that extended into the medieval period when the Masoretes worked. This system arose from a desire to include, not merely side-by-side, but actually within the same word, two variant readings rather than two select ones. The Masoretes provide the consonants of one text option in the vowels of another. They indicated their preferred reading, but did not omit the reading they regarded as inferior, they simply did not localize it.[108]

Differences in Style and Vocabulary: An investigator would not be honest if he were simply to reject these differences out of hand, as though they did not exist. Therefore, rightly, we need to investigate these differences, giving an answer that has substance. I will cite one of their pillar examples, to demonstrate the principle that if they are so far off base here, then we can conclude their foundation in this area is really no foundation at all. Before we get started, let us do a little review of Biblical Hebrew, to be better able to address our example.

---

[108] Douglas K. Stuart, *The New American Commentary: An Exegetical Theological Exposition of Holy Scripture: EXODUS* (Nashville: Broadman & Holman, 2006). See pp. 30–31 for examples of the above four points.

(Qal): Qal is the simple form of the verb, meaning "light" or "easy." This is the simple active stem of the verb.

(Hiphil): This is generally called the *"causative"* form because it reveals the *causative* action of the qal verb. The *"h"* is prefixed to the stem, which modifies the root.

Qal	yalad (to give birth)
Hiphil	holid (he caused to give birth)

Examples:

Gen. 14:18: Irad begat (*yalad*) Mehujael

Gen. 5:4: Adam after he begat (*holid*) Seth

The advocates of the Documentary Hypothesis argue that to find *yalad* in the genealogy of Cain in Genesis chapter 4, the Table of Nations in Genesis chapter 10, and Nahor's family line in Genesis chapter 22 (all being of the "J" author), while finding *holid* in Adam's history down to Noah in Genesis chapter 5 as well as the genealogy of Shem found in Genesis chapter 11 (being of the "P" author) is nothing more than proof positive that there are two authors: "J" and "P."

In short, we are not dealing with a word or phrase that is peculiar to an individual writer like "J" or "P." No, this is nothing more than an example of following the basic rules of Hebrew grammar and syntax. In many cases, it could not have been written in any other way, because it is the socially accepted usage of the Hebrew language. When those who support the Documentary Hypothesis pull Hebrew words or even phrases out of their setting (as I have done above), looking at them in isolation, their reasoning becomes based solely on personal wishes, feelings, or perceptions, rather than on linguistic rules, reasons, or principles of the language itself. Hebrew, like any other language, conforms to the socially accepted style, with the regular and specific order, or arrangement. The Hebrew language has its own rules and allowable combinations of how words are joined together to make sense to the Hebrew mind. Umberto Cassuto, also known as Moshe David Cassuto, (1883–1951), who held the chair of Biblical studies at the Hebrew University of Jerusalem had this to say concerning the usage of *yalad* and *holid*:

> It will suffice to note the fact that the verb *yaladh* occurs in the signification of *holidh* only in the *past tense* [perfect] and the *present* [participle]. We say, "so-and-so *yaladh* [mas. sing. perfect] so-and-so," and we say *yoledh* [participle mas. Sing.: "is begetting"]; but we do not say in the *future tense* [imperfect] so-and-so *yeledh* [to signify: "he will beget"] (or *wayyeledh* [imperfect with *waw* conversive, to connote: "and he begot"]) so-and-so." In the imperfect, the *Qal* is employed only with reference to the mother, for example, so-and-so *teledh* ["will give birth to"] (*watteledh* ["and gave birth to"]) so and so." In connection with the father one can only say, *yolidh* [*hiphil* imperfect; "he will beget"] or *wayyoledh* [*hiphil* imperfect with *waw* conversive; "and he begot"] (although we find in Prov. xxvii 1: what a day may bring forth ["*yeledh*"; *Qal* imperfect] the verb is used there not in connotation of "begetting" but actually in the sense

of "giving birth"). Similarly, we do not say, using the infinitive, Aajare *lidhto* [to signify: "after his begetting"] but only Aajare *lidhtah* ["after her giving birth"]; with regard to the father we can only say Aajare *holidho* ["after his begetting"]. This is clear to anyone who is sensitive to the Hebrew idiom. In the genealogies from Adam to Noah and from Noah to Abraham, it would have been impossible to write anything else but *wayyoledh* and Aajare *hoilidho*; every Hebrew author would have had no option but to write thus and not otherwise. It is not a question of sources but of the general usage of the Hebrew tongue.[109]

Professor K. A. Kitchen, one of the leading experts on Biblical history, notes in his book *Ancient Orient and Old Testament*: "Stylistic differences are meaningless, and reflect the differences in detailed subject-matter." He says that similar style variations can also be found "in ancient texts whose literary unity is beyond all doubt."[110]

A 1981 news report relates to this debate and provides some interesting facts.[111]

TEL AVIV, Israel (UPI)—A five-year long computer study of the Bible strongly indicates that one author—and not three as widely held in modern criticism—wrote the book of Genesis.

"The probability of Genesis' having been written by one author is enormously high—82 percent statistically," a member of the research team said in an article published in Wednesday's *Jerusalem Post*.

Professor Yehuda Radday, a Bible scholar from the Technion, a Haifa university, said more than 20,000 words of Genesis were fed into a computer which conducted a painstaking analysis of its linguistic makeup.

Bible critics widely hold that Genesis had three authors—the Jawhist or "J" author, the Elohist or "E" author and a priestly writer, dubbed "P."

"We found the J and E narratives to be linguistically indistinguishable," Radday told a news conference today. But the P sections differ widely from them.

"This is only to be expected, since dramatic tales and legal documents must necessarily display different 'behavior,'" he said. "If you compared love letters and a telephone directory written by the same person, linguistic analysis would point to different authors."

The team combined statistical and linguistic methods with computer science and Bible scholarship to reach their conclusions. They used 54 analysis criteria, including word length, the use of the definite article and the conjunction "and," richness of vocabulary and transition frequencies between word categories.

"These criteria are a reliable gauge of authorship because these traits are beyond an author's conscious control and furthermore are countable," Radday said.

---

[109] Umberto Cassuto, *The Documentary Hypothesis* (New York, NY: Shalem Press, 2006), 55-56.

[110] K. A Kitchen, *Ancient Orient and Old Testament* (Downers Grove, IL: InterVarsity Press, 1975), 125.

[111] As published in the *St. Petersburg Times:* http://tinyurl.com/noke4m

A mathematics expert on the team ran a computer check against classical German works by Goethe, Herder and Kant and found that the statistical probability of their being the sole authors of their own work were only 22 percent, 7 percent and 9 percent respectively.

As mentioned above, Jewish and Christian conservatives accept one writer for the first five books of the Bible, namely, Moses. The critics, however, argue that although Moses is definitely the main character of the Pentateuch because they are unable to find any *direct mention* within it of Moses having written these five books, it is for them simply a tradition that Moses is the writer. This author is certain that is not the impression you will have after reading the next chapter.

Internal and External Evidence for Moses Authorship

First, it is obvious that Moses did *not* write *every word* of the Pentateuch. Why? The section that relates his death would be something that Joshua could have added after Moses' death. (Deuteronomy 34:1–8) In addition, the critic would argue, it would hardly seem very meek to pen these words about oneself: "Now the man Moses was very meek, more than all people who were on the face of the earth." (Numbers 12:3, *ESV*) Nevertheless, consider that Jesus said of himself: "I am gentle and lowly in heart" (Matthew 11:29, *ESV*), which no one would fault Jesus with as though he were boasting. Both Moses and Jesus were simply stating a fact. The amount of possible material that may have been added by Joshua, another inspired writer is next to nothing and does not negate Moses' authorship.

What Does the Biblical Evidence from the Old Testament Report?

Exodus 17:14 (ASV) ¹⁴ And Jehovah said unto Moses, Write this for a memorial in a book, and rehearse it in the ears of Joshua: that I will utterly blot out the remembrance of Amalek from under heaven.	**Exodus 24:4 (ASV)** ⁴ And Moses wrote all the words of Jehovah, and rose up early in the morning, and builded an altar under the mount, and twelve pillars, according to the twelve tribes of Israel.	**Exodus 34:27 (ASV)** ²⁷ And Jehovah said unto Moses, Write thou these words: for after the tenor of these words I have made a covenant with thee and with Israel.
Leviticus 26:46 (ASV) ⁴⁶ These are the statutes and ordinances and laws, which Jehovah made between him and the children of Israel in mount Sinai by Moses.	**Leviticus 27:34 (ASV)** ³⁴ These are the commandments, which Jehovah commanded Moses for the children of Israel in mount Sinai.	**Numbers 33:2 (ASV)** ² And Moses wrote their goings out according to their journeys by the commandment of Jehovah: and these are their journeys according to their goings out.
Numbers 36:13 (ASV) ¹³ These are the commandments and the	**Deuteronomy 1:1 (ASV)** ¹ These are the words which Moses spake unto	**Deuteronomy 31:9 (ASV)** ⁹ And Moses wrote this law, and delivered it unto the

ordinances which Jehovah commanded by Moses unto the children of Israel in the plains of Moab by the Jordan at Jericho.	all Israel beyond the Jordan in the wilderness, in the Arabah over against Suph, between Paran, and Tophel, and Laban, and Hazeroth, and Di-zahab.	priests the sons of Levi, that bare the ark of the covenant of Jehovah, and unto all the elders of Israel.
Deuteronomy 31:22 (ASV) 22 So Moses wrote this song the same day, and taught it the children of Israel.	**Deuteronomy 31:24 (ASV)** 24 And it came to pass, when Moses had made an end of writing the words of this law in a book, until they were finished,	**Joshua 1:7 (ASV)** 7 Only be strong and very courageous, to observe to do according to all the law, which Moses my servant commanded thee:
Joshua 8:31 (ASV) 31 as Moses the servant of Jehovah commanded the children of Israel, as it is written in the book of the law of Moses, an altar of unhewn stones, upon which no man had lifted up any iron: and they offered thereon burnt-offerings unto Jehovah, and sacrificed peace-offerings.	**1 Kings 2:3 (ASV)** 3 and keep the charge of Jehovah thy God, to walk in his ways, to keep his statutes, and his commandments, and his ordinances, and his testimonies, according to that which is written in the law of Moses, that thou may prosper in all that thou does, and whithersoever thou turn thyself.	**2 Kings 14:6 (ASV)** 6 but the children of the murderers he put not to death; according to that which is written in the book of the law of Moses, as Jehovah commanded, saying, The fathers shall not be put to death for the children, nor the children be put to death for the fathers; but every man shall die for his own sin.
2 Kings 21:8 (ASV) 8 neither will I cause the feet of Israel to wander any more out of the land which I gave their fathers, if only they will observe to do according to all that I have commanded them, and according to all the law that my servant Moses commanded them.	**Ezra 6:18 (ASV)** 18 And they set the priests in their divisions, and the Levites in their courses, for the service of God, which is at Jerusalem; as it is written in the book of Moses.	**Nehemiah 13:1 (ASV)** 1 On that day they read in the book of Moses in the audience of the people; and therein was found written, that an Ammonite and a Moabite should not enter into the assembly of God for ever,
Daniel 9:13 (ASV) 13 As it is written in the law of Moses, all this evil is come upon us: yet have we not entreated the favor of Jehovah our God, that ...	**Malachi 4:4 (ASV)** 4 Remember ye the law of Moses my servant, which I commanded unto him in Horeb for all Israel, even statutes and ordinances.	

To reject Moses as the writer of the Pentateuch is to reject these inspired writers and suggest they are not reliable; moreover, this would mean they were not inspired, because those under inspiration would not make such errors. If these critics are correct, then all the above is merely a great conspiracy. This author hardly thinks so!

What Does the Biblical Evidence from Jesus Christ Report?

Matthew 8:4 (ESV) ⁴And Jesus said to him, "See that you say nothing to anyone, but go, show yourself to the priest and offer the gift that Moses commanded, for a proof to them."	**Matthew 11:23-24 (ESV)** ²³And you, Capernaum, will you be exalted to heaven? You will be brought down to Hades. For if the mighty works done in you had been done in Sodom, it would have remained until this day. ²⁴ But I tell you that it will be more tolerable on the day of judgment for the land of Sodom than for you."
Matthew 19:4-5 (ESV) ⁴He answered, "Have you not read that he who created them from the beginning made them male and female, ⁵and said, 'Therefore a man shall leave his father and his mother and hold fast to his wife, and the two shall become one flesh'?	**Matthew 19:8 (ESV)** ⁸He said to them, "Because of your hardness of heart Moses allowed you to divorce your wives, but from the beginning it was not so.
Matthew 24:37 (ESV) ³⁷ For as were the days of Noah, so will be the coming of the Son of Man.	**Mark 10:5 (ESV)** ⁵And Jesus said to them, "Because of your hardness of heart he wrote you this commandment.
Mark 12:26 (ESV) ²⁶And as for the dead being raised, have you not read in the book of Moses, in the passage about the bush, how God spoke to him, saying, 'I am the God of Abraham, and the God of Isaac, and the God of Jacob'?	**Mark 1:44 (ESV)** ⁴⁴and said to him, "See that you say nothing to anyone, but go, show yourself to the priest and offer for your cleansing what Moses commanded, for a proof to them."
Mark 7:10 (ESV) ¹⁰For Moses said, 'Honor your father and your mother'; and, 'Whoever reviles father or mother must surely die.'	**Luke 5:14 (ESV)** ¹⁴And he charged him to tell no one, but "go and show yourself to the priest, and make an offering for your cleansing, as Moses commanded, for a proof to them."
Luke 11:51 (ESV) ⁵¹from the blood of Abel to the blood of Zechariah, who perished between the altar and the sanctuary. Yes, I tell you, it will be required of this generation.	**Luke 17:32 (ESV)** ³² Remember Lot's wife.
Luke 24:27, 44 English Standard Version (ESV) ²⁷And beginning with Moses and all the Prophets, he interpreted to them in all the Scriptures the things concerning himself. ⁴⁴Then he said to them, "These are my	**John 5:46 English Standard Version (ESV)** ⁴⁶For if you believed Moses, you would believe me; for he wrote of me.

words that I spoke to you while I was still with you, that everything written about me in the Law of Moses and the Prophets and the Psalms must be fulfilled."	
John 7:19 English Standard Version (ESV) ¹⁹ Has not Moses given you the law? Yet none of you keeps the law. Why do you seek to kill me?"	**John 8:58 (UASV)** Jesus said to them, "Truly, truly, I say to you, before Abraham came to be I have been in existence."[112]

How does one ignore the strongest evidence of Moses' writership of these five books, which is specifically referred to by Jesus Christ and numerous other inspired writers? Being on trial by the modern day critic, I am certain Moses would appreciate the numerous witnesses that can be called to the stand on his behalf.[113]

What Does the Biblical Evidence from the Apostles Report?

Acts 2:32 (ESV) ³²This Jesus God raised up, and of that we all are witnesses.	Acts 6:14 (ESV) ¹⁴for we have heard him say that this Jesus of Nazareth will destroy this place and will change the customs that Moses delivered to us."	Acts 15:5 (ESV) ⁵But some believers who belonged to the party of the Pharisees rose up and said, "It is necessary to circumcise them and to order them to keep the law of Moses."
Acts 26:22 (ESV) ²² To this day I have had the help that comes from God, and so I stand here testifying both to small and great, saying nothing but what the prophets and Moses said would come to pass:	Acts 28:23 (ESV) ²³When they had appointed a day for him, they came to him at his lodging in greater numbers. From morning till evening he expounded to them, testifying to the kingdom of God and trying to convince them about Jesus both from the Law of Moses and from the Prophets.	Romans 10:5 (ESV) ⁵For Moses writes about the righteousness that is based on the law, that the person who does the commandments shall live by them.
1 Corinthians 9:9 (ESV) ⁹For it is written in the Law of Moses, "You shall not muzzle an ox when	Hebrews 9:19 (ESV) ¹⁹For when every commandment of the law had been declared by Moses	Hebrews 10:28 (ESV) ²⁸ Anyone who has set aside the law of Moses dies without mercy on the

---

[112] K. L. McKay, A New Syntax of the Verb in New Testament Greek (New York: Peter Lang, 1994), p. 42.

[113] Old Testament witnesses to Moses' writership of the Pentateuch: Joshua 1:7; 8:32–35; 14:10; 1 Kings 2:3; 1 Chronicles 6:49; 2 Chronicles 33:8; 34:14; 35:12; Ezra 3:2; 6:18; 7:6; Nehemiah 1:7, 8; 8:1, 14, 15; Daniel 9:11, 13; Malachi 4:4. New Testament witnesses to Moses' writership of the Pentateuch: Matthew 8:2–4; 19:7; Mark 1:44; 12:26; Luke 2:22; 16:29, 31; 24:27, 44; John 1:45; 7:22; 8:5; 9:29; 19:7 [Leviticus 24:16]; Acts 3:22; 6:14; 15:5; 26:22; 28:23; Romans 10:5; 1 Corinthians 9:9; Hebrews 9:19; 10:28.

| it treads out the grain." Is it for oxen that God is concerned? | to all the people, he took the blood of calves and ... | evidence of two or three witnesses. |

What Does the Internal Evidence Report?

If the writer(s) of the Pentateuch were, in fact, living from the ninth century into the fifth century B.C.E., more than a millennium [1,000 years] after the events described, they would have had to be thoroughly familiar with, even an expert in geology, geography,[114] horticulture, archaeology, toponymy, onomatology (Archer, 1974), botany, zoology,[115] climatology,[116] and history. **Alternatively,** he would have to have been an eyewitness who walked through the events and situations detailed in the Pentateuch; thus, the writer. Here is how I defend these affirmations:

- He would need to have a thorough knowledge of Egyptian names and titles that match inscriptions.

- He would need to have been an expert in toponymy, the study of place-names.

- He would need to have been an expert in onomatology, the study of proper names of all kinds and the origin of names.

- He would need to be aware of the customs and cultures and religious practices of Egypt, desert dwellers, and life in Canaan 1,000 years into the past.

- He would need to have a thorough knowledge of the environment, climate, and the physical features of three regions.

- He would need to have a thorough knowledge of botany, being aware of naturally occurring plant life in three regions 1,000-years before his time.

- He would need to have a thorough knowledge of the environment, climate, and the physical features of three regions.

This internal evidence deals with the proof within the Pentateuch about Moses: the customs and culture of some 3,500 years ago, literary forms used as well as the language itself, and the unity of these five books. As to dating the Pentateuch based on literary forms, one needs look no further than the titles by which God is referred to within the Hebrew Scriptures. From the years of 850–450 B.C.E., we find the Hebrew expression *Yehowah´ tseva'ohth´*, "Jehovah of armies," being used in a significant way. It is found 243 times, with variations, in the Scriptures: 62 times in Isaiah, 77 in Jeremiah, 2 in Micah, 4 in Nahum, 2 in Habakkuk, 2 in Zephaniah, 15 in Haggai, 54 in Zechariah, and 25 in

---

[114] Genesis 13:10; 33:18; Numbers 13:22.

[115] Leviticus 11 and Deuteronomy 14.

[116] Exodus 9:31, 32; Exodus 16–Deuteronomy.

Malachi. This is the same time period, in which higher criticism places the writing of the books of the Pentateuch. If they were penned or constructed during this time period, one would expect to find a high number of occurrences of the expression "Jehovah of armies." Yet, we find just the opposite: there is not one occurrence of this expression to be found in the five books of the Pentateuch. This evidence demonstrates that these books were written prior to the book of Isaiah, before 800 B.C.E., which invalidates the Documentary Hypothesis. Moreover, many aspects of the priesthood that had been adjusted over the centuries, under inspiration, would have been evident if the Pentateuch were written after David[117] and others had made such adjustments.

The building of the tabernacle at the foot of Mount Sinai fits in with the environment of that area. F. C. Cook stated, "In form, structure, and materials, the tabernacle belongs altogether to the wilderness. The wood used in the structure is found there in abundance."[118] The external evidence validates names, customs, and culture, religious practices, geography, places and materials of the book of Exodus, which would have been privy only to an eyewitness. The geographical references by this writer are so vast, detailed, and tremendously precise that it is almost impossible to have him be anyone other than an eyewitness.

Deuteronomy reads, "Then we ... went through all that great and terrifying wilderness." This region in which the annual rainfall is less than 25 cm./10 in. is not different even today, which puts the nomadic traveler on a constant search for water and pasture. In addition, we have meticulous directions as to the encampment of the Israelites (Numbers 1:52, 53), the marching orders (Numbers 2:9, 16, 17, 24, 31), and the signals of the trumpet (Numbers 10:2–6) that directed their every move as evidence that these accounts were written in the "great and terrifying wilderness." Numbers 13:22 makes reference to the time Hebron was built, using the city of Zoan as a reference point: "They went up into the Negeb and came to Hebron. Ahiman, Sheshai, and Talmai, the descendants of Anak, were there. (Hebron was built seven years before Zoan in Egypt.)" Moses "was instructed in all the wisdom of the Egyptians" (Acts 7:22); thus, he would have knowledge of the building of Zoan, an Egyptian city, and of Hebron, a city on one of the trade routes between Memphis in Egypt and Damascus in Syria.

From the internal evidence, it is clearly obvious that the writer must have had an intimate knowledge of the desert, being an eyewitness to that environment. (See Leviticus 18:3; Deuteronomy 12:9; 15:4, 7; Numbers 2:1; Leviticus 14:8; 16:21; 17:3, 9.) The evidence is such because it is something that cannot be retained for a thousand years, but must come from an eyewitness. The details are extremely exact, and some would not have existed hundreds of years later: "Then they came to Elim, where there were twelve wells of water and seventy palm trees, and they camped there by the water," and "ram skins dyed red, fine leather, acacia wood." – Exodus 15:27; 25:5

Again, it should be noted that Moses "was instructed in all the wisdom of the Egyptians." (Acts 7:22) It is also obvious that the writer was quite familiar with Egyptian names: Pithom, meaning "House of Atum;" On, meaning "City of the Pillar" (the Greeks

---

[117] David organized the tens of thousands of Levites into their many divisions of service, including a great chorus of singers and musicians.—1 Chronicles 23:1–29:19; 2 Chronicles 8:14; 23:18; 29:25; Ezra 3:10.

[118] F. C. Cook, *Exodus* (1874), 247.

called the city Heliopolis); Potiphera,[119] meaning "He Whom Ra Has Given;" and Asenath, her name deriving from Egyptian, meaning: "Holy to Anath."

In addition, the writer used Egyptian words generously. "He had Joseph ride in his second chariot, and [servants] called out before him, '*Abrek!*' So he placed him over all the land of Egypt." (Genesis 41:43) The exact meaning of this expression transliterated from Egyptian into Hebrew has not yet been determined. Some feel that it is an Egyptian word meaning (*Attention!*) while others see it as a Hebrew word meaning *Kneel* or *Bow down!* One misstep and the writer will lose credibility. However, this is never the case with the writer of the Pentateuch. He mentions the acacia tree, which is found in Egypt and Sinai but not in the land of Canaan. Moreover, this writer refers to numerous animals that are to be found primarily in Egypt or Sinai. – See Deuteronomy. 14:5; Leviticus 16:11.

The old form of words in the Pentateuch are of the time frame of the fifteenth century B.C.E. as well, and had no longer been in use for centuries by the time of the supposed writer(s) and redactor(s) of the ninth to the sixth centuries B.C.E. Dr. John J. Davis gives us the most widely recognized example, "The pronoun *she*, which appears as *hiw'* instead of *hî'*. Another example is the word *young girl*, spelled *na'ar* instead of *na'ărâ*, the feminine form."[120]

All who engaged in idolatry or prophesying falsely were to be stoned to death, no exceptions. (Deuteronomy 13:2-11) This included not only individuals but also entire communities, every person within a city (verses 12-17). One has to ask, why would a writer include this if it were penned during the time period of 850-450 B.C.E. when most of the time Israel was shoulder deep in idolatry and false prophets abounded? This would mean certain destruction for every city in the kingdom. It would have been mere foolishness to incorporate these laws, which could never be enforced and would cause nothing but resistance to the law. However, it makes perfectly good sense for laws such as these to be given to people living in the time of Moses who had just exited an idolatrous nation and who was preparing to go in and conquer a number of other nations who lived and breathed idolatry.

What Does the External Evidence Report?

"The book of the law of Moses," as Joshua called the Pentateuch, was accepted by Jews, Christians, and Muslims as containing evidence of inspiration. The fact that Moses is the writer of these five books is **not** something that grew up out of tradition; it is something Moses himself claims, saying he wrote under the divine command of Jehovah God. Moreover, the Jewish communities throughout the Roman empire were in total harmony with the fact that Moses was the writer of the Pentateuch, this being supported by the Samaritan Pentateuch, the Palestinian Talmud, the Babylonian Talmud, the Apocrypha, Philo Judaeus (a contemporary of Jesus and Paul and the first century), and by

---

[119] A funeral pillar (stele) discovered in 1935 and now in the Cairo Museum refers to a personage named Potiphare.

[120] John J. Davis, *Paradise to Prison: Studies in Genesis* (Salem: Sheffield, 1975), 26.

Jewish historian Flavius Josephus (37–100 C.E.).[121] What about the early Christian writers, who wrote about Christianity between 150 C.E. and 400 C.E.?

> Moses, the servant of God, recorded, through the Holy Spirit, the very beginning of the creation of the world. First he spoke of the things concerning the creation and genesis of the world, including the first man and everything that happened afterwards in the order of events. He also indicated the number of years that elapsed before the Deluge.–*Theophilus* (c. 180, E), 2.118.[122]

> The origin of that know ledge should not, on that account, be considered as originating with the Pentateuch. For knowledge of the Creator did not begin with the volume of Moses. Rather from the very first it is traced from Adam and paradise.—*Tertullian* (c. 207, W), 3.278.[123]

> What portion of scripture can give us more information concerning the creation of the world than the account that Moses has transmitted?--*Origen* (c. 225, E), 4.341.[124]

> The destruction of Sodom and Gomorrah by fire on account of their sins is related by Moses in Genesis.--*Origen* (c. 248, E), 4.505.[125]

> Moses said, "And the Lord God saw that the wickedness of men was overflowing upon the Earth" [Gen. 6:5–7].--*Novatian* (c. 235, W), 5.658.[126]

> It is contained in the book of Moses, which he wrote about creation, in which is called Genesis.--*Victorinus* (c. 280, W), 7.341.[127]

> If you will look at the books of Moses, David, Solomon, Isaiah, or the Prophets who follow.... You will see what offspring they have left.--*Methodious* (c. 290, E), 6.333.[128]

> Let the following books be considered venerable and holy by you, both of the clergy and the laity. Of the Old Testament: The five books of Moses—Genesis, Exodus, Leviticus, Numbers, and Deuteronomy.....--*Apostolic Constitutions* (compiled c. 390, E), 7.505.[129]

Archaeology and the Bible

Unlike higher criticism, archaeology is a field of study that has a solid foundation in physical evidence, instead of presenting only hypotheses, inferences, and implications.

---

[121] See Ecclesiasticus 45:5; 2 Maccabees 7:30; Philo (*On the Life of Moses* II; III, 12–14; IV, 20; VIII, 45–48, pp. 93–95); Josephus (*The Antiquities of the Jews*, 3.8.10); Exodus 17:14; 24:4.

[122] David W. Bercot, *A Dictionary of Early Christian Beliefs* (Peabody: Hendrickson, 1998), 599.

123. Ibid., 600.
124. Ibid., 600.
125. Ibid., 600.
126. Ibid., 601.
127. Ibid., 601.
128. Ibid., 601.
129. Ibid., 602.

Within archaeology, one has both explicit and direct evidence as well as implicit evidence. There are many great publications that will undoubtedly go into this area in much greater detail, but suffice it to say that the Biblical events, the characters, geography, agriculture, plants and trees and settings are all in harmony with and accessible through archaeology.

While archaeology is not a total vindicator, it has defended God's Word. No one can argue against the fact that our understanding of ancient times has increased tremendously over the past 150 years and is being continuously refined. At present, one could list thousands of events within the Scriptures that are in complete harmony with the archaeological record. In fact, Wellhausen had nothing like what is available to the modern scholar. If he had, one would have to wonder if he would have come to the same conclusions. Conveying this exact point, Dr. Mark F. Rooker, Professor of Old Testament and Hebrew, stated:

> Regarding the issue of differing divine names, it is now clear from archaeological data not available to Wellhausen and early critical scholars that deities in the ancient Near East often had multiple names. This fact is especially clear in the conclusion to the Babylonian Creation account, the *Enuma Elish*, where the god Marduk is declared to be preeminent and his fifty different names are mentioned in celebration of his conquest.[22] No one has suggested that each name represents a different source, as was done in biblical studies. On the contrary, it would have been impossible to attribute these different names to different sources that have been pasted or joined together in the literary account because the Mesopotamian writing system involved inscription in stone! Moreover, it is clear that throughout the Old Testament the occurrence of the names of God as Elohim or Yahweh are to be attributed to contextual and semantic issues, not the existence of sources. This conclusion is borne out by the fact that the names consistently occur in predictable genre. . . . Thus through scientific discovery and analysis the criterion of the differing divine names, which gave rise to the Documentary Hypothesis, has been found wanting. If this information would have been known in the last years of the nineteenth century, it is safe to assume that the critical approach to the Pentateuch would never have seen the light of day.[130]

Much archaeological evidence as well as other forms of evidence has been uncovered to reveal the accuracy of the record. The ziggurat located at Uruk (Erech) was found to be built with clay, baked bricks for stone, and asphalt (bitumen) for mortar.[131] The Egyptian names and titles that Moses penned in the book of Exodus match Egyptian inscriptions. The book of Exodus shows that the Hebrew people were allowed to live in the land of Egypt as foreigners, as long as they kept separate from the Egyptians. Archaeology supports this custom. Likely, you will recall that Pharaoh's daughter bathed in the Nile (Exodus 2:5), which "was a common practice in ancient Egypt," according to Cook's *Commentary*. "The Nile was worshipped as an emanation . . . of Osiris, and a peculiar power of imparting life and fertility was attributed to its waters."

---

130. Mark F. Rooker, *Leviticus: The New American Commentary* (Nashville: Broadman & Holman, 2001), 26–27.

[131] (Genesis 11:3, *ESV*) "And they said to one another, 'Come, let us make bricks, and burn them thoroughly.' And they had brick for stone, and bitumen for mortar."

The fact that a king's daughter should bathe in the open river is certainly opposed to the customs of the modern, Mohammedan East, where this is only done by women of the lower orders, and that in remote places (Lane, *Manners and Customs*); but it is in harmony with the customs of ancient Egypt,[132]* and in perfect agreement with the notions of the early Egyptians respecting the sanctity of the Nile, to which divine honours even were paid (vid., Hengstenberg's *Egypt*, etc. pp. 109, 110), and with the belief, which was common to both ancient and modern Egyptians, in the power of its waters to impart fruitfulness and prolong life (vid., *Strabo*, xv. p. 695, etc., and Seetzen, *Travels* iii. p. 204).[133]

In addition, history also testifies to the fact that magicians were a well-known feature of Egyptian life during the period of Moses.--Genesis 11:1-9; Exodus 8:22; 2:5; 5:6, 7, 18; 7:11.

Bricks have been found made with and without straw. The painting below was found in the private tomb of Vizier Rekhmire (the highest official under Pharaoh) on the west bank of ancient Thebes. Archaeology also supports "taskmasters--Egyptian overseers, appointed to exact labor of the Israelites,"[134] as well as strictly controlled or enforced quotas that had to be met. (Exodus 5:6) Moreover, Egyptian papyri express serious concern for the needed straw (which was lacking at times) to be mixed with the mud to make these bricks. (Exodus 1:13, 14) The Papyri Anastasi, from ancient Egypt, reads, "There was no one to mould bricks, and there was no straw in the neighbourhood."[135]

Furthermore, the historical conditions and surroundings are in accord precisely with the occasions and assertions in the book of Numbers. We have references to Edom, Egypt, Moab, Canaan, Ammon, and Amalek, which are true to the times, and the names of places are free from error.[136] Archaeology is never absolute proof of anything, but it continues to add evidence, weighty at times to the fact that Moses had to be the writer of the Pentateuch. *Halley's Bible Handbook* writes, "Archaeology has been speaking so loudly of late that it is causing a decided reaction toward the conservative view. The theory that writing was unknown in Moses' day is absolutely exploded. And every year there are being dug up in Egypt, Palestine and Mesopotamia, evidences, both in inscriptions and earth layers, that the narratives of the Old Testament are true historical records. And 'scholarship' is coming to have decidedly more respect for the tradition of Mosaic authorship."[137]

The Silver Amulet is one of many archaeological nails in the coffin of the Documentary Hypothesis. Why? This portion of Numbers is argued by the critics to be

---

[132] Wilkinson gave a picture of a bathing scene in which an Egyptian woman of rank is introduced, attended by four female servants.

133. Carl Friedric Keil and Franz Delitzsch, *Commentary on the Old Testament* (Peabody, MA: Hendrickson, 2002), S. 1:278.

134. Robert Jamieson, A. R. Fausset, and David Brown. *A Commentary, Critical and Explanatory, On the Old and New Testaments* (Oak Harbor: Scranton & Company, 1997), 51.

135. Adolf Erman and H. M. Tirard. *Life in Ancient Egypt* (Whitefish: Kessinger, 2003), 117.

136. "Sirion... Senir." These names appear in the Ugaritic texts found at Ras Shamra, Syria, and in the documents from Bogazköy, Turkey.

137. Henry Halley, *Halley's Bible Handbook* (Grand Rapids: Zondervan, 1988), 56.

part of the "P" document that was supposedly penned between 550 and 400 B.C.E. However, initially, it was dated to the late seventh / early sixth centuries B.C.E.

Of course, this dating was subsequently challenged by Johannes Renz and Wolfgang Rollig (*Handbuch der Althebraischen Epigraphik*, 1995) because the silver was cracked and blemished to the point of making many words and a few lines unreadable. This allowed these critics to argue for a date in the third to second centuries B.C.E. period, which would remove this stain on the lifeless body of their Documentary Hypothesis.

Then it was shipped to the University of Southern California to be examined under photographic and computer imaging. The results? The researchers stated that they could "read fully and [had] analyzed with far greater precision," which resulted in the final analysis of being yet another vindication for Moses—the original dating stands: late seventh century B.C.E.

Exodus 14:6, 7 (*ESV*) reads, "So he [the Pharaoh] made ready his chariot and took his army with him, and took six hundred chosen chariots and all the other chariots of Egypt with officers over all of them." Pharaoh, being the god of the world and the supreme chief of his army, personally led the army into battle. Archaeology supports this custom.

Why are there no Egyptian records of the Exodus of the Israelites from Egypt? The critics may also ask why is there no archaeological evidence to support the Israelite's 215-year stay in Egypt (some of which was in slavery) and the devastation that was executed on the gods of Egypt. There is, in fact, one simple answer that archaeology has provided us: Any new Egyptian dynasty would erase any unflattering history prior to their dynasty, if such even existed, as it was their custom never to record any defeats that might be viewed as embarrassing or critical, which could damage the dignity of their people, for they were an extremely prideful empire.[138]

For example, Thutmose III ordered others to chisel Queen Hatshepsut out of the history books when he removed the name and representation of Queen Hatshepsut on a monumental stone record later uncovered at Deir al-Bahri in Egypt as well as from any other monuments she had built. Hatshepsut, daughter of Thutmose I, would eventually gain the throne upon her father's death even though Thutmose II (husband and half-brother to Hatshepsut) technically ascended the throne in name only. At best, Thutmose II lasted only three or four years before dying of a skin disease. Thutmose III was too young to rule, thus, Queen Hatshepsut simply held her own as the first female Pharaoh. Embarrassing for Thutmose III, indeed! Thus, as he grew, his hatred mounted for Hatshepsut and Senmut (her lover). After her death, Thutmose III worked vigorously to remove her name and the name of her lover from Egyptian history. If this was embarrassing, how much more so would be the ten plagues that had humiliated numerous gods of Egypt, including the Pharaoh himself? The exodus of 600,000 male slaves and their families, plus Egyptians who had chosen Jehovah as God instead of the Pharaoh of Egypt would have been quite embarrassing, indeed!

In 1925, discoveries of clay tablets were made at the ancient town of Nuzi in northeastern Mesopotamia; it was here that archaeologists found a tremendous number of legal contracts dating to the fifteenth-century B.C.E. These actually shed much light on the life of people of that time. Due to the slow-moving life condition of the ancient Near East,

---

138. Joseph P. Free, *Archaeology and Bible History* (Grand Rapids, MI: Zondervan Publishing, 1964).

they reflect life conditions for many years on both sides of the fifteenth century. Thus, what we now possess and know from studies of these Nuzi Tablets is that there are numerous customs in the Patriarchal period that were very much in common practice among the ancient Hurrians who lived in northern Mesopotamia, encompassing Haran, which was the home of Abraham after he left Ur and where Isaac later found his wife Rebekah.

Abraham's Contract. Eliezer was to be the legal inheritor of childless Abraham's property and position after Abraham's death. In fact, Abraham referred to Eliezer when he said, "a slave born in my house will be my heir." (Genesis 15:2, 3) Tablets from Nuzi discovered by archaeologists help the modern-day reader understand how a servant could become heir to his master's household. Mesopotamian records from the time of Abraham (2018–1843 B.C.E.); makes mention of the tradition of a childless couple adopting a son in their old age to have him take care of them up unto their death, and thereafter inheriting the household property. But if for some reason the couple would end up having a child, the child would become the primary heir instead, with the adopted servant or son getting a minor portion of the property as well. (Wood, 1996) In a culture that passed history down orally through its generations, we find Moses being only three generations removed from Abraham's great-grandson Levi (Levi, Kohath, Amram, and Moses) while our alleged "J" was a thousand years removed from Abraham, and the redactor even further. It is only by means of modern-day archaeology that we are aware of just how accurate the Genesis account is with minor details such as the legal system of adoption rights in Mesopotamia from 2000 B.C.E. (time of Abraham) to 1500 B.C.E. (time of Moses), knowledge that would not be available to our alleged composers. Thus, archaeology puts the Genesis account right back into the hands of its true writer, Moses.

The Price of a Slave. Joseph was the son of Jacob by Rachel, the grandson of Isaac, and the great-grandson of Abraham, and was sold as a slave to some Midianite merchants for a mere 20 pieces of silver by his jealous brothers in about 1750 B.C.E. (Genesis 37:28; 42:21) Throughout the stream of time, we find inflation in the slave trade, and the Biblical account of the price for Joseph falls exactly where it should to be in harmony with secular archaeology, as you can see in chart 1. Again, our alleged "J," "E," "D," and "P" composers would be a thousand years removed from Abraham, and "R" (the redactor) even further; thus they would have no access to this information so as to have gotten it correct. Only the actual writer, Moses, would be aware of this information by family records or oral tradition.

The Inflation of the Slave Trade in Biblical Times (Wood, 1996)

Source	Date	Price of a Slave in Silver
Akkad and 3rd Ur Dynasties	2000 B.C.E.	8–10 pieces of silver
Joseph (Genesis 37:2, 28)	1750 B.C.E.	20 pieces of silver
Hammurabi Code	1799–1700 B.C.E.	20 pieces of silver
Old Babylonian Tablets	B.C.E.	15–30 pieces of silver
Mari tablets	1799–1600 B.C.E.	20 pieces of silver
Exodus 21:32	1520–1470 B.C.E.	30 pieces of silver

Nuzi tablets	1499–1400 B.C.E.	30 pieces of silver
Ugarit tablets	1399–1200 B.C.E.	30–40 pieces of silver
Assyria	First millennium B.C.E.	50–60 pieces of silver
2 Kings 15:20	790 B.C.E.	50 pieces of silver
Persia	750–500 B.C.E.	90–120 pieces of silver

Seti I began much like his father Ramses, as a military commander. His military prowess led to many triumphs that are recorded on the walls of the temple of Amon-Ra at Karnak. Here Seti I recorded his military triumphs; captives are shown being seized by their hair. As was expressed earlier, victories were proudly recorded on Egyptian monuments, but embarrassing or critical events were ignored, that is, never chiseled into their annals of history.

Concluding Thoughts

I had given much thought to a conclusion that contained quotations from many reputable scholars who use thought-provoking points to support the writership of Moses for the Pentateuch, but what would that prove? Certainly, if you quote a reputable scholar you would add weight to an argument, but it does not make the case. It only validates that you are not alone in your reasoning. Therefore, I have added quotations of only two scholars to make just that point. One does not count the number of people who believe one thing as opposed to another and those with the most votes win. No, the results should be based on evidence. In fact, the higher critics will infer that they are in the right by saying, 'Today, you will hardly find one scholar in the world who will argue for the writership of Moses for the Pentateuch.' If that makes them in the right, it also makes them in the wrong. Why? Because for centuries, for millenniums, the majority of Bible scholars—in the Jewish world, the Christian world, and the Islamic world—accepted Moses' writership; that is, until the Age of Reason within the eighteenth and nineteenth centuries when people started to question not only the writership of Moses but the very existence of God.

Would any Christian living in 1700 C.E. have ever doubted the writership of Moses? Hardly! So how did the Documentary Hypothesis become Documentary Fact? All it took was for some leading professors at major universities to plant seeds of doubt within their students. Being at the entrance of the era of higher criticism and skepticism of the nineteenth century, this Documentary Hypothesis had a well-cultivated field in which to grow. It created a domino effect as a few scholars produced a generation of students, who would then be the next generation of scholars, and so on.

As we moved into the twentieth century, these questions had become "facts" in the eyes of many; in fact, it became in vogue to challenge the Bible. Leading schools and leading scholars of higher criticism were the norm, and soon the conservative Christian was isolated. The twentieth-century student received a lean diet from those few scholars who still accepted God's Word as just that, the Word of God, fully inerrant, with 40 writers of 66 books over a period of about 1,600 years. No, these students would now be fed mostly liberal theology, and any who disagreed were portrayed as ignorant and naïve. This planting of uncertainty or mistrust, with question after question bringing Moses' writership into doubt, with most literature focusing on this type of propaganda, would create the latest generation of scholars, and today they dominate the world of scholarship.

How did this progressive takeover come off without a hitch? The conservative scholarship of the early twentieth century saw these liberal naysayers as nothing more than a fly at a picnic. Most did not even deem it necessary to address their questions, so by 1950–1970, the Documentary Hypothesis machine was in full throttle. It was about this same time that the sleeping giant finally awoke to find that conservative scholarship had taken a backseat to this new creature, liberal scholarship. It is only within the last 30–40 years that some very influential conservative scholars have started to publish books in a move to dislodge this liberal movement.* Is it too little, too late?

> *This is not to say that the 19th and early 20th century did not have any apologist defending against biblical criticism. There were some giants in this field, like R. A. Torrey and others in this publication.

It is possible to displace higher criticism, but many factors stand in the way. For one, any opposition is painted as uninformed and inexperienced regarding the subject matter. Moreover, the books that tear down the Bible with all their alleged critical analysis sell far better than those do that encourage putting faith in God's Word. In addition, many conservative scholars tend to sit on the sideline and watch as a few leading scholars attempt to do the work of the many. In addition, there are liberal scholars continually putting out numerous articles and books, dominating the market. Unlike the conservative scholars in the first part of the twentieth century, these liberal scholars in the first part of the twenty-first century are not slowing down. Moreover, they have become more aggressive.

The book *Introduction to the Bible*, by John Laux, explains just what the Documentary Hypothesis would have meant for the Israelites if it were true:

> The Documentary Theory is built up on assertions which are either arbitrary or absolutely false.... If the extreme Documentary Theory were true, the Israelites would have been the victims of a clumsy deception when they permitted the heavy burden of the Law to be imposed upon them. It would have been the greatest hoax ever perpetrated in the history of the world.[139]

It goes much further than that; it would mean that the Son of God was either fooled by what these higher critics argue, that there was a tradition of Moses being the writer of the Pentateuch, which developed through time and was accepted as reality during Jesus' day, or that Jesus was a liar, because he had lived in heaven prior to his coming down to earth and was aware of the deception but had continued a tradition that he knew to be false. The truth is that the Son of God was well aware that Moses was, in fact, the writer of the Pentateuch and he presented Moses as such because he was there at the time!

So again, because Jesus taught that Moses was, in fact, the writer of the Pentateuch, we have three options:

- Jesus knew Moses was the writer because Jesus was there, in heaven, prior to his Virgin birth and observed Moses as the writer; or

---

139. John Laux, *Introduction to the Bible* (Chicago: Tan Books & Pub., 1992), 186.

- Jesus knew that Moses was not the writer and simply perpetuated a Jewish tradition that Moses was the writer; or
- Jesus possessed a limited knowledge and simply believed something that was a tradition because he was unaware of it being such.

So if Jesus knew Moses was *not* the writer and purposely conveyed misinformation for the sake of Jewish tradition, this makes Jesus a liar and therefore a sinner, which would contradict what Hebrews 4:15 says of him, that "he was without sin." If he was simply in ignorance and was mistakenly conveying misinformation, this certainly does away with Jesus having a prehuman existence. (John 1:1–2; 3:13; 6:38, 62; 8:23, 42, 58; Colossians 1:15–18; Revelation 3:14; Proverbs 8:22–30) Based on the scriptures and other evidence presented, we can conclude that Jesus was well aware that Moses was the writer, and that is what he truthfully taught.

Duane Garrett makes the following observation concerning the Documentary Hypothesis:

> The time has long passed for scholars of every theological persuasion to recognize that the Graf-Wellhausen theory, as a starting point for continued research, is dead. The Documentary Hypothesis and the arguments that support it have been effectively demolished by scholars from many different theological perspectives and areas of expertise. Even so, the ghost of Wellhausen hovers over Old Testament studies and symposiums like a thick fog. . . . One wonders if we will ever return to the day when discussions of Genesis will not be stilted by interminable references to P and J. There are indications that such a day is coming. Many scholars are exploring the inadequacies of the Documentary Hypothesis and looking toward new models for explaining the Pentateuch.[140]

These world-renowned scholars who have gone left of center are witty and able to express thoughts, ideas, and feelings coherently, having conviction that leads unsuspecting ones who are not aware of the facts to accept ideas that are made to appear as smooth-fitting pieces in a large puzzle, thinking that they are nothing more than long-awaited answers. Sadly, many unsuspecting readers have taken their words as absolute truth.

Jesus quotes or alludes to 23 of the 39 books of the Hebrew Scriptures. Specifically, he quotes all five of the books attributed to Moses—the book of Deuteronomy 16 times alone, this obviously being one of his favorites. As we close this chapter, we are going to let our greatest witness take the stand. As you read Jesus' references to Moses and the Law you will undoubtedly notice that he viewed Moses' writership as historically true, completely authoritative, and inspired of God. If one does not accept, Moses, as the writer of the Pentateuch as Jesus did, is that not calling Jesus a liar.

As Christians, we accept what the Bible teaches as true. By way of common sense and sound reasoning, the vast majority of the issues of higher criticism's Social Progressive Christian and Christian Modernists have been answered quite easily by the conservative scholar in absolute terms: for example, F. David Farnell, Gleason L. Archer Jr., C. John Collins, K. A. Kitchen, Norman L. Geisler, and others. For the handful of issues left, we still

---

[140] Garrett, Duane. *Rethinking Genesis: The Sources and Authorship of the First Book of the Pentateuch* (Grand Rapids: Baker Books, 1991), 13.

have reasonable answers, which are not beyond a reasonable doubt at this time; we are quite content to wait until we are provided with the concrete answers that will make these few issues beyond all reasonable doubt. The last 150 years of evidence that has come in by way of archaeological discoveries, a better understanding of the original language, historical-cultural and contextual understanding, as well as manuscripts has answered almost all those doubtful areas that have been called into question by the higher critics. Therefore, because we lack the complete answers for a few remaining issues means nothing.

Consider this: A critic raises an issue, but it is answered by a new archaeological discovery a few years later. The critic runs to another issue, and it is later answered by an improved understanding of the original languages. Then he runs to look for yet another issue, and it is answered by thousands of manuscripts that are uncovered over a period of two decades. This has been the case with thousands of issues. What are we to think the agenda is of those who continue scouring God's Word looking for errors, discrepancies, and contradictions? How many times must they raise objections and be proven wrong before we stop listening to their cries? If that is the case, why do their books still outsell those that expose their erroneous thinking? Does that say something about the Christian community and their desire for tabloid scholarship (sensationalized stories)? Would the average Christian rather read an article or book by Dan Brown on how Jesus allegedly married and had sexual relations with Mary Magdalene and fathered children (false, of course), or read an article or book on the actual, even more fascinating account of Jesus' earthly life, based on the four Gospels?

For today's Christian, there is no more important study than the life and ministry of the real, historical Jesus Christ. The writer of the book of Hebrews exhorts us to **"fix our eyes on** Jesus," to **"consider him** who endured such opposition from sinful men." Moreover, Jehovah God himself commanded: "This is my Son, whom I love; with him I am well pleased. **Listen to him!**" (NIV, bolding added) While an apologetic of the study of the "*Historical Jesus*," or "*The Case for the Resurrection of Jesus*"[141] is certainly fine, the primary source of the four Gospels accounts of Matthew, Mark, Luke, and John should be first place, the starting point of any real investigation of Jesus' life and ministry. A life and ministry that viewed the Old Testament as historically true and of the greatest importance to his followers that he would leave behind after his ascension back to heaven.

We return to Wellhausen, who investigated his documentary hypothesis under the worldview of Israelite religion from an evolutionary model: (1) at the beginning it was animistic and spiritistic, (2) gradually developing into polytheism, (3) moving eventually into henotheism (choosing one god out of many), and finally (4) gravitating to monotheism. Wellhausen could not accept that this development took place in a short period, but was an evolution that took more than a millennium. This evolutionary process is no longer held among today's critical scholarship.

---

141. **Recommended**: Gary R. Habermas, *The Historical Jesus: Ancient Evidence for the Life of Christ* (Joplin, MO: College Press, 1996); Gary R. Habermas, *The Case for the Resurrection of Jesus* (Grand Rapids, MI: Kregel, 2004); Craig A. Evans, *Fabricating Jesus: How Modern Scholars Distort the Gospels* (Downers Grove, IL: IVP Books, 2006); Timothy Paul Jones, *Misquoting Truth: A Guide to the Fallacies of Bart Ehrman's Misquoting Jesus* (Downers Grove, IL: IVP Books, 2007).

Another obstacle was that Wellhausen did not believe in the miraculous and could not accept prophetic statements (for example, Genesis 49) happening before the actual events. This mindset was the catalyst behind his research.[142] Consequently, Wellhausen investigated the text with this way of thinking and that state of mind contributed to his discovering the Documentary Hypothesis issues of different uses of the divine name, discrepancies, repetitions (doublets), and differences in style and language, reading his views into the text (eisegesis).

The above facts of this book have easily demonstrated that the evidence of the documentary hypothesis is really no evidence at all. The modern-day critic has to deal with the lack of consensus on the part of his colleagues, who lack in agreement for the explanation of the sources.

> This failure to achieve consensus is represented by the occasional division of source strata into multiple layers (see Smend's J1 and J2) that often occasions the appearance of new sigla (for instance, Eissfeldt's L [*aienquelle*], Noth's G[*rundschrift*], Fohrer's N [for Nomadic], and Pfeiffer's S [for Seir]. A further indication of the collapse of the traditional documentary hypothesis is the widely expressed doubt that E was ever an independent source (Voz, Rudolph, Mowinckel; cf. Kaiser, IOT, 42 n. 18). Similar disagreements are also found in the dating of the sources. J has been dated to the period of Solomon by Von Rad, though Schmidt would argue for the seventh century, and Van Seters (1992, 34) has advocated an exile date. While most scholars believe P is postexilic, Haran has argued that it is to be associated with Hezekiah's reforms in the eighth century BC.[143]

While the lack of consensus is not in and of itself capable of disproving the proposition of sources other than Moses for the writing of the Pentateuch, it does cast even more doubt on the critical scholar's proposal that the new school of the Documentary Hypothesis has any more to offer than the old school of Wellhausen.

As this book has clearly demonstrated, Moses is the inspired author of the Pentateuch. At best, we can accept that it is likely that Joshua may have updated the text in Deuteronomy chapter 34, which speaks of Moses' death, and it is possible that Joshua may have made the reference in Numbers 12:3 that refer to Moses as being 'the humblest man on the face of the earth.'[144] In addition, we can accept that a later copyist [or even possibly Ezra, another inspired author] updated Genesis 11:28, 31 to read "of the Chaldeans," a name of a land and its inhabitants in the southern portion of Babylonia that *possibly* was not recognized as Chaldea until several hundred years after Moses.

> The origin of the Chaldeans is uncertain but may well be in the west, or else branches of the family may have moved there (cf. Job 1:17). The general name for the area in the earliest period is unknown, since it was part of Sumer (see SHINAR); so it cannot be argued that the qualification of Abraham's home city UR

---

[142] Tremper Longman III, and Raymond B. Dillard, *An Introduction to the Old Testament* (Grand Rapids: Zondervan, 2006), 43-44.

143. Ibid., 49-50.

[144] For the possibility of Moses penning these words, see my comments in the first paragraph of section four.

as "of the Chaldeans" (Gen. 11:28, 31; 15:7; as later Neh. 9:7; cf. Acts 7:4) is necessarily a later insertion in the text.[145]

The same would hold true of a copyist updating Genesis 36:31, which reads: "Now these are the kings who reigned in the land of Edom before *any king reigned over the sons of Israel*." Moses and Joshua were long gone for hundreds of years before Israel ever had a king over them.[146] The same would hold true again for Genesis 14:14, which reads: When Abram heard that his relative had been taken captive, he led out his trained men, born in his house, three hundred and eighteen, and went in pursuit *as far as Dan*. Dan was an area settled long after Moses death, after the Israelites had conquered the Promise Land. This too is obviously an update as well, making it contemporary to its readers.[147]

Reference to "Ur of the Chaldeans"[148] (11:28) identifies the native land of Haran but not necessarily of Terah and his sons Abram and Nahor. In fact, the inclusion of this information for Haran may suggest the ancestral home was elsewhere (for this discussion see comments on 12:1). "Ur of the Chaldeans" occurs three times in Genesis (11:28, 31; 15:7) and once elsewhere (Neh 9:7). Stephen identified the place of God's revelation to Abram as "Mesopotamia" from which he departed: "So he left the land of the Chaldeans and settled in Haran" (Acts 7:3–4). The "land [*chōra*] of the Chaldeans" rather than "Ur of the Chaldeans" is the Septuagint translation, as reflected in Stephen's sermon, which can be explained as either a textual slip due to the prior phrase "land of his birth" or the ancient translator's uncertainty about the identity of the site. J. W. Wevers proposes that due to the apposition of "land of his birth," the translator interpreted "Ur" as a region.[149, 150]

As we have already stated, the critic is fond of finding portions of the text that lack secular support, and then summarily dismissing it as not being a real historical account. Once evidence surfaces to support their dismissal as being wrong and premature, they simply never mention this section again, but move on to another. The question that begs to be asked by the logical and reasonable mind is, how many times must this take place

---

[145] Geoffrey W. Bromiley, vol. 1, *The International Standard Bible Encyclopedia, Revised* (Wm. B. Eerdmans, 1988; 2002), 630.

[146] It should be noted that even this statement could belong to Moses, even though there were no kings in Israel at this time. How? He would be aware that Jehovah had promised Abraham that he would be so great that kings would come out of him (Gen 17:6) and the preparation for such is mentioned at Deuteronomy 17:14-20.

[147] It should be noted that this author does not accept higher criticisms unending desire to find source(s) for a book, because they have dissected it to no end. While there are a few details that may have been updated by a copyist, or even the inspired writer Ezra (writer of Chronicles and the book that bears his name), this does not mean that we accept the update, if it is such, as the inspired material that was originally written, unless it was done by another inspired writer like Joshua, Ezra, or Nehemiah, or even possibly Jeremiah. It is also possible that it could be an explanatory addition.

[148] Hb. "Chaldeans" כַּשְׂדִּים is *kaldu* (Akk.) in Assyrian texts, and the Gk. has καλδαιοι; the original *sd* has undergone a change to *ld* (see R. S. Hess, "Chaldea," *ABD* 1.886–87).

[149] J. W. Wevers, *Notes on the Greek Text of Genesis*, Septuagint and Cognate Studies 35 (Atlanta: Scholars Press, 1993), 158.

[150] K. A. Mathews, vol. 1B, *Genesis 11:27-50:26*, electronic ed., Logos Library System; The New American Commentary (Nashville: Broadman & Holman Publishers, 2007), 99–100.

before they stop and accept the Bible as sound and reliable history? Let us look at the historicity of the above account of Abraham's men defeating the Mesopotamian kings, for it is historically sound. Information had become known in the 20th century that vindicates this account as being historically true, and removes yet another arguing point from those supporters of the documentary hypothesis:

> The name of Chedorlaomer, King of Elam, contains familiar Elamite components: *kudur* meant "servant," and *Lagamar* was a high goddess in the Elamite pantheon. Kitchen (Ancient Orient, p. 44) generally prefers the vocalization Kutir instead of Kudur and gives the references for at least three Elamite royal names of this type. He equates tidal with a Hittite name, Tudkhaliya, attested from the nineteenth century B.C. As for Arioch, one King of Larsa ("El-Larsa") from this era was Eri-aku ("Servant of the Moon-god"), whose name in Akkadian was *Arad-Sin* (with the same meaning). The Mari tablets refer to persons by the name of Ariyuk. The cuneiform of the original of Amraphel, formerly equated with Hammurabi of Babylon, is not demonstrable for the twentieth century (Hammurabi himself dates from the eighteenth century, but there may possibly be a connection with Amorite names like *Amud-pa-ila*, according to H. B. Huffman.... It should be added that according to G. Pettinato, the leading epigraphist of the Ebla documents dating from 2400–2250 B.C., mention is made in the Ebla tablets of Sodom (spelled *Si-da-mu*), Gomorrah (spelled in Sumerian cuneiform *I-ma-ar*), and Zoar (*Za-e-ar*). He feels that quite possibly these may be the same cities mentioned in the Abrahamic narrative.[151]

> W. F. Albright comments: In spite of our failure hitherto to fix the historical horizon of this chapter, we may be certain that its contents are very ancient. There are several words and expressions found nowhere else in the Bible and now known to belong to the second millenium. The names of the towns in Transjordania are also known to be very ancient.[152]

In the final analysis, based on both the internal and external evidence, we can absolute confidence that Moses was the author of the Pentateuch. The minor additions of Joshua, who was himself an inspired writer, as well as the handful of updates in the text to make it clearer to the then-current reader does no harm to the inspired message that God wished to convey.

---

[151]. Gleason L. Archer, *Encyclopedia of Bible Difficulties* (Grand Rapids: Zondervan, 1982), 90–91.
[152]. H. C. Alleman and E. E. Flack, *Old Testament Commentary* (Philadelphia: Fortress, 1954), 14.

CHAPTER XX The Authorship and Unity of Isaiah

Edward D. Andrews

In **Isaiah 1:1**, we are introduced to Isaiah in his own words as **"the son of Amoz,"** informing his readers that he served as God's prophet **"in the days of Uzziah [52 years], Jotham [16 years], Ahaz [16 years] and Hezekiah [28 years], kings of Judah."** The total reign of these four kings would be 112 years, which means that Isaiah likely began toward the end of Uzziah's reign. He was one of the longest serving prophets of the southern kingdom of Judah, no fewer than 46 years, about 778-732 B.C.E.

Very little is known about the personal life of Isaiah, compared to what we know of the other prophets of the Old Testament. He was married to a "prophetess." (8:3) "It is possible that the 'prophetess' simply refers to the prophet's wife, though there are no other examples of this in Scripture. It is possible that Isaiah's wife had a prophetic gift, but this gift is not affirmed elsewhere."[153] There are other women within the Old Testament that held the office of a prophetess, making it likely that Isaiah's wife may very well have had this same assignment. – Judges 4:4; 2 Kings 22:14.

Amoz was Isaiah's father, this being the only detail of Amoz that is known. (1:1) We are not told of Isaiah's birth or death, though strong Jewish tradition has it "that the prophet Isaiah was cut in half with a wooden saw. This happened during the reign of King Manasseh. The Old Testament has no record of this incident."[154] (Compare Heb. 11:37.) His prophetic book places him in Jerusalem with at least two sons with prophetic names and his prophet wife. (Isa. 7:3; 8:1, 3) His years of prophesying for the southern kingdom likely run from 778 B.C.E through the 14th year of Hezekiah's reign, a little after 732 B.C.E. (1:1; 6:1; 36:1) Some contemporary prophets of Isaiah were Micah in the land of Judah and, to the north, Hosea and Oded. – Micah. 1:1; Hos. 1:1; 2 Chronicles 28:6-9.

Life in Judah throughout these 46 years for Isaiah was unstable and chaotic, to say the least. The political element was in constant turmoil, the courts were corrupt to no end, and the religious structure of the nation was filled with pretense and duplicity. Scattered throughout the hill country of Judea were pagan altars to false gods. A case in point would be King Ahaz, who not only allowed this idolatrous worship, "but was an active participant, not only duplicating the sins of Israel's kings, but he also sacrificed his son 'in the fire,' perhaps as an offering to the god Molech."[155] (2 Ki 16:3, 4; 2 Ch. 28:3, 4) Sadly, this is only a continuation of a people that were supposed to be in a covenant relationship with Jehovah. – Exodus 19:5-8.

We need not leave the impression that all was lost, for some of Isaiah's contemporaries were working for the restoration of true worship. For instance, King

---

[153] E. Ray Clendenen, *New American Commentary: Isaiah 1-39* (B & H Publishing Group, 2007), 222.

[154] Simon J. Kistemaker and William Hendriksen, vol. 15, *New Testament Commentary: Exposition of Hebrews*, New Testament Commentary (Grand Rapids: Baker Book House, 1953-2001), 355.

[155] Paul R. House, vol. 8, *1, 2 Kings*, electronic ed., Logos Library System; The New American Commentary (Nashville: Broadman & Holman Publishers, 2001), 336.

Uzziah "did that which was right in the eyes of Jehovah." However, this was not enough, because "the high places were not taken away: the people still sacrificed and burnt incense in the high places." (2 Ki 15:3, 4) King Jotham followed in his father's footsteps and "did that which was right in the eyes of Jehovah." And like in the case of Uzziah, the people of Jotham's reign "followed corrupt practices." (2 Ch. 27:2) Sadly, Isaiah spent much of his career in a spiritually defunct kingdom. While some kings promoted false worship, others worked for the return of pure worship, with no real effect on the people. As one can imagine, presenting this prophetic message to such stiff-necked people was going to prove none too easy.

Some have looked to the style throughout the book of Isaiah and have suggested two Isaiah's, a "Second Isaiah," "the idea of a multiple authorship of Isaiah has arisen only in the last two centuries. Its simplest, most persuasive form is the ascription of chapters. 1–39 to Isaiah and 40–66 to an anonymous prophet living among the sixth-century exiles in Babylonia."[156] There is an enormous amount of evidence that there is only one Isaiah, who penned the entire book, centuries before the Babylonian exile.[157]

Chapters 1 to 6 give the reader the historical setting within Judah and Jerusalem, emphasizing the guilt of Judah before God, as well as the commissioning of Isaiah. Chapters 7 to 12 cover the continuous threats of an invasion, giving the people a hope by means of the Prince of Peace, authorized by Jehovah. Chapters 13 to 35 comprise a succession of announcements against numerous nations and a prophecy of salvation, which is to come from Jehovah. Chapters 36 to 39 cover Hezekiah's reign with significant dealings. Chapters 40 to 66 deal with a release from the Babylonian Empire,[158] and the return of the Jewish people to Judah and Jerusalem restoring Zion.

Multiple Authorship for the Book of Isaiah

> Man is unable to foretell the future with any inevitability. Repeatedly their struggles at prophecy are unsuccessful in the extreme. Therefore, a book full of prophetic books, if true, would attract interest, and even attack. The Bible is just such a book.

The primary cause behind questioning Isaiah's authorship is the same for all other prophetic books. It is their prophetic nature (detailed history written in advance), which is impossible for the Bible critic or liberal scholar to accept as a reality. (Isaiah 41:21-26; 42:8, 9; 46:8-10) If we are to understand the critic, we must examine their thinking. Therefore, let us look at some aspects of their reasoning.

---

[156] D. A. Carson, *New Bible Commentary: 21st Century Edition*, 4th ed. (Leicester, England; Downers Grove, Ill., USA: Inter-Varsity Press, 1994).

[157] For additional verbal agreements and similarities within Isaiah, cf. G.L. Robinson and R.K. Harrison, "Isaiah," in *The International Standard Bible Encyclopedia*, vol. 2 (Grand Rapids: Eerdmans, 1982), pp. 895–898.

[158] The Babylonian Empire at the time of prophecy, late eighth century B.C.E., is merely an unknown entity, who is yet to grow into an Empire, unseating the current Assyrian Empire.

Prophecy is Contemporary, Meaningful and Applicable to the People

The **important truth for the Bible critic lies in** the understanding that for all occurrences, prophecy pronounced or written in Bible times meant something to the people it was spoken or written to; it was meant to serve as a guide for them if they heeded its counsel. Frequently, it had specific fulfillment for that time, being fulfilled throughout the lifetime of that very generation. Thus, it is true that the penned or spoken words always had some application to the very people who heard them. The words of Isaiah's chapters 40 to 66 pointed out that the Jewish people would see the destruction of their beloved Jerusalem, be taken into exile to Babylon for 70-years, yet freed by the Medo-Persians, Cyrus, the leader of Persia specifically. Thereafter, the Jewish people would be released to their homeland, to rebuild. All of this took place 200 years plus after the days of Isaiah. Therefore, for the critic, **there must have been a second Isaiah writing in 540 B.C.E., just before the return of the Israelites to Jerusalem.**[159]

That Isaiah penned the book that bears his name was never thought otherwise until the 12th century C.E. This was not the position of Jewish commentator Abraham Ibn Ezra.[160] "He states in his commentary on Isaiah that the second half of the book, from chapter 40 on, was the work of a prophet who lived during the Babylonian Exile and the early period of the Return to Zion." (Pfeffer 2005, 28) Progressively, throughout the next two centuries, more and more scholars were adopting this view. The New Bible Dictionary notes:

> Many scholars nowadays deny great portions of the book to Isaiah, not only in the sense that he did not write them down, but in the sense that their subject-matter does not come from him at all. Even chapters 1–35 are believed by some to contain much non-Isaianic material. Some scholars go farther than others, but there is a wide measure of agreement that Isaiah cannot be credited with chapters 13:1–14:23; 21; 24–27; 34–35. In addition, critical scholars are

---

[159] It should be noted that the words of Jehovah by way of Isaiah were very much applicable to his audience of the eighth-century B.C.E. The exile to Babylon (150 years away), was applicable for Isaiah and his audience and started the moment he penned the words. It was a process, which began with their guilt before Jehovah, as outlined in chapters 1:1-6:13.

Judah and Jerusalem's guilt; the commission of Isaiah (1:1–6:13)

Hostile intentions of an enemy invasions and promise of relief (7:1–12:6)

Declaring international desolations (13:1–23:18)

Judgment on the whole world, promise of salvation by Jehovah (24:1–35:10)

Jehovah delivers Judah from Assyria; Babylonian exile foretold (36:1–39:8)

Release from Babylon by the Jehovah God through Cyrus, restoration of Israel, Messiah to come (40:1–66:24)

[160] Abraham Ibn Ezra (1089-1164) was a Jewish scholar of the Middle Ages, who penned a commentary on ever Old Testament book, as well as poetry and grammatical treatise, being more read than all, with the exception the greatest Jewish scholar of that period, Rashi.

practically unanimous in the view that chapters 40–66 do not come from Isaiah.[161]

A Dissecting of Isaiah

The Bible critics were not going to stop with this Isaiah II. No, they would go on to challenge Isaiah authorship even further. The above theory, known as the Second Isaiah, or Deutero-Isaiah, only led to a suggested Isaiah III. If Isaiah 40 to 66 could not belong to the First-Isaiah, because of the foreknowledge; then, chapters 13 and 14 must be set aside for the very same reason. The critique goes even further as they continue to cut up the book of Isaiah, with chapters 15 and 16 also receiving a writer of its own, another unknown prophet. Chapters 23 to 27 have been set aside as well, belonging to yet another. Another critic argues that chapters 34 to 35 could not have belonged to the 8th century prophet either, as it resembles chapter 40 to 66 that had already been set aside as not being the First-Isaiah. Bible scholar Charles C. Torrey briefly sums up the result of this irrational reasoning. "The once great 'Prophet of the Exile,'" he says, "has dwindled to a very small figure, and is all but buried in a mass of jumbled fragments." (Blenkinsopp 2003, 27) It should be noted that while Torrey brought down the number of alleged Isaiah writers, he still held many of the liberal positions. Nevertheless, not all scholars agree with such dismembering of the prophetic book that was penned in its entirety by one Isaiah, from the 8th century B.C.E.

The idea that the composer of Isaiah II lived in Babylon was being lost with some scholars. As Dr. Gleason L. Archer points out, "the references to geography, flora, and fauna found in Deutero-Isaiah were far more appropriate to an author living in Syria or Palestine."[162] Professor Bernard Duhm (1847-1928) introduced the world to three Isaiah, with none of them being the Isaiah of the 8th century B.C.E., nor having lived in Babylon. Duhm argues that Isaiah II penned chapters 40-55 about 540 B.C.E., near the region of Lebanon. Isaiah III, in Jerusalem, penned chapters 56 to 66 at the time of Ezra, 450 B.C.E. Duhm would go on to argue that some of the data within Isaiah was even further removed from Isaiah I, some belonging to the first-century B.C.E. Once they settled on a final set of dates for the dissected Isaiah, it was this criticism that George Adam Smith (1856 – 1942), accepted in his *The Book of Isaiah* (*The Expositor's Bible*; 2 vols., 1888, 1890). This criticism would receive one serious blow, only five years after the death of Smith.

Prior to the discovery of the Dead Sea Scrolls, the oldest manuscripts of the Old Testament were dated to about the ninth and tenth centuries C.E., known as the Masoretic texts (MT).[163] The Isaiah scrolls identified as "IQisa^a" and "IQIsa^b" are complete copies of the book of Isaiah, but the latter is the earliest known copy of a complete Bible book, and

---

[161] D. R. W. Wood and I. Howard Marshall, *New Bible Dictionary*, 3rd ed. (Leicester, England; Downers Grove, Ill.: InterVarsity Press, 1996), 514.

[162] Gleason Leonard Archer, *A Survey of Old Testament Introduction*, 3rd. ed.]. (Chicago: Moody Press, 1998), 368.

[163] **Hebrew Bible:** the traditional text of the Hebrew Bible, revised and annotated by Jewish scholars between the 6th and 10th centuries C.E.

dates to about 175 B.C.E. Both are from cave 1 of the Dead Sea area. Thus, the idea that some portion of the book of Isaiah was penned in the first-century B.C.E. is not long attainable. Gleason Archer stated that about the two Isaiah scrolls "proved to be word for word identical with the standard Hebrew Bible in more than 95% of the text. The 5% of variation consisted chiefly of obvious slips of the pen and variations in spelling." (Archer 1994, 19) It should be noted that the earlier criticisms of Isaiah did not go unchallenged as a result of the DSS, as numerous scholars throughout the nineteenth-century established that there was but one Isaiah, and he lived and wrote in the eighth-century B.C.E.

Entering the Twentieth-Century

The twentieth-century scholars have attempted to move the date of Isaiah out of the first-century B.C.E., closer toward Isaiah I, in an attempt to lower the number of Isaiah's. Dr. C. C. Torrey mentioned above, argued for just one writer for chapters 34 to 66, who lived in Jerusalem at the close of the fifth century. Torrey did not see these chapters as addressing the exiles, but addressing the people who lived right there in Palestine. To him the mere five mentions of Cyrus and Babylon, were interpolations,[164] and could be ignored.

Different Themes and Subject Matter

The Bible scholar often uses the Latin term *a priori*, which means to work from something that is already known or self-evident to arrive at a conclusion. Another common term among the scholars can possibly further clarify this biased position. A preconception is an idea; an opinion formed in advance, based on little or no information that reflects bias. The Bible critic approaches the study of the book of Isaiah with his or her own preconception that there is no such thing as advanced knowledge events, history written in advance, prophecy. Therefore, the critic will accept, reject, ignore, or fail to mention evidence based on whether or not it fits the preconceived notion of their antisupernatural mindset. For the critic, it is feasible that a Jewish writer living about 540 B.C.E would be able to surmise the rise of Cyrus the Great, to overthrow Babylon (44:28; 45:1), as he could surmise this from his observation of current affairs. However, it is impossible for the critical mind to accept that a Jewish writer of the eighth century could make such observations because Babylon was not even an empire at that time, and Cyrus was yet to be born for some 150 years.

The idea that God's Word prophesied so specifically as to mention Cyrus by name 150 years in advance may seem foreign to the average Bible reader. However, it is not as uncommon as one might think. God's Word is known to mention people and places hundreds of years in advance. God's prophecy regarding Josiah called for some successor of David to be named as such, and it predicted his acting against false worship in the city of Bethel. (1 Ki 13:1, 2) Over three hundred years later, a king named Josiah fulfilled this prophecy. (2 Ki 22:1; 23:15, 16) Of course, the same critics would just argue that we have another interpolation. However, this argument can be used only so much, before we run

---

[164] An interpolation is to alter or deliberately falsify a text by adding words to it or removing words from it.

into a case where it will not work. In the eighth century B.C.E., Isaiah's contemporary, the prophet Micah predicted that a great leader would be born in the unimportant town of Bethlehem. However, there were two towns in Israel at that time that was named Bethlehem, but this prediction identified which one: Bethlehem Ephrathah, the place of King David's birth. (Micah 5:2; Lu 2:1-7) This is not so easily dismissed, as the Jewish scribes of Herod the Great were aware of these facts. The book *Archaeology and Old Testament Study* states the following concerning the future of Babylon after Cyrus conquered it:

> "These extensive ruins, of which, despite Koldewey's work, only a small proportion has been excavated, have during past centuries been extensively plundered for building materials. Partly in consequence of this, much of the surface now presents an appearance of such chaotic disorder that it is strongly evocative of the prophecies of Isa. xiii. 19–22 and Jer. l. 39 f., the impression of desolation being further heightened by the aridity which marks a large part of the area of the ruins."—Thomas 1967, 41.

Presuppositions

The critic will argue that Isaiah 2:2-4 contains the conversion of the non-Jew, which hardly belongs to the eighth-century B.C.E., but occurs hundreds of years later. Therefore, this passage and all similar ones actually come from a later era in Israelite history. The critic will argue that Isaiah 11:1–9 contains the idea of world peace, and must be removed as belonging to Isaiah I. The critical will argue that a verse like Isaiah 14:26, which speak of judgment that is to befall the whole earth is to be removed, as it is not of the mindset of Isaiah's day. The critic will argue that the apocalyptic nature Isaiah chapters 24 to 27 are of a time in the fifth-century Jewish mindset.

Evidence of One Isaiah

The name of Jehovah God "the Holy One of Israel" is found 12 times in Isaiah chapters 1 to 39 and 13 times in Isaiah chapters 40 to 66, yet this name appears only 6 times in the rest of the Hebrew Old Testament. This interconnects the so-called two Isaiah's together as one. This expression being repeated throughout the whole of the book is of great value in establishing that we have one book, written by one prophet of the eighth-century.—Isa. 1:4; 5:19, 24; 10:20; 12:6; 17:7; 29:19; 30:11, 12, 15; 31:1; 37:23. Also, 41:14, 16, 20; 43:3, 14; 45:11; 47:4; 48:17; 49:7; 54:5; 55:5; 60:9, 14. Compare 2 Kings 19:22; Psa. 71:22; 78:41; 89:18; Jer. 50:29; 51:5.

Another similarity between chapters 1 to 39 and chapters 40 to 66 is a "way" or "highway." (11:16; 35:8; 40:3; 43:19; 49:11; 57:14; 62:10) Yet, another similarity runs through the whole of Isaiah is the idea of a "remnant" or "remaining ones." (1:9; 6:13; 10:20, 21, 22; 11:11, 12, 16; 14:22, 30; 15:9; 16:14; 17:3, 6; 21:17; 28:5; 37:31; 46:3; 65:8, 9) There is also a recurring reference to "Zion," a term used 29 times in chapters 1 to 39 and 18 times in chapter 40 to 66. (2:3; 4:5; 18:7; 24:23; 27:13; 28:16; 29:8; 30:19; 31:9; 33:5, 20; 34:8; 46:13; 49:14; 51:3; 11; 52:1; 57:13; 59:20; 60:14; 62:1; 11; 65:11; 25; 66:8) Even more, there is another distinctive figure of speech such as the expression, "pangs of a woman in labor." 13:8; 21:3; 26:17, 18; 42:14; 54:1; 66:7.

Literary Style

Another expression found only in Jeremiah 9:12 and Micah 4:4 as well as crossing through both chapters 1 to 39 and 40 to 66: "the mouth of Jehovah hath spoken it." (1:20; 40:5; 58:14) Another title found only in Isaiah and appearing throughout the complete book is: "the Mighty One of Israel." (1:24; 49:26; 60:16) Another phrase common to Exodus 7:19; Psalm 1:3, 119:136, Pro 5:16, Lam 3:48, as well as Isaiah is "streams of water." (30:25; 44:4) The style of this author was to use what was known as emphatic duplication. (2:7, 8; 6:3; 8:9; 24:16, 19; 40:1; 43:11, 25; 48:15; 51:12; 57:19; 62:10) This evidence could be repeated with other terms, some less distinctive, yet nevertheless, it authenticates the book as being of one author.

There is another aspect to the Cyrus evidence that actually works against the two Isaiah criticisms. We are to believe that this Second-Isaiah or some redactor[165] of about 540 B.C.E. is so skilled at smoothing out a document, attempting to make it as though it were one document, by having numerous terms and phrases show up throughout the alleged two Isaiah's, to then develop the Cyrus of Persia situation. Throughout chapters 41 to 48, there are numerous specific references to Cyrus, or allusions to him and his kingdom. In these references, Cyrus' character and person is developed, as well as there being a prophetic element to his actions that is presented as though being far into the future. If written in the midst of the current affairs, it would be pointless to build a character that is extremely well known, unless you presented him as being a product of prophecy.

Once we get past the idea that such devious thinking would be within the mind of some mysterious writer, who then had the tremendous skills to carry it out; we then must believe that this composer would have possessed knowledge that was beyond his circumstances. Little does the critic realize that he is giving just as much power to the mysterious composer as was given to Isaiah the prophet by Jehovah God. This redactor or Second-Isaiah would have had an extensive knowledge of Israel's governmental affairs from the eighth-century to the sixth century, the ability to deduce from current affairs that Cyrus would level Babylon, and release a remnant to return to Jerusalem (Zion), to rebuild. Further, he would have possessed a knowledge of Canaanite idolatry that is reflective of the first 39 chapters; a subject that had long been a dead issue to the Israelites of the sixth-century. Moreover, he would have had to see centuries later that the Messiah [Jesus], would have had to die for the transgressions of others.—Matt 4:15-16.

The critic would have his listeners believe that chapters 40 to 66 have no connection to the eighth-century B.C.E. This could not be further from the truth, as one considers Isaiah 44:23f.; 45:8; 50:1; 55:12f.; 56:1; 57:1; 59:3; 61:8; 63:3f.f As was stated earlier Micah is a contemporary of Isaiah, his writing being completed about 16-years after Isaiah, covering 777 – 716 B C.E. There is a great resemblance between what Isaiah wrote in chapters 40 to 66 and what Micah penned: Isaiah 41:15f, and Micah 4:13; Isaiah 47:2f. and Micah 1:11; Isaiah 48:2 and Micah 3:11; Isaiah 49:29 and Micah 7:17; Isaiah 52:12 and Micah 2:13; Isaiah 56:10 and Micah 3:5; Isaiah 58:1 and Micah 3:8. On this Old Testament scholar R. K. Harrison wrote:

---

[165] A redactor is a person who edits or revises a document in preparation for publication.

> Obviously the same glorious expectation of the future under divine providence, the same broad conception of the nations of the Near East, and the confident expectation that a renewed Israel would return from exile, were characteristic of both prophets. (Harrison 2004, 779)

An Anthology of one Author

An anthology is a book that consists of essays, stories, or poems by different writers.[166] If one considers that Isaiah did not write the entire book that bears his name in one setting, but different sections over a forty-six-year prophetic career; his book become a collection of his different writings throughout his life. For instance, Isaiah may have penned a section of his work at the age of twenty, and another at the age of thirty, and another at forty-three, and another at fifty-two and the final at sixty-five. This could explain the differences in style and literary expression as we are literally different people through our seventy to eighty-year life. As a result, this anthology of the book of Isaiah would have had each section being written under different circumstances and in different historical settings, making the critics argument not relevant.

The following analogy illustrates in modern terms how the book of Isaiah was written over time. Imagine a newspaper writer, at the age of twenty-three, writing an assignment in 1935 about The Great Depression. Then imagine the same writer, in his forties, embedded with the troops and writing articles about World War II from 1942-1945. Next, imagine the writer in his seventies being asked to come out of retirement to cover the Vietnam Conflict in 1969. Then, in 1991, this same writer in his nineties, who had seen the fall of the Soviet Union and the end of the Cold War, decides to pen one last article in his life. The writer dies in 1995 and several years after his death, a compilation of his articles is published in an anthological book about life in the twentieth-century.

Isaiah 1:1 Updated American Standard Version (UASV)

The vision of Isaiah the son of Amoz, which he saw concerning Judah and Jerusalem in the days of Uzziah, Jotham, Ahaz, and Hezekiah, kings of Judah.

Isaiah 2:1 Updated American Standard Version (UASV)

The word that Isaiah the son of Amoz saw concerning Judah and Jerusalem.

Isaiah 13:1 Updated American Standard Version (UASV)

The prophetic utterance concerning[167] Babylon which Isaiah the son of Amoz saw.

The Bible Takes the Witness Stand for Isaiah

As the Bible is a collection of 66 smaller books, all of which are inspired of God, it deserves the opportunity to get on the stand for itself, to testify in its own behalf. It is obvious that first-century Christians believed that the book of Isaiah had just one author.

---

[166] Inc Merriam-Webster, *Merriam-Webster's Collegiate Dictionary.*, Eleventh ed. (Springfield, Mass.: Merriam-Webster, Inc., 2003).

[167] Or *oracle*; a serious, lengthy address kind of prophetic message

Luke was the writer of the Gospel bearing his name, as well as the Book of Acts. In Acts, Luke tells of an Ethiopian official, who "had come to Jerusalem to worship and was returning, seated in his chariot, and he was reading the prophet Isaiah." (Chapter 53) This is the very portion of Isaiah that is attributed to the Deutero-Isaiah." Acts 8:26-28

Luke 1:1-4 Updated American Standard Version (UASV)

¹ Inasmuch as many have undertaken to compile an account of the things accomplished among us, ² just as they were handed down to us by those who from the beginning were eyewitnesses and servants of the word, ³ it seemed good to me also, **having followed all things accurately** from the beginning, to **write an orderly account** for you, most excellent Theophilus, ⁴ so that you may know fully the certainty of the things that you have been taught orally.

Acts 1:1-2 Updated American Standard Version (UASV)

¹ The first account, O Theophilus, I composed about all that Jesus began to do and teach, ² until the day when he was taken up, after he had given commands through the Holy Spirit to the apostles whom he had chosen.

"The general consensus of both liberal and conservative scholars is that Luke is very accurate as a historian. He's erudite, he's eloquent, his Greek approaches classical quality, he writes as an educated man, and archaeological discoveries are showing over and over again that Luke is accurate in what he has to say."—John McRay (Strobel 1998, 97)

Luke Wrote

Luke 4:17 Updated American Standard Version (UASV)

¹⁷ And the scroll[168] of the prophet Isaiah was given to him. And he unrolled the scroll and found the place where it was written,

The words that Jesus would go on to read in verse 18-19 of Luke chapter 4 are found in Isaiah 61:1-2. Does Luke attribute this to the alleged Deutero-Isaiah? No, he specifically says "the prophet Isaiah."

Matthew wrote

Matthew 3:1-3 Updated American Standard Version (UASV)

¹ Now in those days John the Baptist came preaching in the wilderness of Judea, saying, ² "Repent, for the kingdom of heaven has come near."[169] ³ For this is the one referred to by Isaiah the prophet when he said,

"The voice of one crying out in the wilderness,
'Make ready the way of the Lord,
  make his paths straight.'"[170]

---

[168] Or *roll*

[169] Matt. 4:17

These prophetic words come from Isaiah 40:3. Does Matthew attribute these prophetic words to some unknown prophet, some Deutero-Isaiah? No, he clearly states that it was "Isaiah the Prophet."

Mark wrote

Mark 1:1-3 Updated American Standard Version (UASV)

¹ The beginning of the gospel of Jesus Christ, [the Son of God].[171]

² As it is written in Isaiah the prophet;[172]

"Behold, I send my messenger before your face,
who will prepare your way,

³ the voice of one crying in the wilderness:
'Make ready the way of the Lord,
make his paths straight.'"

The latter portion of that quotation comes from Isaiah 40:3. Peter played a major role in helping Mark with his Gospel. Therefore, in one verse, we can get the assessment of two prominent Christians. Neither shows any knowledge of there being another Isaiah, the so-called Deutero-Isaiah.

John Wrote

John 12:36-43 Updated American Standard Version (UASV)

³⁶ While you have the light, trust[173] in the light, so that you may become sons of light."

The Jews' Lack of Faith Fulfills Isaiah's Prophecy

Jesus said these things, and he went away and was hidden from them. ³⁷ But though He had performed so many signs before them, yet they were not trusting[174] in him. ³⁸ So that the word of Isaiah prophet might be fulfilled, which he said:

---

[170] Isa. 40:3

[171] Son of God (υἱοῦ θεοῦ) is absent in ℵ* Θ 28ᶜ al by either a human error in copying or an addition by the copyist adding to the title – B D W al (e.g., Rev. 1:1). Because of the strong witnesses and the fact that "Son of God" is a theme throughout Mark, it could have been original; thus, it is retained in brackets.

[172] Some manuscripts that carry no textual weight have *in the prophets*; however, the first part of Mark's quote is actually from Malachi 3:1, the second portion from Isaiah 40:3, which makes it easy to see why some copyist would have altered "Isaiah the prophet." Comfort suggests that Mark's attributing all of it to Isaiah may have been because his Roman audience would like be more familiar with Isaiah. Regardless, Mark does not acknowledge any Deutero-Isaiah.

[173] The grammatical construction of *pisteuo* "believe" followed by *eis* "into" plus the accusative causing a different shade of meaning, having faith into Jesus.

[174] The grammatical construction of *pisteuo* "believe" followed by *eis* "into" plus the accusative causing a different shade of meaning, having faith into Jesus.

"Lord, who has trusted in the thing heard from us,
and to whom has the arm of the Lord been revealed?"[175]

39 For this reason they could not believe, for Isaiah said again,

40 "He has blinded their eyes
and he hardened their heart,
so that they would not see with their eyes,
and understand with their heart, and turn,
and I might heal them."[176]

41 These things Isaiah said because he saw his glory, and he spoke about him. **42** Nevertheless many even of the rulers believed in him, but because of the Pharisees they were not confessing him, so that they might not be put out of[177] the synagogue; **43** for they loved the glory of men more than the glory of God.

The apostle John drew from both sides of the alleged two Isaiah's: John 12:38 in Isaiah 53:1 and John 12:40 in Isaiah 6:1. There is no indication that two separate writers were being considered.

Paul wrote

Romans 10:16, 20; 15:12 Updated American Standard Version (UASV)

16 But they have not all obeyed the gospel. For Isaiah says, "Lord,[178] who has believed what he has heard from us?"

20 And Isaiah is very bold and says,

"I was found by those who did not seek me;
I became manifest to those who did not ask for me."[179]

12 And again Isaiah says,

"There shall come the root of Jesse,
And he who arises to rule over the Gentiles,
In him shall the Gentiles hope."[180]

---

[175] Quotation from Isaiah 53:1

[176] Quotation from Isaiah 6:10

[177] Or *expelled from*

[178] Quotation from Isaiah 53:1, which reads, "Who has believed our message? And to whom has the arm of Jehovah been revealed?"

[179] Quotation from Isa 65:1, which reads, "I have let myself be sought by those who did not ask for me; I let myself be found by those who did not seek me."

I said, 'Here I am; here I am!' to a nation that was not calling on my name.

[180] A quotation from Isa 11:10, which reads, "In that day the root of Jesse, who shall stand as a signal for the peoples, to him shall the nations inquire, and his resting place shall be glorious."

In Paul's letter to the Romans, Paul refers to Isaiah 53:1 in Romans 10:16, Isaiah 65:1 in Romans 10:20, and Isaiah 11:10 in Romans 15:12. Thus, we can see that Paul makes references to both chapters 1-39 and chapters 40-66. The context is quite clear that he is referring to the same writer throughout. Obviously, the writers of the New Testament never had any idea of two, three, or more writers for the Book of Isaiah.

Let us look again to the Dead Sea Scrolls, particularly the Isaiah scroll mentioned earlier, which dates to about 175 B.C.E. This one scroll especially refutes the critical claim of a Deutero-Isaiah. How? Within this document, chapter 40 begins on the last line of a column, with the opening sentence being completed in the next column. Therefore, this suggests that the copyist was not aware of a change from a Proto-Isaiah to a Deutero-Isaiah, or some sort of division at this point.

First-Century Jewish Historian

Flavius Josephus, the first-century Jewish historian makes it quite clear that the prophecies pertaining to Isaiah belonged to Isaiah the prophet, but come from the eighth-century B.C.E. as well. "These things Cyrus knew," Josephus writes, "from reading the book of prophecy which Isaiah had left behind two hundred and ten years earlier." It is also Josephus' position that these very prophecies may have been what contributed to Cyrus releasing the Jews, to return to their homeland, for Josephus writes that Cyrus was "seized by a strong desire and ambition to do what had been written." *Jewish Antiquities*, Book XI, chapter 1, paragraph 2.

Isaiah the Prophet—Trustworthy

Having looked at a small portion of the evidence, what conclusions should we draw? One inspired writer, who lived in the eighth-century B.C.E., whose father was Amoz, penned the book of Isaiah. This book for 2,000 years was never questioned as belonging to more than one writer. Yes, we openly acknowledge that there is a style shift from chapter 40 forward. However, as was stated earlier, the prophet worked on sections of this writing for 46 years, living in different historical settings. In a lifetime, all of us are different people. Therefore, the way this writer may express something at 21 years of age, would certainly be penned differently at the age of 44. Moreover, Isaiah was commissioned to deliver a variety of messages, some coming as warnings, others as judgment, still others as: "Comfort, comfort my people, says your God." (Isaiah 40:1) There is no doubt that the Israelites were comforted by the promise that they would be released after 70-years of exile in Babylon, to return to their homeland. Below the reader will find four specifically selected books, which offer a far more extensive amount of evidence that the Book of Isaiah is but one Isaiah, from the eight-century B.C.E.

CHAPTER XXI Daniel Misjudged

Edward D. Andrews

You have a critical body that has formulated an opinion of the Bible, especially prophetic books, long before they have ever looked into the evidence. The liberal critical scholar is antisupernatural in their mindset. In other words, any book that would claim to have predicted events hundreds of years in advance are simply misrepresenting itself, as that foreknowledge is impossible. Therefore, the book must have been written after the events, yet written in such a way, as to mislead the reader that it was written hundreds of years before.

This is exactly what these critics say we have in the book of Daniel. However, what do we know about the person and the book itself? Daniel is known historically as a man of uprightness in the extreme. The book that he penned has been regarded highly for thousands of years. The context within says that it is authentic and true history, penned by Daniel, a Jewish prophet, who lived in the seventh and sixth centuries B.C.E. The chronology within the book shows that it covers the time period of 616 to 536 B.C.E., being completed by the latter date.

The New Encyclopædia Britannica acknowledges that the book of Daniel was once "generally considered to be true history, containing genuine prophecy." However, the *Britannica* asserts that in truth, Daniel "was written in a later time of national crisis—when the Jews were suffering severe persecution under [Syrian King] Antiochus IV Epiphanes." This encyclopedia dates the book between 167 and 164 B.C.E. *Britannica* goes on to assert that the writer of the book of Daniel does not prophesy the future but merely presents "events that are past history to him as prophecies of future happenings."

How does a book and a prophet that has enjoyed centuries of a reputable standing, garner such criticism? It actually began just two-hundred years after Christ, with Porphyry, a philosopher, who felt threatened by the rise of Christianity. His way of dealing with this new religion, was to pen fifteen books to undercut it, the twelfth being against Daniel. In the end, Porphyry labeled the book as a forgery, saying that it was written by a second-century B.C.E. Jew. Comparable attacks came in the 18th and 19th centuries. German scholars, who were prejudiced against the supernatural, started modern objections to the Book of Daniel.

As has been stated numerous times in this section, the higher critics and rationalists start with the presupposition that foreknowledge of future events is impossible. As was stated earlier in the chapter on Isaiah, the **important truth for the Bible critic is** the understanding that in all occurrences, prophecy pronounced or written in Bible times meant something to the people of the time it was spoken or written to; it was meant to serve as a guide for them. Frequently, it had specific fulfillment for that time, being fulfilled throughout the lifetime of that very generation. This is actually true; the words always had some application to the very people who heard them. However, the application could be a process of events, starting with the moral condition of the people in their relationship with Jehovah God, which precipitated the prophetic events that were to unfold, even those prophetic events that were centuries away.

However, it must be noted that while Daniel and Isaiah are both prophetic books, Daniel is also known as an apocalyptic book, as is the book of Revelation. This is not to say that Isaiah does not contain some apocalyptic sections (e.g., Isa 24–27; 56–66) What is assumed by the critical scholar here is that there is a rule that a prophet is understood in his day, to be only speaking of the immediate concerns of the people. They are looking at it more like a proclamation, instead of a future event that could be centuries away. Before addressing this concern, let us define apocalyptic for the reader:

Apocalyptic

This is a term derived from a Greek word meaning "revelation," and used to refer to a pattern of thought and to a form of literature, both dealing with future judgment (eschatology).

Two primary patterns of eschatological thought are found in the Bible, both centered in the conviction that God will act in the near future to save his people and to punish those who oppress them. In prophetic eschatology, the dominant form in the OT, God is expected to act within history to restore man and nature to the perfect condition which existed prior to man's fall. Apocalyptic eschatology, on the other hand, expects God to destroy the old imperfect order before restoring the world to paradise.

Origins of Apocalypticism

In Israel, apocalyptic eschatology evidently flourished under foreign domination.

From the early 6th century B.C., prophetic eschatology began to decline and apocalyptic eschatology became increasingly popular. The Book of Daniel, written during the 6th century B.C., is the earliest example of apocalyptic literature in existence.[181]

The problem with the modern critic is that he is attempting to look at the Biblical literature through the modern-day mindset. His first error is to believe that a prophetic book was viewed only as a proclamation of current affairs. The Jewish people viewed all prophetic literature just as we would expect, as a book of prophecy. The problem today is that many are not aware of the way they viewed the prophetic literature. While we do not have the space to go into the genre of prophecy and apocalyptic literature extensively, it is recommended that you see Dr. Stein's book in the bibliography at the end of the chapter.

Some Rules for Prophecy

- One needs to identify the beginning and end of the prophecy.
- The reader needs to find the historical setting.

---

[181] Walter A. Elwell and Barry J. Beitzel, *Baker Encyclopedia of the Bible* (Grand Rapids, Mich.: Baker Book House, 1988), 122.

- The Bible is a diverse book when it comes to literary styles: narrative, poetic, prophetic, and apocalyptic; also containing parables, metaphors, similes, hyperbole, and other figures of speech. Too often, these alleged errors are the result of a reader taking a figure of speech as literal, or reading a parable as though it is a narrative.

- Many alleged inconsistencies disappear by simply looking at the context. Taking words out of context can distort their meaning.

- Determine if the prophet is foretelling the future. On the other hand, is he simply proclaiming God's will and purpose to the people. (If prophetic, has any portion of it been fulfilled?)

- The concept of a second fulfillment should be set aside in place of implications.

- Does the New Testament expound on this prophecy?

- The reader needs to slow down and carefully read the account, considering exactly what is being said.

- The Bible student needs to understand the level that the Bible intends to be exact in what is written. If Jim told a friend that 650 graduated with him from high school in 1984, it is not challenged, because it is all too clear that he is using rounded numbers and is not meaning to be exactly precise.

- Unexplained does not equal unexplainable.

Digging into the ancient Jewish mindset, we find that it is dualistic. It views all of God's creation, either on the side of God or Satan. Further, the Jewish mind was determined that regardless of how bad things were, God would come to the rescue of his people. The only pessimistic thinking was their understanding that there had to be a major catastrophe that precipitated the rescue. In combining this way of thinking, they believed that there are two systems of things: (1) the current wicked one that man lives in, and (2) the one that is to come, where God will restore things to the way it was before Adam and Eve sinned. Jehovah impressed upon his people, to see His rescue as imminent. The vision that comes to Daniel in the book of Daniel and John in the book of Revelations, comes in one of two ways: (1) in a dreamed vision state or (2) the person in vision is caught up to heaven and shown what is to take place. Frequently, Isaiah, Daniel and John did not understand the vision; they were simply to pen what they saw. (Isa 6:9-10; 8:16; 29:9-14; 44:18; 53:1; Dan 8:15–26; 9:20–27; 10:18–12:4; Rev 7:13–17; 17:7–18) The people readily recognized the symbolism in most of the prophetic literature, and the less common symbolisms in apocalyptic literature were far more complex, which by design, heighten the desire to interpret and understand them. There are two very important points to keep in mind: (1) some were not meant to be understood fully at the time, and (2) only the righteous ones would have insight into these books, while the wicked would refuse to understand the spiritual things.

Daniel 8:26-27 Updated American Standard Version (UASV)

²⁶ The vision of the evenings and the mornings that has been told is true,¹⁸² but seal up the vision,¹⁸³ for it refers to many days from now."¹⁸⁴

²⁷ And I, Daniel, was exhausted and sick for days. Then I got up and carried out the business of the king, and I was disturbed over the vision and no one could understand it.¹⁸⁵

Daniel 10:14 Updated American Standard Version (UASV)

¹⁴ Now I have come to give you an understanding of what will happen to your people in the end of the days, for it is a vision yet for the days to come."

Daniel 12:3-4 Updated American Standard Version (UASV)

³ And the ones who are wise will shine brightly like the brightness of the expanse of heaven; and those who turn many to righteousness, like the stars forever and ever. ⁴ But as for you, O Daniel, conceal these words and seal up the book until the time of the end; many will go to and fro,¹⁸⁶ and knowledge will increase."

Daniel 12:9-10 Updated American Standard Version (UASV)

⁹He said, "Go your way, Daniel, for the words are shut up and sealed until the time of the end. ¹⁰Many shall purify themselves and make themselves white and be refined, but the wicked shall act wickedly. And none of the wicked shall understand, but those who are wise shall understand.

2 Corinthians 4:3-4 Updated American Standard Version (UASV)

³ And even if our gospel is veiled, it is veiled to those who are perishing. ⁴ In their case the god of this world has blinded the minds of the unbelievers, to keep them from seeing the light of the gospel of the glory of Christ, who is the image of God.

One of the principles of interpreting prophecy is to understand judgment prophecies. If a prophet declares judgment on a people, and they turn around from their bad course, the judgment may be lifted, which does not negate the trueness of the prophetic judgment message. There was simply a change in circumstances. There is a principle that most readers are not aware of:

Jeremiah 18:7-8 Updated American Standard Version (UASV)

⁷ At one moment I might speak concerning a nation or concerning a kingdom to uproot, to tear down, and to destroy it; ⁸ and if that nation which I have spoken against

---

[182] Lit *truth*; Heb., *'emet*

[183] I.e., keep the vision secret; Heb., *satar*

[184] Lit *for to days many*; I.e., to the distant future

[185] Lit *make me understand*

[186] I.e. examine the book thoroughly

turns from its evil, I will also feel regret over[187] the calamity that I intended to bring against it.

Another principle that needs to be understood is the language of prophecy. It uses imagery that is common to the people, with the exception of the highly apocalyptic literature. One form of imagery is the cosmic.

Isaiah 13:9-11 Updated American Standard Version (UASV)

⁹ Behold, the day of Jehovah is coming,
  cruel, with wrath and burning anger,
to make the land a desolation;
  and he will destroy its sinners from it.
¹⁰ For the stars of the heavens and their constellations
  will not flash forth their light;
the sun will be dark when it rises,
  and the moon will not shed its light.
¹¹ And I will punish the world for its evil,
  and the wicked for their iniquity;
I will put an end to the arrogance of the proud,
  and lay low the haughtiness of tyrants.

It is often assumed that this sort of imagery is talking about the end of the world, and this is not always the case. Using Isaiah 13 as our example, it is talking about a pronouncement against Babylon, not the end of the world, as can be seen in verse 1. This type of terminology is a way of expressing that God is acting in behalf of man. At times, figurative language can come across as contradicting for the modern-day reader. For example, in chapter 21 of Revelation the walls of Jerusalem are described as being 200 feet thick. The walls are an image of safety and security for the New Jerusalem. However, in verse 25 we read that the gates are never shut. This immediate leads to the question of why have walls that cannot be penetrated, and then leave the gates open? Moreover, if gates are the weakest point to defend, why have twelve of them (vs. 12)? To the modern militaristic mind, this comes off as contradictory, but not to the Jewish-Christian mind of the first-century. Both present the picture of safety. It is so safe that you can leave the gates open. What about the idea of a "fuller meaning" that the prophet was not aware of? As we saw in the above there would be symbolism meant for a day far into the future, but generally speaking, most prophets proclaimed a message that was applicable to their day, and implications for another day. Dr. Robert Stein addresses this issue:

> There are times when a prophetic text appears to have a fulfillment other than what the prophet himself apparently expected. (The following are frequently given as examples: Matt. 1:22–23; 2:15, 17–18; John 12:15; 1 Cor. 10:3–4.) Is it possible that a prophecy may have a deeper meaning or "fuller" sense than the prophet envisioned? . . . Rather than appealing to a "fuller sense" distinct and different from that of the biblical author, however, it may be wiser to see if the supposed *sensus plenior* is in reality an implication of the author's conscious meaning. Thus, when Paul in 1 Corinthians 9:9 quotes Deuteronomy 25:4 ("do not muzzle an ox while it is treading out the grain") as a justification

---

[187] Lit *repent of*; .e., *I will change my mind concerning*; or *I will think better of*, or *I will relent concerning*

for ministers of the gospel living off the gospel, this is not a "fuller" meaning of the text unrelated to what the author sought to convey. Rather, it is a legitimate implication of the willed pattern of meaning contained in Deuteronomy 25:4. If as a principle animals should be allowed to share in the benefits of their work, how much more should the "animal" who is made in the image of God and proclaims the Word of God be allowed to share in the benefits of that work! Thus, what Paul is saying is not a fuller and different meaning from what the writer of Deuteronomy meant. On the contrary, although this specific implication was unknown to him, it is part of his conscious and willed pattern of meaning. Perhaps such prophecies as Matthew 1:22–23 and 2:15 are best understood as revealing implications of the original prophecies in Isaiah 7:14 and Hosea 11:1. Whereas in Isaiah's day the prophet meant that a maiden would give birth to a son who was named "Immanuel," that willed meaning also allows for a virgin one day to give birth to a son who would be Immanuel. Whereas God showed his covenantal faithfulness by leading his "son," his children, back from Egypt to the promised land in Moses' day so also did he lead his "Son," Jesus, back from Egypt to the promised land.[188]

Getting back to Daniel, we can clearly see that his book is prophetic and the only Old Testament apocalyptic book at that, which makes him a special target for the Bible critic. The critic has deemed that Daniel did not pen the book that bears his name, but another writer penned the words some centuries later.[189] These attacks have become such a reality that most scholars accept the late date of 165 B.C.E., by a pseudonym. As we have learned throughout this book, it is never the majority that establishes something as being true, simply for the fact of being the majority; it is the evidence. If the evidence proves that Daniel did not write the book, then the words are meaningless, and the hope that it contains is not there.

For example, take the allegation made in *The Encyclopedia Americana:* "Many historical details of the earlier periods [such as that of the Babylonian exile] have been badly garbled" in Daniel. Really? We will take up three of those alleged mistakes.

Claims That Belshazzar Is Missing From History

Daniel 5:1, 11, 18, 22, 30 Updated American Standard Version (UASV)

¹ Belshazzar the king made[190] a great feast for a thousand of his nobles, and he was drinking wine in the presence of the thousand.

---

[188] Robert H. Stein, *A Basic Guide to Interpreting the Bible: Playing by the Rules* (Grand Rapids, MI: Baker Books, 1994), 97.

[189] Some Bible critics attempt to lessen the charge of forgery by saying that the writer used Daniel as a false name (pseudonym), just as some ancient noncanonical books were written under assumed names. In spite of this, the Bible critic Ferdinand Hitzig held: "The case of the book of Daniel, if it is assigned to any other [writer], is different. Then it becomes a forged writing, and the intention was to deceive his immediate readers, though for their good."

[190] I.e., held

11 There is a man in your kingdom in whom is a spirit of the holy gods;[191] and in the days of your father, enlightenment, insight and wisdom like the wisdom of the gods were found in him. And King Nebuchadnezzar, your father, your father the king, appointed him chief of the magic-practicing priests, conjurers, Chaldeans and diviners.

18 You. O king, the Most High God granted the kingdom and the greatness and the glory and the majesty to Nebuchadnezzar your father.

22 "But you, his son[192] Belshazzar, have not humbled your heart, although you knew all of this,

30 That same night Belshazzar the Chaldean king was killed.

In 1850 German scholar Ferdinand Hitzig said in a commentary on the book of Daniel, confidently declaring that Belshazzar was "a figment of the writer's imagination."[193] His reasoning was that Daniel was missing from history, only found in the book of Daniel itself. Does this not seem a bit premature? Is it so irrational to think that a person might not be readily located by archaeology, a brand new field at the time, especially from a period that was yet to be fully explored? Regardless, in 1854, there was a discovery of some small cylinders in the ancient city of Babylon and Ur, southern Iraq. The cuneiform documents were from King Nabonidus, and they included a prayer for "Belshazzar my firstborn son, the offspring of my heart." This discovery was a mere four years after Hitzig made his rash judgment.

Of course, not all critics would be satisfied. H. F. Talbot made the statement, "This proves nothing." The charge by Talbot was that Belshazzar was likely a mere child, but Daniel has him as being king. Well, this critical remark did not even stay alive as long as Hitzig's had. Within the year, more cuneiform tablets were discovered, this time they stated he had secretaries, as well as a household staff. Obviously, Belshazzar was not a child! However, more was to come, as other tablets explained that Belshazzar was a coregent king while Nabonidus was away from Babylon for years at a time.[194]

One would think that the critic might concede. Still disgruntled, some argued that the Bible calls Belshazzar, the son of Nebuchadnezzar, and not the son of Nabonidus. Others comment that Daniel nowhere mentions the name of Nabonidus. Once again, both arguments are dismantled with a deeper observation. Nabonidus married the daughter of Nebuchadnezzar, making Belshazzar the grandson of Nebuchadnezzar. Both Hebrew and Aramaic language do not have words for "grandfather" or "grandson"; "son of" also means "grandson of" or even "descendant of." (See Matthew 1:1.) Moreover, the account in Daniel does infer that Belshazzar is the son of Nabonidus. When the mysterious handwriting was on the wall, the horrified Belshazzar offered the *third* place in his

---

[191] Spirit of … gods Aram., *ruach-'elahin'*; Or possibly *the Spirit of the holy God*

[192] Or *descendant*

[193] *Das Buch Daniel*. Ferdinand Hitzig. Weidman (Leipzig) 1850.

[194] When Babylon fell, Nabonidus was away. Therefore, Daniel was correct in that Belshazzar was the king at that time. Critics still try to cling to their Bible difficulty by stating that no secular records state that Belshazzar was a king. When will they quit with this quibbling? Even governors in the Ancient Near East were stated as being kings at times.

kingdom, to whoever could interpret it. (Daniel 5:7) The observant reader will notice that Nabonidus held first place in the kingdom, while Daniel held the second place, leaving the third place for the interpreter.

Darius the Mede

One would think that the critic would have learned his lesson from Belshazzar. However, this is just not the case. Daniel 5:31 reads: "and Darius the Mede received the kingdom, being about sixty-two years old." Here again, the critical scholar argues that Darius does not exist, as he has never been found in secular or archaeological records. Therefore, *The New Encyclopædia Britannica* declares that this Darius is "a fictitious character."

There is no doubt that in time; Darius will be unearthed by archaeology, just as Belshazzar has. There is initial information that allows for inferences already. Cuneiform tablets have been discovered that shows Cyrus the Persian did not take over as the "King of Babylon" directly after the conquest. Rather he carried the title "King of the Lands."[195] W. H Shea suggests, "Whoever bore the title of 'King of Babylon' was a vassal king under Cyrus, not Cyrus himself." Is it possible that Darius is simply a title of a person that was placed in charge of Babylon? Some scholars suggest a man named Gubaru was the real Darius. Secular records do show that Cyrus appointed Gubaru as governor over Babylon, giving him considerable power. Looking to the cuneiform tablets again, we find that Cyrus appointed subgovernors over Babylon. Fascinatingly, Daniel notes that Darius selected 120 satraps to oversee the kingdom of Babylon.—Daniel 6:1.

We should realize that archaeology is continuously bringing unknown people to light all the time, and in time, it may shed more light on Darius. However, for now, and based on the fact that many Bible characters have been established, it is a little ridiculous to consider Darius as "fictitious," worse still to view the whole of the book of Daniel as a fraud. In fact, it is best to see Daniel as a person, who was right there in the midst of that history, giving him access to more court records.

After Belshazzar (King of Babylon), Sargon (Assyrian Monarch), and the like have been assailed with being nonexistent, the Bible critic and liberal scholars do the same with Darius the Mede, and Mordecai in the book of Esther. This illustrates the folly of assigning boundless confidence in the ancient secular records, while we wait in secular sources to validate Scripture. Most outside of true conservative Christianity carry the presupposition that the Bible is myth, legend and erroneous until secular sources support it.

Bible critics argued profusely that Belshazzar was not a historical person. Then, evidence came in that substantiated Belshazzar, and the Bible critic just move on to another like Sargon, saying that he was not a real historical person, as though they had never raised such an objection for Belshazzar. Then, evidence came in that substantiated Sargon and the Bible critic would silently move on yet again. This is repeated time after time.

---

[195] This evidence is found in royal titles in economic texts, which just so happens to date to the first two years of Cyrus' rule.

The Bible critics, liberal and moderate Bible scholars believe the Bible is wrong until validated by secular history. They move the goal post of trustworthiness as they please, so that Scripture will never be authentic and true, it will never be trustworthy, and to theses one, it is not the inspired, fully inerrant Word of God, as far as they are concerned.

Why do we continue to cater to these ones, as though we need to appease them somehow?

King Jehoiakim

Daniel 1:1 Updated American Standard Version (UASV)

¹ In the third year of the reign of Jehoiakim king of Judah, Nebuchadnezzar king of Babylon came to Jerusalem and besieged it.

Jeremiah 25:1 Updated American Standard Version (UASV)

¹ The word that came to Jeremiah concerning all the people of Judah, in the fourth year of Jehoiakim the son of Josiah, king of Judah (that was the first year of Nebuchadnezzar king of Babylon),

Jeremiah 46:2 Updated American Standard Version (UASV)

² About Egypt, concerning the army of Pharaoh Neco king of Egypt, which was by the Euphrates River at Carchemish, which Nebuchadnezzar king of Babylon defeated in the fourth year of Jehoiakim the son of Josiah, king of Judah:

The Bible critic finds fault with Daniel 1:1 as it is not in harmony with Jeremiah, who says "in the fourth year of Jehoiakim the son of Josiah, king of Judah (that was the first year of Nebuchadnezzar king of Babylon)." The Bible student who looks a little deeper will find that there is really no contradiction at all. Pharaoh Necho first made Jehoiakim king in 628 B.C.E. Three years would pass before Nebuchadnezzar succeeded his father as King in Babylon, in 624 B.C.E. In 620 B.C.E., Nebuchadnezzar conquered Judah and made Jehoiakim the subordinate king under Babylon. (2 Kings 23:34; 24:1) Therefore, it is all about the perspective of the writer and where he was when penning his book. Daniel wrote from Babylon; therefore, Jehoiakim's third year would have been when he was made a subordinate king to Babylon. Jeremiah on the other hand, wrote from Jerusalem, so he is referring to the time when Jehoiakim was made a subordinate king under Pharaoh Necho.

This so-called discrepancy really just adds more weight to the fact that it was Daniel, who penned the book bearing his name. In addition, it must be remembered that Daniel had Jeremiah's book with him. (Daniel 9:2) Therefore, are we to believe that Daniel was this clever forger, and at the same time, he would contradict the well-known book of Jeremiah, especially in verse 1?

Positive Details

There are many details in the book of Daniel itself, which give credence to its authenticity. For example, Daniel 3:1-6 tells us that Nebuchadnezzar set up a huge image of gold, which his people were to worship. Archaeology has found evidence that credits Nebuchadnezzar with attempts to involve the people more in nationalistic and religious practices. Likewise, Daniel addresses Nebuchadnezzar's arrogant attitude about his many construction plans. (Daniel 4:30) It is not until modern-day archaeology uncovered evidence that we now know Nebuchadnezzar was the person who built much of Babylon. Moreover, his boastful attitude is made quite evident by having his name stamped on the bricks. This fact would not have been something a forger from 167-63 B.C.E. would have known about because the bricks hadn't at that time been unearthed.

The writer of Daniel was very familiar with the differences between Babylonian and Medo-Persian law. The three friends of Daniel were thrown into the fiery furnace for disobeying the Babylonian law, while Daniel, decades later under Persian law, was thrown into a lion's pit for violating the law. (Daniel 3:6; 6:7-9) Archaeology has again proven to be a great help, for they have uncovered an actual letter that shows the fiery furnace was a form of punishment. However, the Medes and Persians would have not used this form of punishment; as fire was sacred to them. Thus, they had other forms of capital punishment.

Another piece of inside knowledge is that Nebuchadnezzar passed and changed laws as he pleased. Darius on the other hand was unable to change a law once it was passed, even one that he himself had commissioned. (Daniel 2:5, 6, 24, 46-49; 3:10, 11, 29; 6:12-16) Historian John C. Whitcomb writes: "Ancient history substantiates this difference between Babylon, where the law was subject to the king, and Medo-Persia, where the king was subject to the law."

Daniel 5:1-4 Updated American Standard Version (UASV)

¹ Belshazzar the king made[196] a great feast for a thousand of his nobles, and he was drinking wine in the presence of the thousand.

² Belshazzar, when he tasted the wine, commanded that the vessels of gold and of silver that Nebuchadnezzar his father[197] had taken out of the temple in Jerusalem be brought, that the king and his nobles, his wives, and his concubines might drink from them. ³ Then they brought the gold vessels that had been taken out of the temple, the house of God which was in Jerusalem; and the king and his nobles, his wives and his concubines drank from them. ⁴ They drank the wine and praised the gods of gold and silver, of bronze, iron, wood and stone.

Archaeology has substantiated these kinds of feasts. The fact that stands out is the mention of women being present at the feast, the "wives, and his concubines" were present as well. Such an idea would have been repugnant to the Greeks and Jews of 167-67 B.C.E. era. This may very well be why the Greek Septuagint version of Daniel removed the mention of these women.[198] This so-called forger of Daniel would have live during this same time of the Septuagint.

---

[196] I.e., held

[197] Or *predecessor*; also verses 11, 13, 18

[198] Hebrew scholar C. F. Keil writes of Daniel 5:3: "The LXX. have here, and also at ver. 23, omitted mention of the women, according to the custom of the Macedonians, Greeks, and Romans."

Do External Factors Prove Daniel Is A Forgery?

Even the place of Daniel in the canon of the Hebrew Old Testament is evidence against his having written the book, so says the critics. The Jewish scribes (like Ezra) of ancient Israel arranged the books of the Old Testament into three groups: the Torah, the Prophets, and the Writings. Naturally, we would expect that Daniel would be found among the Prophets, yet they placed him among the Writings. Therefore, the critic makes the argument that Daniel had to of been an unknown when the works of the prophets were being collected. Their theory is that it was placed among the writings, because these were collected last.

However, not all Bible scholarship agree that the ancient scribes placed Daniel in the Writings, and not the Prophets. However, even if it is as they claim, Daniel was added among the Writings; this does nothing to prove that it was penned at a later date. Old Testament Bible scholar Gleason L. Archer states that . . .

> It should be noted that some of the documents in the Kethubhim [Writings] (the third division of the Hebrew Bible) were of great antiquity, such as the book of Job, the Davidic psalms, and the writings of Solomon. Position in the Kethubhim, therefore, is no proof of a late date of composition. Furthermore the statement in Josephus (Contra Apionem. 1:8) quoted previously in chapter 5 indicates strongly that in the first century A.D., Daniel was included among the prophets in the second division of the Old Testament canon; hence it could not have been assigned to the Kethubim until a later period. 349 The Masoretes may have been influenced in this reassignment by the consideration that Daniel was not appointed or ordained as a prophet, but remained a civil servant under the prevailing government throughout his entire career. Second, a large percentage of his writings does not bear the character of prophecy, but rather of history (chaps. 1-6), such as does not appear in any of the books of the canonical prophets.350 Little of that which Daniel wrote is couched in the form of a message from God to His people relayed through the mouth of His spokesman. Rather, the predominating element consists of prophetic visions granted personally to the author and interpreted to him by angels.[199]

The critic also turns his attention to the Apocryphal book, Ecclesiasticus, by Jesus Ben Sirach, penned about 180 B.C.E., as evidence that Daniel did not pen the book that bears his name. Ecclesiasticus has a long list of righteous men, of which, Daniel is missing. From this, they conclude that Daniel had to of been an unknown at the time. However, if we follow that line of reasoning; what do we do with the fact that the same list omits: Ezra and Mordecai, good King Jehoshaphat, and the upright man Job; of all the judges, except Samuel.[200] Simply because the above faithful and righteous men are missing from a list in

---

[199] Archer, Gleason (1996-08-01). A Survey of Old Testament Introduction (Kindle Locations 7963-7972). Moody Publishers.

[200] If we turn our attention to the Apostle Paul's list of faithful men and women found in Hebrews chapter 11; it does appear to mention occasions recorded in Daniel. (Daniel 6:16-24; Hebrews 11:32, 33) Nevertheless, the list by Paul is not an exhaustive list either. Even within his list, Isaiah, Jeremiah, and Ezekiel are not named in the list, but this scarcely demonstrates that they never existed.

an apocryphal book, are we to dismiss them as having never existed? The very idea is absurd.

Sources in Favor of Daniel

Ezekiel's references to Daniel must be considered to be one of the strongest arguments for a sixth-century date. No satisfactory explanation exists for the use of the name Daniel by the prophet Ezekiel other than that he and Daniel were contemporaries and that Daniel had already become widely known throughout the Babylonian Empire by the time of Ezekiel's ministry.[201]

We have in chapter 9 a series of remarkable predictions which defy any other interpretation but that they point to the coming of Christ and His crucifixion [about] A.D. 30, followed by the destruction of the city of Jerusalem within the ensuing decades. In Dan. 9:25–26, it is stated that sixty-nine heptads of years (i.e., 483 years) will ensue between a "decree" to rebuild the walls of Jerusalem, and the cutting off of Messiah the Prince. In 9:25–26, we read: "Know therefore and understand, that from the going forth of the commandment to restore and to build Jerusalem unto the Messiah the Prince shall be seven weeks, and threescore and two weeks.... And after threescore and two weeks shall Messiah be cut off, but not for himself: and the people of the prince that shall come shall destroy the city and the sanctuary."[202]

The Greatest Evidence for Daniel

First of all, we have the clear testimony of the Lord Jesus Himself in the Olivet discourse. In Matt. 24:15, He refers to "the abomination of desolation, spoken of through [*dia*] Daniel the prophet." The phrase "abomination of desolation" occurs three times in Daniel (9:27; 11:31; 12:11). If these words of Christ are reliably reported, we can only conclude that He believed the historic Daniel to be the personal author of the prophecies containing this phrase. No other interpretation is possible in the light of the preposition *dia*, which refers to personal agency. It is significant that Jesus regarded this "abomination" as something to be brought to pass in a future age rather than being simply the idol of Zeus set up by Antiochus in the temple, as the Maccabean theorists insist.[203]

While this has certainly been an overview of the evidence in favor of the authenticity of Daniel, there will never be enough to satisfy the critic. One professor at Oxford University wrote: "Nothing is gained by a mere answer to objections, so long as the original prejudice, 'there cannot be supernatural prophecy,' remains." What does this

---

[201] Stephen R. Miller, vol. 18, *Daniel*, electronic ed., Logos Library System; The New American Commentary (Nashville: Broadman & Holman Publishers, 2001), 42-43.

[202] Gleason Leonard Archer, *A Survey of Old Testament Introduction*, 3rd. ed.]. (Chicago: Moody Press, 1998), 445.

[203] Gleason Leonard Archer, *A Survey of Old Testament Introduction*, 3rd. ed.]. (Chicago: Moody Press, 1998), 444.

mean? It means that the critic is blinded by his prejudice. However, God has given them the choice of free will.

The Bible critics are ever so vigilant today. They are more prepared than most Christians, and witness about their doubts far more than your average Christian witnesses about his or her faith.

1 Peter 3:15 Updated American Standard Version (UASV)

¹⁵ but sanctify Christ as Lord in your hearts, always being prepared to make a defense[204] to anyone who asks you for a reason for the hope that is in you; yet do it with gentleness and respect;

Peter says that we must be prepared to make a *defense*. The Greek word behind the English "defense" is *apologia* (apologia), which is actually a legal term that refers to the defense of a defendant in court. Our English apologetics is just what Peter spoke of, having the ability to give a reason to any who may challenge us, or to answer those who are not challenging us but who have honest questions that deserve to be answered.

To whom was the apostle Peter talking? Who was Peter saying needed always to be prepared to make a defense? Was he talking only to the pastors, elders, servants, or was he speaking to all Christians? Peter opens this letter saying, "to the chosen who are residing temporarily in the dispersion in Pontus, Galatia, Cappadocia, Asia, and Bithynia." Who are these "chosen" ones? The College Press NIV Commentary gives us the answer,

The Greek text does not include the word "God's," but the translation is a fair one since the clear implication is that God did the choosing. The word Peter uses has a rich biblical heritage. The Jews found their identity and the basis of their lives in the fact that they were God's chosen people (see, e.g., Deut 7:6–8). The New Testament frequently identifies Christians as elect or chosen. In 1 Peter 2:9 Peter will identify Christians as "a chosen people," using the same word ἐκλεκτός (*eklektos*) here translated "elect." The same word is also used of Christ in 2:4 and 6 (where it is translated "chosen"). Christians are chosen or elect through the chosen or elect One, Jesus Christ. The idea that Christians are God's chosen people is fundamental to Peter's thinking, as is apparent in 1:13–2:10. Peter is already laying the foundation for his appeals to these Christians to live up to their holy calling. (Black and Black 1998)

The "chosen who are residing temporarily in the dispersion" were Christians, who were living among **non-**Christian Jews and Gentiles. This letter, then, is addressed to all Christians, but the context of chapters 1:3 to 4:11 is mostly addressed to newly baptized Christians. Therefore, all Christians are obligated to 'be prepared to make a defense to anyone who asks us for a reason for the hope that is in us.' Yes, we are all required to defend our hope successfully. If any have not felt they were up to the task, this author by way of Christian publishing House are publishing books to help along those lines. Here is what is available at present, including this publication you are reading,

CONVERSATIONAL EVANGELISM Defending the Faith, Reasoning from the Scriptures, Explaining and Proving, Instructing in Sound Doctrine, and Overturning False Reasoning (Sept. 16, 2015) by Edward D. Andrews

---

[204] Or *argument*; or *explanation*

THE CHRISTIAN APOLOGIST: Always Being Prepared to Make a Defense (September 27, 2014) By Edward D. Andrews

THE EVANGELISM HANDBOOK: How All Christians Can Effectively Share God's Word in Their Community (Aug 28, 2013) by Edward D Andrews

OVERCOMING BIBLE DIFFICULTIES Answers to the So-Called Errors and Contradictions (Aug. 04, 2015) by Edward D. Andrews

These first-century Christians in Asia Minor were in a time of difficulty. They were at the time of Peter's letter; about 62-64 C.E. going through some trials, not knowing that many far more severe lie in the not too distant future. Within a few years, the persecution of Christians by Emperor Nero would begin. These new converts had given up former religions, idols, cults and superstitions, their 'the futile ways inherited from your forefathers.' (1 Pet. 1:18) These one's were taking of their old person, and bringing their lives in harmony with God's Word, such as 'malice and deceit and hypocrisy and envy and slander.' (1 Pet. 2:1) Now they were 'no longer living for the lusts of men, but for the will of God.' (1 Pet. 4:2) Their former pagan friends now hated these new Christians, because 'they were surprised when these chosen ones do not join them in the same flood of debauchery, and they maligned them.' (1 Pet. 4:4) In fact, Peter informs us that Satan, the Devil is enraged when one is converted from their former life of debauchery, conformed instead to the Word of God. Peter warned them, "Be sober-minded; be watchful. Your adversary the devil prowls around like a roaring lion, seeking someone to devour." 1 Peter 5:8

Christians have never really had it easy in defending their hope. Peter counsels these new ones, who have next to no experience in coping with trials and persecutions to rejoice, albeit distressed by numerous trials. "**Keep your conduct among the Gentiles honorable**, so that when they speak against you as evildoers, they may see your good deeds and glorify God on the day of visitation." (1 Pet. 2:12) "The end of all things is at hand; therefore **be self-controlled and sober-minded for the sake of your prayers**." 1 Pet. 4:4) "Be sober-minded; be watchful" in the midst of men who continue "living in sensuality, passions, drunkenness, orgies, drinking parties, and lawless idolatry." (1 Pet. 4:3) They should be united under Christ as they 'Have purified their souls by their obedience to the truth for a sincere brotherly love, love one another earnestly from a pure heart." (1 Peter 1:22) "Above all, [they were to] keep loving one another earnestly, since love covers a multitude of sins. Show hospitality to one another without grumbling. As each has received a gift, use it to serve one another, as good stewards of God's varied grace." (1 Pet 4:8-10) 'Finally, all of them, had unity of mind, sympathy, brotherly love, a tender heart, and a humble mind. They did not repay evil for evil or reviling for reviling, but on the contrary, they blessed, for to this they were called, that you may obtain a blessing.' (1 Pet. 3:8-9) If they heeded this counsel, it would have kept them from falling or drifting back into their former ways.

There was one more obligation, if they were to preserve on the right path of conduct, namely, being prepared to make a defense for their hope. "It was revealed to [the prophets] that they were serving not themselves but you, in the things that have now been announced to you through those who preached the good news to you by the Holy Spirit sent from heaven, things into which angels long to look. Therefore, preparing your minds for action, and being sober-minded, set your hope fully on the grace that will be brought to you at the revelation of Jesus Christ." (1 Pet. 1:12-13) Peter went on to tell them that they were "a chosen race, a royal priesthood, a holy nation, a people for his own possession, that you may proclaim the excellencies of him who called you out of darkness into his marvelous light." (1 Pet. 2:9) When should they "proclaim these excellencies"? He writes, "but in your hearts honor Christ the Lord as holy, **always being prepared** to make a defense to anyone who asks you for a reason for the hope that is in you; yet do it with gentleness and respect." 1 Peter 3:15

The world in which we live today is much more vast than that of the first-century up unto the 21st-century. The trials and persecution today are much more intense, which unfortunately we ca watch around the world, by way of the media and social media. The greatest threat to Christianity is Islam, which has been an ardent enemy of Christianity since the seventh-century C.E. They are slaughtering Christians the world over. They view Christians as the big Satan and the Jews as little Satan. In their theology, they are looking to turn the world into one big Islamic state, governed by the Quran. For the more radical aspects of Islam, it is convert to Islam or be killed as an infidel.

The second greatest threat to tradition and conservatism is liberal Christianity. Their continued dissecting of the Scriptures until Moses did not pen the first five books, Isaiah is not the author of the book that bears his name, nor is Daniel the author of the book that bears his name, and the Bible is full of myths and legends, errors and contractions.

Then, as we have seen throughout this publication, there are moderate and liberal Bible scholars, who are advocates of Historical Criticism Methodology, and its sub-criticisms: Source Criticism, Tradition Criticism, Form Criticism, Redaction Criticism, among others.

2 Timothy 2:24-25 Updated American Standard Version (ASV)

[24] For a slave of the Lord does not need to fight, but needs to be kind to all, qualified to teach, showing restraint when wronged, [25] instructing his opponents with gentleness, if perhaps God may grant them repentance leading to accurate knowledge [*epignosis*][205] of the truth,

Look at the Greek word (*epignosis*) behind the English "knowledge" from above. "It is more intensive than *gnosis*, knowledge, because it expresses a more thorough participation in the acquiring of knowledge on the part of the learner."[206] The requirement of all of the Lord's servants is that they be able to teach, but not in a quarrelsome way, but in a way to correct opponents with mildness. Why? The purpose of it all is that by God, yet through the Christian teacher, one may come to repentance and begin taking in an accurate knowledge of the truth.

> Some Christians see apologetics as pre-evangelism; it is not the gospel, but it prepares the soil for the gospel.[207] Others make no such distinction, seeing apologetics, theology, philosophy, and evangelism as deeply entwined facets of

---

[205] *Epignosis* is a strengthened or intensified form of *gnosis* (*epi*, meaning "additional"), meaning, "true," "real," "full," "complete" or "accurate," depending upon the context. Paul and Peter alone use *epignosis*.

206. Spiros Zodhiates, *The Complete Word Study Dictionary: New Testament*, Electronic ed. (Chattanooga, TN: AMG Publishers, 2000, c1992, c1993), S. G1922.

[207] Norman Geisler and Ron Brooks, When Skeptics Ask (Grand Rapids: Baker Books, 1996), 11.

the gospel.[208] Whatever its relation to the gospel, apologetics **is an extremely important enterprise that can profoundly impact unbelievers** and be used as the tool that clears the way to faith in Jesus Christ. (Bold mine.)

Many Christians did not come to believe as a result of investigating the Bible's authority, the evidence for the resurrection, or as a response to the philosophical arguments for God's existence. They responded to the proclamation of the gospel. Although these people have reasons for their belief, they are deeply personal reasons that often do not make sense to unbelievers. **They know the truth but are not necessarily equipped to share or articulate the truth in a way that is understandable** to those who have questions about their faith. It is quite possible to believe something is true without having a proper understanding of it or the ability to articulate it. (Bold mine.)

Christians who believe but do not know why are often insecure and comfortable only around other Christians. Defensiveness can quickly surface when challenges arise on issues of faith, morality, and truth because of a lack of information regarding the rational grounds for Christianity. At its worst, this can lead to either a fortress mentality or a belligerent faith, precisely the opposite of the Great Commission Jesus gave in Matthew 28:19–20. The Christian's charge is not to withdraw from the world and lead an insular life. Rather, we must be engaged in the culture, to be salt and light.

The solution to this problem requires believers to become informed in doctrine, the history of their faith, philosophy, logic, and other disciplines as they relate to Christianity. Believers must know the facts, arguments and theology and understand how to employ them in a way that will effectively engage the culture. Believers need Christian apologetics. One of the first tasks of Christian apologetics provides information. A number of widely held assumptions about Christianity can be easily challenged with a little information. This is even true for persons who are generally well-educated.[209]

The ability to reason with others will take time, practice and patience. For example, if someone reasons with others successfully, that person must be reasonable. In a discussion about the historicity about Jesus, a believer knows the other person denying the existence of Jesus is wrong. Moreover, believers possess a truckload of evidence to support this position. However, it is best sometimes to not unload the truck by dumping the entire load at a listener's feet in one conversation, or in one breath. Being reasonable does not mean that a believer compromises the truth because he or she does not unload on the listener.

The other person will likely make many wrong statements in the conversation, and we should let most of them go unchallenged; rather, focus on a handful of the most crucial pieces of evidence and do not get lost by refuting every wrong statement. He may

---

[208] Greg Bahnsen, Van Til Apologetic (Phillipsburg, NJ: Presbyterian and Reformed, 1998), 43.

[209] Powell, Doug (2006-07-01). *Holman QuickSource Guide to Christian Apologetics* (Holman Quicksource Guides) (p. 6-7). B&H Publishing. Kindle Edition.

make bold condemnatory statements about many Christian beliefs, but we need to remain calm and not make a big deal of those statements. Listen carefully to the other person, and stay within the boundaries of the evidence in the conversation. For example, in a conversation on the historicity of Jesus when the listener states, "The New Testament manuscripts were completely corrupted in the copying process for a millennium, to the point that we do not even have the supposed Word of God." The evidence for the historicity of Jesus rests in the first and second century, so it would be a fool's errand to get into an extensive side subject about the restoration of the New Testament text, which took place over the centuries that followed the first two centuries C.E. There will be another day to talk about the history of the Greek New Testament, but today focus on the historicity of Jesus Christ.

God has given humanity free will, meaning each human has the right to choose, even if that choice is unwise. Believers have the assignment of proclaiming "the good news of the kingdom," as well as "making disciples" of redeemable humankind. Therefore, we must not pressure, coerce, or force people to accept the truth of that "Good News." However, all Christians have an obligation to reason with anyone by respectfully, gently, and mildly overturning their false reasoning, in the attempt that being used by God we may save some.

Other Books By Christian Publishing House Classics

Exapanded and Updated

www.ingramcontent.com/pod-product-compliance
Lightning Source LLC
Chambersburg PA
CBHW050458110426
42742CB00018B/3293